Remembering May Fourth

Ideas, History, and Modern China

Edited by

Ban WANG (*Stanford University*)
WANG Hui (*Tsinghua University*)

VOLUME 23

The titles published in this series are listed at *brill.com/ihmc*

Remembering May Fourth

The Movement and Its Centennial Legacy

Edited by

Carlos Yu-Kai Lin, *City University of Hong Kong*
Victor H. Mair, *University of Pennsylvania*

BRILL

LEIDEN | BOSTON

Calligraphy by Shen Wen-Chun.

The Library of Congress Cataloging-in-Publication Data

Names: Mair, Victor H., 1943- editor. | Lin, Carlos Yu-Kai, editor.
Title: Remembering May Fourth : the movement and its centennial legacy / edited by Carlos Yu-Kai Lin, City University of Hong Kong, Victor H. Mair, University of Pennsylvania.
Description: Leiden ; Boston : Brill, [2020] | Series: Ideas, history, and modern China, 1875-9394 ; vol. 23 | Summary: "Remembering May Fourth: The Movement and its Centennial Legacy is a collective work of thirteen scholars who reflect on the question of how to remember the May Fourth Movement, one of the most iconic socio-political events in the history of modern China. The book discusses a wide range of issues concerning the relations between politics and memory, between writing and ritualizing, between fiction and reality, and between theory and practice. Remembering May Fourth thus calls into question the ways in which the movement is remembered, while at the same time calling for the need to create new memories of the movement"—Provided by publisher.
Identifiers: LCCN 2019059239 (print) | LCCN 2019059240 (ebook) | ISBN 9789004424722 (hardback) | ISBN 9789004424883 (ebook)
Subjects: LCSH: China—History—May Fourth movement, 1919. | Chinese literature--20th century--History and criticism. | China--Intellectual life--20th century.
Classification: LCC DS777.43 .R46 2020 (print) | LCC DS777.43 (ebook) | DDC 951.04/1—dc23
LC record available at https://lccn.loc.gov/2019059239
LC ebook record available at https://lccn.loc.gov/2019059240

Typeface for the Latin, Greek, and Cyrillic scripts: "Brill". See and download: brill.com/brill-typeface.

ISSN 1875-9394
ISBN 978-90-04-42472-2 (hardback)
ISBN 978-90-04-42488-3 (e-book)

Copyright 2020 by Koninklijke Brill NV, Leiden, The Netherlands.
Koninklijke Brill NV incorporates the imprints Brill, Brill Hes & De Graaf, Brill Nijhoff, Brill Rodopi, Brill Sense, Hotei Publishing, mentis Verlag, Verlag Ferdinand Schöningh and Wilhelm Fink Verlag.
All rights reserved. No part of this publication may be reproduced, translated, stored in a retrieval system, or transmitted in any form or by any means, electronic, mechanical, photocopying, recording or otherwise, without prior written permission from the publisher.
Authorization to photocopy items for internal or personal use is granted by Koninklijke Brill NV provided that the appropriate fees are paid directly to The Copyright Clearance Center, 222 Rosewood Drive, Suite 910, Danvers, MA 01923, USA. Fees are subject to change.

This book is printed on acid-free paper and produced in a sustainable manner.

Contents

List of Contributors   VII
Introduction   1
   Carlos Yu-Kai Lin

PART 1
Histories and Politics

1. May Fourth as Affect   25
   Gloria Davies

2. The May Fourth Liberal Legacy in Chan Koonchung's *Jianfeng ernian*   53
   Josephine Chiu-Duke

3. Two Versions of Modern Chinese History: a Reassessment of Hu Shi and Lu Xun   75
   Chih-p'ing Chou

4. Chinese Renaissance, Other Renaissances   95
   Gang Zhou

5. Hu Shi and the May Fourth Legacy   113
   Yung-chen Chiang

6. Theory and Practice in the May Fourth Period   137
   Shakhar Rahav

PART 2
Literature and Languages

7. Nature and Critique of Modernity in Shen Congwen: an Eco-Critical Reading   159
   Ban Wang

8. A New Vision of Life in Xiao Hong's *The Field of Life and Death*   183
   Todd Foley

9 Aesthetic Cognition and the Subject of Discourse in Lu Xun's Modern-Style Fiction 207
Nicholas Kaldis

10 Literary Bombs: a Sketch of the May Fourth Generation and Bomb as Metaphor 227
Chien-hsin Tsai

11 Utopian Language: from Esperanto to the Abolishment of Chinese Characters 247
Chih-p'ing Chou

12 The Immortality of Words: Hu Shi's Language Reform and His Reflection on Religion 265
Gina Elia & Victor H. Mair

13 A Historical and Bilingual Perspective on the Concept of Vernacular 283
Carlos Yu-Kai Lin

Index 301

Contributors

Josephine Chiu-Duke
is a professor in the Department of Asian Studies of the University of British Columbia. She is the author of *To Rebuild the Empire: Lu Chih's His Confucian Pragmatist Approach to Mid-Tang Predicament* (SUNY Press, 2000), and numerous essays on Tang China and contemporary Chinese thought. She has also edited, co-edited and co-translated *Liberalism and the Humanistic Tradition—Essays in Honor of Professor Lin Yü-sheng* (Yun Chen Publishing, 2005), Ying-shih Yü, *Chinese History and Culture* (2 vols., Columbia University Press, 2016), Ge Zhaoguang *An Intellectual History of China* (2 vols., Brill, 2014, 2018). Her edition of *Lin Yü-sheng's Recent Works in Chinese Intellectual History* is forthcoming soon.

Yung-chen Chiang
is a professor of History at DePauw University. His major publications include *Social Engineering and the Social Sciences in China, 1919–1949* (Cambridge University Press, 2001), a biographical tetralogy on Hu Shi, *Shewo qishei: Hu Shi* (*The Titan: Hu Shi*), published by the Linking Publishing Company in Taiwan (2011, 2013, 2018, and 2018), and *Xingxing, Yueliang, Taiyang: Hu Shi de qinggan shijie* (*The Stars, the Moons, and the Sun: the Women in Hu Shi's Life*), revised edition, (Beijing: New Star Press, 2012).

Chih-p'ing Chou
is a professor of East Asian Studies at Princeton University, specializes in modern Chinese intellectual history and late Ming literature. His publication includes *Yuan Hung-tao and the Kung-an School* (Cambridge University Press, 1988), *A Pragmatist and His Free Spirit: The Half-Century Romance of Hu Shi and Edith Clifford Williams* (Co-authored with Susan Chan Egan, Chinese University of Hong Kong Press, 2009), *The Sparks of Freedom: Hu Shi and Lin Yutang* (Taipei: Yunchen, 2018). His *Hu Shi's Thought and Modern China* (Beijing: Jiuzhou, 2012) was selected as one of the best 100 publications of the year by several media in China.

Gloria Davies
is a professor of Chinese Studies at Monash University and has published widely on modern Chinese intellectual politics and Chinese literary and cultural topics, including *Worrying About China: On Chinese Critical Inquiry* (Harvard University Press, 2007) and *Lu Xun's Revolution: Writing in a Time of Violence*

(Harvard University Press, 2013). She is a regular contributor to the China Story Yearbook project based at the Australian Centre on China in the World (CIW), ANU.

Gina Elia

is an adjunct professor at Broward College in Fort Lauderdale, Florida. She received her PhD in Chinese Literature from the University of Pennsylvania in 2018. Before that, she completed her undergraduate studies at Cornell University. She was a Taiwan Fulbright Fellow for the 2016–2017 academic year, and has also received a Foreign Language and Area Studies Grant from the Department of Education. Her essay on Yunte Huang's poetry collection *SHI* appears in the online journal *Jacket2*. She has also published popular articles in the digital magazine *CommonWealth* and on the website *SupChina*.

Todd Foley

is a faculty fellow in the departments of Comparative Literature and East Asian Studies at New York University, where he teaches courses on modern Chinese literature, film, and critical theory.

Nicholas Kaldis

is the Director of Chinese Studies at Binghamton University (SUNY). He is author of *The Chinese Prose Poem: A Study of Lu Xun's Wild Grass (Yecao)* (Cambria Press, 2014), and has published essays on Lu Xun and world literature, modern Chinese fiction and poetry, Taiwan nature writing, contemporary Chinese cinemas, and numerous translations.

Carlos Yu-Kai Lin

is an assistant professor in the Department of Linguistics and Translation at the City University of Hong Kong. His research focuses on modern Chinese intellectual history, modern Chinese literature and culture, and the history of Chinese fiction. He has taught at UC Berkeley, Davis, University of Pennsylvania, and Princeton University and he currently teaches at the City University of Hong Kong.

Victor H. Mair

is a professor of Chinese language and literature at the University of Pennsylvania. He is the founder and editor of Sino-Platonic Papers and General Editor of the ABC Chinese Dictionary Series at the University of Hawaii Press. He has been a fellow or visiting professor at the University of Hong Kong (2002–2003), the Institute for Advanced Study (Princeton, 1998–1999), the

Institute for Research in Humanities (Kyoto University, 1995), Duke University (1993–1994), and the National Humanities Center (Research Triangle Park, North Carolina, 1991–1992).

Shakhar Rahav
is a historian of China in the department of Asian Studies at the University of Haifa. He is the author of *The Rise of Political Intellectuals in Modern China: May Fourth Societies and the Roots of Mass-Party Politics* (Oxford University Press, 2015) and of several articles about intellectuals and politics in twentieth-century China.

Chien-hsin Tsai
was an associate professor of Modern Chinese Society and Culture at the University of Texas at Austin. He is the author of *A Passage to China: Literature, Loyalism, and Colonial Taiwan* (Harvard University Asia Center Press, 2017) and co-editor of *Sinophone Studies: A Critical Reader* (Columbia University Press, 2013).

Ban Wang
is the William Haas Professor in Chinese Studies in East Asian Languages and Cultures and Comparative Literature at Stanford University. His major publications include *The Sublime Figure of History* (Stanford University Press, 1997), *Illuminations from the Past* (Stanford University Press, 2004) and *History and Memory* (*Lish yu jiyi*) (Oxford University Press, 2004). He has edited and co-edited 8 books on Chinese film, memory studies, Chinese studies in the US, the Chinese Revolution, socialism, and the New Left, including *Chinese Visions of World Order: Tianxia, Culture and World Politics* (Duke University Press, 2017). He has taught at SUNY-Stony Brook, Harvard, Rutgers, East China Normal University, Yonsei, and Seoul National University.

Gang Zhou
is an associate professor of Chinese in the Department of Foreign Languages and Literatures at Louisiana State University. She is the author of *Placing the Modern Chinese Vernacular in Transnational Literature* (Palgrave Macmillan, 2011) and the editor of *Other Renaissances: A New Approach to World Literature* (Palgrave/Macmillan, 2006).

Introduction

Carlos Yu-Kai Lin

It was a beautiful sunny day in late spring Beijing. Thousands of students from thirteen different colleges and universities, mostly from Peking University, marched toward the Gate of Heavenly Peace, the symbolic center of the country as well as the city. The light spring breeze that mixed with a fresh smell of newly-budded flowers and green plants offered a sharp contrast with the solemn atmosphere of the large student groups whose members held up tall white banners, handed out flyers, and passionately shouted out slogans that demanded the Chinese government fight for its sovereignty when dealing with foreign imperial powers. That date was May 4, 1919. A series of strikes and boycotts was organized soon afterwards across the country by workers, merchants, and like-minded students to support the Beijing protest, eventually forcing the government to readjust its political stance and withdraw the troops sent to crack down on the student protestors. This chain reaction of socio-political activities was later collectively known as the May Fourth Movement.

The international situation that China faced at the time has often been said to be the immediate cause of the movement. Only a few years before the demonstration, Japan had sought to take economic and administrative control of Manchuria, Inner Mongolia, Shandong, and China's southeast coast, by imposing the notorious Twenty-One Demands on the Chinese authorities in 1915. Not only did China's warlord president, Yuan Shikai 袁世凱 (1859–1916), accept the demands, he also managed to temporarily restore monarchy by appointing himself an emperor in the same year. While Yuan's monarchical restoration was short-lived, the domestic disorder and diplomatic failure had led many Chinese intellectuals to realize that the downfall of the Qing dynasty (1644–1911) and the establishment of a Republic of China did not guarantee the maturation of a modern society.

In a larger historical context, after World War I (1914–1918) was over, American president Woodrow Wilson (1856–1924) announced a famous policy at the Congress known as the Fourteen Points that emphasized the spirit of self-determination, freedom, and democracy as the guidelines for rebuilding the postwar international society. President Wilson's vision had won the support of many, including the liberal Chinese scholars and students who believed that, under the guidance of the Fourteen Points, China would be given fair treatment in the ensuing Paris Peace Conference convened by the victorious countries that sought to settle the peace terms with the defeated ones.

Nevertheless, the Wilsonian idealistic vision eventually failed to appeal to other major powers, and the decisions made at the conference ultimately only favored the major winning countries. The German concessions in Shandong, instead of returning to China, were transferred to Japan; the Twenty-One Demands were not annulled; and the Chinese delegates were unable to reverse the decisions made at the conference. This diplomatic failure, together with the domestic disorder mentioned above, are often said to be the main and immediate cause of the May Fourth student protest in Beijing.[1]

The political movements in Russia and Korea also played a role in inspiring the rise of the nationalistic sentiment instrumental in facilitating the May Fourth student protests. The success of the 1917 Russian Revolution which put an end to the Tsarist autocracy, and the 1919 March 1st Movement in Korea that protested against the Japanese colonization and called for Korean national independence, gave the Chinese people a sense of hope that a political change is possible if the people are successfully mobilized to engineer a social movement.

While the standard narrative of the May Fourth Movement often portrays the Paris Peace Conference as an outright brutal power play of the few major winning countries, Arno J. Mayer suggested that the conference was really a result of the struggle between what he called the "Old Diplomacy" represented by the alliance system that relies on the use of secrete treaties and power politics, and the "New Diplomacy" represented by Woodrow Wilson's Fourteen Points of 1918 and Vladimir Lenin's Decree on Peace of 1917 that seek to advocate a more rational and peaceful diplomatic handling. In particular, Mayer emphasizes that the domestic politics in both the winning and defeated countries, were crucial to the debates and decisions at the conference, since the delegates and diplomats of each country had to play the role of a politician at the same time who need to constantly and carefully weight on the political situations in their own respective countries that were often troubled by an intensifying struggle between left and right, or in some cases, the diminishing

---

[1] It is therefore not surprising that early discourses on the May Fourth Movement were often imbued with the ideas of nationalism, patriotism, or individualism defined in nationalistic terms. For example, Sun Yat-sen (1866–1929), in a letter to the overseas members of the Nationalist Party in 1920, defines the protest as a "patriotic movement" (愛國之運動) that calls for a radical renovation of the mind. Hu Shi (1891–1962), a cultural leader at the time, also referred to this protest as a "patriotic movement of Peking students" (北京學生界的愛國運動). Cai Yuanpei 蔡元培 (1868–1949), the president of Peking University, also called this demonstration a "movement of national salvation" (救國之運動). See Zhang Zhongdong 張忠棟 et al., eds., *Wusi yu xuesheng yundong* 五四與學生運動 (May Fourth and student movement) (Taipei: Tangshan chubanshe, 1999), 11, 15, 273.

role of a central government. In other words, the task of peacemaking was actually more difficult and intricate than how it was often perceived to be—a simple and one-sided power play of the major winning Western countries. Mayer's observation is valuable since it provides a more complex international perspective on the multi-faceted development of the Peace Conference, with which China's May Fourth Movement is often said to be associated.[2]

However, the reason the term "May Fourth" has assumed a symbolic stature in the history of modern China is not simply because of the international situation in which the movement took place. There are many other political events and uprisings that occurred in China during the early twentieth century, yet none had received the kind of long-standing scholarly attention as did the May Fourth Movement. The student protest in 1919 had indeed garnered the attention of the entire country, thereby engendering a series of social and political responses that in turn made the protest memorable. Yet what gives the term "May Fourth" its lasting historical as well as theoretical significance is perhaps the burgeoning cultural discourses that facilitated and outlived the protest *per se*, which had become an intellectual resource that allowed the Chinese to reflect on and respond to the ever-changing political situation on both the domestic and international fronts. These discourses, which manifested themselves in the form of a radical cultural-intellectual-literary movement that sought to consider and examine a nation's past as a project, that needs to be actively shaped and repeatedly reflected upon through various new narratives, according to a set of modern and universal values, are what make the May Fourth Movement an important milestone in modern Chinese history. This is also why the movement is often associated with, or even simply remembered as, the May Fourth new culture movement, in which "literature" and "culture" were gradually seen as new sites for political and ideological struggles.

The May Fourth Movement has long been compared to other major cultural trends or movements in the West. For example, to some, it represents a Chinese "Renaissance" that seeks to free the individual from the constraints of a tradition marked by dogmatism and superstition. To others, it stands for a Chinese "Age of Enlightenment" that emphasizes the power of reason and methods of science. Still others relate it to the "Sturm and Drang" in late eighteen-century Germany or even most ambitious and creative attempts of Chinese intellectuals to negotiate the difference between Western and Chinese civilizations. This trope of a cross-cultural and comparative analysis is a key feature of May Fourth cultural and intellectual discourses.

---

2   See Arno J. Meyer, *Politics and Diplomacy in Peacemaking* (New York: Alfred A. Knopf, 1967).

1   From Late Qing to May Fourth

From a culturalist's perspective, the origin of May Fourth discourses can be traced back to the late nineteenth century, to a time in which modern Western knowledge was introduced to China in an unprecedented scale and manner. Late Qing intellectuals such as Yan Fu 嚴復 (1854–1921), Kang Youwei 康有為 (1858–1927), Liang Qichao 梁啟超 (1873–1929), Lin Shu 林紓 (1852–1924), and Zhang Taiyan 章太炎 (1869–1936) had all participated in this massive movement of Western learning, seeking to engender social changes through an intellectual revolution. After the Opium Wars (1839–1842, 1856–1860), the defeated Qing government was forced to recognize the superiority of Western technologies, and as a result subsequently set up many offices and institutes to take charge of all foreign affairs and train its officials to learn from Western modern knowledge. A huge number of foreign works thus had been brought to China as early as the mid-nineteenth century. This series of governmental efforts was later known as the Self-strengthening Movement (a.k.a., the Western Affairs Movement; 1861–1895), which was proposed and implemented by a few high-ranking government officials who aimed to modernize the empire's military and industrial strength.[3]

But the newer trend of Western learning was different. First, it was no longer spearheaded only by a few government elites but participated by a large group of intellectuals who were not necessarily affiliated with one another. Second, the late Qing reformers had served a greater variety of roles in carrying out their various social aims and political agendas, including that of journalist, writer, educator, translator, social activist, and even revolutionary. For instance, some late Qing intellectuals, most notably Kang Youwei and Liang Qichao, were believers in a constitutional monarchy and had striven to urge the government to initiate institutional reform in an attempt to remodel the entire country. Others such as Yan Fu and Zhang Taiyan did not want to challenge the political authority of the Qing court and sought instead to advocate a fundamental and bottom-up intellectual reform as a means to achieving national salvation. Still others such as Sun Yat-sen and Chen Duxiu 陳獨秀 (1879–1942) had doubts on the plan for an institutional reform and pondered the possibility of a political revolution. It was not uncommon, moreover, for late Qing intellectuals to switch their cultural-political stances at different stages of their lives. For instance, Liang Qichao, a political reformist and a long-term ally with Kang Youwei who was a Qing loyalist, had temporarily chosen to side

---

3 Some of the key proponents of this movement include Prince Gong 奕訢 (1833–1880), Wenxiang 文祥 (1818–1876), Zeng Guofan 曾國藩 (1811–1872), Li Hongzhang 李鴻章 (1823–1901), and Zuo Zongtang 左宗棠 (1812–1885).

with the revolutionaries such as Sun Yat-sen and Chan Siu-bak 陳少白 (1869–1946) during his exile in Japan in 1902. Later in his life, however, Liang grew more conservative culturally as well as politically. After his visit to postwar Europe in 1918–1919, he began to critique the limit of science and technology and returned to the value of Chinese tradition, which he claimed can supplement the Western model of modernity. Zhang Taiyan, for another example, used to be a supporter of Kang Youwei and Liang Qichao's political agenda of achieving a constitutional monarchy, but later in his life became a strong advocate of political revolution and a foremost propagandist for the anti-Manchu movement. The third feature of the newer trend of Western learning is that, unlike the government elites in the Self-strengthening Movement, which focused primarily on the adoption of Western technology, the late Qing intellectuals had begun to shift their attention to what they perceived as the core values of a truly matured civilization, such as a modern political structure, a constitutionalized legal system, and more importantly, the cultivation of the mindset of a modern individual characterized by his or her awareness of a cosmopolitan world. Such an emphasis on the value of cosmopolitanism and inquiry into the nature of modern society, nation-state, individual, and the relationship among the three had become the ethos of the May Fourth Movement as a cultural-intellectual movement.

Among the late Qing intellectuals who sought to renovate the Chinese society through a more thorough learning about the West, Yan Fu was perhaps the most influential. Throughout his life, Yan Fu had translated some of the most important European sociological works such as T. H. Huxley's *Evolution and Ethics*, Adam Smith's *The Wealth of Nations*, Herbert Spencer's *The Study of Sociology*, John Stuart Mill's *On Liberty*, Edward Jenks's *A History of Politics*, and Montesquieu's *The Spirit of the Laws*. While Yan Fu's translation, from a modern standard, is not entirely faithful to the original—he often mixed his own interpretation with his translations, and created many neologisms in classical Chinese in order to negotiate the epistemological differences between the Chinese and Western cultural traditions—his translated works had a significant and far-reaching impact on the Chinese intellectual circles at the time, challenging as well as changing the way the Chinese conceptualized their identity and history. Questions such as what it means to be a modern individual, and his or her relation to the society, had started to emerge in this period. In particular, Yan Fu's translation of *Evolution and Ethics*, which expounds the social and moral implication of Darwin's theory of evolution, was widely circulated among the Chinese intelligentsia, revolutionizing the way in which they viewed themselves as well as the bigger world.

While Yan Fu's translations were widely read in the late nineteenth century, many of the neologisms that he coined did not survive in modern Chinese.

For example, Yan Fu translated "evolution" as "*tianyan*" (天演), which literally means "changes of the Heaven." But in modern Chinese, the term for "evolution" is "*jinhua*" (進化), which was actually a Japanese translation. For another example, the modern Chinese term for "society" is "*shehui*" (社會), which was again a Japanese creation. But Yan Fu had translated it as "*qun*" (群), which literally means "group." In this case, Yan Fu's translation is perhaps more accurate, for it captures the idea of "society" as a collective entity that consists of individuals.

Yan Fu's translation of "liberty" is particularly interesting. He translated "liberty" as "*qunji quanjie*" (群己權界), which literally means "the boundary between the group and the self." In this example, Yan Fu obviously highlights the boundary between an individual and other social members by reflecting the inherent relations between "liberty" and "society" in his translation of "liberty"—a connection that is not altogether clear in the modern Chinese translations of the same concepts ("*shehui*" and "*ziyou*"). It is especially noteworthy to point out that in Yan Fu's translation of *On Liberty*, he renders the book title as "On the boundary between the group and the self," but in the actual content of the work, he translated "liberty" as "*ziyao*" (自繇), in which case an ancient Chinese word "*yao*" (繇) was used to differentiate it from the more common Japanese rendering of "liberty" as "*ziyou*" (自由).

Although many of Yan Fu's translated words or neologisms were not adopted, many of the new concepts or ideas that he introduced such as "evolution," "natural selection," and "survival of the fittest" gave the Chinese intellectuals new vocabularies and forms of logic to articulate China's cultural past and to envision its future. The idea of evolution that presupposes an origin and an infinite possibility for the future, in particular, had allowed the Chinese to reconsider their culture from a historical and cross-cultural perspective. Such an evolutional-historical perspective permeated the writings of many May Fourth scholars, many of whom later produced paradigm-shifting scholarship based on this evolutionist framework. Lu Xun (1881–1936), for instance, wrote *A Brief History of Chinese Fiction* (中國小說史略; 1923/4), *The Historical Development of Chinese Fiction* (中國小說的歷史的變遷; 1924), and *An Outline of Chinese Literary History* (漢文學史綱要; 1926). Hu Shi (1891–1962), too, had published "The Concept of Literary Evolution and the Reform of Drama" (文學進化觀念與戲劇改良; 1918), *Outline of the History of Chinese Philosophy* (中國哲學史大綱; 1919), "An Introduction to Chinese Grammar" (國語文法概論; 1921), "Chinese Literature of the Past Fifty Years" (五十年來中國之文學; 1923), and *History of Vernacular Literature* (白話文學史; 1928). These works all concern the cultural specificity and the development of Chinese literature and situated China's cultural tradition in a historical and transnational context.

Perhaps it might not be an exaggeration to say that before the rise of Marxism and socialist thought as a dominant ideology in the 1930s, China had gone through a period of Social Darwinism, during which almost all Chinese intellectual writings were influenced by the idea of evolution.[4] Liang Qichao, the foremost late Qing public intellectual, journalist, and activist whose works and words had inspired an entire generation of May Fourth writers, for example, had repeatedly relied on the logic of evolution in articulating the importance of the establishment of a modern nation-state that is regulated by a constitutionalized legal system. Together with his mentor Kang Youwei, Liang had urged the Qing government to implement an institutional political reform that would renovate the entire country. Liang and Kang had petitioned the Guangxu emperor in 1895 in order to communicate their visions and agendas. While their petition was not accepted at the time, their call for a legal and institutional reform had garnered the attention of many like-minded literati who decided to join them in the cause of political reformation. A few years later, in 1898, Liang and Kang had successfully persuaded the emperor to launch a series of reform program that aimed to modernize the empire's political structure. This reform, however ambitious it was, only lasted for about a hundred days and was ended by the powerful Empress Dowager Cixi, who was known for her conservative and anti-foreign positions.

While the 1898 political reform was unsuccessful, the cultural discourse excited by this political event was abundant. After the reform failed, Liang fled to Japan and Kang to Canada where the two began to diverge in their visions of China's future. While Kang remained a loyalist to the Qing court and the emperor throughout his life and thus continued to promote the idea of a monarchical system, his former student and most-trusted comrade, Liang, had started to express doubts on the efficacy of a political reformation. During his exile to Japan, he envisioned an alternative path for China's modernization in which the dynastic rule of China must end. From 1899 onwards, Liang wrote a series of essays that introduced a variety of modern political thought, including concepts such as the nation-state, sovereignty, and constitutionalism, that he considered to be a "universal law" (公理) that can be applied in all cultural contexts.

---

4   While Social Darwinism was an extremely influential presence at the time, voices of dissent could still be heard. For example, Zhang Taiyan, a late Qing scholar, critiqued the Darwinian ideas of progress and evolution by drawing on Buddhist concepts in order to formulate a theory of history that challenges a linear model of time and development associated with capitalist modernity. See Viren Murthy, *The Political Philosophy of Zhang Taiyan: The resistance of Consciousness* (Brill: Leiden, Boston, 2011), 135–167.

For example, he wrote "Lun jinshi guomin jingzheng zhi dashi ji Zhongguo qiantu" 論近世國民競爭之大勢及中國前途 ("On recent trends of the competition between peoples and the future of China") in which he argued that the idea of "people of a nation" or "citizens" (國民) had never previously existed in China, and the idea of a "state" (國) as a public asset owned by the people was equally absent in the Chinese tradition. He thus lamented, "The Chinese did not know about people of a nation. Over the past thousands of years, there is only the concept that consists of the two words, family-state, and not the two words, national-people" (中國人不知有國民也, 數千年來通行之語, 只有國家二字並稱者, 未聞有以國民二字並稱者). This essay perhaps reveals the early divergence between Liang and Kang as two pioneering thinkers.

To further separate the idea of a dynasty from that of a nation-state, Liang described China as a budding nation-state that was still in the process of forming and growing, and that, as a result, contains a great potential for developing an alternative and better future. In his famous essay, "On a Young China" (少年中國說), Liang wrote in a figurative language, "The Japanese are used to calling our China an old empire over and over again. They might get this idea from the Westerners. Alas! Is China indeed old? Liang Qichao says: Oh, how can they say that! How can they say that! In my heart there is a China that is young" (日本人之稱我中國也, 一則曰老大帝國, 再則曰老大帝國. 是語也, 蓋襲譯歐西人之言也. 嗚呼! 我中國其果老大矣乎? 梁啟超曰: 惡, 是何言! 是何言! 吾心目中有一少年中國在). Elsewhere in the essay, he also claimed, "Dynasty and nation-state are different entities" (朝與國既異物). Liang's depiction of China as a youth and a budding nation was important at the time as it separated the idea of China as an age-old empire and as a modern-nation-state-to-be, the significance of which can only be revealed when one examines it in the historical and political context of the time.

The late Qing reformer's cultural-intellectual discourses had thus inspired and facilitated the rise of May Fourth intellectuals, many of whom grew up reading Yan Fu's and Liang Qichao's works. Nevertheless, the most sustaining influence that the May Fourth intellectuals received from their late Qing predecessors was not political or scientific knowledge, but the ways in which this knowledge was introduced and interpreted.[5] As the late Qing intellectuals have shown us, introducing a foreign concept in classical Chinese was never an easy process capable of being completed by a simple act of translation; there

---

5 The existence of some scientific or political terms and concepts—such as nation-state, sovereignty, and constitutionalism—had become common knowledge by the end of the 1910s. The outbreak of the Beijing student protest in 1919 was fueled by a strong sense of national identity. Given the political and intellectual atmosphere of the time, it might not have seemed very daunting to elaborate on the necessity of the notion or the nation-state or the scientific findings of evolution.

were no corresponding terms or concepts in the host culture. Under such circumstances, Chinese intellectuals can only re-appropriate existing Chinese terminology or concepts to articulate originally different cultural systems. In other words, what the May Fourth generation had inherited and eventually exemplified is actually a highly creative interpretive model for cross-cultural analysis, which they continued to develop in their own right and for other purposes. Such an experimental and adventurous spirit is essential to and characteristic of the works of May Fourth intellectuals, who have in their turn shaped the contour of modern Chinese literature and culture, history and politics.

2   From Political Discourses to Literary Revolution

So how did the scientific and political discourses produced by the late Qing intellectuals translate into a cultural movement in which "literature" was gradually seen as a new site for political struggle? It is noteworthy that many of the late Qing intellectuals' works had actually produced a kind of literary effect that began to be noticed and appreciated by Chinese readers at the time, including those who later became the backbone of the May Fourth Movement. For example, those who admitted to having been influenced by Liang Qichao, instead of remembering him as a politician who sought to introduce various new political ideas, tended to remember him simply as a great writer! Compared to the effect of his relentless efforts in introducing Western political thoughts, it appears that it was Liang Qichao's style in writing that had the greater appeal to his Chinese readers. Huang Zunxian 黃遵憲 (1848–1905), a late Qing scholar, for example, described Liang Qichao's writing as: "Breathtaking and soul-stirring; a word is worth a thousand pieces of gold. He writes in a way that no one else can, but speaks to the mind of every man. Even a cold-hearted person shall be moved. The power of words, since the ancient times, has never achieved this height" (驚心動魄，一字千金，人人筆下所無，卻為人人意中所有，雖鐵石人亦應感動. 從古至今，文字之力之大，無過於此者矣). One might be amused by the way Huang described Liang's political writings, since nothing was mentioned about the new concepts that Liang had introduced into China. What amazed Huang was the mesmerizing literary quality of Liang's words. The expression that "he [Liang Qichao] writes in a way that no one else can, but speaks to the mind of every man" is clearly, one might argue, a perfect definition of "literature" *per se*, which is by nature a kind of telepathic activity that connects a writer with a group of anonymous readers. The idea of achieving a social and political change in the realm of culture and literature therefore had its roots in the late nineteenth century.

Hu Shi, a leading May Fourth scholar, also commented on Liang's exceptional skill in writing: "Were it not for the pen of Liang, even were there hundreds of Sun Yat-sens and Huang Keqiangs, could the success [of the Xinhai revolution] arrive so soon? A recent poet thus wrote, 'Revolution begins when language reveals its power.' Only Liang can be an example of this"[6] (使無梁氏之筆, 雖有百十孫中山, 黃克強, 豈能成功如此之速耶? 近人詩 "文字收功日, 全球革命時", 此二語惟梁氏可以當之無愧). While Hu Shi often claimed that the May Fourth literary movement was different from many other literary and cultural movements in the history of China since it was consciously promoted, perhaps the idea of a cultural-literary revolution had been articulated almost a decade before the May Fourth period. Even Mao Zedong 毛澤東 (1893–1976) complimented Liang's writings; "His *Bianfa tongyi* (General discussions on the reform of laws) was serialized on the *Shiwubao* (Contemporary news). His writings are sharp in argument, clear in reasoning, overflowing with emotion, and thoroughly satisfying to read" (他寫的《變法通議》在《時務報》上連載, 立論鋒利, 條理分明, 感情奔放, 痛快淋漓). If Mao did not specify what he was commenting on, which was actually a serious piece of writing on the necessity of a legal reform, one might think that he was complimenting the writer on a piece of literature. What amused Mao most was obviously not Liang's proposal for a legal reform, but the literary effect of his exceptional writings. From the late Qing to the early Republican period, it is clear that, in the eyes of many, Liang Qichao was more significant as a writer than as a politician.

To be sure, Liang himself was also aware of the power of language. During his exile to Japan, he wrote "Lun xiaoshuo yu qunzhi zhi guanxi" 論小說與群治之關係 (On the relationship between fiction and the government of the people) in 1902, in which he proposed a "revolution of fiction" (小說界革命) that seeks to elevate the writing of fiction to be an exemplary form of literary creation.[7] Many scholars had pointed out that this article might be considered the precursor of the May Fourth new literature movement. But judging from the evaluations of Liang given by Chinese intellectuals and their comments on his work, the series of political essays that he wrote between 1896 and 1902 had perhaps the greatest influence on Chinese literary circles and the

---

6 The Xinhai revolution was the revolution that overthrew the Qing dynasty in 1911.
7 See Liang Qichao, "Lun xiaoshuo yu qunzhi zhi guanxi" 論小說與群治之關係 (On the relationship between fiction and the government of the people), translated and collected in Kirk Denton, *Modern Chinese Literary Thought: Writings on Literature 1893–1945* (Stanford, CA: Stanford University Press, 1996), 72.

ensuing May Fourth generation. The political writings of Liang that are full of new ideas and new views on a new world order amazed the Chinese and gave them a fresh look at international reality.

Lin Shu 林紓 (1852–1924) is another figure who contributed to the rise of May Fourth cultural discourses that started to consider "literature" as a new site for ideological contestation. A prominent classical essayist, Lin had translated more than one hundred and fifty foreign literary works (mostly novels) from France, Britain, Russia, Norway, Spain, Switzerland, Japan, and the United States. Some of the most important writers that he translated include William Shakespeare, Daniel Defoe, Jonathan Swift, Charles Dickens, Washington Irving, Alexander Dumas, Alexander Dumas *fils*, Leo Tolstoy, and Henrik Ibsen. Lin himself, however, did not speak any foreign languages, but had to rely on others to translate and interpret the content of the novels for him, and he would then put down what he heard in literary Chinese (i.e., classical Chinese). Lin Shu's translations are thus necessarily full of errors, mistranslations, and even his or his co-translator's own rewritings of the original stories. While Lin's translations are far from being accurate according to modern standards, his translated works were incredibly popular and well received in his time. In particular, his translation of Alexander Dumas *fils*'s *La Dame aux Camélias* as *Bali chahua nü yishi* 巴黎茶花女遺事 (Past stories of the Lady of the Camellias in Paris) in 1899 was an immediate commercial success. According to a biographical account of Lin, it is said that this book had "revealed to the Chinese what they had never seen before, and hundreds of thousands of copies were sold" (國人見所未見, 不脛走萬本).[8] Many Chinese readers at the time even wrote poems to lament the tragic fate of the protagonist. Yan Fu, for example, who typically wrote on and translated only serious sociological and scientific works, responded to the novel in a poetic way, "The story of the poor Lady of the Camellias had broken the hearts of many Chinese men" (可憐一卷茶花女, 斷盡支那盪子腸).[9] While Lin was eventually targeted and criticized by the May Fourth intellectuals for defending the value of literary Chinese—a view that contradicted the overall aim of many May Fourth writers who sought to promote vernacular Chinese and vernacular literature, it is undeniable that his translated works had demonstrated a new kind of literature that was different from the norm of classical Chinese writing and that reflects the traits of both Chinese and foreign narrative traditions.

---

8 See A Ying 阿英, "Guanyu bali chahua nü yishi" 關於巴黎茶花女遺事 (On the past stories of the camellia-woman in Paris), in Qian Zhongshu 錢鐘書 et al., *Lin Shu de fanyi* 林紓的翻譯 (Lin Shu's translations) (Beijing: Shangwu chubanshe, 1981), 53–59.

9 Ibid., 53.

Leo Ou-fan Lee once argued that Lin Shu's translation of *La Dame aux Camélias* was instrumental to the rise of May Fourth writers, who, despite their ostensibly rational and scientific slogans, were guided by a romantic spirit that continued to shape their revolutionary language even in the 1950s and 60s. In order to highlight the romantic temper of the May Fourth generation, Lee juxtaposed the scientific rationalism represented by Yan Fu, Liang Qichao, and Chen Duxiu 陳獨秀 (1879–1942), who glorified the image of "science," "new people," and "new youth," with the subjective sentimentalism represented by Lin Shu and Su Manshu 蘇曼殊 (1884–1918), among others, who stressed the positive value of the emotions of individual humans.[10] Such an interpretation is illuminating because it opens up the possibility of understanding the May Fourth Movement not simply as a political movement or a form of historical objectivism and collectivism, but as a dynamic literary movement that embraces the various imaginings and desires of mankind. With this logic in mind, if we consider the large number of emotional responses aroused by Lin's translated works, we can go on to argue that Lin's translation had even helped his readers foster a kind of cosmopolitan consciousness that allowed them to connect spiritually and emotionally to a larger world, thereby making them feel that they were part of a global community and that they, too, possessed a kind of sensibility common to all human beings. This emphasis on a cosmopolitan consciousness dovetails with the scientific rationalism championed by Yan Fu, Liang Qichao, and Chen Duxiu, who had consciously sought to cultivate a modern mindset among the Chinese, raising their awareness of a new and changing international world.

As a literary movement, the tale commonly told of the May Fourth new culture movement often starts with Hu Shi's call for literary reform in 1917. In January 1917, Hu Shi published "Wenxue gailiang chuyi" 文學改良芻議 (Some modest proposals for the reform of literature) in *New Youth* 新青年, a progressive magazine that sought to introduce modern social thought to China. In the next month, the magazine's founder and chief editor, Chen Duxiu, published "Wenxue geming lun" 文學革命論 (On literary revolution) in support of Hu Shi, using a more radical language to call for a fundamental reevaluation of China's cultural tradition. Other writers, such as Qian Xuantong 錢玄同 (1887–1939), Liu Bannong 劉半農 (1891–1934), and Fu Sinian 傅斯年 (1896–1950), all wrote in response to both Hu's and Chen's proposals for a literary revolution. Since the aim of these writers was to create a new literature in

---

10 See Schwartz, B. (ed.) *Reflections on the May Fourth Movement: A Symposium*. (Cambridge, Mass: Harvard University Asia Center, 1972), 70.

vernacular Chinese, this literary revolution is also known as the New Literature Movement or Vernacular Literature Movement.

This literary movement, which had its roots in the late Qing and blossomed in the May Fourth period, is important, for it signals a process in which the Chinese began to reflect on the question of national character and the cultural psychology of the Chinese in a serious manner. Lu Xun's often-quoted passage from the *Outcry* 吶喊 perhaps best summarizes the vision of this literary movement: "I no longer believed in the overwhelming importance of medical science. However rude a nation was in physical health, if its people were intellectually feeble, they would never become anything other than cannon folder or gawping spectators, their loss to the world no cause for regret. The first task was to change their spirit; and literature and the arts, I decided at the time, were the best means to this end. And so I reinvented myself as a crusader for cultural reform" (醫學并非一件緊要事, 凡是愚弱的國民, 即使体格如何健全, 如何茁壯, 也只能做毫無意義的示眾的材料和看客, 病死多少是不必以為不幸的. 所以我們的第一要著, 是在改變他們的精神, 而善于改變精神的是, 我那時以為當然要推文藝, 于是想提倡文藝運動了).[11]

Zhou Zuoren 周作人 (1885–1967), Lu Xun's younger brother and another leading May Fourth writer, had it right when he commented on the nature of the May Fourth literary revolution: "In this literary revolution, script reform is the first step, and thought reform the second, which is more important than the first step" (文學革命上, 文字改革是第一步, 思想改革是第二步, 卻比第一步更為重要).[12] Fu Sinian 傅斯年, a student leader in the 1919 Beijing student protest who later became an important scholar, even portrayed this literary revolution as a "psychological change" (心理改換),[13] since an individual's psychological development, as Fu maintained, is equally important to his or her intellectual growth. This emphasis on cultural-psychological-intellectual reformulation thus characterizes the literary discourses in the early May Fourth period in which the idea of "literature" emerged as a new concept that was intellectually and ideologically contested.[14]

---

11   Lu Xun, "Preface," in *The Real Story of Ah-Q and Other Tales of China: The Complete Fiction of Lu Xun*, trans. Julia Lovell (New York: Penguin, 2010), 17.
12   Zhou Zuoren, "Sixiang geming" 思想革命 (Thought reform), in Hu Shi, ed., *Zhongguo xin wenyi daxi: wenxue lunzhan yiji* 中國新文學大系: 文學論戰一集 (Taipei: Dahan, 1976), 274.
13   Ibid., 280.
14   Some May Fourth intellectuals noticed a possible connection between the May Fourth new literature and the Ming dynasty's vernacular literature. Particularly, Zhou Zuoren, in a long essay, pointed out that the May Fourth literary movement might actually derive from a late Ming literary school, the Gong'an school, which also emphasized a natural and vernacular literary expression. Zhou's observation is valuable since it places and

3   The Transnational and Cross-Cultural Flow of May Fourth Discourses

While the intention of creating a national literature and a standardized Chinese language underlies the May Fourth new culture movement, the transnational and cross-cultural flow that facilitated the rise of such a movement should merit our attention. Take Hu Shi, the initiator of the May Fourth literary revolution, for instance. Hu Shi had pointed out time and again that he had started to ruminate on the idea of a literary revolution when he was still studying in the United States. The debate between him and his friends over the question of whether Chinese poetry can be written in vernacular Chinese, in particular, led him to believe that a literary revolution would eventually be needed in the Chinese context to foster a new literary practice that is free from the shackles of classical Chinese tradition.[15] While Hu's debate with his friends in the U.S. is a well-known story, the multicultural and translingual nature of the May Fourth discourses deserves more attention from researchers, because it demonstrates a useful example for cross-cultural analysis.

In fact, as a scholar who was born and raised in China but trained in America, Hu Shi, like many others at that time, had read and written extensively in both English and Chinese throughout his life. In particular, he had elaborated his theory of a literary revolution in both languages for different audiences on various occasions. A multicultural and bilingual mode of reading and writing thus characterizes his intellectual discourses. In his English writings, one can see how he sometimes modifies the meanings of certain English words through Chinese. In his Chinese writings, one can also notice how he

---

examines the May Fourth literary revolution in a larger historical context. While the May Fourth writers and the Gong'an scholars appear to have shared the same goal of vernacularizing Chinese literary writing, the two groups still differed from each other in that the May Fourth writers associated their practice with an agenda to modernize the country, a trend that only began to emerge in the late Qing period, as this introduction has previously shown. In addition, contrary to the cultural-psychological-intellectual approach, the late Ming scholars did not express any intention to probe into the psychology of the Chinese people and to create a national culture. From this perspective, the May Fourth literary movement is more akin to the late Qing literati's political agenda than the late Ming's Gong'an school, which simply aims for a more natural way of writing and leaves the foundation of Chinese culture intact and unchallenged. See Zhou Zuoren, *Zhongguo xin wenxue de yuanliu* 中國新文學的源流 (The origin of new Chinese literature) (Shanghai: Huadong shifan daxue chubanshe, 1995), 17–65.

15   Mei Guangdi 梅光迪 (1890–1945) and H. C. Zen (Jen Hung-chun) 任鴻雋 (1886–1961) often debated with Hu Shi, who suggested that vernacular Chinese could also be used in poetic writing. Mei later established an important magazine of cultural conservatism, *Xueheng* 學衡 (The Critical Review), the antithesis of *New Youth*.

resorted to English at times as an alternative knowledge system to reintroduce or articulate a new or foreign concept. In his diaries, one can also observe how he repeatedly compared the Chinese culture to others, reevaluating the latter in order to make sense of the former. Yuen Ren Chao 趙元任 (1892–1982), another leading scholar of the time, also studied in the U.S. and also wrote many works in English that later changed the course of Chinese linguistics studies. His *A Grammar of Spoken Chinese* and *Language and Symbolic System*, originally composed in English, for example, were two of the most important modern scholarly works on Chinese languages.[16]

The transnational and cross-cultural discourses of May Fourth scholars hence reflected a larger debate on the cultural origin of the May Fourth Movement. Many had debated whether the literary revolution in the May Fourth period could be seen as a derivative of Western literary trends. For instance, as early as 1955, Achilles Fang argued that Hu Shi's famous proposals for a literary reform were principally based on Ezra Pound's and Amy Lowell's poetic works of Imagism—an early twentieth-century English and American literary movement that concerns the writing of poetry. Other scholars, such as Wang Runhua and Luo Qing in the 1970s, also agreed that there is a connection between Hu Shi's proposition and American Imagism. Wang, in particular, described this connection as "a missing footnote in the history of new Chinese literature" (中國新文學史中一個被遺漏的註腳).[17] It was not until the 1980s that Chou Chih-p'ing began to emphasize Hu's background in classical Chinese learning, arguing that his years of training in classical Chinese literature were instrumental to his theory of vernacular literature.[18] In fact, scholars had in a sense long noted the transnational and cross-cultural nature of May Fourth discourses. Merle Goldman, for example, in her 1977 volume, *Modern Chinese Literature in the May Fourth Era*, maintained,

---

16　See Yuen Ren Chao, *A Grammar of Spoken Chinese* (Berkeley, University of California Press, 1968), and *Language and Symbolic System* (Cambridge, Cambridge University Press, 1868).

17　See Wang Runhua 王潤華, "Cong 'xinchao' de neirong kan zhongguo xinshi geming de qiyuan—zhongguo xin wenxue shi zhong yige bei yilou de zhujiao" 從「新潮」的內涵看中國新詩革命的起源—中國新文學史中一個被遺漏的註腳 (The origin of revolution of Chinese new poetry from the perspective of *New Tide*—A missing footnote in the history of new Chinese literature), in *Zhongxi wenxye guanxi yanjiu* (Taipei: Dongda, 1978), 227–245. Also see Luo Qing's 羅青〈各取其所需影響—胡適與印象派〉《中外文學》八卷七期（1987）頁, 48–69.

18　Chou Chih-p'ing, "Hu Shi wenxue lilun tanyuan" 胡適文學理論探源 (The origin of Hu Shi's literary theory), in Chou Chih-p'ing, ed. *Hu Shi and Lu Xun* 胡適與魯迅 (Taipei: Shibao chubanshe, 1988), 77–101.

At no other time, even in the period of Buddhist influence, was China so exposed to an alien culture. There is also no question that the impetus for change was already in motion before the May Fourth period ... The complex interaction between Western themes and Chinese material, and between Western techniques and Chinese inclinations, triggered the May Fourth creative explosion.[19]

Mau-sang Ng, for another example, foregrounded the influence of the Russian literary tradition on the May Fourth intellectuals who sought to build a modern literature that addresses the Chinese reality.[20] While different views on the cultural origin of the May Fourth Movement exist, it seems fair to say that the May Fourth literary revolution, from its beginning, was marked and facilitated by a transnational and cross-cultural flow of ideas and knowledge that can and should be examined in a global context and cannot be traced back to an absolute source of origin.

One may relate this volume to Goldman's 1977 *Modern Chinese Literature in the May Fourth Era*, a highly valuable volume that consists of several interesting papers which similarly highlighted the interactions and relations between foreign and native cultural traditions in shaping the May Fourth literary discourses. Yet this present volume has dealt with a number of issues and authors that were previously under-explored. For example, while Goldman's volume puts a stronger emphasis on the transformation of the modern Chinese literature in the May Fourth era, this volume highlights more how contemporary scholarship and newer historical materials can help us shed light on the cultural-intellectual discourses essential to the May Fourth Movement in general. Moreover, while Goldman's volume discusses more the aesthetic qualities of the May Fourth literature, this volume explores more the political memories and affective histories of May Fourth studies. Lastly, while the 1977 volume mainly investigates a group of writers traditionally labeled as "left-winged" such as Lu Xun, Mao Dun, and Qu Qiubai, this new volume on "May Fourth" investigates writers sometimes associated with "liberalism" such as Hu Shi and Shen Congwen. This, however, does not mean that this new volume has run the risk of reinforcing the dichotomy of the left and right, or between the revolutionary and reactionary. Instead, it attempts to complicate the story and memory of the May Fourth Movement by revealing its complexities and

---

19   See Merle Goldman, *Modern Chinese Literature in the May Fourth Era* (Cambridge: Harvard University Press, 1977), 11.
20   See Mau-sang Ng, *The Russian Hero in Modern Chinese Fiction* (New York: SUNY Press, 1988).

sometimes self-contradictory nature—a quality that makes the movement still relevant and useful to researchers nowadays.

More than a century has passed since Hu Shi and Chen Duxiu called for a literary revolution in 1917, a symbolic event that initiated a fundamental reevaluation and reformulation of China's cultural roots. Those who devoted themselves to the cause of this revolution are known as the May Fourth intellectuals because they are associated with the student protest that took place in Beijing on May 4, 1919. It was their works and words that set a new course for the development of Chinese culture and history. To date, the movement's legacy is still being contested and debated, and the effect of the paradigm that it created is still being invoked and discussed by those who seek to affirm and criticize it. Certain slogans that sprang forth from the movement are also time and again subject to interpretation and re-contextualization for various different purposes. The Chinese president Xi Jinping's recent remark on how the spirit of "May Fourth" should be applied to the Chinese government's agenda for the "great revival of the Chinese nation" is only one of many examples of how a simple evocation of the term "May Fourth" is still considered useful in contemporary political arena.[21]

The questions of what constitutes and how to evaluate the legacy of "May Fourth" has and will continue to generate a tremendous amount of debates and emotions, reflecting the various ways in which Chinese history and politics are interpreted and understood. While the conventional definitions of the legacy of "May Fourth" often refer to the ideas of science and democracy, anti-imperialism and patriotism, the essays collected in this volume aim to widen our scope of understanding by including various cultural, political, and historical forces that were aroused and facilitated by the May Fourth Movement, both as a historical event and a political symbol, from which many later social activists and political organizations gained their inspiration and momentum. The "May Fourth legacy," from this perspective, is necessarily historically-contingent and personally-invested. With the volume of discourse and emotion created by and invested in this time-honored tradition, it may be wise not to pin down

---

21 In the keynote speech delivered at the Great Hall of the People in Beijing on April 30th, 2019 that commemorates the 100th anniversary of the May Fourth Movement, Xi Jinping defined the core value of "May Fourth" to be the "spirit of patriotism". He asserted, "as long as the banner of patriotism is being held high, the Chinese people can unleash great powers in the endeavors to transform China and the world." Xi thus linked the movement with the cause of the great revival of the Chinese nation, and called for the mobilization of the young people of the entire country to have an "ardent love for the country" and "to obey and follow the party". For the full text of Xi's speech, see http://www.xinhuanet.com/politics/leaders/2019-04/30/c_1124440193.htm.

"May Fourth" with any single or sloganized definition. It is perhaps better to see it as an interpretative and analytical model that always welcomes and points to an alternative way of thinking and engaging with the past, and through which the future can be acted upon.

4   Contemporary Repercussions

This volume brings together thirteen essays by thirteen scholars from different fields to address the various aspects of the May Fourth Movement. One major goal of this book is to explore the possibilities of the May Fourth discourses, revealing their interdisciplinary nature and cross-cultural perspective, which are crucial to our humanities studies today. This book is divided into two parts, each of which contains chapters that address the main theme of the title of each part.

The first part examines the historical and political issues revolving around interpretations of "May Fourth." Some of the questions that we explore in this part include: How do we evaluate the May Fourth legacy in a global context? What is at stake in our current understanding of the "May Fourth" tradition and modern Chinese history? What are the gains and losses of comparing the movement to other major cultural movements in the Western context, such as the Renaissance and Enlightenment? And how do we reappraise the theoretical significance of "social practices" that seem to be left out in our current scholarship on the May Fourth Movement?

This first part, which addresses these questions, begins with chapter one exploring the memorability of "May Fourth" writings in relation to their capacity to arouse emotion. Gloria Davies argues that our understanding of "May Fourth" will be impoverished if we do not heed the affective power of its textual legacy and treat "May Fourth" instead as an object of analysis. Drawing on J. L. Austin's "speech act theory," Davies addresses the performative dimension of expressions, statements, and key texts that have come to be subsumed under "May Fourth." This take on "May Fourth" is thus illuminating in that it demonstrates that the discursive history of "May Fourth" can *de facto* and *de jure* be read as a history of emotions and affects, whose factors perhaps have yet to be fully explored in light of our reflection and commemoration of the May Fourth Movement.

Josephine Chiu-Duke, in chapter two, introduces and explores an important intellectual tradition of the May Fourth Movement—liberalism. Through the lens of Chan Koonchung's most recent novel, *Jianfeng ernian: An Uchronia of New China*, which limns an alternative history of a modern China, Chiu-Duke

INTRODUCTION

demonstrates the continual relevance of May Fourth liberal ideas and ideals, and suggests that Chan's depiction of a uchronia not only exposes the ills of Chinese society, but also signals a novelist's creative responses to the future of China after it has become a formidable world power. Chiu-Duke's discussion on the relationship between the May Fourth liberal legacy and Chan's fictional writing is thus important, as it sheds light on the connection between historical writing and political reality, thereby revealing the discursivity and elasticity of historical reality, which is always articulated through political languages.

Chih-p'ing Chou in chapter three demonstrates the two versions of modern Chinese history separately written and endorsed by the Nationalist and Chinese Communist Parties. As Chou lucidly points out, the political difference between the two parties has generated very different evaluations of many May Fourth intellectuals, among whom Lu Xun and Hu Shi are perhaps the best examples. While Lu Xun was hailed by Mao Zedong as "the greatest and most courageous fighter of the new cultural army," Hu Shi was denounced by many Chinese historians as "the most persistent and uncompromising enemy of Marxism and socialist thought." This bias against Hu Shi and the idolization of Lu Xun had permeated the Chinese scholarship of the May Fourth Movement for decades. The fact that these two major May Fourth thinkers are evaluated in radically different ways also reveals the complexity of the cultural-political landscape of modern China.

In chapter four, Gang Zhou revisits a long-standing debate on the question of whether Renaissance or Enlightenment is a more appropriate and useful term to describe the May Fourth Movement. Zhou proposes a renewed interest in using "Renaissance" as a conceptual category to evaluate the movement so as to situate it in a transnational context. Appropriating Franco Moretti's concept of "distant reading," Zhou ambitiously compares May Fourth China with historical junctures in other civilizations or cultures such as the Arabic, Indian, Turkish, Japanese, and Korean cultures, in order to emphasize the multiple and transnational practices of Renaissance. As the recent movement of world literature has challenged any analytical framework that focuses on a singular national literary tradition, chapter four is a timely intervention and response to such a challenge, and it demonstrates how the theoretical model of world literature can actually help us reshape and refresh our understanding of "May Fourth" in a global context.

In chapter five, Yung-chen Chiang discusses the historical significance of "May Fourth" through the lens of Hu Shi, who is perhaps the most vigilant and active May Fourth writer in re-interpreting and "safeguarding" this movement's legacy. In this chapter, Chiang guides us through the various stages of Hu Shi's work, wherein interpretations of "May Fourth" not only reflect his evolving cultural-political positions, but also reveal the possibility of understanding modern China's history in light of Cold War geopolitics. The fact that Hu Shi had always situated the movement in its historical context, even as his political position shifted, as Chiang elucidates in great detail, should alert us to read carefully his deceptively dispassionate writings, encouraging us to follow him in continuing to reinterpret the meanings of "May Fourth" in its various historical and global contexts without reifying any ideological historical perspective.

This first part of the book ends with chapter six, which raises an interesting question on the notion of "social practices" as an important aspect of the May Fourth Movement. Shakhar Rahav suggests that scholars of modern Chinese studies can focus more on the connection between May Fourth intellectuals' "social practices" and the "theoretical doctrines" they offered, which are more extensively researched. Rahav highlights the tension between "theory" and "practice," and he considers it crucial to our understanding of May Fourth theorists, who are often social activists themselves. In particular, Rahav discusses the example of an early leader of the Chinese Communist Party, Yun Daiying, and shows that Yun as a social activist was not only inspired by the socialist and anarchist ideology but also motivated by the religious practices of foreign missionaries who were traveling across China in the early twentieth century.

Following the discussions of the historical and political issues revolving around the May Fourth Movement, the second part of this volume brings its readers to the realm of language and literature, in which the May Fourth intellectuals played a significant role in establishing modern Chinese literature and language. While much ink has been spilt on topics related to the May Fourth new culture movement, and many works of May Fourth writers have also been canonized, this volume seeks to put the May Fourth literary discourses in dialogue with such contemporary literary trends as ecocriticism, sound studies, and postcolonial theories, in hope of renewing our understanding as well as applying the research methods of May Fourth studies. In particular, the second part of the volume aims to challenge some of the assumptions or concepts that are hitherto unchallenged by the existing scholarship, particularly those related to language reform and vernacular literature.

For this effort, chapter seven opens the discussion by introducing a new way of investigating May Fourth literature: problematizing the modern concept of the "self" that started to emerge in China during the early twentieth century. In chapter seven, Ban Wang maintains that this modern trend of individualism implied a negation of premodern human—nature and human—human relations, as well as a kind of anthropocentrism that is essential to a capitalistic modernity characterized by its division of labor, consumerism, urbanism, and corrosive commodity production. Yet this anthropocentrism had long been pondered and criticized by the great May Fourth writer Shen Congwen. Through a close reading of Shen's essays and stories, Wang argues that Shen's works actually contain a variety of mythical and cosmic insights that dissolve the modern "self" into a vast ecological chain of beings, uncovering a comprehensive, interconnected, resonant universe of plants, mountains, rivers, crops, and animals, to which the human body is organically linked.

Continuing chapter seven's inquiry into the ecological writings of Shen Congwen, Todd Foley, in chapter eight, proposes to examine Xiao Hong's *The Field of Life and Death* through the lens of both ecocriticism and animal studies. While this novella was initially framed in terms of its immediate social relevance—namely, its nationalist, anti-Japanese sentiment—Foley shows how the work effectively operated as a broader critique and subversion of the patriarchal order. By focusing on Xiao Hong's presentation of animals and the natural world in relation to humans, the author contends that her critique not only extends to the very conception of the human, but also suggests that the only way to overcome the problems of human society is to reformulate this conception from its basic grounding in the animal.

Nick Kaldis, in chapter nine, explores some of Lu Xun's best-known stories, examining the configuration of Lu Xun's characters and their relationship to then-dominant ideological discourses, in order to tease out the heretofore seldom-observed or altogether unremarked-upon vital features of his canonical works. Kaldis's chapter is grounded in the conviction that an attunement to the insights internal to a text can expand our understanding of a literary work, its intellectual-historical context, and its author. This chapter also affirms the relevance of the concept of aesthetic cognition and the value of a hermeneutics of engagement in the study of modern Chinese literature.

Chapter ten explores the works of Ding Ling and seeks to point to a new way of studying modern Chinese literature. In this chapter, Chien-hsin Tsai points out that, due to the political turmoil in early twentieth-century China, many May Fourth writers frequently documented bombing incidents in their diary entries, essays, and novels. Despite the intense military situation, the May Fourth writers did not hesitate to use sound-inflected metaphors such as "bomb" and "bombing" to praise an author or work that had a huge impact on the literary scene at the time. Tsai provides a review of Ding Ling's works and her relationship with other May Fourth writers with a focus on other sound-related metaphors. By treating Ding Ling as a synecdoche for May Fourth writers, this chapter seeks to highlight the literary and social effects of these sound-related metaphors in the May Fourth literary writings.

Chapter eleven discusses an interesting case of language reform in early twentieth-century China. Chih-p'ing Chou traces the way in which Esperanto, a European artificial language invented in 1887, was introduced into China and perceived by Chinese intellectuals as a convenient tool for articulating the differences between Chinese and Western civilizations. Chou particularly details the different stages of the introduction of Esperanto into China from the late nineteenth to the mid-twentieth century, explaining how anarchism, utilitarianism, and social Darwinism facilitated the reception of the artificial language by Chinese intellectuals. This chapter even extends its discussion to the contemporary period by discussing the way in which a Chinese writer such as Ba Jin has proposed Esperanto as a moral medium instead of a political tool for various purposes.

In chapter twelve, Victor Mair and Gina Elia examine Hu Shi's notion of "religion" as a self-styled, rhetorical device that enables him to engage in philosophical thinking. While scholars such as Jerome B. Grieder have examined Hu Shi's notion of "religion" in great depth, Mair and Gina appropriate the perspectives of religious studies, arguing that Hu Shi's use of the term "religion" in describing his worldview, is actually a rhetorical strategy that helps him enact his philosophy on a formal level as the content of what he writes simultaneously explains what his philosophy entails. By providing an overview of Hu Shi's theory of social immortality, this chapter shows that Hu Shi's reference to "religion" worked to emphasize the significance he attributed to it.

Chapter thirteen re-examines the concept of "vernacular" in the May Fourth context. Carlos Yu-Kai Lin argues that the Chinese term for the vernacular, *baihua*, was not a self-evident concept in the May Fourth context, since its meanings were still being contested and redefined. By tracing the connotations of the term from the Ming to Qing and early Republican periods, this chapter shows that what we take as *baihua* now is actually a modern invention. Chapter thirteen also investigates the transformation of the concept of *baihua* in the May Fourth context by using Hu Shi's writings as a primary example. The author argues that concept of *baihua* in the May Fourth period was not just a new instrument or medium of writing, but actually a kind of quality, property, and potentiality that could be used to evaluate or predict the health or lifespan of a living language.

Proposed in 2017, this volume invites scholars and teachers and all those who are interested in the development of modern Chinese literature, culture, and history, to ponder the May Fourth Movement's discursive utility and relevancy to our twenty-first-century world. It is our sincere and collective hope that the "spirit" of May Fourth, whatever form and content it embodies, can continue to be an illuminating source for our various inquiries into the world of humanities.

PART 1

Histories and Politics

CHAPTER 1

May Fourth as Affect

Gloria Davies

Will we ever know enough about "May Fourth"? Not likely, if the ever-expanding textual edifice that is "May Fourth" is anything to go by. In Chinese-language scholarship, "May Fourth studies" (*Wusi yanjiu* 五四研究) is practically a research field in its own right, one covering a spectrum of cultural and literary, political and social issues, centering on the historic protest movement of 1919 and extending from the mid-1910s to the mid-late 1920s.[1] What this massive academic interest in "May Fourth" demonstrates is the contingency of historical significance on textual production. So long as "May Fourth" attracts public and research interest and continues to receive institutional funding, it will remain historically relevant.

Many of those who participated in or supported the student-led street protest in Beijing on May 4, 1919, evidently sought to keep "May Fourth" discursively alive. By the protest's first anniversary in 1920, expositions on "May Fourth" and its "spirit" had already appeared in abundance. Commemorative essays by prominent academics of the day such as Chen Duxiu 陳獨秀 (1879–1942), Hu Shi 胡適 (1891–1962), and Jiang Menglin 蔣夢麟 (1886–1964), and leading student activists such as Fu Sinian 傅斯年 (1896–1950) and Luo Jialun 羅家倫 (1897–1969) ensured that the idea of "May Fourth" gained currency among their contemporaries. These earliest commemorations lauded the protestors, among other things, for having taken "direct action" (直接行動) (Chen; Fu), for having "summoned forth a sense of public responsibility" (喚起公眾責任心) (Fu), for their "spirit of self-motivation" (Hu and Jiang), their "spirit of sacrifice" (犧牲精神) (Chen; Luo), and their "spirit of [invoking] social sanctions" (社會制裁的精神) (Luo). The May Fourth protestors were also praised for having "raised the consciousness of the masses" (民眾自決的精神) (Luo) and fostering among themselves "an interest in society and the nation" (對於社會國家的興趣) as well as "an ability to write essays and give speeches, to organize

---

1   See for instance, Zhao Qian, "A Review of Studies of the May Fourth Movement in China over the Past Decade," *Chinese Studies in History* 43, no. 4 (2010): 73–89.

and get things done" (引出學生的作文演說的能力, 組織的能力, 辦事 的能力) (Hu and Jiang).[2]

These early rhetorical evocations, together with statements or expressions from numerous other essays by noted intellectual figures of the time have, in turn, been widely quoted in subsequent decades as textual evidence of one or another "May Fourth spirit" at work, propelling modern China forward. Yet different motivations and different ways of writing about "May Fourth" have generated multiple and varied responses to the question, "What does 'May Fourth' mean?"

This question presupposes the importance of "May Fourth." It also assumes that a cogent and meaningful account of "May Fourth" can always be produced if one studies the textual evidence closely enough, equipped with the right theoretical and analytical tools. However, this begs corollary and debate-generating questions such as: Who decides (or is authorized to decide) what is cogent and meaningful? What constitutes adequate textual evidence? How many and what kinds of texts have authority? Which theoretical and analytical tools are the right ones, and according to whom or which authorities?

State censorship in mainland China, first under Chiang Kai-shek's Nationalist (KMT) government from 1928 to 1949, then under Chinese Communist Party rule (CCP) after 1949 and to the present, and under censorship in Taiwan from 1949 to the early 1980s, together with the official accounts of "May Fourth" produced by China's Communist party-state since 1949, have politicized and complicated interpretations of "May Fourth" across the Taiwan Strait and throughout the Chinese-speaking world. For one thing, "May Fourth" commands far greater official and public attention in mainland China than in

---

[2] I have included links to online resources that I accessed while researching this essay. The availability of "May Fourth" publications online and the interest they attract is indicative not only of their present-day relevance but the extent to which digital technology has transformed scholarship and public debate about "May Fourth." Chen Duxiu 陳獨秀, "Wusi yundongde jingshen shi shenme?" 五四運動的精神是什麼 (What was the spirit of the May Fourth Movement?), *Shi bao* 時報, April 22, 1920, online at: http://blog.renren.com/share/222018481/10589389434; Fu Sinian 傅斯年, "Zhongguo gou he zhongguoren" 中國狗和中國人 (Chinese dogs and Chinese people), *Xin qingnian* 新青年 (New Youth), vol. 6, no. 6 (November 1, 1919), online at https://www.edubridge.com/erxiantang/l2/fusinian_gouren.htm; Hu Shi 胡適 and Jiang Menglin 蔣夢麟, "Women duiyu xuesheng de xiwang" 我們對於學生的希望 (Our hope for the students), *Chenbao fukan* 晨報副刊 (Morning Post Supplement), May 4, 1920, online at: http://data.book.hexun.com/chapter-18093-3-1.shtml; Luo Jialun, "Yinianlai women xuesheng yundongde chenggong shibai he jianglai ying qu de fangxiang" 一年來我們學生運動的成功失敗和將來應採取的方針 (The successes and failures of our student movement over the past year, and the policy to be adopted in the future), *Xinchao* 新潮 (New Tide), 2, no. 4 (1920): 846–861. Online at: www.cnthinkers.com/thinkerweb/literature/29124.

Taiwan. Lung-kee Sun, among others, has noted the singular influence of Mao Zedong's 1940 essay "New Democracy" in shaping mainland perceptions of "May Fourth." By describing "May Fourth" as the starting point of China's "history of 'cultural revolution,'" Mao effectively elevated it to the moment when "modern China" began in earnest.[3] In 1939 the CCP designated May Fourth a public holiday, calling it China's "National Youth Day." It has ever since been celebrated officially as that in the People's Republic of China. In Taiwan, "May Fourth" has been more modestly remembered and, until at least the late 1970s, its history was carefully stripped of any association with Chinese Communism.

It is precisely because the violent politics of the KMT and the CCP dominated the decades *after* May 4, 1919, that sinophone scholars have frequently historicized "May Fourth" as the promise of what came *before*. The Taiwan-based author and social commentator Li Ao 李敖 (1935–2018) highlighted the event's prelapsarian significance when he wrote in April 1989:

> Unfortunately, after the May Fourth Movement, as both the Nationalists and the Communists adopted Soviet-style organizational methods and party discipline under the tutelage of the Soviet Union, the goal of "healthy individualism" was abandoned for that of collectivism. This foreign import brought disaster on China, for it stifled intellectual liberation.[4]

A decade earlier, the editorial introduction to the May 1979 issue of the prominent Taipei-based magazine *Biographical Literature* 傳記文學, published to commemorate the event's sixtieth anniversary, asked a series of questions to draw attention to "May Fourth" as a moment of possibility, prior to the various agitative directions taken by Chinese politics from that moment onward:

> Was it a New Thought movement? A New Culture Movement? A New Arts Movement? A Vernacular Language movement? A Modernization movement? A Westernization movement? A Reform movement? An Enlightenment movement? A movement for Science and Democracy? A Women's Rights movement? A Youth movement? A Mass movement? ... Those who love it are only afraid they are not close enough to it, those

---

3 Lung-kee Sun, "The *Other* May Fourth," in *Beyond the May Fourth Paradigm: In Search of Chinese Modernity*, ed. Kai-wing Chow, Tze-ki Hon, Hung-yok Ip, and Don C. Price (Lanham: Lexington Books, 2008), 275.

4 Quoted and translated in *New Ghosts, Old Dreams: Chinese Voices of Conscience*, ed. Geremie R. Barmé with Linda Jaivin (New York: Times Books, 1992), 344. Online at: http://chinaheritage.net/journal/may-fourth-at-ninety-nine/.

who distance themselves from it are only afraid they are not far enough. How fortunate is May Fourth! How guilty is May Fourth![5]

The key words listed in this excerpt constitute ways of historicizing "May Fourth" that were first introduced in the 1920s, with "New Culture," "Modernization," "Enlightenment," and "Science and Democracy" (especially "Democracy") receiving great attention from scholars both in China and internationally. As concepts, these key words also provide an organizational fiction (to use Fredric Jameson's useful notion) around which academic authors present their arguments about "May Fourth."[6] Contingent upon how we thematize and structure our accounts of May Fourth, whether we accentuate, say, "New Culture" over "Science and Democracy," the received explanations and interpretations on which we draw, the individuals and organizations we discuss, the primary and archival materials we assemble in support of our argumentation, will differ.

To engage with "May Fourth" in its centenary year is to confront a formidable hermeneutical enterprise: analyses abound under each of its many key words (ideas and events) and key figures (individuals and groups). "May Fourth" is researched under History, Cultural Studies, Literary Studies, Politics, and Sociology, to name just the main disciplines, setting aside sub-disciplines and interdisciplinary areas of research. The sense we make of "May Fourth" constitutes its "constative" dimension, to use John Austin's term.[7] These are the evidence-based (or factual) accounts we produce, in which we grant significance to selected actions, ideas, persons, and texts as representative of "May Fourth."

Take, for example, Rudolf Wagner's summary of a retrospective 1940 account by Luo Jialun: "On the morning of May 4, the head of the organizing committee at Peking National University, Di Fuding (1895–1964), stormed into the office of the journal *New Tide* [...], then edited by Luo Jialun (1896–1969), and declared: 'Today's movement cannot do without a public appeal.'"[8] Di's role in the protest, his visit to the office of *New Tide* that morning, and what he said when he was there, are statements for which we can look for evidence to corroborate

---

5 Quoted and translated by Wang Gungwu, *The Chineseness of China: Selected Essays* (Hong Kong: Oxford University Press, 1991), 240.
6 As Jameson writes, "Texts come before us as the always-already-read," such that the "sedimented reading habits and categories developed by ... inherited interpretive traditions" dictate the approach and methods we use. Fredric Jameson, *The Political Unconscious: Narrative as a Socially Symbolic Act* (London: Methuen, 1981), 9–10.
7 J. L. Austin, *How to Do Things with Words*, ed. J. O. Urmson and Marina Sbisà (Cambridge MA: Harvard University Press, 1975), 6, 47.
8 Quoted and translated in Rudolf Wagner, "The Canonization of May Fourth" in *The Appropriation of Cultural Capital: China's May Fourth Project*, ed. Milena Doleželová-Velingerová and Oldřich Král (Cambridge MA: Harvard University Asia Center, 2001), 69–70.

Luo's account. They are constative if we simply want to know whether these things happened. The statements are either true or false.

However, the overall picture of Di "storming" in, declaring what he did, is also a subjective construction. Insofar as the constative dimension consists of descriptions or true/false statements, it does not include communications of perception or persuasion, which are best described as "performative," a term that Austin used to refer to utterances that "perform" or accomplish an action (of which clear examples include "I declare the meeting open," "I pronounce you husband and wife", or "I promise to ...").[9]

Performative utterances are neither true nor false. Instead, they "do something in saying something" and are judged as either "felicitous" or "infelicitous."[10] John Searle explains:

> If I make a statement that I am in no position to make, my utterance will be infelicitous in exactly the same sense that a promise can be infelicitous if, for example, I am unable to do the thing I promised to do.[11]

Searle's explanation is based on Austin's definition of the performative as depending on "the intentions or sincerity of the one who speaks."[12] However, J. Hillis Miller, among others, provides a fuller and more productive understanding of the performative as depending instead "on ignoring whatever goes on secretly in people's hearts and holding them to the rule that says our word is our bond." Hence,

> The words themselves must do the work, not the secret intentions of the speaker or writer. For civil order to be maintained, we must be able to hold speakers and writers responsible for their words, whatever their intentions at the time.[13]

Just as the credibility (and performative force) of Di's declaration, "Today's movement cannot do without a public appeal," depended upon whether his peers accorded him the authority to so instruct them on that occasion, the extent to which we, as latter-day readers today, regard Luo's recollection as felicitous, rests on whether we (like Wagner) perceive him as a reliable narrator.

---

9   Austin, *How to Do Things with Words*, 6, 47.
10 J. Hillis Miller, *Speech Acts in Literature* (Stanford CA: Stanford University Press, 2001), 12.
11 John Searle, "J. L. Austin," in *A Companion to Analytic Philosophy*, ed. A. P. Martinich and E. David Sosa (Malden and Oxford: Blackwell Publishers), 220.
12 Miller, *Speech Acts*, 28.
13 Miller, *Speech Acts*, 32.

The constative and performative are intricately combined in human communications. Luo's account of that morning when Di entered *New Tide*'s office becomes meaningful for us when we take Luo at his word, for it triggers an affective image that shapes and colors how we see "May Fourth." The constative and performative serve us well as a heuristic device. However, it is important to note that Austin was unable to develop a systematic theory out of the "dichotomy of performatives and constatives" and abandoned it "in favor of more general *families* of related and overlapping speech acts."[14] As long as we do not treat the constative and performative as key elements of a grand theory, the dichotomy is helpful in highlighting the difference between the truth-value of what is said (constative) and the effects achieved by what is said and how it is said (performative).

The constative dimension of "May Fourth" is what my opening question alludes to: Will we ever *know* enough about "May Fourth"? A general answer would be that we seem to be always discovering more and better ways of explaining the known "facts" or finding new ones, and subjecting what we cumulatively know to ever more refined analysis. However, this constative view of "May Fourth" is never the whole picture. Far from it. What has sustained the interpretive fervor surrounding "May Fourth" is not simply a case of knowing more or knowing better. As indicated by *Biographical Literature*'s 1979 editorial introduction (cited earlier), it is because "May Fourth" arouses the passions that readers decades later remain inclined to either "love" or "distance themselves from" what they discover in its textual remnants. Authors (long dead) who invoked spirits of "self-motivation," "sacrifice," and "social sanctions" and so on, were not relaying known or verifiable facts. They used emotion-charged language. They wrote to elicit a reaction.

The performative power of the writings signed "May Fourth" is implicit in the extent to which readers past and present have responded to them. An utterance such as: "How fortunate is May Fourth! How guilty is May Fourth!" conveys a felt experience of reading "May Fourth" texts, as does this remark by the literary historian Chen Pingyuan 陳平原 (b. 1954) in 2017: "I wager that three hundred years from now, the whole of [China's] twentieth century would be viewed as the era of 'May Fourth'" (我猜測，三百年後再看，整個 20 世紀就是一個 "五四" 的時代)[15] To date, however, scholarly attention has focused on the constative dimension of "May Fourth": to identify and account

---

14　Quoted in Miller, *Speech Acts*, 15.
15　Chen Pingyuan, "Zhengge ershi shiji doushi Wu Si xin wenhua de shiji" 整個 20 世紀都是五四新文化的世紀 (The whole of [China's] twentieth century is the century of May Fourth and New Culture), an interview with Chen Pingyuan by Xu Zhiyuan 許知遠 and Zhuang Qiushui 莊秋水, *Dongfang lishi pinglun* 東方歷史評論 (Oriental History Review), 3 May 2017, online at: http://cul.qq.com/a/20170503/035915.htm.

for the significance of events, persons, and texts connected with one or another aspect of "May Fourth," to relate what happened, analyze why things happened the way they did, and even to provide would-be fact patterns (as if to establish the "innocence" or "guilt" of a given action or decision).[16] Yet, causal narratives cannot account for the intensity of affect associated with "May Fourth" by those who commemorate it (whether in 1919, 1920, or in subsequent decades up to the present).

The performative dimension of the key texts that have come to be subsumed under "May Fourth" (their emotion-arousing capacity; their memorableness) is resistant to analysis (if analysis presupposes getting-to-the-bottom of performativity by attempting to pin down its effects in words).

Affect is infectious. A poetics (rather than a method of analysis) is required if we want to discern the ways in which a text quickens the heartbeat and excites the mind. To summarize, we cannot understand the historical significance of "May Fourth" (its constative value) without appreciating its affective (performatively produced) power. The two go together insofar as one feels compelled to make sense of "May Fourth" only if one has been affected by what one reads as "May Fourth." An exploration of this basic proposition follows.

1   Making History

Representing May 4, 1919, as an historic turning point for China was the focus of many of the earliest commemorative essays. Take for instance the reflective essay by Luo Jialun, writing as a co-organizer of the protest, in which he judged the protest, one year on, as having significantly "advanced the reform of ideas," "increased social organization," and "increased the power of the masses."[17] Having explained how the protest had contributed in these three ways, Luo declared with a flourish, "In sum, the China before May Fourth was a China struggling to breathe, and silent. The China after May Fourth is a spirited, lively, and dynamic China. The achievement of the May Fourth Movement is that it made China 'move'" (總之五四以前的中國是氣息奄奄的靜的中國; 五四以後的中國是天機活潑的動的中國. 五四運動的功勞就在使中國 "動").[18]

Luo, however, also pointed out the protest's many "failures." He wrote that the success of "June Third" (the series of workers' strikes organized, with the help of student activists, in support of the May Fourth protest and occurring

---

16   A key example of this approach is Li Zehou 李澤厚 and Liu Zaifu 李澤厚, *Gaobie geming* 告別革命 (Bidding farewell to the revolution) (Hong Kong: Cosmos Books Ltd., 1996).
17   Luo, "Yinianlai women xuesheng yundongde chenggong shibai," *Xin chao*, 847–850.
18   Ibid., 850.

a month after it) had given rise to "a most popular and most dangerous idea" (自從六三勝利以來，我們學生界有一種最流行而最危險的觀念). This was "the idea that 'students are all-powerful,' which has led us to think that we can do anything; that we should therefore intervene into everything, and which has also caused us to intervene badly" (就是 "學生萬能" 的觀念，以為我們什麼事都能辦，所以什麼事都要去過問，所以什麼事都問不好). Moreover, because "there are definitely neither all-powerful people nor an all-powerful society in this world" and because "China today is so filthy and corrupt, so primitive and gloomy and so ridden with sores, it would not matter who you gave the job to, no one would do it well" (世界上決沒有萬能的人，也決沒有一種特殊的萬能的社會. 平心而論，以現在這樣齷齪腐敗，草昧蒙塞，百孔千瘡的中國交給誰也是辦不好的).[19] Luo noted further on that "the final awakening for those of us involved in the cultural movement is that we should know that China does not have any kind of knowledge that is world-class. A nation without its own basic culture will not exist in the world of the future" (我們做文化運動的最後覺悟，是要知道現在中國沒有一樣學問，可以在世界上占得位置的；無基本文化的民族，在將來的世界上不能存在的).[20]

In diction and sentiment, Luo's essay was characteristic of the then-burgeoning avant-garde discourse conducted in *baihuawen* (or *baihua* 白話), the experimental modern Chinese written vernacular. The essay appeared in *New Tide*, which Luo had co-founded, and which, as a leading outlet for *baihua* writings, reflected a cosmopolitan embrace of all things "new" (*xin* 新). Rhetorically at least, *baihua* became inseparable from the range of concepts and "isms" (*zhuyi* 主義) that it was used to promote, such as (to list several of the key ones alphabetically): "democracy," "enlightenment," "humanism," "liberalism," "literary revolution," "Marxism," "movement," "new culture," "new literature," "new thought," "patriotism," "realism," "renaissance," "romanticism," "science," "socialism," "the masses," and "youth." *Baihua* in its early years consisted of a profusion of literary creativity, translations of foreign works, and many and varied forms of cultural and political critique. It was first introduced into schools in Beijing as a medium of instruction in 1920. For the better part of the 1920s, amid the turbulence of warlord politics, *baihua* publications grew popular and influential. Moreover, with most of China's major and progressive presses located in Shanghai's foreign concessions, *baihua* publications also enjoyed substantial protection from state censorship.

The intellectual freedom of the "May Fourth" era is an important context for the melancholy behind such remarks as "How fortunate is May Fourth! How guilty is May Fourth!" Appearing in a Taipei publication in 1979, this

---

19 Ibid., 851.
20 Ibid., 861.

remark addressed, in the first instance, readers who had lived under the dictatorship of Chiang Kai-shek in Taiwan for almost three decades. In mainland China, Mao's dictatorship lasted a year longer. By 1979, readers on both sides of the Taiwan Strait had regained a limited measure of intellectual freedom following the deaths of Chiang (in April 1975) and Mao (in September 1976). In this shifting politics, readers were suffused with a heightened awareness of historical change when they read or re-read "May Fourth" texts.

Affective reading, unlike analytic reading, is unsystematic, immediate, and ungeneralizable. The feelings and impressions created varied from reader to reader, contingent upon their depth of engagement with and attunement to "May Fourth." To closely read Luo's 1920 essay as a "May Fourth" document—that is, to consider the author's purpose, the ideas he presented, and his word choice in relation to other writings of the day—is one thing. To find oneself dwelling on the nervous energy of a twenty-three-year-old student leader as one reads the essay, and to recall, simultaneously, the statements he made in his fifties about "May Fourth" in KMT-ruled Taiwan, when Luo served as chairman of the KMT's party history committee, is something else.

"May Fourth" most haunts those readers who encounter a discourse of hope than those who examine an object of study *per se*. The latter approach, however, is what scholarship demands and accordingly, it is what academics have heeded far more, that is, when they write *as* academics. They may say quite different things in interviews or in personal essays that they post on their blogs. As academics, we have contextualized Luo's 1920 essay in our research and teaching, relating it to student activism at Peking University (where Luo studied), the *baihua* "literary revolution," the protest itself and developments leading to and following from it, as it were, to establish the facts-of-the-matter. Conversely, writers who privilege "May Fourth" as a discourse of hope often highlight the gulf between what was hoped for and how badly things turned out, or else they defend "May Fourth" as perennially relevant. Chinese expressions such as *muji daocun* 目擊道存 ("the truth hit me," whatever the object perceived) give a name to this way of reading "May Fourth" as a source of inspiration and spiritual guidance, and the availability of such expressions in Chinese indicates a cultural attentiveness to, if not a privileging of, insight as felt immediacy.[21]

The saying *muji daocun* first appeared in the Daoist classic *Zhuangzi* 莊子 in a statement attributed to Confucius. Confucius was explaining to his

---

21 *Zhuangzi* 21: 2. Many of the standard Chinese expressions that present insight as felt immediacy, such as a "sudden flash of understanding" (*huangran dawu*) and "awakening" (*juewu* or *yijue*), are derived from Buddhism. I have chosen this older Daoist expression to indicate the longevity of this attitude.

disciple Zilu why no words were exchanged between himself and a man named Wenbo Xuezi 溫伯雪子 (whom Confucius admired) when they met. It was because Confucius saw at once (*muii*) that Wenbo Xuezi embodied the Way (*dao cun*).[22] Thus, because the saying signifies a truth so palpable that words are not needed, *muji daocun* offers a useful caption for the following excerpts from a 2017 *Oriental History Review* interview with Chen Pingyuan.

> Chen: I am from the Class of '77, the main characteristic of which was that we encountered the Movement to Liberate Thinking the minute we entered university. In 1978, many students who were Chinese literature majors at famous universities set up their own literary magazines. At the time, it was the easiest thing to plant yourself in the discursive realm of "May Fourth." In our imaginations, 1978 *was* 1919. It was all about liberating thinking, we were all discussing democracy, science and freedom ... I'm flooded with emotions when I think about the magazines. Those of 1978 were not a patch on those of 1919, though they were all student publications. If you take Sun Yat-sen University's *Red Bean* [*Hongdou*] and Peking University's *Morning* [*Zaochen*] and compare them with *New Tide*, *The National Past* [*Guo gu*] and *The Citizen* [*Guomin*] as magazines published by students from Peking University's Chinese department in 1919, you'll see a striking gap.

> 我是 77 級級大學生，77 級的特點是一進學校就碰上了思想解放運動. 1978 年, 很多名校中文系學生, 在各自校園裡創辦文學雜誌, 那時候, 很容易把自己置身於 "五四" 的語境裡面. 在我們的想像中, 1978 年就是 1919 年, 都是思想解放, 都講民主, 科學, 自由 ... 回頭看這些雜誌, 還是蠻感慨的. 同樣是學生刊物, 1978 年比不上 1919 年. 拿中大的《紅豆》, 北大的《早晨》, 來跟 1919 年北大中文系學生為主創辦的《新潮》,《國故》和《國民》對比, 差距很明顯.

> [...]

> *Oriental History Review*: Let's go back to 1979. Did you see yourselves as the continuation of "May Fourth"? What materials informed your understanding? Did you have access to, say, copies of *New Tide*? As for the materials you were able to read, where did they come from?

---

22   *Zhuangzi* 21: 2.

回到 1979 年, 您把當時的你們自比為 "五四" 的延續嗎? 你們對他們的理解從哪些材料來? 比如當時能看到《新潮》雜誌嗎? 能看到的材料又是從哪裡來?

Chen: It ought to be said that students from the Class of '77 and the Class of '78 did not receive a good educational foundation. We were able to get hold of *New Youth* but not *New Tide*, and journals such as *The National Past* and *The Citizen* were well beyond our reach. At the time our minds raced with ideas and it was if we had returned to that turbulent and exciting era. As for why it all felt so familiar, that was because, from 1920, year after year without fail, teachers and students at Peking University had commemorated "May Fourth." In one sense, "May Fourth" is a "story" that has been thoroughly told. The capacity of a historical event to "renovate itself once and to be renewed daily thereafter" [*gou ri xin, riri xin*], to continuously exercise a direct influence, necessarily owes to its ongoing narration and richly inventive interpretation.

應該說, 77, 78 級大學生當時並沒有那麼好的學養, 我們能看到《新青年》, 並沒有讀《新潮》, 更不會考慮《國故》,《國民》等. 當時只是馳想, 自己似乎是回到那個風雲激盪的年代. 之所以感覺很熟悉, 那是因為, 自 1920 年開始, 北大師生就不斷地, 年復一年地紀念 "五四". 某種意義上, "五四" 是一個說出來的 "故事". 一個歷史事件之所以能 "苟日新, 日日新," 不斷影響當下, 必須靠不斷的陳述以及富有創意的闡釋.[23]

To more fully appreciate Chen's remarks requires familiarity not only with "May Fourth" as received history but also an inkling of the histories of the magazines Chen named and their importance (*New Youth, New Tide, The National Past,* and *The Citizen*). One must also sense the continuities and discontinuities between the *guwen* and *wenyan* of premodern China, *baihua* during "May Fourth," and *putonghua* in the People's Republic. All of this is necessary if we are to appreciate Chen's witty use of a saying from the early classic *The Great Learning* (大學 traditionally used to exhort a disciplined attitude to "renewing" or improving oneself) to figure the ongoing "renewal" of "May Fourth" through a complex politics of narration and re-narration.

The felt nature of insight (of being moved by what one reads) that sayings like *muji daocun* evoke, resonates with what Charles Taylor calls "catching on" to an idea. Insight, as the experience of a sudden understanding, involves "the whole of language." As Taylor explains:

---

23 The Class of '77 (77 *ji*) refers to the first group of students to attend university in China following the re-introduction of the national university entrance examination that year.

The condition for this catching on is that one is already in the linguistic dimension: linguistic in the wider sense that includes body language, tone of voice, urgency of communication, the whole mood which surrounds the exchange ... Each new word supposes the whole of language. But in this case, it is not just our whole power of describing objects: it is our whole linguistic capacity, including its enactive dimension.[24]

The enactive dimension of a given language (the expression or acting out of an idea, sentiment or value, whether through existing formulations, new coinages, or reinventions of the already-said) often coincides with its performative power. In Chen's play on the premodern saying, its capacity to mean something new is enacted, the performative effect of which is strengthened if the saying, as used, also elicits from readers a knowing chuckle or an appreciative smile.

Readers "catch on" to what we write because we (writers and readers) have been inducted into a "whole of language" through our upbringing, education, and socialization. Chen, as a student at Sun Yat-sen University in Guangzhou in 1978, "plants" himself with ease "in the discursive realm of 'May Fourth'" because reading, discussing, and citing from "May Fourth" had become newly fashionable (departing from the mandated Mao-era account of "May Fourth" as a "cultural revolution"). In intellectual and official circles, a post-Maoist state-supported "Movement to Liberate Thinking" was underway, displacing the former Maoist discourse of class struggle with that of "reform and opening up." It was a time when the appearance of big-character posters calling for social, political, and cultural change, on a brick wall at the Xidan-Chang'an intersection in Beijing, was being hailed as the "Xidan Democracy Wall" (*Xidan minzhu qiang* 西單民主牆). The whole mood of public and private communications had visibly shifted from the High Maoism of the previous decade such that May Fourth-inspired talk of "democracy, science, and freedom" could catch on, with greatly diminished fear of ostracization and persecution.

To date, rich empirical studies have appeared in and outside China of key concepts and themes associated with "May Fourth," together with abundant analysis of how these were reintroduced and used in post-Maoist discourse of the late 1970s and 1980s.[25] However, the performative force of "May Fourth" discourse, whether in its day or in subsequent decades, generally falls outside

---

24   Charles Taylor, *The Language Animal: The Full Shape of the Human Linguistic Capacity* (Cambridge MA: Harvard University Press, 2016), 229.
25   A useful summary account of post-Maoist understandings of "May Fourth" appears in Xu Jilin, "The Fate of an Enlightenment—Twenty Years in the Chinese Intellectual Sphere (1978–1998)", trans. Geremie R. Barmé and Gloria Davies, in Edward Gu and Merle Goldman, eds., *Chinese Intellectuals between State and Market* (London and New York: Routledge/Curzon, 2004), 183–203.

the analytical purview of these meaning-seeking endeavors. When we encounter the evocative language that Chen used (in the cited interview excerpts above) to express the affective response that "May Fourth" texts triggered in him, we see that analysis alone is inadequate. We need a poetics to appreciate what Chen meant by being "flooded with emotions" when comparing student magazines from 1978 with those of 1919. By poetics, I mean an inquiry that attunes us to how wordings from the "May Fourth" period have caught the eye (*muji*) of readers (past and present), causing them to feel intuitively convinced (*dao cun*) by these wordings, and how these readers have, in turn, articulated their feelings.

One way of doing this is to read "May Fourth" writings as constitutive of a poetics of hope, which would help us to focus attention as much on their experiential mood as their semantic content. Hope is writ large in the title of Hu Shi's and Jiang Menglin's "May Fourth" first-anniversary commemorative essay, "Our Hope for the Students." Like Luo Jialun's 1920 essay cited earlier, Hu and Jiang commended the protest for its many positive outcomes. Unlike Luo, however, they avoided hyperbole, confining themselves, as educators, to personal observations of how the protest had "increased the desire of many students to gain more knowledge" (引起許多學生求知識的慾望) while also "enhancing their experience of collective life" (使學生增加團體生活的經驗).[26]

Just as Luo warned his fellow-students away from luxuriating in an inflated sense of their own power, Hu and Jiang reminded their readers: "This kind of movement is an extraordinary thing, the unavoidable result of a society in transition. Moreover, precisely because it could not be avoided, it was also an uneconomical and unfortunate thing" (這種運動是非常的事, 是變態的社會裡不得已的事. 但是他又是很不經濟的不幸事, 因為是不得已). Their essay ended with the following plea: "If the student movement is to preserve the glory of 'May Fourth' and 'June Third,' there is only one thing to be done. The direction of the movement must change. [The students] must put the spirit of 'May Fourth' and 'June Third' into every beneficial and useful student activity both in and out of school. What we've said is blunt and candid, but these are all honest words" (學生運動如果要想保存 "五四" 和 "六三" 的榮譽, 只有一個法子, 就是改變活動的方向, 把 "五四" 和 "六三" 的精神用到學校內外有益有用的學生活動上去. 我們講的話, 是很直率, 但這都是我們們的老實話).[27]

Early essays on "May Fourth" published in 1919 and 1920 were often didactic yet personal. Hu and Jiang referred to their "blunt and candid … honest

---

26   Hu and Jiang, "Women duiyu xuesheng de xiwang" http://data.book.hexun.com/chapter-18093-3-1.shtm.
27   Ibid.

words" to accentuate the heartfelt nature of their exhortations. The authors sought not only to capture what the protest had achieved and inspired. They also expressed apprehension about an as-yet unknown future, for which they hoped the myriad "spiritual" qualities that "May Fourth" had fostered in themselves and their fellow-citizens would equip them better to face. In these writings, "May Fourth" is presented as historic (history-in-the-making): that is, as not yet historical. The urgency of immediate action is integral to "May Fourth's" discursive mood. Hence, Luo urged his readers to undergo a "final awakening" to remedy China's cultural deficiencies while Hu and Jiang urged their student readers to "put the spirit of 'May Fourth'" to work in "every beneficial and useful student activity."

The present, as historic and happening "now," is a time of hope, for hope involves a deeply affective experience of time, in which one's sense of the past, present, and future acquires an acute personal significance. (To quote the madman in Lu Xun's 魯迅 [1881–1936] seminal 1918 short story: "I can't bear to think of it. It has only just dawned on me that all these years I have been living in a place where for four thousand years human flesh has been eaten."[28]) To hope for the future is to see the present as the "now" of opportunity and peril. (To quote the madman again: "Perhaps, there are still children who haven't eaten men? Save the children …"[29])

To see the present as the "now" of true insight and as time for action is to see history anew: to make history. Walter Benjamin wrote in his 1940 essay "On the Concept of History": "History is the subject of a construction whose site is not homogeneous, empty time, but time filled by now-time [*Jetszeit*]."[30] The number and range of citations and readings to date of Benjamin's enigmatic statement amply demonstrate its performative force and that of "now-time." However, readers must be receptive to Benjamin's statement as a felicitous form of words if it is to jolt them into seeing the difference between "homogeneous, empty time" (devoid of excitement and purpose) and fully lived (revolutionary) "now-time." Extemporizing on Benjamin, Jean-Luc Nancy writes:

---

28 Lu Xun, "A Madman's Diary," in *Lu Xun: Selected Works* vol. 1, trans. Yang Xianyi and Gladys Yang (Beijing: Foreign Languages Press, 1985), 51. In a 1951 essay, Sun Fuyuan 孫伏園, a protégé of Lu Xun's, noted: "For many years now, when meetings are held to commemorate May Fourth, someone would recite from 'A Madman's Diary.' I feel that this is most appropriate as the story and the May Fourth Movement are forever connected." Sun Fuyuan, "Wu Si yundong he Lu Xun xiansheng de 'Kuangren riji'" 五四運動和魯迅先生的《狂人日記》 (The May Fourth Movement and 'A Madman's Diary' by Mr Lu Xun), *Xin jianshe* 新建設, vol. 4, no. 2 (1951).
29 Ibid.
30 Walter Benjamin, *Selected Writings, vol. 4: 1988–1940*, ed. Howard Eiland and Michael W. Jennings (Cambridge MA: Harvard University Press, 2003), 395.

"Now" does not mean the present, nor does it represent the present. "Now" presents the present, or makes it *emerge* ... "now" as a performed word, as the utterance that can be ours, performing the "we" as well as the "now" ... is also the coming of "we" and of history. A time full of "now" is a time full of openness and heterogeneity. "Now" says "our time" and "our time" says "We, filling the space of time with existence." This is not an accomplishment: this is happening.[31]

Openness and heterogeneity are the operative words here. "May Fourth" signifies many things because its language is of lived experiential "now-time." Julian Thomas's Heideggerian distinction between "existential time" and "pragmatic time" (or public time) is helpful for highlighting the difference between "May Fourth" as historic (as it was presented in the writings of the day) and as the stuff of history textbooks that "May Fourth" subsequently became. As Thomas puts it, existential time "possesses ... a 'mine-ness,' a certain immediacy of direct relevance to the person and their existence." In existential time,

particular events have passed me by and are lost, but I am who and what I am, and I am in a particular mood because I 'have' a past ... The past is conceivable in terms of my having-been and the future is significant as 'not yet'.[32]

In presenting themselves as spokespersons for their age, for their chosen causes, and for China, "May Fourth" authors were encumbered by neither political doctrine nor party directive. They celebrated and interrogated "May Fourth" in existential time. "May Fourth" had yet to be subjected to the "laws" of historical development that would locate it in the meta-narrative time of Marxism-Leninism. The latter began only in the mid-1920s, with Qu Qiubai's 瞿秋白 (1899–1935) 1925 essay, "Commemorating 'May Fourth' and the National Revolutionary Movement" 五四紀念與民族革命運動, as an early Communist attempt to locate "May Fourth" within a narrative of national revolutionary progress.[33]

---

31   Jean-Luc Nancy, *The Birth to Presence*, trans. Brian Holmes and others (Stanford CA: Stanford University Press, 1993), 165.
32   Julian Thomas, *Time, Culture and Identity: An Interpretative Archaeology* (London: Routledge, 2002), 44. What Thomas calls "pragmatic time" conversely "is not 'mine' ... it is a public time ... it can extend onward for ever and ever but I don't *care* about it." (Ibid.)
33   See Ouyang Zhesheng's 歐陽哲生 discussion of Qu's 1925 essay in *Wu Si yundong de lishi quanshi* 五四運動的歷史詮釋 (The May Fourth Movement: A historical interpretation) (Taipei: Showwe Information Co., 2011), 163–164.

According to Qu, "The eruption of the May Fourth movement within world history effectively divided politics, economics, thought, and other aspects of life in China into what came before and after the movement" (五四運動爆發, 在世界史上實在是分割中國之政治經濟思想等為前後兩時期的運動). In Qu's description, "May Fourth" was no longer a historic turning-point but a stage of historical development: it was "the first time after the Xinhai Revolution [1911] where the various social classes in China energetically took part in politics and showed a mass character in doing so" (的確是辛亥革命之後, 中國社會裡各階級努力以行動干預政治而且帶著群眾性質的第一次).[34] With growing support for the Chinese Communist Party among intellectuals and university students from the mid-1920s onward, the experiential notion of "May Fourth" presented by Luo, Hu, and Jiang in their 1920 essays, as the moment when Chinese students achieved a heightened awareness of the world around them and their purpose, was increasingly displaced by a Marxist-informed view of "May Fourth" as a stage along a historically inevitable path.

This was also a discursive shift from history as possibility (open to interpretation) to history as necessity (in accord with the so-called science of historical materialism).[35] Paulo Freire outlines the incommensurability between possibility and necessity in this way:

> In a history as possibility, there is no room for the inexorable future. On the contrary, the future is always problematic.... History as a time of *possibility* presupposes human beings' capacity for observing, discovering, comparing, evaluating, deciding, breaking away, and for being responsible. It implies their ability to be ethical as well as their capacity for ethical transgression. It is not possible to educate for democracy, for freedom, for ethical responsibility within a deterministic understanding of history.[36]

To the extent that an event acquires historic stature when it continues to receive significant written attention, we should note the importance that Luo, Hu, and Jiang ascribed to "June Third" (六三) in 1920. Today, "June Third" barely rates a mention in scholarship and public discourse. Unlike "May Fourth's" continuing "renewal" through "richly inventive interpretation" (to recall Chen Pingyuan's words), "June Third," once important, now signifies little if anything

---

34   Quoted in ibid., 163.
35   The idea of historical materialism as a "science" took hold from the Second International (1889–1916). Gavin Kitching, *Marxism and Science: Analysis of an Obsession* (University Park PA: Pennsylvania State University Press, 1994), 59.
36   Paolo Freire, *Pedagogy of Indignation* (Boulder: Paradigm Publishers, 2004), 113.

for the few who have written about it. "June Third" bears poignant testament to the performative powers of language: having fallen out of history, how can it evoke possibility?

2   A Poetics of the Possible

In mainland scholarship since the late 1970s, the use of concepts and expressions associated with "May Fourth" has often served writers as a means of indicating their antipathy to official history and the CCP's highly deterministic narrative. For instance, when extolling "Enlightenment" as a lasting achievement of "May Fourth" in a 1998 essay, the philosopher and advocate of Chinese liberalism Xu Youyu 徐友漁 enjoined his readers to aspire to be like those "progressive Chinese intellectuals" of the "May Fourth" period who "made Enlightenment their personal responsibility" (*yi qimeng wei jiren* 以啟蒙启蒙為己任). By adapting the Mencian motto of "assuming personal responsibility for all under Heaven" (*yi tianxia wei ji ren* 以天下為己任), Xu implied that Enlightenment (that is, democratic thinking, human rights, and humanitarian values) was China's true intellectual tradition. Hence, "although conservative forces and rulers in different eras have spared no effort in their attempts to obstruct or strangle Enlightenment … they have not dared to act as if they had truth on their side directly to negate it, much less to denounce it intellectually" (各個時代的守舊勢力或統治者雖然竭力阻止或扼殺啟蒙. 未敢正面理直氣壯地否定, 更無能力在思想理論上加以貶斥). He wrote that, though the "discourse of Enlightenment" (啟蒙的話語) that emerged out of "May Fourth" had been reduced to "a bare thread" (不絕如縷), it remained nonetheless indestructible.[37]

Conversely, the historian Wang Hui 汪暉, with whom Xu disagreed vociferously in the 1990s and 2000s, presented May Fourth discourse as suffering from a flawed "emotionalism" (情感性), resulting from the self-imposed estrangement of May Fourth intellectuals from their "native soil" (鄉土).[38] Wang described the defense of a prelapsarian "May Fourth" by Chinese intellectuals

---

37   Xu Youyu 徐友漁, "'Houzhuyi' yu qimeng" "後主義" 與啟蒙 ("Postisms" and Enlightenment) in Xu Youyu, *Ziyoude yanshuo* (Changchun: Changchun chubanshe, 1999), 359. Online at: http://www.literature.org.cn/article.aspx?id=5913 Xu's essay was a rebuttal of postmodern criticisms of Enlightenment in 1990s' mainland scholarship.

38   Wang Hui 汪暉, "Zhongguo xiandai lishi zhongde 'Wu Si' qimeng yundong" 中國現代歷史中的 "五四" 啟蒙運動 (The May Fourth Enlightenment Movement in modern Chinese history) in Wang Hui, *Zixuan ji* (Selected works) (Nanning: Guangxi shifan daxue chubanshe, 1997), 318.

living in post-Mao China as akin to a "radiant daydream" (一個輝輝煌的夢想), one that "signifies freedom of thought, the liberation of human nature, the return of reason, and eternal justice, but in the sense that these things arrived belatedly and proved to be short-lived" ('它意味著思想的自由, 人性的解放, 理性的復歸, 永恒正義的為時已晚卻又匆匆而去的來臨.)[39]

We can discern the haunting power of "May Fourth" as a linguistic legacy in Xu's and Wang's formulations. In mainland intellectual discourse at least, the affective intensity of this legacy remains bound up with state censorship. People who write about democracy as a "May Fourth" ideal know they must avoid challenging the CCP's highly qualified definitions of democracy as the "people's democratic dictatorship" and "socialist democracy."[40] They know to hint obliquely at the prospect of a liberal democracy in China, as Xu did when referring to the "May Fourth" legacy of Enlightenment as indestructible yet hanging by "a bare thread," which Wang likened to a short-lived "radiant daydream." These coded formulations remind readers that "May Fourth" cannot be freely remembered; that any attempt (to recall Freire) to "educate for democracy, for freedom, for ethical responsibility" is pre-emptively state-constrained.

Yet, happier affects of linguistic play are also involved in remembering "May Fourth." Take for instance the rhetorical inseparability of "democracy" from "May Fourth," which owes in no small part to Chen Duxiu's coinage, "Messrs Democracy and Science" (*Demokelaxi he Saiyinsi liangwei xiansheng* 德莫克拉西和賽因斯兩位先生). Through sheer frequency of citation, the expression has practically become a byword for "May Fourth" even though it predated the May fourth protest and became representative of "May Fourth" only retrospectively. "Messrs Democracy and Science" first appeared in a polemical article published on January 1, 1919, titled "In reply to charges made against *New Youth*." In the article, Chen, as the magazine's founding editor, expressed, on behalf of *New Youth*'s contributors, "infinite pessimism" about the prospect of reform in China.

He wrote that attacks against the magazine had come from two different groups of people. The first group consisted of supporters who felt that the magazine's uncompromising radicalism prevented it from reaching a wider readership. Chen described these people as like-minded progressives whose comments he appreciated. The second group however sought to preserve everything "old" and hated everything the magazine stood for. Chen wrote that

---

39   Ibid., 306.
40   See the 2004 Constitution of the People's Republic of China at http://english.gov.cn/archive/laws_regulations/2014/08/23/content_281474982987458.htm.

"the fellows of our organization freely accept these charges but when all's said and done, we are not guilty" (這幾條罪案, 本社同人當然直認不諱。但是追本溯源, 本志同人本來無罪). He continued:

> It is only because we sought to defend Messrs Democracy [*Demokelaxi*] and Science [*Saiyinsi*] that we committed these heinous crimes. To defend Mr De, we had to oppose Confucianism, ritual laws, chastity, old morality, and old politics. To defend Mr Sai, we had to oppose old art and old religion. To support both Mr De and Mr Sai we cannot help but oppose "national essence" and old literature. So, let's be calm and think things through. Besides defending Messrs De and Sai, has this magazine committed any other crime? If it hasn't, you should refrain from targeting our magazine and oppose Messrs De and Sai vigorously and boldly instead. That would make you true heroes with a clear plan.[41]

> 只因為擁護那德莫克拉西 (Democracy) 和賽因斯 (Science) 兩位先生, 才犯了這幾條滔天的大罪, 要擁護那德先生, 便不得不反對孔教, 禮法, 貞節, 舊倫理, 舊政治; 要擁護那賽先生, 便不得不反對舊藝術, 舊宗教; 要擁護德先生又要擁護賽先生, 便不得不反對國粹和舊文學. 大家平心細想, 本誌除了擁護德, 賽兩先生之外, 還有別項罪案沒有呢? 若是沒有, 請你們不用專門非難本誌, 要有氣力有膽量來反對德賽兩先生, 才算是好漢, 才算是根本的辦法.

In Chen's witty anthropomorphism "Messrs Democracy and Science," we see the performative force of a transfiguration: the concepts of democracy and science are embodied—made flesh—with the simple addition of "*xiansheng*" (Mr, Esq.) and "*liang (wei) xiansheng*" (Messrs). *Xiansheng* is also a way of addressing one's teacher. The anthropomorphism works by playing off the normative importance of self-cultivation and self-improvement in premodern Chinese scholarship. The emphasis that Confucian thought placed on correct social conduct and the privileging of a cultivated dispassion in Daoist and Buddhist thinking were key elements of a premodern knowledge to which Chen and his *New Youth* readers were deeply acculturated. The effectiveness of "Messrs Democracy and Science" relies on its mock-serious imitation of

---

41 Chen Duxiu, "Ben zhi zui'an zhi dabian shu" 本志罪案之答辯書 (In defense of *New Youth* against its accusers), in *Chen Duxiu wenzhang xuanpian* (*Chen Duxiu: Selected essays*) (Beijing: Shenghuo, dushu, xinzhi, sanlian shudian, 1984) 1:317. Online at: https://www.marxists.org/chinese/chenduxiu/marxist.org-chinese-chen-19190115.htm.

this self-cultivating reverential discourse. Mr De and Mr Sai are nothing like the sagely exemplars of premodern China, yet by commending them as true teachers whom one should emulate in aid of one's self-cultivation, Chen created a locution that to Chinese readers sounded (and still sounds) "right." The rightness of defending Messrs De and Sai is then set in contrast to the botched self-cultivation of *New Youth*'s critics, whom Chen disparaged for failing to be "true heroes with a clear plan."

The "expressive rightness" of a locution is inextricable from how we make "liveable sense" of things within the normative dimension of our communications and social conduct.[42] That the gleeful irony of "Messrs Democracy and Science" has enjoyed currency in post-Maoist discourse, generating an abundance of playful variations, indicates that its performative effects have altered but not diminished over time. For instance, there are numerous online articles calling on readers to remember "Miss Freedom" (*Fei xiaojie* 費小姐) as a contemporary of "Messrs Democracy and Science." The historian Yang Nianqun 楊念群 (b. 1964) wrote in 2016 that people had grown weary of "Messrs Democracy and Science" because they had been continually "worshipped," with the "spirit tablet" for Mr Science being revered far more than Mr Democracy's. He continues:

> It's not that the two "gentlemen" are not worthy but that the actors presenting them have poor acting skills and appear far too frequently, turning the audience off. It wasn't until the 1980s that someone reminded us that during "May Fourth," there was also a huge celebrity by the name of "Miss Fei" (Freedom) and that we should let her have the limelight. It was because of this that the customary annual commemoration [of "May Fourth"] acquired new meaning and ceased being old and hackneyed.[43]

> 不是兩位"先生"不好,而是演員的演技太差,出場頻頻率過高反而會倒了欣賞者的胃口. 直到20世紀80年代, 才有人提醒別忘了"五四"還有個大明星叫"費小姐"(自由), 應該讓她登場亮相, 才使得當年的祭拜風情蘊出些新意而不至於陳腔依舊.

With "Miss Freedom" signifying the liberatory mood of the post-Maoist 1980s, Yang wrote that "Miss Freedom" gave rise to readings of "May Fourth" as a

---

42 Taylor, *Language Animal*, 62–64.
43 Yang Nianqun 楊念群, "'Wu Si' yanjiu huisu yu fansi" "五四"研究回溯與反思 (Retracing and reflecting on "May Fourth" studies), *Zhongguo jingying bao*, 12 May 2016, online at: http://history.people.com.cn/n1/2016/0512/c372329-28346234.html.

"movement of cultural reform" (文化改造運動) that "transformed the Chinese people in spirit and soul" (中國人靈魂和精神變化). As with Xu's and Wang's formulations cited above, Yang merely hints that a dramatic shift away from the previous Maoist description of "May Fourth" as an "anti-imperialist and anti-feudal revolutionary movement" had occurred.

Insofar as the verve and eloquence of post-Maoist essays and commentaries on "May Fourth" is, to varying degrees, conditioned by pre-emptive self-censorship and state-imposed strictures, their affective quality is always complex. The literary historian Wen Fengqiao 溫奉橋 sought to capture the metaphysical ache of invoking "Messrs Democracy and Science" in China in 2008 as follows:

> The "May Fourth" New Culture Movement happened almost ninety years ago. However, the two "foreign gentlemen" [*yang xiansheng*] to whom that generation volubly appealed—Mr De (*Demokelaxi, Democracy, minzhu*) and Mr Sai (*Saiyinsi, Science, kexue*) have, to date, not been able to come to China. How many Chinese heads have turned white with age, how many Chinese hearts have been broken as people waited in vain for these two "foreign" gentlemen. How difficult the waiting. To quote from the song: I waited till the flowers withered away!

> "五四" 新文化運動過去已近 90 年, 但是, 那一代人所大聲呼喚的兩位 " 洋先生"—德先生 (德莫克拉西, Democracy, 民主) 和賽先生 (賽因斯, Science, 科學) 至今未能來到中國. 等待這兩位 "洋" 先生, 等白了多少中國人的頭髮, 也等碎了多少中國人的心. 等得苦哇. 套用一句歌詞: 我等到花兒也謝了!

> Could the two "foreign" gentlemen be playing hide-and-seek with us? Last year, Mr Yu Keping's *Democracy Is a Good Thing* fired so many Chinese imaginations, with certain people reading it as "signifying" this or that thing. In fact, it's that "Mr De" that our New Culture warriors summoned and defended ninety years ago. Now, ninety years later, we finally learn that he has been, all along, "a good thing." History is filled with things about which we can do nothing.[44]

---

44   Wen Fengqiao 溫奉橋, "Guilai xi: De xiansheng, Sai xiansheng" 歸來兮: 德先生, 賽先生 (Come back, Mr De and Mr Sai!), *Wen Fengqiao de boke*, 15 May 2008. Online at: http://blog.sina.com.cn/s/blog_4cb0c88301008i21.html.

莫非這兩位 "洋" 先生在與我們捉迷藏? 去年, 俞可平先生的一本書:《民主是個好東西》, 曾激發了多少中國人的想像, 被某些人解讀為什麼什麼的 "標誌" 等等. 也就是 90 年前, 我們的新文化鬥士們為之呼喊, 奮鬥的 "德先生," 90 年後, 我們才認識到他原來還是個 "好東西". 歷史充滿了無奈.

Wen's figuration of romantic longing via motifs drawn from Tang poetry and a 1994 Jacky Cheung Canto-pop hit; his mention of Yu Keping's much-discussed defense of gradual institutional and political reform under CCP rule, published with the Party leadership's approval, gesture to a "whole of language" to which readers must be sensitive and attuned, that is, if they want to savor the melancholy of the concluding remark: "History is filled with things about which we can do nothing." History, so understood, is also the very opposite of history envisaged as "a time full of 'now' ... a time full of openness and heterogeneity."

The performative force of "Messrs Democracy and Science" owes, perhaps above all, to the transliteration of these two concepts, to which Wen draws attention in the passage above. The experimental zeal of *baihua*'s advocates generated neologisms, loanwords, foreign words and extravagant transliterations like *demokelaxi* and *saiyinsi*, all of which piled into Chinese together with all manner of literary invention. These linguistic phenomena evince an optimism about language as a vehicle of societal change and a confidence in the democratizing properties of *baihua*. The explanation Li Dazhao 李大釗 (1888–1927) gave in 1921 as to why he sometimes wrote Democracy as a capitalized English word is nothing if not a demonstration of the openness and heterogeneity needed for thinking democracy as possibility:

> This word Democracy is not easy to translate. To translate it as a political term allows us to call it a system. If we investigate the idea from various aspects of social life, we can see that it is the trend of recent times, the tide of the present world. There isn't one area of social life in which Democracy doesn't appear. This name hence qualifies as representing the spirit of the age. If we translate it as "the politics of the ordinary people," we would only illuminate its political dimension and not the many different elements making up the lived social dimension beyond politics. So, while it may seem more fitting to translate it as "the principles of ordinary people," we should nonetheless consider transliterating it as *demokelaxi* so as not to reduce its scope.[45]

---

45   Li Dazhao 李大釗, *Li Dazhao wenji* 李大釗文集 (The works of Li Dazhao) (Beijing: Renmin chubanshe, 1984), 2: 501. These remarks were part of a public lecture by Li first

> Democracy 這個字最不容易翻譯. 由政治上解釋他, 可以說為一種制度. 而由社會生活的種種方面去觀察, 他實在是近世紀的趨勢, 現世界的潮流, 遍社會生活的各方面幾無一不是 Democracy 底表現. 這名詞實足以代表時代精神. 若將他譯為 "平民政治," 則只能表明政治, 而不能表明政治以外的生活各方面. 似不如譯為 "平民主義," 較妥帖些. 但為免掉弄小他的範圍起見, 可以直譯為 "德謨克拉西".

Fragments from the life histories of "May Fourth" authors flitted through my mind as I re-read their essays to write this paper. While translating the excerpt from Li Dazhao above, I recalled that he was hanged in Beijing on April 28, 1927, under the orders of the Fengtian warlord Zhang Zuolin 張作霖. I re-read Lu Xun's 1933 preface to an anthology of Li's essays, in which Lu Xun recalled that he first met Li (whom he referred to as Mr Shouchang 守常先生, Li's style) at a meeting organized by Chen Duxiu to discuss *New Youth*'s operations. Of Li's essays, Lu Xun wrote: "Evidently, his arguments may no longer fit the times ... however, even if this were so, the writings he left behind are everlasting as the legacy of a pioneer and a monument in revolutionary history" (他的理論, 在現在看起來, 當然未必精當的 ... 是雖然如此, 他的遺文卻將永住, 因為這是先驅者的遺產, 革命史上的豐碑). Lu Xun then contrasted the value of Li's writings with "the stack upon stack of books by swindlers living and dead, which are about to fall over, and isn't this why even the traders now 'put up with the loss' by giving a twenty or thirty per cent discount on these books?" (一切死的和活的騙子的一迭迭的集子, 不是已在倒塌下來, 連商人也 "不顧血本" 的只收二三折了麼).[46]

While re-reading Chen Duxiu on "Messrs De and Sai," I found myself reflecting on the changes he underwent, from being *New Youth*'s celebrated founding editor and Dean of Arts at Peking University in 1919 to becoming by 1921 the inaugural General Secretary of the Chinese Communist Party that he and Li co-founded that year, to his growing estrangement from Comintern and Stalin in the mid-1920s, his deposal in 1927 and eventual expulsion from the CCP in 1929. I recalled that Qu Qiubai replaced Chen as General Secretary in 1927 and that Qu had earlier served as Chen's interpreter at a Comintern meeting in Moscow in 1922. I thought too of the protest banners raised on May 4,

---

published as "You pingmin zhengzhi dao gongren zhengzhi" 由平民政治到工人政治 (From the politics of ordinary people to the politics of workers) in *Chenbao fukan* (15–17 December 1921).

46 Lu Xun 魯迅, "*Shouchang quanji* ti ji" 守常全集題記 (A preface to the *Collected Works of Shou Chang*), in *Lu Xun quanji* (Beijing: Renmin wenxue chubanshe, 1991), 4: 524–525.

1989, in Tiananmen Square that read: "Hello Mr Democracy" in English and *De xiansheng ni hao* (德先生你好) in Chinese.

There is no way of measuring the extent to which these and other details that form my contextual knowledge have contributed to my affective response to "May Fourth" writings. Moreover, I would not be able to accurately describe my response: emotions (and impressions) are ultimately resistant to analysis unless we confine analysis to mean the study of brain activity maps. Yet, re-reading "May Fourth" writings has evidently put me in an experimental mood which, at writing's end, I discern in my attempt to create a complementarity between Zhuangzi's *muji daocun* and Taylor's "catching on" and in my reading of passages from Luo, Hu, and Jiang in 1920 in the cadence of Benjamin's "now time."

These interpretive acts bear traces of my "May Fourth" infection as a reader who first encountered "May Fourth" while a student and who now teaches and writes about different aspects of it as a professional academic, but who has done so outside mainland China and Taiwan. "May Fourth" affects me arguably in a less complex way than the mainland scholars I have cited above, whose meditations on "May Fourth" in post-Maoist times and since are bound up with the far more elemental question of what "being Chinese" means and how, over time, one's changing reception of "May Fourth" might have aided or hindered one's answer to this perennial question. Moreover, the fact that mainland scholars risk punishment if they openly challenge the determinism of official history has meant that remarks such as the following delivered by China's President and the CCP's General Secretary Xi Jinping at Peking University on May 2, 2018, are seldom interrogated:

> From the May Fourth era to the advent of the New Epoch of Socialism with Chinese Characteristics [announced at the National CCP Congress in November 2017, together with the inauguration of Xi Jinping Thought], the Chinese Race has experienced a Great Leap from Standing Up, to Getting Rich and Becoming Powerful. This is epoch-making not only in terms of the history of the Chinese race but in terms of human history itself.[47]

---

47 Xi Jinping, "Zai Beijing daxue shisheng zuotanhui shang de jianghua" 在北京大學師生座談會上的講話 (A speech presented at a Peking University seminar for faculty and students) (May 2, 2018), *Renmin ribao*, May 3, 2018, online at: http://politics.people.com.cn/n1/2018/0503/c1001-29961481.html. Quoted and translated in Geremie R. Barmé, "May Fourth at Ninety-Nine," *China Heritage*, May 4, 2018, online at: http://chinaheritage.net/journal/may-fourth-at-ninety-nine/.

This caricature of "May Fourth" as "the Chinese Race ... Standing Up" exercises performative force through the mandated repetition of Xi's speeches in the media, schools, and workplaces. Yet it has not (or not yet) displaced the elegiac remembrances by mainland scholars (such as the ones quoted above) of "May Fourth's" hope- and anxiety-filled utterances.

Throughout this essay I have followed the convention adopted by many Chinese scholars of putting quotation marks around "May Fourth." The practical explanation for this convention is that the quotation marks act as a disambiguation device. Readers see at once that "May Fourth" refers to the protest of May 4, 1919, and all that has come to be associated with this date. However, the quotation marks also evoke a sense of "May Fourth" as eminently citable for this capacious term (or date, name, or sign) subsumes a dizzying range of mostly *baihua* writings that have been repeatedly quoted, and whose cosmopolitan or internationalist disposition has been repeatedly invoked. To read the quotation marks around "May Fourth" as reflecting the citational power of its textual remains is to appreciate the grip that these remains continue to have on us as readers. As Alan Bennett wrote in *The History Boys*:

> The best moments in reading are when you come across something—a thought, a feeling, a way of looking at things—that you'd thought special, particular to you. And here it is, set down by someone else, a person you've never met, maybe even someone long dead. And it's as if a hand has come out, and taken yours.[48]

The heart-racing linguistic play of the writings we now associate with "May Fourth" presented, or made emerge, a "now" in anticipation of a *demokelaxi* yet to come. Through citation, these remains of a poetics of the possible continue, a century on, to bespeak their performative resilience.

---

48   Alan Bennett, *The History Boys* (London: Faber & Faber, 2006), 60.

Bibliography

Austin, J. L. *How to Do Things with Words*, edited by J. O. Urmson and Marina Sbisà. Cambridge MA: Harvard University Press, 1975.

Benjamin, Walter. *Selected Writings vol. 4: 1988–1940*, edited by Howard Eiland and Michael W. Jennings. Cambridge MA: Harvard University Press, 2003.

Bennett, Alan. *The History Boys*. London: Faber & Faber, 2006.

Chen Duxiu 陳獨秀. "Ben zhi zui'an zhi dabian shu" 本志罪案之答辯書 (In defense of *New Youth* against its accusers). In *Chen Duxiu wenzhang xuanbian* 陳獨秀文章選編 (Chen Duxiu: Selected essays), Vol. 1. Beijing: Shenghuo, dushu, xinzhi, sanlian shudian, 1984. https://www.marxists.org/chinese/chenduxiu/marxist.org-chinese-chen-19190115.htm.

Chen Duxiu. "Wusi yundongde jingshen shi shenme?" 五四運動的精神是什麼 (What was the Spirit of the May Fourth Movement?), *Shi bao* 時報, April 22, 1920. http://blog.renren.com/share/222018481/10589389434.

Chen Pingyuan 陳平原. "Zhengge ershi shiji doushi Wu Si xin wenhua de shiji" 整個 20 世紀都是五四新文化的世紀 (The whole of [China's] twentieth century is the century of May Fourth and New Culture), an interview with Chen Pingyuan by Xu Zhiyuan 許知遠 and Zhuang Qiushui 莊秋水. *Dongfang lishi pinglun* 東方歷史評論 (Oriental History Review), May 3, 2017. http://cul.qq.com/a/20170503/035915.htm.

Freire, Paolo. *Pedagogy of Indignation*. Boulder: Paradigm Publishers, 2004.

Fu Sinian 傅斯年. "Zhongguo gou he zhongguoren" 中國狗和中國人 (Chinese dogs and Chinese people). *Xin qingnian* 新青年 (New Youth), vol. 6, no. 6 (November 1, 1919). https://www.edubridge.com/erxiantang/l2/fusinian_gouren.htm.

Hu Shi 胡適 and Jiang Menglin 蔣夢麟. "Women duiyu xuesheng de xiwang" 我们對於學生的希望 (Our hope for the students). *Chenbao fukan* 晨報副刊 (Morning Post Supplement), May 4, 1920. http://data.book.hexun.com/chapter-18093-3-1.shtml.

Jameson, Fredric. *The Political Unconscious: Narrative as a Socially Symbolic Act*. London: Methuen, 1981.

Li Ao 李敖. "A High Price." In *New Ghosts, Old Dreams: Chinese Voices of Conscience*, ed. Geremie R. Barmé with Linda Jaivin, 344–345. New York: Times Books, 1992.

Li Dazhao 李大釗. "You pingmin zhengzhi dao gongren zhengzhi" 由平民政治到工人政治 (From the politics of ordinary people to the politics of workers), *Chenbao fukan* (December 15–17 1921). In *Li Dazhao wenji* 李大釗文集 (The works of Li Dazhao), vol. 2. Beijing: Renmin chubanshe, 1984.

Lu Xun 魯迅. "*Shouchang quanji* ti ji" 守常全集題記 (A preface to the *Collected Works of Shou Chang*), in *Lu Xun quanji* 魯迅全集 4: 523–526. Beijing: Renmin wenxue chubanshe, 1991.

Lu Xun. "A Madman's Diary." In *Lu Xun: Selected Works*, vol. 1, trans. Yang Xianyi and Gladys Yang. Beijing: Foreign Languages Press, 1985.

Luo Jialun 羅家倫. "Yinianlai women xuesheng yundongde chenggong shibai he jianglai ying qu de fangxiang." 一年來我們學生運動的成功失敗和將來應採取的方針 (The successes and failures of our student movement over the past year, and the policy to be adopted in the future). *Xinchao* 新潮 (New Tide), 2, no. 4 (1920): 846–861. www.cnthinkers.com/thinkerweb/literature/29124.

Miller, J. H. *Speech Acts in Literature*. Stanford: Stanford University Press, 2001.

Nancy, Jean-Luc. *The Birth to Presence*, trans. Brian Holmes and others. Stanford: Stanford University Press, 1993.

Ouyang Zhesheng 歐陽哲生. *Wu Si yundong de lishi quanshi* 五四運動的歷史詮釋 (The May Fourth Movement: A Historical Interpretation). Taipei: Showwe Information Co., 2011.

Searle, John. "J. L. Austin." In *A Companion to Analytic Philosophy*, ed. by A. P. Martinich and E. David Sosa. Malden and Oxford: Blackwell Publishers, 2005.

Sun Fuyuan 孫伏園. "Wu Si yundong he Lu Xun xiansheng de 'Kuangren riji'" 五四運動和魯迅先生的《狂人日記》(The May Fourth Movement and "A Madman's Diary" by Mr Lu Xun), *Xin jianshe* 新建設, vol. 4, no. 2 (1951).

Sun, Lung-kee. "The *Other* May Fourth." In *Beyond the May Fourth Paradigm: In Search of Chinese Modernity*, ed. Kai-wing Chow, Tze-ki Hon, Hung-yok Ip, and Don C. Price, 271–292. Lanham: Lexington Books, 2008.

Taylor, Charles. *The Language Animal: The Full Shape of the Human Linguistic Capacity*. Cambridge MA: Harvard University Press, 2016.

Thomas, Julian. *Time, Culture and Identity: An Interpretative Archaeology*. London: Routledge.

Wagner, Rudolf G. "The Canonization of May Fourth." In *The Appropriation of Cultural Capital: China's May Fourth Project*, ed. Milena Doleželová-Velingerová and Oldřich Král, 66–120. Cambridge MA: Harvard University Asia Center, 2001.

Wang Gungwu. *The Chineseness of China: Selected Essays*. Hong Kong: Oxford University Press, 1991.

Wang Hui 汪暉. "Zhongguo xiandai lishi zhongde 'Wu Si' qimeng yundong" 中國現代歷史中的 "五四" 啟蒙運動 (The May Fourth enlightenment movement in modern Chinese history). In Wang Hui, *Zixuan ji* 自選集 (Selected works), Nanning: Guangxi shifan daxue chubanshe, 1997.

Wen Fengqiao 溫奉橋. "Guilai xi: De xiansheng, Sai xiansheng" 歸來兮: 德先生, 賽先生 (Come back Mr De and Mr Sai!), *Wen Fengqiao de boke*, 15 May 2008. http://blog.sina.com.cn/s/blog_4cb0c88301008i21.html.

Xi Jinping 習近平. "Zai Beijing daxue shisheng zuotanhuishang de jianghua" 在北京大學師生座談會上的講話 (A speech presented at a Peking University seminar for faculty and students). *Renmin ribao* 人民日報, 3 May 2018. http://politics.

people.com.cn/n1/2018/0503/c1001-29961481.html. Translated in Geremie R. Barmé, "May Fourth at Ninety-Nine," *China Heritage*, May 4, 2018. http://chinaheritage.net/journal/may-fourth-at-ninety-nine/2002.

Xu Youyu 徐友漁. "'Houzhuyi' yu qimeng" "後主義" 與啟蒙 ("Postisms" and Enlightenment). In Xu Youyu, *Ziyoude yanshuo* 自由的言說 (Speaking freely). Changchun: Changchun chubanshe, 1999. http://www.literature.org.cn/article.aspx?id=5913.

Yang Nianqun 楊念群. "'Wu Si' yanjiu huisu yu fansi" "五四" 研究回溯與反思 (Retracing and reflecting on "May Fourth" studies). In *Zhongguo jingying bao* 中國經營報, 12 May 2016. http://history.people.com.cn/n1/2016/0512/c372329-28346234.html.

Zhuangzi 莊子. 中國哲學書電子化計劃. https://ctext.org/zhuangzi/zh21:2.

CHAPTER 2

The May Fourth Liberal Legacy in Chan Koonchung's *Jianfeng ernian*

Josephine Chiu-Duke

In a 2017 interview discussing the historical development of the one hundred years of the new literature movement and its dynamic relationship with Chinese intellectuals, Chen Pingyuan (陳平原), a leading scholar in Chinese literary studies, stated that "the entire twentieth century was the May Fourth new culture century" (整個二十世紀都是五四新文化的世紀).[1] It is obvious that the "twentieth century" here should be understood as referring to the unfolding of the century in the Chinese historical context, but what is striking about the statement, is that the May Fourth new culture, or rather the New Culture Movement, was selected as the single most dominant event to characterize the entire one hundred years of Chinese history. Apparently, this characterization has something to do with the fact that this movement was regarded as marking the real turning point for the beginning of China's modernity.

Whether or not one agrees with such a characterization is not a concern here, but it reveals, at the least, the unquestionable importance of the May Fourth New Culture Movement in China's path to modernity in that it continues to emerge in the Chinese intellectual discourse and inspire reflective dialogues, even though it took place a century ago. As is well known, the past becomes important only when it speaks to the living in the present. In this sense, it is not surprising that the May Fourth New Culture Movement is still considered relevant to many Chinese intellectuals, or rather, to their concerns about China's current development and where it is heading in the future.[2] It is

---

1 See "Fangtan Chen Pingyuan: Zhengge ershi shiji doushi Wusi xin wenhua de shiji 訪談陳平原：整個二十世紀都是五四新文化的世紀 (Interviewing Chen Pingyuan: The entire 20th century was the century of the May Fourth New Culture)," conducted by Xu Zhiyuan and Zhuang Qiushui 許知遠, 莊秋水, *Dongfang lishi pinglun*, May 6, 2017 https://chinadigitaltimes.net/chinese/2017/05/东方历史评论｜访谈-陈平原：整个20世纪都是五四/.

2 For these concerns, see, for example, the essays covered in a special section on "Wusi yu dangdai Zhongguo 五四與當代中國 (The May Fourth and contemporary China)," in *Ershiyi shiji*, no. 113 (June 2009), 4–73. Especially relevant is Gao Quanxi's 高全喜 essay entitled "Chongxin fansi Wusi yi xiang de Zhongguo qimeng 重新反思五四以降的中國啟蒙 (Re-reflection on the Chinese 'Enlightenment' since the May Fourth)," 13–17.

also from this angle of historical relevance that I find the continued significance of the May Fourth liberal legacy can be further explored through the lens of Chan Koonchung's innovative novel *Jianfeng ernian: xin Zhongguo wuyoushi, An Uchronia of New China*.

The term May Fourth Movement has long been defined from both narrow and broad perspectives. In the narrow sense, the movement's name refers only to the college students' patriotic demonstration in Beijing on May Fourth 1919 against the then Chinese government's consent to a humiliating policy toward Japan assented to at the Versailles Peace Conference. However, seen from a broader perspective, this movement has been defined as a new cultural movement that spans roughly from 1917 through 1921, and includes different developments calling for reforms in almost all major aspects of Chinese society. Some of these reforms were so radical in nature that they can certainly be described as amounting to an "intellectual revolution in modern China."[3] Defined in this broad sense, the May Fourth Movement no longer appears to represent only a single important patriotic protest at one particular point in time, but instead it comes to denote a complex historical phenomenon extending throughout a certain period.

Indeed, many scholars agree that the May Fourth Movement should be understood as a movement that includes multiple sides and many levels of complex literary, cultural, social and political "projects." For example, Yü Ying-shih points out in his essay "Neither Renaissance nor Enlightenment: A Historian's Reflections on the May Fourth Movement," that "… the May Fourth intellectual world consisted of many communities of changing minds. Consequently, not only were there several May Fourth projects constantly undergoing changes and often conflicting with one another but each project also had different versions. Perhaps the safest generalization one can make about May Fourth is that it must always be understood in terms of its multidimensionality and multidirectionality."[4] Leaving aside this astute observation, what becomes

---

3 For this particular description and the interpretation of this movement from narrow and broad angles, see Chow Tse-tsung's well-known study and the sub-title of this discussion: *The May Fourth Movement: Intellectual Revolution in Modern China* (Stanford, CA: Stanford University Press, 1960), chap. 1, esp. pp. 1–6.

4 Yü Ying-shih, "Neither Renaissance nor Enlightenment: A Historian's Reflection on the May Fourth Movement," in his *Chinese History and Culture, vol. 2 Seventeenth Century Through Twentieth Century*, with the editorial assistance of Josephine Chiu-Duke and Michael S. Duke (New York: Columbia University Press, 2016), 198–219. On the complexity of the various intellectual developments in the May Fourth era, also see Yü-sheng Lin, *The Crisis of Chinese Consciousness: Radical Antitraditionalism in the May Fourth Era* (Madison: University of Wisconsin Press, 1979); and Vera Schwarcz, *The Chinese Enlightenment: Intellectuals and the Legacy of the May Fourth Movement* (Berkeley: University of California Press, 1986).

clear is that the May Fourth Movement gradually lost its multi-dimensional and multi-directional character and became increasingly radicalized after 1919. It eventually ended actually with the victory of radicalism, that is, it ended with the victory of its famous "radical anti-traditionalism" that was embodied in the victory of radical revolution over the earlier reform-oriented liberalism that advocated the importance of "Mr. Democracy."[5]

What needs to be clarified is that to those who advocated revolution as China's correct path to modernity, democracy was now perceived as "a form of radicalism" in the sense that representative institutions were no longer valued, but direct democracy was emphasized instead. This eventually paved the way for the emergence of "people's democracy" in Mao's China after 1949. Even so, before 1949 the option of liberal democracy was kept alive by various individuals who had participated in or were the leaders of the early May Fourth movement, and also by some thinkers of the younger generation. They continued to uphold liberal values and explore the possibility of building a democratic political system in place of the then one-party dictatorial rule of the Nationalist Party (Kuomintang, KMT, or Guomin Dang, GMD) from 1927 to 1949 before the KMT was forced by the Chinese Communist Party (CCP) to escape to Taiwan as a result of the civil war between these two most important political parties in modern Chinese history. Their efforts to continue the search for liberal democracy have been characterized as a "prodemocracy movement" starting in 1929 with those liberal minded individuals' "civil opposition" to the KMT dictatorship, but these efforts basically ended when the KMT lost control of China in 1949. Like their counterparts in the early stage of the May Fourth, or even earlier when the Chinese under the Manchu Qing rule began to search for representative institutions to restrain the arbitrary power of the Manchu government in the late nineteenth century, this "prodemocracy movement"

---

5 See Yü Ying-shih, "The Radicalization of China in the Twentieth Century," in his *Chinese History and Culture*, 2 (2016): 178–197, esp. 182–191; Lin Yü-sheng 林毓生, "Ershi shiji Zhongguo jijinhua fan chuantong sichao, Zhongshi MaLie zhuyi yu Mao Zedong de wutuobang zhuyi 二十世紀中國激進化反傳統思潮，中式馬列主義與毛澤東的烏托邦主義 (Radical anti-traditional intellectual trend in the 20th century, Chinese style Marxism-Leninism and Mao Zedong's utopianism)" in *Gongmin shehui jiben guannian* 公民社會基本觀念 (The basic ideas of civil society), edited by Lin Yü-sheng (Taipei: Zhongyang yanjiuyuan renwen shehui kexue yanjiu zhongxin, 2014) 2: 785–863; also see Jin Guantao and Liu Qingfeng 金觀濤, 劉青峰, *Guannian shi yanjiu: Zhongguo xiandai zhongyao zhengzhi shuyu de xingcheng* 觀念史研究: 中國現代重要政治術語的形成 (A study of the history of ideas: The formation of the important political terms in modern Chinese history) (Beijing: Falü chubanshe, 2010), 281–283.

continued on in the post-May Fourth period to articulate the importance of the core values of liberal democracy, values such as individual rights, constitutionalism with a limited government as well as checks and balances to prevent any abuses of political power.[6]

The advocacy of democracy in the early May Fourth period and the similar efforts afterwards are what I take to be the May Fourth liberal legacy that remains in the historical memory of modern Chinese intellectuals, writers, and scholars including obviously scholars like Chen Pingyuan, quoted at the beginning of this essay.

To be specific, "liberal legacy" is used here to refer to those ideas and ideals propagated most ardently during the early stage of the May Fourth New Culture Movement and the similar efforts that continued on afterwards. As we know, Chen Duxiu 陳獨秀 (1879–1942) and Hu Shi 胡適 (1891–1962), the two leading pioneer intellectuals of the May Fourth New Cultural Movement, both advocated individual freedom, and both believed that the purpose of a nation-state, or *guojia* 國家, was to protect and enhance the well-being of its citizens. In an essay published in late 1914, Chen Duxiu wrote specifically that the purpose of a nation-state is "to protect individual rights and to enrich individual happiness" (保障權利, 共謀幸福).[7] Hu Shi's life-long insistence that government must protect basic individual rights is no doubt widely known, and this insistence has recently also been described as having sowed the seeds of liberty in the consciousness of modern Chinese intellectual.[8] Hu Shi of course was

---

6 For the "prodemocracy movement" that continued the push to build a liberal democracy during the period of Nationalist rule, and for the Chinese quest for democracy in the late Qing, see the important work by Edmund S. K. Fung, *In Search of Chinese Democracy: Civil Opposition in Nationalist China, 1929–1949*, Cambridge University Press, 2000, esp. Chapters 1–4.

7 Chen's essay is entitled "Aiguo xin yu zijue xin 愛國心與自覺心 (Patriotism and self-consciousness)," and the citation is from: Lin Yü-sheng 林毓生, *The Crisis of Chinese Consciousness* (1979), 60; also see Lin Yü-sheng, "Renshi 'Wusi', rentong 'zaoqi' 'Wusi'—wei jinian 'Wusi yundong' jiushi zhounian er zuo 認識 '五四', 認同 '早期五四'—為紀念 '五四運動' 90 周年而作 (Knowing 'the May Fourth', identifying with the 'Early May Fourth'—in Commemoration of the 90th Anniversary of the 'May Fourth Movement')," in his *Zhongguo chuantong de chuangzao xing zhuanhua*, zengding ben 中國傳統的創造性轉化 (增訂本) (The creative transformation of the Chinese tradition [expanded edition]) (Beijing: Shenghuo, Dushu, Xinzhi Sanlian Shudian, 2011), 565–569; Gao Like 高力克, "Chen Duxiu de guojia guan 陳獨秀的國家觀 (Chen Duxiu's idea of the nation-state)," *Ershiyi shiji*, no. 94 (April 2006), pp. 63–72, esp. 66.

8 See the title of Chou Chih-p'ing's 周質平 new anthology, *Ziyou de Huozhong* 自由的火種 (The seeds of liberty) (Taipei: Yunchen wenhua, 2018), and how he discusses Hu Shi's liberal position in chap. 4 and 9, esp. pp. 137–195, 307–334. Also see Yü Ying-shih 余英時, *Chongxun Hu Shi licheng: Hu Shi shengping yu sixiang zai renshi* 重尋胡適歷程: 胡適生

also the leading intellectual of the "prodemocracy movement," but what needs to be underscored is that those liberal ideas and ideals were further upheld and preserved after 1949 through the efforts of Hu Shi and numerous other courageous intellectuals and individuals in Taiwan, and they have contributed to the formation of a liberal tradition in the Sinophone world.[9]

In *Jianfeng ernian,* one finds that Chan Koonchung not only discusses Hu Shi's persistent efforts after 1949 to render his full support of the publication of the *Free China Bimonthly* to keep alive May Fourth liberal ideals, but specifically mentions "the elevation of individuality and the tradition of liberalism during the May Fourth period" as a basic motif of the May Fourth new literature (171). Of course, Chan himself may not have intended his novel to be taken as being in line with the May Fourth liberal tradition, but his mentioning in the novel of "the tradition of liberalism during the May Fourth period" already serves to confirm that the May Fourth liberal legacy continues to have its modern relevance.[10] Furthermore, in both an interview and an essay, Chan Koonchung defines himself as what I would call a "social liberal" (*shehui ziyou zhuyizhe* 社會自由主義者), but he says he is a "middle-of-the-road" (*zhongdao* 中道) liberal with "left-wing" (左翼) leanings, understood here as valuing liberty while also advocating a government role in ensuring social welfare and preventing the monopoly of the market by hegemonic transnational capital. Thus, he clearly holds that liberal values protected by constitutional democracy are the necessary foundation for social and economic equality. In other

---

平與思想再認識 (Re-visiting Hu Shi's Life Journey: A New Understanding of Hu Shi's Life and Thought) (Taipei: Lianjing & Zhongyang yanjiuyuan, 2004), especially the chapter on "Hu Shi yu Zhongguo de minzhu yundong 胡適與中國的民主運動 (Hu Shi and Chinese democratic movement)," 255–263; Yang Zhende's 楊貞德 discussion in her *Zhuanxiang ziwo—jindai Zhongguo zhengzhi sixiang shang de geren* 轉向自我—近代中國政治思想上的個人 (Turning toward the self—The individual in modern Chinese political thought) (Taipei: Zhongyang yanjiuyuan Zhongguo wenzhe suo, 2009), esp. chap. 5, pp. 167–173.

9 See Chou, *Ziyou de Huozhong* (2018); Yü, *Chongxun Hu Shi lichen* (2004), 255–263; Xue Huayuan 薛化元, *"Ziyou Zhongguo" yu minzhu xianzheng—1950 niandai Taiwan sixiangshi de yige kaocha* "自由中國" 與民主憲政— 1950 年代台灣思想史的一個考察 (*Free China* and constitutional Democracy—A study of Taiwan's intellectual history in the 1950s) (Taipei: Daoxiang chubanshe, 1996), 75–176 and 229–231.

10 For its modern relevance, Gao Quanxi's essay, mentioned in n. 3 above, can serve as another useful example. Gao's main point is that the constitutional democracy advocated in the early stage of the May Fourth era should still serve as the "unfinished" goal for China's path to modernity in the 21st century.

words, despite Chan's dislike of the downplaying of equality in traditional liberal democracy, based on the tragic results of the disastrous socialist experiments in Mao's China, he obviously also does not believe social and economic equality can be achieved without first securing basic rights under the rubric of liberal democracy.[11]

In this sense, Chan's "middle-of-the-road" liberal with "left-wing" leanings easily remind us of the ideas upheld by the members of the "Third Force" group within the "prodemocracy movement." This "Third Force", represented by the notable Chinese Democratic League (*Zhongguo minzhu tongmeng* 中國民主同盟), was active from 1941 to 1945 just a year before the full-scale civil war broke out between the Nationalist and Chinese Communist Parties. While the members of the "Third Force" only constituted a minor political group at the time, they nevertheless tried to mediate the differences between the KMT and the CCP, or one can perhaps say, to balance the tension between liberty and equality in their efforts to build a modern China. In that sense, it is understandable why they have also been characterized as "middle-of-the-road intellectuals." Even so, they never stopped pressing the Nationalist Party to establish constitutional rule.[12] In other words, they never believed that one should push for equality at the risk of loosing one's liberty. From this perspective then, we can say that a parallel does exist between their views and Chan Koonchung's "middle-of-the-road" liberal position. In fact, I should note that Chan's persona in *Jianfeng ernian* actually employs the name of a notable member of the "Third Force" group.[13]

At the same time, it is also interesting to note that, whether by design or just coincidence, Chan's Jianfeng ernian was published in 2015, exactly one hundred years after the launch of the *New Youth* magazine that marked the beginning of the May Fourth New Culture Movement.

---

11 See Chan's "Xin Zuoyi sichao de tujing 新左翼思潮的圖景 (A map of the New Left-wing intellectual trend)," and his "Zhongdao ziyou zhuyi yu fan zhuanzhi de zuoyi 中道自由主義與反專制的左翼 (Middle of the road liberalism and anti-dictatorial liberalism)," both are in Chan Koonchung (Chen Guanzhong) 陳冠中, *Wutuobang, etuobang, yituobang: Chen Guanzhong de shidai wenpingji* 烏托邦, 惡托邦, 異托邦: 陳冠中的時代文評集 (Utopia, dystopia, and heterotopia: Chen Guanzhong's selected essays) (Taipei: Maitian, 2018), 349–406, 160–166, esp., 162–163 and 166.

12 For the emergence of the "Third Force" and their "middle-of-the-road" ideas and position during this period as well as their split and failure after 1946, see Edmund Fung, *In Search of Chinese Democracy*, 2000, pp. 2, 11–12, 19, 21, and Chs. 6, 7 and 8.

13 The name of this notable member is Zhang Dongsun 張東蓀 (1886–1973). For his thought on democracy, see Edmund Fung, *In Search of Chinese Democracy*, 2000, pp. 93–94, 134–136, and esp. pp. 216–218.

Chan Koonchung did not become a full-time novel writer until after he had chosen Beijing as his regular residence around 2000. He was born in Shanghai in 1952, but soon was taken to Hong Kong and grew up in that free city under the British colonial rule. For Chan, Hong Kong is his home through and through, and he started to write about this city and began, at the same time, to engage himself in various cultural endeavors long before he became a full-time novelist. His most recent novel was published in January 2018 with the title of *Make Boluo* (馬可波囉 or Marco Polettes).[14] *Make Boluo* is not related to my discussion of *Jianfeng ernian*, but Chan's two earlier novels are. It is thus necessary to provide first some brief comments on these two novels.

For one thing, although Chan's two previous novels—*Shengshi: Zhongguo, Erlingyisan nian* 盛世: 中國, 二零一三年 (2009), translated as *The Fat Years*, and *Luo Ming* 裸命 (2013), translated as *The Unbearable Dreamworld of Champa the Driver*—do not seem to have any direct bearing on the May Fourth liberal legacy, they may both be seen as carrying on the May Fourth tradition of social criticism. That is, they disclose the dark side of Chinese life and allow us to see an understated longing for a China that would open itself to liberal reforms.[15]

When reading *Shengshi*, or *The Fat Years*, one easily follows the fictional narrative that describes how China's path to "wealth and power" in post-Mao China has brought China to its "age of prosperity, or *shengshi*" (盛世) but at the same time, the narrative also makes it clear that China's "*shengshi*" actually was achieved by making its people forget their previous efforts in search of a different China. Through the voice of the narrator, we understand that Chan here unquestionably is referring to the June 1989 democracy movement, the huge peaceful demonstration demanding a democratic reform from the government, which eventually ended with a bloody military suppression on June Fourth. We can say that this "*shengshi*," as Chan presents it in an ironic mode, represents the political reality of China that continues to depart from the May Fourth dream of liberal (or constitutional) democracy, and

---

14　For Chan's background and his works, see Wikipedia: https://zh.wikipedia.org/wiki/陳冠中 Also see Kuang Qiao 匡翹, "Du Chen Guanzhong Make Boluo qian huigu Chen Guanzhong de xiaoshuo rensheng 讀陳冠中《馬可波囉》前回顧陳冠中的小說人生 (A review of Chan Koonchung's life as a novelist before reading his *Marco Polettes*)" https://bkb.mpweekly.com/cu0001/20180131-65545.

15　*Shengshi: Zhongguo, Erlingyisan nian* 盛世: 中國, 二零一三年 (Taipei: Maitian, 2009; Hong Kong: Oxford University Press, 2013). Translated by Michael S. Duke as *The Fat Years* (London: Random House Group Ltd., 2011). *Luo ming* 裸命 (Taipei: Maitian, 2013). Translated by Nicky Harman as *The Unbearable Dreamworld of Champa the Driver* (London: Doubleday 2014; London: Black Swan, 2015).

simultaneously also unfolds a China that is not an imagined dystopia and certainly not a utopia either. In this sense, one can agree that Chan Koonchung has created a fictional China that serves to expose the real nature and possible extent of the Party-State control and repression. Aspiring to be a total state in total control and to become the leading superpower in the world, this Party-State has brought about a *"shengshi,"* but in the end, it turns out that the real China today is a "counterfeit paradise."[16] I should perhaps add that the Chinese scholars who sent the novel to me, and many other Chinese intellectuals I talked to at the time, considered it the best description of the way they were actually living.

Like *Shengshi, Luoming* also exposes Chinese life under the rule of the Chinese Party-State. It depicts the fabricated nature of the Chinese Communist Party's so-called "harmonious society" through the story of a Tibetan chauffeur in Lhasa who becomes the boy-toy lover, or "Tibetan Mastiff puppy," of a Han Chinese businesswoman. As one reviewer describes the novel in a review of the translation, Chan Koonchung:

> ... paints disturbing vignettes. An apartheid-in-the-making. The eerie death wish of a would-be self-immolator. The Kafkaesque "black jails" where provincial petitioners who dare air their grievances to the Beijing Mandarins are brutalized, then sent home. If they're lucky, that is.

This reviewer concludes that the novel artfully manages to

> sensitize the casual reader, i.e., [one] who may have no previous knowledge of the Tibetan "question," to how China is micromanaging and marginalizing Tibetans in their own homeland, and suggests that the Chinese Police State is no less active—and no less evil—in Beijing than it is in Lhasa.[17]

---

16   The phrase "counterfeit paradise" is from page 20 of the "Preface" to *The Fat Years* by Julia Lovell. For the comments on this novel being a realistic exposé that reveals the dark side of the *"shengshi"* created by the Party-State, see the "translator note" 300–307. Also see Charles Foran's review "An Audacious View of a Counterfeit Paradise," *Global and Mail*, Jan. 2012; it can be downloaded from: http://charlesforan.com/wordpress/writings-reviews/the-fat-years-by-chan-koochung/.

17   Bruce Humes, "Champa the Driver: Tibetan Dreamer in an Alien Land," May 9, 2014, http://bruce-humes.com/archives/558.

Whether or not one accepts this reviewer's interpretation of Chan's novel, Chan Koonchung's serious concerns about the way the Chinese Party-State treats its Tibetan minority, and the way it treats its people in general as shown in this novel as well as in the *Shengshi*, is certainly not missed by his readers.

Like many works of almost all the major May Fourth writers, and certainly similar to the two novels discussed above, Chan Koonchung's *Jianfeng ernian* continues to disclose what the late Professor C. T. Hsia described as an "obsession with China." To be sure, this "obsession" is no longer related to the May Fourth sense of *jiuwang* 救亡, or saving China from the imperialist powers, but is instead concerned again with China's present socio-political reality and its future orientation, since China has already become a leading economic and military superpower. In this sense, it is only natural to view *Jianfeng ernian* together with Chan's other two novels mentioned above as his China "trilogy," even though they are banned in China.[18]

Since Chan's imagined literary world is intended to undergird reality from multiple angles, one can see this literary imaginary as signifying again Chan's critical reflections on China's recent path to "wealth and power" and the various serious problems that have come with it.[19] However, unlike his two earlier novels, in *Jianfeng ernian: An Uchronia of New China*, Chan, through his persona in the novel, starts to envision an alternative path for China's development by affirming repeatedly the May Fourth liberal ideas and ideals as the "right" ones for China's future development. Intentionally or unintentionally, such an affirmation undoubtedly reinvigorates the May Fourth liberal legacy, and it also leads me to argue that *Jianfeng ernian* is not just about exposing the

---

18 The term "trilogy about China" in its original Chinese is "Zhongguo sanbuqu 中國三部曲." It emerged in an interview with Chen Guanzhong: see A Lo 阿 Lo, "Zhuanfang Chen Guanzhong tan xinshu: *Jianfeng ernian* … Jiaru Guomindang meiyou shudiao dalu 專訪陳冠中談新書: 建豐二年 … 假如國民黨沒有輸掉大陸 (An interview with Chan Koonchung discussing his new work: *Jianfeng ernian* … If the KMT had Not lost mainland China)" https://theinitium.com/article/20150922-culture-feature-chankoonchung/.

19 Chan is of course not alone in this regard. One can see such concerns in many works of contemporary Chinese writers, even in those well received science fictions in recent time. Some of these science fictions reveal these concerns in their "reflections on social reality and power maneuvering," or in presenting migrant peasant workers' lack of any basic rights, and environmental devastation. Although science fictions focus on telling fantastic stories, many stories do have multilevel implications. See Song Mingwei 宋明煒, "Zaixian 'bu ke jian' zhi wu: Zhongguo kehuan xin langchao de shixue wenti 再現 '不可見' 之物: 中國科幻新浪潮的詩學問題 (Re-emerging 'invisible' matter: The problem of poetics in the new Chinese wave of science fiction)," *Ershiyi shiji* 157 (October 2016), 41–56, esp. 52 and 54.

ills of Chinese society, but rather it represents Chan's creative response to the question of where China should be heading after having become a formidable world power.

To bring forth Chan Koonchung's reflections and responses, I will present my readings of the novel on the basis of the two obvious meanings of the word "uchronia," and, at the same time, I will further suggest that the key to unraveling the embedded message in Chan's uchronia lies not merely in grasping the significance and implications of the novel's title, but perhaps more importantly, in unpacking the meaning imbricated in the headings of its two major sections.

In his "Preface" to *Jianfeng ernian*, David Dewei Wang points out that the strength of uchronia lies in its attempt to change the historical trajectory through a mediated temporality and thus make history right.[20] Here making history right understandably refers to Chan Koonchung's imagined historical picture in which the Nationalist regime defeated the Chinese Communist Party and became the ruling party on the Mainland since 1949. In short, everything that actually happened on Taiwan during the Nationalist rule in Taiwan since 1949 is transposed to China in this fictional world. Such a transposed world includes the KMT's first toleration but eventual suppression of the *Free China Bimonthly* that was under the wing of the leading May Fourth liberal intellectual Hu Shi, its white terror, its remarkable economic achievements, and its increasing inclination toward political reforms.

Before I discuss the novel further, it should be helpful to point out a common denominator that binds together Chan Koonchung's China trilogy. In his two novels mentioned above as well as in *Jianfeng ernian*, we see that Chan's fictional narratives, either in a cool and deadpan tone, or in a sarcastic and mocking voice, all in their different ways show that after China finally has become the world's second largest economic entity, the Chinese people are, however, still trapped in what Lu Xun described almost a century ago as an "iron house," though one may say that the "house" is no longer made of "iron" but is rather a gilded cage.[21] And yet, there is a big difference between Lu Xun's

---

20 David Dewei Wang, "Preface" to *Jianfeng ernian* (Taipei: Maitian, 2015), 1. The title of the "Preface" is: "Shitong san, xiaoshuo xing 史統散, 小說興 (The tradition of historical writing is disappearing and fiction is emerging)," but Wang's "Preface" is not in the 2015 edition published by Oxford University Press (Hong Kong). My thanks to Professor Wang for sending me this "Preface" essay.

21 For Lu Xun's famous metaphor, see his "Zixu 自序 (Preface)" to *Nahan* 吶喊 (Call to arms), in *Lu Xun quanji* 魯迅全集 (The complete works of Lu Xun), (Beijing: Renmin wenxue chubanshe, 1981) 1: 419.

conceptualization of the Chinese people being trapped in that "iron house" and Chan's way of portraying the Chinese people as trapped in a gilded cage. To put it simply, In Lu Xun's work, the sick Chinese "national character" was a fundamental cause for their being trapped. This is because, as embodied by the fictional character Ah Q, they had no inner self. They lived like animals by their instincts, and had no ability whatsoever to reflect on their own predicament, let alone to escape from it, or to help save their country from foreign invasion during that particular period of Chinese history. Ah Q then is the epitome of the slave mentality of the Chinese people who are totally unfit to carry out the task of saving their country.

In Chan's works, by contrast, the Chinese people are not portrayed as being similar to Ah Q. Nor is their "national character" the cause of their predicament. Rather, it is the Chinese state, or the Chinese ruling party, that deliberately makes its people live in a gilded cage despite the fact that China is no longer under any imminent threat from foreign powers. This poignant message is made crystal clear in Chan's two earlier novels as we learn that most of the people in *Shengshi* enjoy their age of prosperity. They have lost their memory of the June Fourth tragedy not because they wanted to but because the water they drank in Beijing had been tempered with by the Party-State by adding some sort of chemical. The most important character in *Luoming* also gradually becomes aware of his existence as purely instrumental and thus realizes the nature of the rule of the Party-State. By contrast, such a poignant message did not appear so directly, but rather emerges as an embedded one in *Jianfeng ernian*.

Bearing this in mind, let me now discuss how Chan Koonchung in this third novel of his "China trilogy" presents us with an example of the continuous line of May Fourth liberal ideas and ideals in the consciousness of many concerned intellectuals in today's Chinese language speaking world. Through a mediated imagined past history, Chan's novel envisions a future that seems to be pure fiction, but with close examination one can link this fictional future with what actually happened on the two sides of the Taiwan Strait, but during different time periods. For Taiwan, one can link this with what actually happened from 1949 down to the late 1980s, that is, with Taiwan's successful transformation from one-party authoritarian rule to a new democratic polity. For China, however, the link is not about what happened during the same time period, but rather is implied in what happened from 1979 to 1989, or really all the way down to the present. The novel's central concern about China here then is that what could have happened for China during these past thirty some years never took place, that is, a kind of transformation similar to Taiwan's path to constitutional democracy never emerged, but history is not preordained and an imagined future may just serve as a better alternative for China's future path to modernity. In short, an imagined fictional future can still serve as China's chosen path to the establishment of a constitutional democracy in which the basic rights of Chinese citizens could be protected by the rule of law (*fazhi* 法治) in which everyone is equal before the law and not simply by a rule by law (*fazhi* 法制) in which the state uses the law to control society, or even just by the will or whim of political leaders (*renzhi* 人治) who can ignore the law of anytime.

Meanwhile, as the novel unfolds, we see the author either asserting through his persona, or implying through the changes in some ordinary people that the idea of a liberal democracy has taken root in the consciousness of many Chinese, and that this will continue with the passage of time.

In reality, as is well known, the early May Fourth liberal ideas and ideals were almost completely eradicated in China during Mao's extreme form of socialism, but the fact is that they never disappeared in Taiwan even in the era after the KMT's "white terror." They were carried forward and kept alive in Taiwan by Hu Shi and other intellectuals such as Lei Zhen and Yin Haiguang through the publication of the *Free China Bimonthly*. Their efforts throughout the 1950s made this magazine the most influential voice advocating and calling for the implementation of liberal democracy. Later magazines with similar aspirations published in the 1970s and 1980s basically all followed the intellectual spirit and ideals of this pioneer magazine.[22] These successive waves of intellectual efforts thus provided Taiwan society with what Qian Yongxiang calls "narrative resources" based on liberal values.[23] These

---

22 For this complex historical development, see Xue, *"Ziyou Zhongguo"* (1996); Yin Haiguang jijinhui 殷海光基金會編, ed., *Ziyou zhuyi yu Xin shiji Taiwan* 自由主義與新世紀台灣 (Liberalism and Taiwan in a new century) (Taipei: Yunchen wenhua, 2007), particularly the first two chapters in section one; Chengshe 澄社編, ed., *Taiwan minzhu ziyou de quzhe licheng* 台灣民主自由的曲折歷程 (The zigzag journey of Taiwan's democracy and liberty) (Taipei: Zili wanbao, 1992), esp. see the chapter "Fandui shiye de di-er tiao zhenxian—cong dangwai dao Minjin dang de neibu fenqi 反對事業的第二條陣線－從黨外到民進黨的內部分歧 (The second front of the opposition activities—From the *Dangwai* to the internal split in the Democratic Progressive Party)," by Wu Naide 吳乃德 and the comments by Chen Zhongxin 陳忠信, 77–110; Jay Taylor, *The Generalissimo's Son: Chiang Ching-kuo and the Revolutions in China and Taiwan* (Harvard University Press, 2000), esp. 259–261, 306–308, and 348–349.

23 Qian Yongxiang 錢永祥, "Gongmin, Gonggong lingyu, gonggongxing zhishifenzi 公民, 公共領域, 公共型知識份子 (Citizens, public realm, and public intellectuals)," in *Zaizao gong yu yi de shehui yu lixing kongjian* 再造公與義的社會與理性空間 (Rebuilding a

"narrative resources" played a role in Taiwan's eventual transformation to a democratic polity. They also formed a tradition based on an unbroken line with the May Fourth liberal legacy. In this sense, we can say that it is precisely this tradition that Chan Koonchung appropriated to offer an imaginary China in *Jianfeng ernian*.

Moreover, the early May Fourth liberal concerns are crafted and woven together in Chan's narrative structure in such a way that readers can be engaged to ponder some built-in but not-so-specified questions in the narrative, questions such as: Will China let go of its Party-State dictatorial rule and implement a real political reform based on the rule of law that will eventually lead to constitutional democracy as advocated at the beginning of the May Fourth New Culture Movement? Or, will it follow the path of the Nationalist regime led by Chiang Kai-shek after it was forced to escape to Taiwan in 1949, especially after Chiang Ching-kuo's presidency starting in 1978, when Taiwan's journey to democratic transformation gradually came into being? Or, did it miss its best moment to do so when its military suppression of June 4, 1989, smashed the best hope of its patriotic and liberal-minded citizens? And ultimately, despite missing this best moment, will China be able to launch a long-awaited political reform aimed at the establishment of constitutional democracy? These are the questions that one can sense between the lines when reading *Jianfeng ernian*.

To be sure, no direct answers to the above questions are offered in the novel, but the questions themselves clearly suggest the direction that the author anticipates his readers will take when giving their answers. What I attempt to do next is to examine some important details that lead me to my interpretation of the novel.

Many of us know that "Jianfeng" is the courtesy name of Chiang Ching-kuo and *Jianfeng ernian* refers to the second year of Chiang's presidency in Taiwan under the KMT or Nationalist rule that corresponded in fact to the year 1979. The novel starts specifically with December 10, 1979, and strangely ends exactly also with the same day of the same year. The curious thing is that, except for December 10, 1979, the novel does not at all mention any other time in Chiang's presidency, but instead, it focuses on offering a story about KMT rule from 1949 up to December 10, 1979. Thus, throughout we see how Chan underscores the KMT's successful land reform and its "economic miracle," and how he also

---

fair and just society and a rational realm), edited by Yu Jianchuan and Huang Shushen 于建洲, 黃淑慎編 (Taipei: Shibao wenjiao jijinhui, 2003), 466.

criticizes the KMT's dictatorial rule when it comes to suppression and persecution of its critics, including its treatment of the *Free China Bimonthly*, the only magazine, as already mentioned above, that had been continuing since late 1949 (November 1949–September 1960) to promote the May Fourth liberal ideas and ideals.

What is intriguing is of course that everything Chan Koonchung portrays about KMT rule in this novel, as also mentioned above, does not take place in Taiwan, but is recorded as happening in China. Chan of course already makes it clear that whatever happens in this novel is meant to be understood as an "uchronia," or a history that has never taken place. Yet, an imagined historical narrative can also be understood, on the implicit level, as an ideal alternative to the extant historical trajectory, or as a reminder of what could have happened if the opportunity of the Weberian idea of a railroad track switch had been seized at a particularly critical moment.[24] In this sense, as David Wang has pointed out, Chan's imagined history of KMT rule on mainland China from 1949 to 1979 clearly brings out the crucial question underscoring this whole uchronia. That is, what would have happened if the KMT, instead of the CCP, had ruled China after 1949?[25] Following this question, we can further ask: Might the Chinese people as a whole have been better off under KMT rule? Chan's answer as seen in the novel is clearly a positive one since, at the very least, they would not have had to go through the "purgatory" created by Mao's extreme form of socialist experimentation. Moreover, might China not have long since developed a much healthier economic situation, and, as a nation-state, have already established itself as a reasonable and respectable superpower that treats every other country as an equal member of the international community?

Leaving aside these questions, Chan, through the voice of one of his major characters, actually spares no criticism of the KMT's ruthless suppression of any dissenters, and he discusses the difference between the KMT and CCP as a matter of degree and not of kind (20). Nevertheless, I will argue that when we understand that December 10, 1979, is meant to be a specific time point in this novel, then we can see that this key temporality is intended as a boundary when the two most notable political parties in modern Chinese history would begin to take two fundamentally different roads.

---

24 For Weber's idea of the railroad track switch, see *From Max Weber: Essays in Sociology*, translated by H. H. Gerth and C. Wright Mills (New York: Oxford University Press, 1958), 280.
25 David Dewei Wang, "Shitong san, xiaoshuo xing," in his "Preface" to the Taiwan edition of Chen Guanzhong's *Jianfeng ernian* (2015), 4–19.

So, on December 10, 1979, at the very beginning of the first chapter of *Jianfeng ernian*, we read that a group of people who include almost all the notable intellectual dissenters and political criminals from China and Taiwan are all invited to get together in a Beijing restaurant named Beautiful Taiwan Guest Friendship Cafe (Meili Taikeqing shitang 美麗台客情食堂). Their gathering is meant to celebrate the United Nations-designated Human Rights Day, but they end up being arrested on that same day by the party-state as the novel reaches its end. What deserves our attention is that the chapter itself ends with the statement that "this is really the important moment of democracy in our country, and it will be remembered in history" (這是我國民主發展之重要時刻, 歷史是會記下一筆的) (8).

With this statement, we can safely say that Chan Koonchung is suggesting that China should take the KMT's rule in Taiwan after 1979 as a reference for its future development. Why? Because it was during the second year of Chiang Ching-kuo's presidency that Taiwan gradually started its relatively peaceful process toward democratization.[26]

Chan is careful when portraying how the hard work of ordinary people helped make the "economic miracle" come true. He describes their determination to change their lives as a result of their transformation after suffering in what he calls "purgatory." Yet, this transformation through "purgatory" (*lianyu bian* 煉獄變) (218), made them strong-willed, but also made them care for nothing but their material conditions and for a the new age of mass entertainment culture or other peculiar obsessions. We could take the term "lianyu bian" as referring to those people who experienced the KMT's "white terror." Chan's subsequent description of the Chinese people's "transformation" does not, however, fit the picture of what the people of Taiwan transformed themselves into after Taiwan's economic take-off throughout the 1970s and 80s. It fits better when applied to the general condition of the Chinese people that we know from various scholarly reports.[27] Thus, in the last section of the last

---

26   For the history of Taiwan in general, and Chiang Ching-kuo's presidency in particular, see Murray A. Rubinstein, ed., *Taiwan: A New History* (Armonk, New York: M. E. Sharpe, 1999, 2007), esp. chap. 16 on Chiang Ching-kuo's presidency, 437–447; Jay Taylor, *The Generalissimo's Son* (2000), esp. from chap. 18 onward.

27   See for example, Sun Liping's 孫立平 report: "zhongguo zuida de weixie bushi shehui dongdang ershi shehui fuhua 中國最大的問題不是社會動盪, 而是社會腐化 (The biggest threat to China is not social turmoil but social decay)" chinadigitaltimes. net/2009/03/sun-liping-孫立平, translated by Linjun Fan for China Digital Times. Also see Sun's "Jide liyi tuanti dui gaige de tiaozhan hai Meiyou zhenzheng daolai 既得利益團體對改革的挑戰沒有真正到來 (The real challenge of the vested interest groups to the reform has yet to come)," *Gaige neican* 改革內參 (Internal References for the

chapter of *Jianfeng ernian*, we see how Chan portrays the coming of the age of mass entertainment in which some individuals can suddenly become popular television hosts as long as their strangeness or peculiarity can amuse the masses to their hearts' content. On the one hand, we see how Chan describes, in a journalistic and yet empathetic tone, the way that Mai Shinai 麥師奶 strives mightily if comically to improve the living standards of her son Mai A-dou 麥阿斗 (183–198), just a might many Chinese people, but on the other hand, we also sense that Chan's description actually implies that one should take these people seriously, since they clearly never want to go back to living as before in "purgatory."

In light of Chan's description of this "lianyu bian," I will suggest that what is described in the novel about the KMT's rule from 1949 to 1979, can equally be interpreted as what happened in China in the past three decades under Deng Xiaoping's policy of opening up and reform. The only difference is that after December 10, 1979, the KMT under Chiang Ching-kuo in Taiwan began to embark on a different road that eventually led to a peaceful path to constitutional democracy, whatever flaws and problems it still has to struggle with. To substantiate this claim, I will attempt to unpack the meanings and implications of the headings of the first and last sections.

The heading of the first section is "Zhongju de kaiju: jinri heri (The beginning of an end: what day is today?" 終局的開局: 今日何日); the heading of the last section is: "Kaiju de zhongju: jinxi hexi (The end of a beginning: what night is tonight?" 開局的終局: 今夕何夕). But what "end (*zhongju* 終局)" and what "beginning (*kaiju* 開局)" is Chan referring to? And why does he use "day" and "night" in two almost identical headings?

Many of us know that December 10, 1979, was in reality a dark moment in Taiwan's history: on that day, the infamous "Formosa Incident" (*Meilidao shijian* 美麗島事件) broke out. But ironically it also marked "the turning point" in Taiwan's long journey to democracy due to a series of policies implemented afterwards.[28] From this, I suggest that we read the heading of the first section "Zhongju de kaiju" as implying the "beginning" of the "ending" the KMT's

---

Reform) (April 19, 2014) theory.gmw.cn/2014-04/19/content_11079446.htm; also see Zhou Lian 周濂, "Liusha zhuangtai de dangdai Zhongguo zhengzhi wenhua 流沙狀態的當代中國政治文化 (The quicksand of contemporary Chinese political culture)," *Ershiyi shiji* 158 (December 2016): 28–37.

28   Jay Taylor, *The Generalissimo's Son*, 2000. For Chiang Ching-kuo's policies see chap. 18 and after; for the Formosa Incident in particular, see chap. 21, esp. pp. 348–353.

one-party rule on the island, and thus pointing to a new chapter in Taiwan history. Subsequently, adding the question "what day is today" to the heading can be understood as Chan's logical way to emphasize that the dawn is approaching.

As for the heading of the last section: "Kaiju de zhongju 開局的終局," or "the end of a beginning," I interpret it as meaning "the end of a new era." This means we cannot apply the "new era" here to the KMT rule from 1949 to 1979 because its rule during that particular period was still a one-party dictatorship. However, if we apply it to China's development in the last thirty years under Deng Xiaoping, then it makes sense to say that the economic "opening up" part of the reform era under Deng constitutes a "new era." But the "opening up" soon reached "an end" when the expected political reforms were never really delivered. In fact, by December 10, 1979, Wei Jingshen, one of the notable leaders of the first wave of the Democracy Wall Movement, was already under arrest, not to mention what happened in June 1989.[29] From this point of view, I will argue that it is by no means an accident that Chan Koonchung names the heading of his last chapter "the end of a beginning." Since on December 10, 1979, the dawn of political reform in China was still far off, it is only natural for Chan Koonchung to add the question: "what night is tonight? 今夕何夕" after the phrase "the end of a beginning." In so doing, we can see how he deliberately contrasts the rule of the KMT and CCP by using December 10, 1979, as a divisive temporality through the rearrangement of the wording in the first and the last sections of *Jianfeng ernian*. In short, Taiwan by December 10, 1979, was heading toward a new day, or a new beginning, even though it had to suffer a dark moment on that day. In this sense, one can also say that the May Fourth liberal ideals finally found their way to daylight in Taiwan, while China's future direction after December 10, 1979, is still in the dark and far away from those ideals. As the ending of *Jianfeng ernian* tells us, the authorities are still hunting down those who dare to push for liberal democracy.

Is this the final answer that Chan Koonchung has to offer us in *Jianfeng ernian*? Perhaps not. As dark as the ending of the *Jianfeng ernian* is, Chan clearly does not want this dark night to continue. In fact, in the last section,

---

29   Wei Jingsheng 魏京生 was the author of a critical manifesto entitled "Diwuge xiandaihua 第五個現代化 (The fifth modernization)" calling for democracy in China. He was incarcerated as a political prisoner from March 1979 to 1993 and again in 1994–1997. He now lives in the United States. See Orville Schell, *Discos and Democracy: China in the Throes of Reform* (New York: Pantheon Books, 1988; Anchor Books, 1989), 278–279.

Chan's persona, the third person narrator who assumes the name of a leading member of the "Third Force" group within the "prodemocracy movement" as mentioned above, repeatedly affirms that, compared with Mao, his belief in constitutional democracy, civic rights and restraints on political power will in the end prove to be the right path for China. Meanwhile, Chan also relies on this third person narrator's wife to tell us that she is going to tell their children and grandchildren and all of her husband's friends what her husband had affirmed before he passed away. As a writer, Chan Koonchung, like most writers, embodies his personal beliefs in his imagined literary history in hopes of passing on the May Fourth liberal ideas and ideals. Through his uchronia, this May Fourth liberal legacy can be said to be once again revived. It is also in this sense that we can say that Chan does not believe China will forever be trapped in the same historical mode of rule; instead, his message is that an individual political leader's choices as well as the persistent efforts of concerned intellectuals and citizens can, and do, make a difference in history, at least as he knows it from the history of Taiwan's struggle for constitutional democracy, and as he implies in his uchronia of *Jianfeng ernian*.

Acknowledgement

I would like to thank an anonymous reviewer of this essay whose important suggestions helped to strengthen my arguments.

Bibliography

A Lo 阿 Lo. "Zhuanfang Chen Guanzhong tan xinshu: *Jianfeng ernian* … Jiaru Guomindang meiyou shudiao dalu 專訪陳冠中談新書《建豐二年》: 假如 … 國民黨沒有輸掉大陸 (An Interview with Chan Koonchung Discussing His New Work: *Jianfeng Ernian* … If the KMT Had Not Lost Mainland China)" https://theinitium.com/article/20150922-culture-feature-chanKoonchung/.

Chan, Koonchung 陳冠中. *Shengshi: Zhongguo, erlingyisan nian* 盛世: 中國, 二零一三年. Taipei: Maitian, 2009; Hong Kong: Oxford University Press, 2009.

Chan, Koonchung 陳冠中. *Luo ming* 裸命. Taipei: Maitian, 2013.

Chan, Koonchung 陳冠中. *Jianfeng ernian: xin Zhongguo wuyoushi*, 建豐二年: 新中國烏有史 (The Second Year of *Jianfeng*: An Uchronia of New China). Hong Kong: Oxford University Press, 2015; Taipei: Maitian, 2015.

Chan, Koonchung 陳冠中. "Xin zuoyi sichao de tujing 新左翼思潮的圖景 (A Map of the New Left-wing Intellectual Trend)," in *Wutuobang, etuobang, yituobang*: *Chen*

Guanzhong (Chan Koonchung) de shidai wenpingji 烏托邦, 惡托邦, 異托邦: 陳冠中的時代文評集 (Utopia, Dystopia and Heterotopia: Chen Guanzhong's Selected Essays), 349–406. Taipei: Maitian, 2018.

Chan, Koonchung 陳冠中. "Zhongdao ziyou zhuyi yu fan zhuanzhi de zuoyi 中道自由主義與反專制的左翼 (Middle of the Road Liberalism and Anti-Dictatorial Liberalism)," in *Wutuobang, etuobang, yituobang: Chen Guanzhong de shidai wenpingji* 烏托邦, 惡托邦, 異托邦: 陳冠中的時代文評集 (Utopia, Dystopia and Heterotopia: Chen Guanzhong's [Chan Koonchung's] Selected Essays). Taipei: Maitian, 2018, 160–166.

Chengshe, ed. 澄社編. *Taiwan minzhu ziyou de quzhe licheng* 台灣民主自由的曲折歷程 (The Zigzag Journey of Taiwan's Democracy and Liberty). Taipei: Zili wanbao, 1992.

Chou Chih-p'ing 周質平. *Ziyou de Huozhong* 自由的火種 (The Seeds of Liberty). Taipei: Yunchen wenhua, 2018.

Chow Tse-tsung. *The May Fourth Movement: Intellectual Revolution in Modern China.* Stanford, CA: Stanford University Press, 1960.

Duke, Michael S. *The Fat Years.* London: Random House Group Ltd., 2011.

Ershiyi shiji 二十一世紀, no. 113 (June 2009). "Wusi yu dangdai Zhongguo" 五四與當代中國 (The May Fourth and Contemporary China), 4–73.

Foran, Charles. "An Audacious View of a Counterfeit Paradise," *Global and Mail*, Jan.2012, http://charlesforan.com/wordpress/writings-reviews/the-fat-years-by-chan-koochung/.

Fung, Edmund S. K. *In Search of Chinese Democracy: Civil Opposition in Nationalist China, 1929–1949.* Cambridge: Cambridge University Press, 2000.

Gao, Like 高力克. "Chen Duxiu de guojia guan 陳獨秀的國家觀 (Chen Duxiu's Idea of the Nation-State)," *Ershiyi shiji* 二十一世紀, no. 94 (April 2006), 63–72.

Gao Quanxi 高全喜. "Chongxin fansi Wusi yi xiang de Zhongguo qimeng 重新反思五四以降的中國啟蒙 (Re-reflection on the Chinese 'Enlightenment' Since the May Fourth)," *Ershiyi shiji* 二十一世紀, no. 113 (June 2009), 13–17.

Gerth, H. H., and C. Wright Mills, trans. *From Max Weber: Essays in Sociology.* New York: Oxford University Press, 1958.

Harman, Nicky. *The Unbearable Dreamworld of Champa the Driver.* London: Doubleday, 2014; London: Black Swan, 2015.

Humes, Bruce. "Champa the Driver: Tibetan Dreamer in an Alien Land." May 9, 2014, http://bruce-humes.com/archives/558.

Jin Guantao 金觀濤, and Liu Qingfeng 劉青峰. *Guannian shi yanjiu: Zhongguo xiandai zhongyao zhengzhi shuyu de xingcheng* 觀念史研究: 中國現代重要政治術語的形成 (A Study of the History of Ideas: The Formation of the Important Political Terms in Modern Chinese History), 281–283. Beijing: Falü chubanshe, 2010.

Kuang Qiao 匡翹. "Du Chen Guanzhong (Chan Koonchung) Make Boluo qian huigu Chen Guanzhong de xiaoshuo rensheng 讀陳冠中馬可波囉前回顧陳冠中的小說人生 (A Review of Chan Koonchung's Life as a Novelist Before Reading His *Marco Polettes*)," https://bkb.mpweekly.com/cu0001/20180131-65545.

Lin Yü-sheng 林毓生. "Ershi shiji Zhongguo jijinhua fan chuantong sichao, Zhongshi MaLie zhuyi yu Mao Zedong de wutuobang zhuyi 二十世紀中國激進化反傳統思潮，中式馬列主義與毛澤東的烏托邦主義 (Radical Anti-traditional Intellectual Trend in the the 20th Century, Chinese Style Marxism—Leninism and Mao Zedong's Utopianism)," in *Gongmin shehui jiben guannian* 公民社會基本觀念 (The Basic Ideas of Civil Society), ed. Lin Yü-sheng 林毓生編 2: 785–863. Taipei: Zhongyang yanjiuyuan renwen shehui kexue yanjiu zhongxin, 2014.

Lin Yü-sheng 林毓生. "Renshi 'Wusi', rentong 'zaoqi' 'Wusi'—wei jinian 'Wusi yundong' jiushi zhounian er zuo 認識 '五四', 認同 '早期五四'—為紀念 '五四運動' 90 周年而作 (Knowing 'the May Fourth,' Identifying with the 'Early May Fourth'—in Commemoration of the 90th Anniversary of the 'May Fourth Movement')," in his *Zhongguo chuantong de chuangzao xing zhuanhua*, zengding ben 中國傳統的創造性轉化 (增訂本) (The Creative Transformation of the Chinese Tradition, expanded edition), 565–569. Beijing: Shenghuo, Dushu, Xinzhi Sanlian Shudian, 2011.

Lin, Yü-sheng. *The Crisis of Chinese Consciousness: Radical Antitraditionalism in the May Fourth Era*. Madison: University of Wisconsin Press, 1979.

Lu Xun 魯迅. "Zixu 自序 (Preface)," to *Nahan* 呐喊 (Call to Arms), *Lu Xun quanji* 魯迅全集 (The Complete Works of Lu Xun), vol. 1 (Beijing: Renmin wenxue chubanshe, 1981).

Qian Yongxiang 錢永祥. "Gongmin, gonggong lingyu, gonggongxing zhishifenzi 公民, 公共領域, 公共性知識分子 (Citizens, Public Realm, and Public Intellectuals)," in *Zaizao gong yu yi de shehui yu lixing kongjian* 再造公與義的社會與理性空間 (Rebuilding a Fair and Just Society and a Rational Realm), ed. Yu Jianchuan and Huang Shushen 于建洲 黃淑慎編. Taipei: Shibao wenjiao jijinhui, 2003.

Rubinstein, Murray A., ed. *Taiwan: A New History*. Armonk, New York: M. E. Sharpe, 1999, 2007.

Schell, Orville. *Discos and Democracy: China in the Throes of Reform*. New York: Pantheon Books, 1988; Anchor Books, 1989.

Schwarcz, Vera. *The Chinese Enlightenment: Intellectuals and the Legacy of the May Fourth Movement*. Berkeley: University of California Press, 1986.

Song Mingwei 宋明煒. "Zaixian 'bu ke jian' zhi wu: Zhongguo kehuan xin langchao de shixue wenti 再現 '不可見' 之物: 中國科幻新浪潮的詩學問題 (Re-emerging 'Invisible' Matter: The Problem of Poetics in the New Chinese Wave of Science Fiction)," *Ershiyi shiji* 二十一世紀 157 (October 2016): 41–56.

Sun Liping 孫立平. "Jide liyi tuanti dui gaige de tiaozhan hai Meiyou zhenzheng daolai 既得利益團體對改革的挑戰還沒有真正到來 (The Real Challenge of the Vested Interest Groups to the Reform Has Yet to Come)," *Gaige neican* 改革內參 (Internal References for the Reform), April 19, 2014, theory.gmw.cn/2014-04/19/content_11079446.htm.

Sun Liping 孫立平. "Zhongguo zuida de weixie bushi shehui dongdang er shi shehui fuhua 中國最大的威脅不是社會動盪而是社會腐化 (The Biggest Threat to China Is Not Social Turmoil but Social Decay)," translated by Linjun Fan for China Digital Times. chinadigitaltimes.net/2009/03/sun-liping-孫立平.

Taylor, Jay. *The Generalissimo's Son: Chiang Ching-kuo and the Revolutions in China and Taiwan.* Cambridge, MA: Harvard University Press, 2000.

Wang, David Dewei (Wang Dewei) 王德威. "Shitong san, xiaoshuo xing 史統散, 小說興 (The Tradition of Historical Writing Is Disappearing and Fiction Is Emerging)," "Preface" to the Taiwan edition of Chen Guanzhong's *Jianfeng ernian: Xin Zhongguo wuyoushi* 4–19.

Xu Zhiyuan 許知遠 and Zhuang Qiushui 莊秋水. "Fangtan Chen Pingyuan: Zhengge ershi shiji doushi Wusi xin wenhua de shiji 訪談陳平原: 整個二十世紀都是五四新文化的世紀 (Interviewing Chen Pingyuan: The Entire 20th Century Was the Century of the May Fourth New Culture)," *Dongfang lishi pinglun*, May 6, 2017. https://chinadigitaltimes.net/chinese/2017/05/东方历史评论 ｜ 访谈-陈平原: 整个20世纪都是五四/.

Xue Huayuan 薛化元. *"Ziyou Zhongguo" yu minzhu xianzheng—1950 niandai Taiwan sixiangshi de yige kaocha* "自由中國" 與民主憲政 1950 年代台灣思想史的一個考察 (*Free China* and Constitutional Democracy—A Study of Taiwan's Intellectual History in the 1950s). Taipei: Daoxiang chubanshe, 1996.

Yang Zhende 楊貞德, *Zhuanxiang ziwo—jindai Zhongguo zhengzhi sixiang shang de geren* 轉向自我近代中國政治思想上的個人 (Turning toward the Self—the Individual in Modern Chinese Political Thought). Taipei: Zhongyang yanjiuyuan Zhongguo wenzhe suo, 2009.

Yin Haiguang jijinhui, ed. 殷海光基金會編. *Ziyou zhuyi yu xin shiji Taiwan* 自由主義與新世紀台灣 (Liberalism and Taiwan in a New Century). Taipei: Yunchen wenhua, 2007.

Yü Ying-shih 余英時. *Chongxun Hu Shi licheng: Hu Shi shengping sixiang zai renshi* 重尋胡適歷程: 胡適生平思想再認識 (Re-visiting Hu Shi's Life Journey: A New Understanding of Hu Shi's Life and Thought). Taipei: Lianjing & Zhongyang yanjiuyuan, 2004.

Yü, Ying-shih. "Neither Renaissance nor Enlightenment: A Historian's Reflection on the May Fourth Movement," in *Chinese History and Culture, vol. 2, Seventeenth Century through the Twentieth Century*, with the editorial assistance of Josephine Chiu-Duke and Michael S. Duke, 198–219. New York: Columbia University Press, 2016.

Yü, Ying-shih. "The Radicalization of China in the Twentieth Century," in his *Chinese History and Culture* 2 (2016): 178–197.

Zhou Lian 周濂. "Liusha zhuangtai de dangdai Zhongguo zhengzhi wenhua 流沙狀態的當代中國政治文化 (The Quicksand of Contemporary Chinese Political Culture)," *Ershiyi shiji* 二十一世紀 158 (December 2016): 28–37.

CHAPTER 3

Two Versions of Modern Chinese History: a Reassessment of Hu Shi and Lu Xun

Chih-p'ing Chou

There are two versions of modern Chinese history. One is the account by the Nationalist Party, the Guomindang (KMT), and the other by the Chinese Communist Party (CCP). Historical figures are portrayed very differently depending on which version is being referenced. This is especially true after 1949. Scholarship is hardly independent from politics. The best example of this divergence can be found in the study of Hu Shi and Lu Xun.

Hu Shi (1891–1962) and Lu Xun (1881–1936) were two of the most influential intellectuals in modern Chinese history. They were closely identified with the Guomintang and the Communist Party respectively, even though neither was actually a member of these parties. After Lu Xun's death in 1936, he was praised by Mao Zedong 毛澤東 (1893–1976) as the greatest cultural hero that China had ever known, and was portrayed as a spokesman for the proletariat class. In contrast, Hu Shi's close dealings with the Guomintang and the United States of America led people to associate him with the opposite end of the political spectrum.

From 1949 to 1979 the Communist government in China carefully planned to create an image of Lu Xun as a "positive model" (正面教材) and Hu Shi a "negative model" (反面教材) for Chinese intellectuals. While Lu Xun's thought was officially interpreted as an ideology that served the proletariat class, Hu Shi's was said to help the bourgeois class. Thus, Lu Xun was said to be "the most correct, most courageous, most persistent, most loyal and most enthusiastic national hero ever known" (最正確，最勇敢，最堅決，最忠實，最熱忱的空前的民族英雄)[1] while Hu Shi was "the earliest, the most persistent and most uncompromising enemy of Chinese Marxism and socialist thought,"[2]

---

[1] Mao Zedong, "Xin minzu zhuyi lun" 新民主主義論 (On new democracy), *Mao Zedong xuanji* (Beijing: Renmin chubanshe, 1966), 2: 658.

[2] Hu Shi, "Sishinian lai Zhongguo wenyi fuxing yundong liuxia de kangbao xiaodu Liliang—Zhongguo Gongchandang qingsuan Hu Shi sixiang de lishi yiyi" 四十年來中國文藝復興運動留下的抗暴消毒力量—中國共產黨清算胡適思想的歷史意義 (The legacy of the forty years of Chinese Renaissance Movement—The historical significance of the Chinese Communist Party purging Hu Shi's thought) 胡適手稿 (Hu Shi hand written manuscript), (Taipei: Hu Shi Memorial, 1970), 9: 492–493.

(中國馬克思主義和社會主義思想的最早的，最堅決的，不可調和的敵人) who "intended to thoroughly destroy the basis of Marxism" (企圖從根本上拆毀馬克思的基礎).[3] The Communist campaign against Hu Shi during these three decades was a blatant example of the extent to which an intellectual could be purged and distorted by a government. It was unprecedented in Chinese history that a government would mobilize people from all walks of life to criticize one intellectual for several years.[4]

The way Lu Xun was received after his death was indeed unique. Mao Zedong had never praised any Chinese intellectual as effusively as he did Lu Xun, and Lu Xun's *Complete Works* 魯迅全集 were annotated and published as early as 1958 and later in 1981. A revised edition of eighteen volumes was published again in 2005. Museums dedicated to Lu Xun were built in Beijing and Shanghai, and his statue was erected. Lu Xun's works were designated as required reading for Chinese students from elementary schools to colleges. It is this sharp contrast that makes a comparative study of Lu Xun and Hu Shi not only interesting but politically significant in modern Chinese intellectual history.

The political differences between Hu Shi and Lu Xun have, unfortunately, overshadowed their ideological similarities, such as their dedication to promoting the vernacular as the medium for literature and education, their belief in freedom of speech and the emancipation of women, and their critical attitude toward traditional Chinese culture, etc. Furthermore, there is a significant coincidence in their educational backgrounds that warrants our attention. Both of them went abroad to study in their youth. Lu Xun studied in Japan, while Hu Shi studied in America. Their original interests were in fields other than literature. While Lu Xun was a student of medical science, Hu Shi was a student of agriculture. Later in their lives, both abandoned their initial interests and dedicated themselves to the life of a literary writer. Their motives differed, but the fact that both underwent a radical career change reveals the common traits in their personalities that have profound implications in understanding their respective thoughts and ideologies.

However, these similarities neither narrowed the gap between these two May Fourth scholars nor lessened their conflicts. In fact, the chasm between them widened with the passing of time. Hu Shi's seven years of college education at Cornell and Columbia University led him to adopt a Western philosophy

---

3　Ibid.
4　Most articles published during this smear campaign were collected in *Hu Shi sixiang pipan* 胡適思想批判 (Criticisms on Hu Shi's thought), (Beijing: Sanlian shudian, 1955).

that shaped his thinking and led him to advocate a Western model for China's intellectual advancement. Hu Shi became a lifelong advocate of Western liberalism, constitutional parliamentarianism, and individual rights. Lu Xun, on the other hand, was more influenced by the revolution in Russia and the ideology of Eastern European thinkers. This led him to become a left-wing writer and a Communist sympathizer.

The three most often quoted posthumous titles given to Lu Xun by Mao Zedong were "the great hero of the Chinese cultural revolution" (中國文化革命的偉人),[5] "the greatest and most courageous fighter of the new cultural army" (文化新軍的最偉大和最英勇的旗手),[6] and "a cow for the proletariat and the people" (無產階級和人民大眾的牛).[7] These labels remind us of one of Lu Xun's articles titled "Masha yu pengsha" 罵殺與捧殺 (To kill by curse and to kill by praise) in which he argued that Xu Zhimo's 徐志摩 (1896–1931) and Lin Changmin's 林長民 (1876–1925) flattering of the Indian poet Rabindranath Tagore (1861–1941) when he visited China in 1924, actually drove the Chinese young people away from this Indian poet. Lu Xun poignantly wrote, "If our poets did not portray him as a living god, the young people would not have felt so alienated from him" (如果我們的詩人諸公不將他製成一個活神仙,青年們對於他是不至於如此隔膜的).[8]

But after Lu Xun's death, he himself was deified and was considered an unearthly figure. The critics in China may have forgotten that excessive praise is just as damaging as condemnation. In a letter to Bao Yaoming 鮑耀明 written in 1965, Lu Xun's younger brother, Zhou Zuoren 周作人 (1885–1966), wrote:

> Nowadays, everyone praises Lu Xun. His statue was recently built near his tomb in Shanghai—I saw that in a picture. The statue has a high platform. On the top of it, Lu Xun sits alone on a chair. Although this statue was intended as a form of respect, it turned out to be a caricature of him. This is precisely what Lu Xun described as a paper-made crown of the intellectual authority. If he knew this happened to him, he would probably laugh at it. Praising for someone must not go overboard; otherwise it could be very embarrassing.

---

5 Mao Zedong, "Xin minzhu zhuyi lun," *Mao Zedong xuanji*, 1: 695.
6 Ibid., 1: 691.
7 Ibid., 3: 878.
8 Lu Xun, "Masha yu pengsha," 罵殺與捧殺 (To kill by curse and by praise), *Lu Xun Quanji* (hereafter: *LXQJ*), 5: 586.

現在人人捧魯迅, 在上海墓上新立造像——我只在照片上看見, 是高高的台上, 兀坐椅上. 雖是尊崇他, 其實是挖苦他的一個諷刺畫, 即是他生前所謂思想界的權威的紙糊高冠是也. 恐九原有知, 不免要苦笑的吧. 要恭維人不過火, 即不至於獻醜.[9]

In a letter to Cao Juren 曹聚仁 (1900–1972), Zhou Zuoren also indicated that Lu Xun's legacy was manipulated and exploited.[10] To a large extent, Zhou Zuoren's concern is true and profound: the distinction between an idol and a puppet is sometimes hard to make. The most sacred idol could be turned into a puppet through zealous worship and praise.

In 1926, ten years before Lu Xun's death, he published an article entitled "Wuhua de qianwei" 無花的薔薇 (Roses without flowers), in which Lu Xun indicated that "When a great figure became a fossil, and people started to regard him as a great hero, he was turned into a puppet" (待到偉大的人物成為化石, 人們都稱他偉人時, 他已經變了傀儡了).[11] If we examine how Lu Xun was idolized after he died, we might be surprised to find how accurate his words are in depicting his own fate.

1   Lu Xun and Mao Zedong, Hu Shi and Chiang Kai-shek

One might wonder why Mao had praised Lu Xun to such an extent. Was there anything special about Lu Xun's writings or thoughts that fit Mao's political needs? During the May Fourth period, all Confucian values such as filial piety, loyalty to the rulers, and chastity for women were either attacked or reassessed. Only one value was not under criticism, and that is forgiveness. However, this value was derided by Lu Xun, who interpreted Confucian forgiveness as weak and hypocritical. He promoted the idea of vengeance, embracing the concept of "an eye for an eye, and a tooth for a tooth" (以眼還眼, 以牙還牙).[12] Under such an interpretation, revenge and hatred were promoted as a virtue.

In 1937, at the anniversary of Lu Xun's death, Mao Zedong delivered a talk entitled, "On Lu Xun," in which he highly complimented Lu Xun's article "Lun feie polai yinggai huanxing" 論費厄潑賴應該緩行 (Do not conduct fair play yet). In this article, Mao extolled Lu Xun as a cultural saint in China.

---

9   Zhou Zuoren and Cao Juren, *Zhou Cao tongxinji* 周曹通信集 (Letters between Zhuo Zuoren and Cao Juren) (Hong Kong: Nantian, 1973), 1: 32.
10   Ibid., 49.
11   Lu Xun, "Wuhua de qiangwei" 無花的薔薇 (Rose without bloom), in *LXQJ*, 3: 256.
12   Lu Xun, "Si" 死 (Death), *LXQJ*, 6: 612.

Comparing Lu Xun to Confucius, Mao argued that "Confucius was a saint in a feudal society and Lu Xun is a saint in modern China" (孔夫子是封建社會的聖人, 魯迅則是現代中國的聖人).[13] This is the first step that Mao took to mold Lu Xun into a role model for Mao's political agenda.

According to Lu Xun's philosophy, all forgiveness is obligatory. Forgiveness and resentment are two sides of the same token. If one is not powerful enough to seek revenge, then the only thing to do is to forgive. In Lu Xun's will, he warned his son, "Have nothing to do with those [hypocrites] who injure others but oppose revenge and advocate tolerance ... I have a lot of enemies ... let them hate me and I will forgive no one" (損著別人的牙眼, 卻反對報復, 主張寬容的人, 萬勿和他接近 ... 我的怨敵可謂多矣 ... 讓他們怨恨去, 我也一個都不寬恕).[14]

To be sure, this kind of cynicism and callousness is characteristic of Lu Xun's writings. But this does not prevent his works from being integrated into all levels of curriculum in China. After 1949, Lu Xun's writings were included in middle school and high school textbooks, and Lu Xun became one of the most influential writers in China. As a result, for decades, Lu Xun became a role model for generations, and cynicism and malice were regarded as a virtue.

In the 1981 version of Lu Xun's complete works, the term "fair play" (費厄潑賴) was defined as a slogan for the bourgeoisie, who wanted to conceal their class nature and numbness to the proletariat public. Under such a circumstance, the word "fair play" was considered derogatory.

The way Hu Shi was received in China after his death greatly differed from that of Lu Xun. Hu Shi's books were banned in Mainland China for nearly three decades after 1949. Even to date, his name has yet to be officially restored by the Chinese authority. *The Complete Works of Hu Shi*, published in 2003, were far from being complete. Dozens of his articles that criticize Communism and the Communist Party are still not allowed to be included.[15] Ironically, Hu Shi was not well received in Taiwan either. There has never been any government-sponsored activity or publication in memory of Hu Shi in Taiwan. This lack of any "official endorsements" perhaps reflects his political independence, for neither the Guomintang nor the Communist Party could mold him into a role that served their political interests. It was this independence that prevented him from being used as a puppet in political struggles, something that Lu Xun was unable to avoid.

---

13 Mao Zedong, "Lun Lu Xun" 論魯迅 (On Lu Xun), in *Mao Zedong wenji* (hereafter: MZWJ) (Beijing: Renmin chubanshe, 1993), 2: 43.
14 *LXQJ*, 6: 612.
15 Hu Shi, *Hu Shi quanji* (hereafter: HSQJ). (Anhui: Anhui jiaoyu chubanshe, 2003).

For at least thirty years, during the smear campaign against Hu Shi from 1950 to 1980, the Communist critics had tried every possible way to depict Hu Shi as an intellectual who was used and manipulated by the Nationalist Party that was led by Chiang Kai-shek. Nevertheless, one would be surprised to see that there was an incredible tension between Hu Shi and Chiang Kai-shek, after Chiang's diary was open to the public at the Hoover Institute at Stanford University. Throughout his life, Hu Shi had never stopped trying to transform China into a more democratic country and Chiang into a more democratic leader.[16]

The conflict between Chiang and Hu reached its height after Hu returned to Taiwan to assume the position of the President of Academia Sinica in 1958. At Hu's inaugural ceremony, aside from congratulating him, Chiang remarked that part of the Academia Sinica's mission was to restore the traditional Chinese culture in Taiwan.[17] Hu Shi disagreed and openly challenged Chiang's statement.[18] Chiang later wrote in his diary that he considered Hu's comments as one of the greatest humiliations in his life, and consequently suffered insomnia for several nights.[19]

---

16 See Chih-p'ing Chou 周質平, "Zhangchi zai ziyou yu weiquan zhijiznz" 張弛在自由與威權之間—胡適林語堂與蔣介石 in *Ziyou de huozhong* 自由的火種 (Seeds of freedom—Hu Shi and Lin Yutang) (Taipei: Yunchen 允晨 publishing Co., 2018), 137–195.

17 Hu Songping 胡頌平, ed. *Hu Shizhi xiansheng nianpu changbian chugao* 胡適之先生年譜長編初稿 (First draft of an extended chronological biography of Hu Shi) (Taipei: Linking, 1984), 2662. Chiang Kai-shek remarked in his speech delivered at Hu Shi's inaugural ceremony:

> Academia Sinica is the leading research institute in this country; it should take up the responsibility of completing the difficult task of reviving the national culture. The only objective that we should all strive for now is to fight against Communists and resist Russia. If this task cannot be completed, all our efforts will be in vain. Thus, I hope our academic research in the future can be developed according to this task ... [I] hope that everyone in the fields of education, culture, and academia may assume responsibility of reviving and advocating the culture of our country.
>
> 中央研究院不但為全國學術之最高研究機構，且應擔負起復興民族文化之艱鉅任務，目前大家共同努力的唯一工作目標，為早日完成反共抗俄使命，如果此一工作不能完成，則我人一切努力均將落空，因此希望今後學術研究，亦能配合此一工作求其發展 …… 期望教育界，文化界與學術界人士，一致負起恢復並發揚我國固有文化與道德之責任。

18 Ibid.: 2663, 2665. Hu Shi responded to Chiang's statement in his inaugural speech at the ceremony:

> I believe, regarding the mission of fighting against Communists ... our job is still about academic works. We should promote academic research.
>
> 我個人認為，我們學術界和中央研究院挑起反共復國的任務，我們做的工作，還是在學術上，我們要提倡學術。

19 See *Chiang Kai-shek diaries*, [Box/Folder 66: 13.], Hoover Institution Archives. April 10, 1958.
> This is the second greatest insult that I had in my life. The first is when Bao Erting (Mikhail Borodin) humiliated me at the banquet during the winter of 1926 and early

Hu Shi had regarded the dominant power of the KMT as the greatest obstacle to the development of democracy in China. Before 1949, he had urged Chiang to divide the KMT into several parties. In Hu's April 8, 1948, diary entry, he recounted the meeting with Chiang, in which he suggested splitting the KMT into two or three "sections" or "sub-parties" (國民黨最好分化作兩三個政黨).[20] In a letter to Chiang dated May 31, 1951, he again proposed that the KMT should be divided into a few independent political parties and that Chiang should resign from the KMT's chairmanship.[21]

Hu Shi's most radical suggestion was mentioned in a letter to Lei Zhen 雷震 (1897–1979), dated August 29, 1957, in which he wrote:

> A few years ago, I openly expressed one wish: I hoped some of the strongest factions within the KMT could form several new political parties, so that a two-party system can be gradually fostered. This is what I hoped a few years ago. But last year I told some of my KMT friends that I had given up this idea that KMT can be divided up and form new parties freely. I now rather lean towards the idea of "destroy the party, save the country" or "destroy the party, build the country."

> 我前幾年曾公開的表示一個希望： 希望國民黨裡的幾個有力的派系能自由分化成幾個新政黨, 逐漸形成兩個有力的政黨. 這是我幾年前的一個希望. 但去年我曾對幾位國民黨的朋友說, 我對於國民黨自由分化的希望, 早已放棄了. 我頗傾向於 "毀黨救國," 或 "毀黨建國" 的一個見解.[22]

1927. Today, hearing Hu Shi's insult at the inaugural ceremony at Academia Sinica is another insult. I don't know why he is arrogant and ridiculous to such an extent. What a bigot! I now have another experience of making the wrong friend. I befriended him and praised him with generosity, treating him with excessive modesty, but instead I was insulted by him. I should refrain from doing him so. I am very worried that he has serious psychological problem and his days are numbered ... Because of this incident, I felt quite unhappy. I have suffered from insomnia, and could only sleep by taking sleeping pills.

今天實為我平生所遭遇的第二次最大的橫逆之來. 第一次乃是民國十五年冬—十六年初在武漢受鮑爾廷宴會中之侮辱. 而今天在中央研究院聽胡適就職典禮中之答辭的侮辱, 亦可說是求全之毀, 我不知其人之狂妄荒謬至此, 真是一妄人. 今後又增我一次交友不易之經驗. 而我輕交過譽, 待人過厚, 反為人所輕侮, 應切戒之. 惟仍恐其心理病態已深, 不久於人世為慮也 ...... 因胡事終日抑鬱, 服藥後方可安眠.

20 Hu Shi, *Hu Shi riji quanji* (hereafter: *HSRJQJ*), 8: 356.
21 Ibid.: 589.
22 Hu Shi, "Hu Shi to Lei Zhen" 胡適致雷震 (Hu Shi to Lei Zhen) in *Wanshan buxu yixi ben: Hu Shi Lei Zhen laiwang shuxin xuanji* 萬山不許一溪奔: 胡適雷震來往書信選集 (Mountains that have no rivers: Selected letters between Hu Shi and Lei Zhen). ed. Wang Lijian and Pan Kuang-che (Taipei: Institute of Modern History, Academia Sinica, 2001), 116.

Upon learning about Hu's radical idea, Chiang was astonished and puzzled. He wrote in his dairy dated June 3, 1958, that Hu's idea was "arrogant" (狂妄) and "absurd and evil" (愚劣), and that he "did not know Hu's hatred against him was even greater than the communist's" (不知其對我黨之仇恨甚於共匪之對我也).[23]

In 1960, Chiang intended to campaign for the third term of his presidency of the Republic of China, but the Constitution limited the tenure of a president to two terms at maximum. Chiang thus sought to add an amendment to the constitution, which would allow him to serve as a president indefinitely. Hu Shi was the only intellectual at the time to openly denounce Chiang.[24] Ignoring Hu's opposition, Chiang started his third term of presidency, and the relationship between Hu and Chiang thus reached its lowest point.

A few years later, Hu Shi suffered a severe heart attack and suddenly passed away on February 24, 1962. The death of Hu gave Chiang a great relief. In his March 3rd diary entry, Chiang wrote, "The death of Hu Shi had removed the obstacle to the restoration of the nation" (胡適之死, 在革命事業與民族復興的建國思想言, 乃除了障礙也).[25] From these examples, we can see that Hu Shi was not in accordance with the KMT and was never used and manipulated by Chiang Kai-shek.

2   Friendship and Impressions

Upon his return from America in 1917, Hu Shi started teaching at Peking University and became a friend of Lu Xun the following year. In his diary entry dated August 12, 1918, Lu Xun noted that he received a letter from Hu Shi. This is the first record of the correspondence between these two May Fourth writers.[26]

In January 1921, several communications were exchanged between Hu Shi and Lu Xun, discussing the question of whether the magazine *New Youth* 新青年 should address political issues. While Hu Shi contended that the *New Youth* should not be a politically oriented publication, Lu Xun did not see anything wrong with the magazine addressing political issues. This was the first confrontation between them; however, it did not affect their friendship, at least not at that time.

---

23   *Chiang Kai-shek diaries*, [Box/Folder 66: 14], Hoover Institution Archives.
24   Wang Shijie, *Wang Shijie riji shougaoben* 王世傑日記手稿本 (Manuscript of the diaries of Wang Shijie) (Taipei: Institute of Modern History, Academia Sinica, 1990), 6: 344–5; 358.
25   *Chiang Kai-shek diaries* [Box/Folder 69: 9], Hoover Institution Archives. March 3, 1962.
26   *LXQJ*, 14: 324.

Lu Xun's early attitude toward Hu Shi was rather skeptical and cautious. In 1934, Lu Xun recalled his impression of Hu Shi in the early 1920s when both of them were editors of the *New Youth*:

> When a new issue of the *New Youth* was released, the editors would hold a meeting to discuss the contents of the next issue. At that time, Chen Duxiu 陳獨秀 (1880–1942) and Hu Shi caught most of my attention. If we were to compare a person's strategy to a warehouse, a big banner was hung outside Chen Duxiu's warehouse with a warning written in large characters—"This place is full of weapons. Be careful!" Yet the gate of his warehouse is wide open; one could clearly see how many rifles and swords were placed inside, and no one needed to guard against him. However, the gate of Mr. Hu Shi's warehouse was tightly closed and there was a small note on the gate that reads "Don't worry, there are no weapons inside." Of course, this could be true, but some people—at least someone like me—could not help but wonder for a moment.

> 《新青年》每出一期，就開一次會，商定下一期的稿件. 其時最惹我注意的是陳獨秀和胡適之. 假如將韜略比作一間倉庫罷, 陳獨秀先生的是外面豎一面大旗, 大書道: "內皆武器, 來者小心!" 但那門卻開著的, 裡面有幾枝槍, 幾把刀, 一目了然, 用不著提防. 適之先生的是緊緊的關著門, 門上粘一條小紙條道: "內無武器, 請勿疑慮." 這自然可以是真的, 但有些人—至少是我這樣的人—有時總不免要側頭想一想.[27]

What Lu Xun intended to indicate here is that Chen Duxiu is formidable but candid and frank, while Hu Shi, who appeared to be peaceful, might be a dangerous and tricky person. It was this skeptical attitude that kept Lu Xun from developing a more intimate relation with Hu Shi.

However, Hu Shi's impression of Lu Xun and his brother Zhou Zuoren was quite different. In his diary entry dated August 11, 1922, Hu Shi noted that the Zhou brothers were most "pleasant" (可愛) and that both of them were highly talented. Hu Shi also indicated that Lu Xun often displayed great critical insight and was able to write short stories.[28] Hu Shi never developed a cautious attitude toward the Zhou brothers in his campaign to promote vernacular literature. On the contrary, Hu Shi actually treated them as comrades.

---

27 Lu Xun, "Yi Liu bann" 憶劉半農君 (Reminiscence of Liu Bannong), *LXQJ*, 6: 71–2.
28 Hu Shi, *Hu Shi de riji* (Diaries of Hu Shi) (Hong Kong: Zhonghua shuju, 1985), 424.

In January 1917, Hu Shi published his famous article, "Wenxue gailiang chuyi" 文學改良芻議 (Some modest proposals for the reform of literature),[29] which is considered the manifesto of the movement of vernacular literature. Four months later, he published a second article entitled "Lishi de wenxue guannianlun" 歷史的文學觀念論 (On the historical concept of literature).[30] In this article, Hu Shi expressed his basic idea that the development of literature could be understood as a kind of evolution. He believed that each historical period should have its own literature and that "wenyan" (文言), the classical Chinese language, was simply a dead language that could no longer serve the multiple purposes of literature in modern society. What we needed to do and had to do, he believed, was to promote "baihua" (白話), the vernacular, which was much closer to the daily speech of the common people.

Lu Xun supported Hu Shi's proposal for a literary reform by writing his first vernacular story, "The Diary of a Madman" 狂人日記. This story appeared in the May 1918 issue of the *New Youth*, sixteen months after Hu Shi's publication of his "Some modest proposals for the reform of literature." Before 1918, Lu Xun had never written anything in vernacular Chinese. Therefore, it is fair to say that Lu Xun's conversion from a writer who used classical Chinese to one who adopted vernacular Chinese is a result of Hu Shi's influence. In 1932, Lu Xun admitted that he had begun to write short stories in vernacular Chinese in order to respond to the voices of the "forerunners" (前驅) of the vernacular literary movement. He jokingly referred to his own works written around 1918 as "obedient literature" (遵命文學) rather than "revolutionary literature" (革命文學). He further pointed out that he was happy to follow the orders of these "forerunners." It is needless to say that Hu Shi was one of the "forerunners" that Lu Xun referred to here.[31]

Lu Xun's vernacular stories not only marked the inception of modern Chinese fiction, but also represented as a turning point in his own life. Before 1918, he was a relatively minor figure in the literary circle in Beijing; but after 1918 he became a household name in literary circles all over China.

Had Hu Shi not initiated the movement of vernacular literature in 1917, and had Lu Xun continued to write in classical language as he always did, Lu Xun would have had little chance of becoming a national figure in such a short period of time. Lu Xun was really a hero created by the vernacular movement, and Hu Shi was the one who initiated this movement. I do not mean to say that

---

29 Hu Shi, *Hu Shi wencun* (Collected works of Hu Shi; hereafter: *HSWC*) (Taipei: Yuandong tushu gongsi, 1968), 1: 5–17.
30 Ibid., 33–36.
31 *LXQJ*, 4: 456.

if it had not been for Hu Shi there would be no Lu Xun. I am simply suggesting that Lu Xun's transition from classical Chinese to vernacular Chinese in his writing is a decisive factor that makes him a writer of historical significance.

Lu Xun's short stories had greatly strengthened the momentum of the vernacular literary movement. During the early phase of this movement, Hu Shi, Chen Duxiu, and Qian Xuantong 錢玄同 (1887–1939), the three major advocates of the May Fourth literary movement, were all critics and theorists; none of them was a creative writer. Therefore, in the first few years of the movement, there was no shortage of theoretical discourses. The predicament was that there was no corresponding vernacular literary works that could prove Hu Shi's argument that vernacular Chinese was more effective than classical Chinese in writing different genres. Hu Shi's own efforts in writing poetry, fiction, and drama were not altogether successful.[32]

It was not until Lu Xun published short stories such as "The Diary of a Madman," "Kong Yiji," and "Medicine" that the vernacular movement began to demonstrate its true potential.[33] Hu Shi gave full credit to Lu Xun for his achievement in short story writing. In his article "Wushinian lai zhongguo zhi wenxue" 五十年來中國之文學 (Chinese literature over the past fifty years), Hu Shi praised Lu Xun as the greatest short story writer in the early phase of the vernacular movement, and claimed that "almost all his works are good" (差不多沒有不好的).[34]

Lu Xun's promotion of vernacular Chinese was without reservation, and it was sometimes rendered in a rather militant language. He once wrote that "I have been searching everywhere for the darkest magic spell to curse anyone who opposed and hindered the development of vernacular Chinese" (我總要上下四方尋求，得到一種最黑，最黑，最黑的咒文，先來詛咒一切反對白話，妨害白話者).[35] At some point, Lu Xun even said that those who opposed the vernacular should be destroyed.[36]

---

32 In 1919, Hu Shi wrote a short story titled "Yige wenti" 一個問題 (A problem) as well as a playscript called "Zhongshen dashi" 終身大事 (The greatest event in life), which was originally written in English and later translated into Chinese by Hu Shi himself. In 1958, Hu Shi admitted that his attempts in creative writing were a failure. See Hu Shi, "Zhongguo wenyi fuxing yundong" 中國文藝復興運動, in *Hu Shi yanjiangji* 胡適演講集 (Collected speeches of Hu Shi) (Taipei: Hu Shi ji'nianguan, 1970), 385–386.

33 *LXQJ*, 6: 238.

34 *HSWC*, 2: 259.

35 Lu Xun, "Ershisixiao tu" 二十四孝圖 (The twenty-four cases of filial piety), *LXQJ*, 2: 251.

36 Ibid., 257.

In an article titled "Wusheng de zhongguo" 無聲的中國 (A muted China), Lu Xun, like other May Fourth writers, had pointed out that classical Chinese is so difficult and incomprehensible that few people in China could actually read and write it. Furthermore, he argued that classical Chinese was not suitable for oral communication, and that is why he would like to describe China as "muted". Lu Xun suggested that the movement of vernacular literature led by Hu Shi would transform the entirety of China from being "muted" (無聲) to "full of voices" (有聲).[37]

It was also under Hu Shi's influence that Lu Xun started to write "new poetry" in 1918. At the beginning of this literary movement, Hu Shi's interest was on poetry. He was eager to prove that both prose and poetry could be written in vernacular Chinese, and this was why he published his *Changshiji* 嘗試集 (Experimental collections) in 1920.

As for Lu Xun, he published four vernacular poems in 1918, under the pseudonym of Tangsi (唐俟). Seventeen years later, he recalled this event in the preface of his *Jiwaiji* 集外集 (Uncollected works), "Actually, I did not enjoy writing vernacular poetry.... It was only because the literary circle at that time was so bleak that I wanted to make some contribution [in order to stir up liveliness in the circle]" (我其實是不喜歡做新詩的—但也不喜歡做古詩—只因為那時詩壇寂寞, 所以打打邊鼓, 湊些熱鬧).[38]

Clearly Lu Xun was referring to the vernacular movement at the time. Hu Shi appreciated this support by praising Lu Xun's poetic works as the true new poetry unaffected by classical literature.[39]

In Hu Shi's own preface to *Changshiji*, he mentioned Lu Xun and his brother Zhou Zuoren together with Shen Yinmo 沈尹默, Liu Bannong 劉半農, Fu Sinian 傅斯年, Yu Pingbo 俞平伯, Kang Baiqing 康白情, and Chen Hongzhe 陳衡哲. Hu Shi called them "my friends" (我的朋友) and said that "they all made great efforts in writing new poetry" (都努力作白話詩).[40] It seemed that during the early phase of the vernacular movement, the relationship between Hu Shi and Lu Xun was quite congenial. In the context of the vernacular movement, Hu Shi was the forerunner and theorist, and Lu Xun the novelist and critic. Their cooperation greatly strengthened the momentum of the campaign and hastened its success.

Hu Shi and Lu Xun not only cooperated in promoting the vernacular, but also shared a common interest in the study of classical Chinese novels.

37   *LXQJ*, 4: 11–25.
38   *LXQJ*, 7: 4.
39   Hu Shi, "Tan xinshi" 談新詩 (On new poetry), *HSWC*, 1: 171.
40   Hu Shi, "Changshiji zixu" 嘗試集自序 (Preface to Changshiji), *HSWC*, 1: 203.

However, their approaches were different. Hu Shi was more interested in the authorship and structure of the novel, while Lu Xun emphasized the content more. Take the novel *Rulinwaishi* 儒林外史 (The scholars) for instance. Lu Xun spoke highly about the novel because it reflected the life of intellectuals under the Manchu rule and described their attitudes toward the civil examination system. Lu Xun particularly admired the author Wu Jingzi's 吳敬梓 (1701–1754) satiric technique, regarding it as an unprecedented success in Chinese literary history.[41] Hu Shi, however, indicated that *Rulinwaishi* was a poorly constructed novel, and the plot was fragmented and inconsistent.[42] Based on their comments on *Rulinwaishi*, we can suggest that Lu Xun had a higher social awareness of literature than Hu Shi. Lu Xun wrote:

> "Honglou meng kaozheng" 紅樓夢考證 (The study of the *Dream of the Red Chamber*), published in 1921, was one of the most important scholarly works on *Hongloumeng*. In this article, Hu Shi proved that the author of *Hongloumeng* was Cao Xueqin 曹雪芹 and that the entire story was in part based on Cao's actual life and the history of his family. Hu Shi repeatedly demonstrates in this article how important "evidence" (證據) is to the analysis of this Chinese novel.[43] Lu Xun commented on Hu Shi's Kaozheng ("looking for evidence"; 考證) approach to the study of *Hongloumeng*:

> If a writer is highly skilled and his work was circulated for a long time, the readers will only remember the characters from this novel and not the real persons on which these characters were based. For example, in *Hongloumeng*, Jia Baoyu is based on the author himself, Cao Zhan. In *Rulinwaishi*, Mr. Ma Er is based on Feng Zhizhong. Now, we only remember Jia Baoyu and Ma Er. Only a special scholar like Hu Shi will think about Cao Zhan and Feng Zhizhong.

> 如果作者手腕高妙,作品久傳的話,讀者所見的就只是書中人,和這曾經實有的人倒不想乾了. 例如《紅樓夢》里賈寶玉的模特兒是作者自己曹霑,《儒林外史》裡的馬二先生的模特兒是馮執中, 現在我們所覺得的卻只是賈寶玉和馬二先生, 只有特種學者如胡適之先生之流, 這才把曹霑和馮執中念念不忘的記在心裡.[44]

---

41   *LXQJ*, 9: 220–226.
42   Hu Shi, "Wushinian lai zhongguo zhi wenxue," *HSWC*, 2: 233–234; 243; 260.
43   *HSWC*, 1: 575–620.
44   Lu Xun, "Chuguan de guan" 出關的關 (Pass in "Leaving the Pass"), *LXQJ*, 6: 519.

Lu Xun thus criticized Hu Shi's "evidential scholarship" as "often relying on rare books and secret materials as a means of astonishing the readers" (往往恃孤本秘笈為驚人之具).[45] Lu Xun also indicated that "My way of research is a little different [from Hu's]. The books I read and the material I use are all common copies, therefore, I am out of the academic world" (我法稍不同, 凡所泛覽, 皆通行之本, 易得之書, 故遂孑然於學林之外).[46] This of course is only a tongue-in-cheek comment.

3   Views on the Tradition

Right after he returned to China from the United States, Hu Shi not only began to promote the movement of vernacular literature, he also took the lead in criticizing traditional Chinese culture. Several of Lu Xun's important articles were written under Hu Shi's influence. For example, Hu Shi published an article entitled "Zhencao wenti" 貞操問題 (On chastity) in the July issue of *New Youth* in 1918, in which he argued that the unilateral demand of chastity for women was unfair and inhuman. Society should not ask a young widow to keep her widowhood for the rest of her life or (as was sometimes even asked of her) to commit suicide for her deceased husband.[47] A month later, Lu Xun followed Hu Shi's lead, and published "My Views on Chastity" 我的節烈觀. In this article, Lu Xun's argument was basically an elaboration of Hu Shi's points.[48]

In May of 1918, Hu Shi wrote a poem "My Son" 我的兒子, which was published in August 1919:

> I really did not want a son,
> Yet the son came anyway.
> The signboard of "no-posterity-ism,"
> I can no longer hang.
> Like flowers blooming on trees,
> Seeds are fortuitously conceived when flowers fall.
> That seed is you,
> That tree is I.

---

45   Lu Xun, "Zhi Tai Jingnong" 致台靜農 (To Tai Jingnong), *LXQJ*, 12: 102.
46   Ibid.
47   *HSWC*, 1: 665–675.
48   *LXQJ*, 1: 116–125.

The tree has no intent to conceive the seed.
Nor have I done any favor to you.
But since you have already come.
I cannot but feed you and educate you.
This is my duty towards humanity,
Not a special favor to you.
When you grow up,
Don't forget how I teach my son.
I want you to be an upright man.
Not a filial son of mine.

我實在不要兒子,
兒子自己來了.
"無後主義" 的招牌,
於今掛不起來了!
譬如樹上開花,
花落偶然結果.
那果便是你,
那樹便是我.
樹本無心結子,
我也無恩於你.
但是你既來了,
我不能不養你, 教你,
那是我對人道的義務,
並不是待你的恩誼.
將來你長大時,
莫忘了我怎樣教訓兒子:
我要你做一個堂堂的人,
不要你做我的孝順兒子.

This poem was read by millions, and it provoked many debates on how parents should raise and educate their children. As we know, Hu Shi himself was a typical filial son. He married an almost illiterate woman with bound feet, chosen for him by his mother, and his married life of forty-two years served as a sacrifice to filial piety. When he wrote this poem, he was not only talking to his son, but also to his deceased mother and perhaps even himself. He tried to free all of them from the bondage of filial piety. In this poem, Hu Shi criticized the traditional concept of filial piety. He indicated that giving birth to a child was only a biological matter, not something to be regarded as a "favor"

(恩) that parents gave to children. Therefore, the child should not be burdened with the feeling of guilt because s/he did not repay his/her parents for the "favor."[49]

Two months later, Lu Xun published an article entitled "How to Be a Father at the Present Time" 我們現在怎樣做父親,[50] in which Lu Xun echoed Hu Shi's poem to a large extent. The content of these articles and the timing of their publication strongly suggested that Lu Xun had willingly followed Hu Shi's ideas from 1918 to 1920.

Of all the Confucian values, filial piety is the foundation. It has a profound influence on every Chinese man or woman, literate or illiterate. Filial piety has often been equated to "original sin" in Christianity. Once you are born, you are indebted to your parents. Your parents created you, gave you life, fed you, and educated you. You thus owed everything to them. No matter what you do, you can never pay off your debt. Thus, to a large extent, filial piety was based on a deep sense of guilt and it prevented children from achieving individuality. Generally speaking, this was how the May Fourth intellectuals interpreted filial piety, and for the leaders of the New Cultural Movement, such as Chen Duxiu, filial piety was regarded as an evil in Chinese culture.

Right after Lu Xun's death in 1936, Su Xuelin 蘇雪林 (1897–1899) wrote two lengthy open letters to Hu Shi and Cai Yuanpei 蔡元培 (1868–1940), in which she severely criticized Lu Xun as being an unscrupulous person who was obsessed by fame and used by the Communists. She further indicated that though Lu Xun was critical toward the Western imperialistic in China, he never dared to criticize the Japanese imperialism, which was an immediate threat to China at that time.[51] In Hu Shi's response to her open letters, he wrote:

> I am quite sympathetic to your indignation; however, I do not think that we should attack [Lu Xun] on a personal level.... He is dead, and we should not be bogged down with trivialities. Let's talk about what his thought actually was, and consider the many different phases through which it was transformed. What he actually believed in and what he was

---

49 Hu Shi, *Changshiji* (Taipei: Hu Shi jinianguan, 1971), 177–799. For a discussion of this poem, see HSWC, 1: 687–693. This English translation is quoted from Ming-chih Chou, *Hu Shih and Intellectual Choice* (Ann Arbor, MI: The University of Michigan Press, 1984), 77.
50 *LXQJ*, 1: 129–240.
51 Su Xuelin, "Su Xuelin zhi Hu Shi" 蘇雪林致胡適 (Su Xuelin to Hu Shi), "Su Xuelin zhi Cai Yuanpei" 蘇雪林致蔡元培 (Su Xuelin to Cai Yuanpei) in *Hu Shi laiwang shuxin xuan* 胡適來往書信選 (Selected letters of Hu Shi) (Hong Kong: Zhonghua shuju, 1983), 2: 325–334.

opposed to. What were the valuable elements and what was worthless trash [in his thought]? This kind of criticism will certainly be effective.[52]

我很同情於你的憤慨, 但我以為不必攻擊其私人行為. 魯迅猖狂攻擊我們, 其實何損於我們一絲一毫? 他已死了, 我們盡可以撇開一切小節不談, 專討論他的思想究竟有些什麼, 究竟經過幾度變遷, 究竟他信仰的是什麼, 否定的是些什麼, 有些什麼是有價值的, 有些什麼是無價值的.

In his response, Hu Shi again recognized Lu Xun's contribution to the study of Chinese novels, and his achievement in creative writing.[53] Although Lu Xun attacked Hu Shi personally on many occasions, Hu Shi never responded with personal criticism. This is an important difference in their styles of writing. Hu Shi never published any articles in memory of Lu Xun; his response to Su Xuelin should be read as his comments on Lu Xun after Lu Xun's death.

In 1956, when the smear campaign against Hu Shi reached its peak, Hu Shi wrote in a letter to his friend, "If Lu Xun were still alive today, he would be beheaded" (魯迅若不死, 也會砍頭的).[54] As Hu Shi suggested, it was in a sense fortunate for the reputation of Lu Xun that he died in 1936. Had he lived for twenty more years, he would certainly be charged as a "rightist."[55]

In 1958, twenty-two years after Lu Xun's death, in a speech honoring the May Fourth Movement, Hu Shi recognized that Lu Xun played a leading role in the New Culture Movement in the 1920s. However, he also indicated that Lu Xun was a person who enjoyed constant applause and flattery, and that was why he had gradually "taken a devious road" (變質的路子). By "devious road," Hu Shi was referring to the fact that Lu Xun had joined the League of Left-Wing Writers in 1930.[56] In order to demonstrate how much Lu Xun regretted involving himself in the League, Hu Shi referenced a letter written by Lu Xun in 1935, in which Lu Xun answered Hu Feng's 胡風 (1902–1985) question on whether Xiao Jun 蕭軍 (1907–1988) should join the League or not. Lu Xun's answer was direct and clear:

---

52 Ibid., 339.
53 Ibid.
54 Hu Shi, "Hu Shizhi xiansheng de yifeng xin" 胡適之先生的一封信 (A letter from Mr. Hu Shi) *Ziyou Zhongguo* 自由中國 (Free China), 14: 8 (April 16, 1956), 273.
55 Ibid.
56 Hu Shi, "Zhongguo wenyi fuxing yundong" 中國文藝復興運動 (A Chinese Renaissance), *Hu Shi yanjiangji*, 2: 388.

> I don't even have to think to tell you my opinion: Don't join now.... In recent years I have come to realize that several new writers have emerged in outside circles, and they have accomplished some new achievements. Once you are in the League, you are immediately stuck in trivialities, and you will be "suffocated" to death.[57]

> 我幾乎可以無須思索, 說出我的意見來, 是: 現在不必進去 ... 近幾年, 還是在外圍的人們裡, 出幾個新作家, 有一些新鮮的成績, 一到裡面去, 即醬在無聊的糾紛中, 無聲無息.

In the same letter Lu Xun talked about himself:

> As for myself, I always feel that I am locked with iron fetters, and that there is a foreman behind my back who keeps whipping me. No matter how hard I work, he just keeps whipping me. When I turn my head and ask what have I done wrong, he [the foreman] politely replies that I am doing just fine.... As you can see, what a dilemma I am in now![58]

> 以我自己而論, 總覺得縛了一條鐵索, 有一個工頭在背後用鞭子在背後打我, 無論我怎麼起勁的做, 也是打, 而我回頭去問自己的錯處時, 他卻拱手客氣的說, 我做得好極了 ... 你看這是怎樣的苦境.

After having mentioned this letter, Hu Shi commented that Lu Xun was in great agony in his later years, and was unable to free himself from the situation in which he was involved.[59] Hu Shi's frequent citing of this letter in his writings of the late 1950s revealed that, on the one hand, he felt fortunate that he had not taken the "devious road" to join the Left-Wing Writers Association, but, on the other hand, he showed deep sympathy to Lu Xun for what he suffered in the last several years of his life.[60]

After Hu Shi's death in 1962, Lin Yutang 林語堂 (1895–1976) wrote a short article in memory of his late friend, in which he compared Hu Shi with Lu Xun:

> Lu Xun was quite political and could not free himself from the desire to become a leader. Shizhi [Hu Shi] did not care too much whether the young people admired him or not, while Lu Xun wanted to be admired

---

57 Lu Xun, "Zhi Hu Feng" 致胡風 (To Hu Feng), *LXQJ*, 13: 211.
58 Ibid.
59 Hu Shi, "Zhongguo wenyi fuxing yundong," *Hu Shi yanjiangji*, 2: 389.
60 From 1955 to 1959, Hu Shi mentioned this letter at least four times.

by the youth.... Therefore Lu Xun aligned himself with [the left-wing writers], and was hence trapped and he regretted this.[61]

魯迅政治氣味甚濃, 脫不了領袖欲. 適之不在乎青年之崇拜, 魯迅卻非做得給青年崇拜不可 ... 故而靠攏, 故而上當, 故而後悔無及.

Lin Yutang concluded that Hu Shi's vision and judgment were superior to those of Lu Xun.

Without a doubt, Lu Xun was one of the leading writers in the May Fourth period. However, after he joined the League of Left-wing Writers in 1930, he lost his political independence. Instead of continuing to lead the intellectual trend, Lu Xun was led by the Communist Party.

The story of Hu Shi has been misinterpreted in China for too long a time. It is necessary for us to reexamine his thought and influence in twenty-first century China. Over the past three decades, we have witnessed some relaxation in the political restriction in China, but the study of Hu Shi and Lu Xun is still very much under the influence of Communist ideology. Breaking these ideological shackles is not only a challenge for the government, but also for the Chinese intellectuals as well.

Bibliography

Hu Shi 胡適. *Changshiji* 嘗試集. Taipei: Hu Shi jinianguan, 1971.
Hu Shi 胡適. *Hu Shi de riji* 胡適的日記. Hong Kong: Zhonghua shuju, 1985.
Hu Shi 胡適. *Hu Shi laiwang shuxin xuan* 胡適來往書信選. Hong Kong: Zhonghua shuju, 1983.
Hu Shi 胡適. *Hu Shi quanji* 胡適全集. Anhui: Anhui jiaoyu chubanshe, 2003.
Hu Shi 胡適. *Hu Shi riji quanji* 胡適日記全集. Taipei: Linking, 2004.
Hu Shi 胡適. *Hu Shi wencun* 胡適文存. Taipei: Yuandong tushu gongsi, 1968.
Hu Shi 胡適. *Hu Shi yanjiangji* 胡適演講集. Taipei: Hu Shi jinianguan, 1970.
Hu Shi 胡適 and Lei Zhen 雷震. *Wanshan buxu yixi ben: Hu Shi Lei Zhen laiwang shuxin xuanji* 萬山不許一溪奔: 胡適雷震來往書信選集. Ed. Wang Lijuan 萬麗鵑 and Pan Kuang-che 潘光哲. Taipei: Institute of Modern History, Academia Sinica, 2001.
Hu Songping 胡頌平, ed. *Hu Shizhi xiansheng nianpu changbian chugao* 胡適之先生年譜長編初稿 (Taipei: Linking, 1984).

---

61   Lin Yutang, "Zhuidao Hu Shizhi xiansheng" 追悼胡適之先生, *Haiwai luntan* 海外論壇, 3:4 (April 1, 1962), p. 2.

Hu Songping 胡頌平. *Hu Shi xiansheng nianpu jianbian* 胡適先生年譜簡編. Taipei: Daluzazhishe, 1971.

Kai-shek Chiang 蔣介石. *Chiang Kai-shek Diaries*. Hoover Institution Archives.

Lu Xun 魯迅. *Lu Xun quanji* 魯迅全集. Beijing: Renmin wenxue chubanshe, 1981.

Mao, Zedong 毛澤東. *Mao Zedong xuanji* 毛澤東選集. Beijing: Renmin chubanshe, 1953.

Mao Zedong 毛澤東. *Mao Zedong wenji* 毛澤東文集. Beijing: Renmin chubanshe, 1993.

Sanlian Shudian editors 三聯書店編輯. *Hu Shi sixiang pipan* 胡適思想批判. Beijing: Sanlian shudian, 1955.

Wang Shijie 王世傑. *Wang Shijie riji shougaoben* 王世傑日記手稿本. Taipei: Institute of Modern History, Academia Sinica, 1990.

Zhou Zuoren 周作人 and Cao Juren 曹聚仁. *Zhou Cao tongxinji* 周曹通信集. Hong Kong: Nantian shuye chubanshe, 1973.

CHAPTER 4

Chinese Renaissance, Other Renaissances

Gang Zhou

In his influential essay "Neither Renaissance nor Enlightenment: A Historian's Reflections on the May Fourth Movement," Yu Ying-shih challenges the conventional understanding of the May Fourth Movement by calling for a multidimensional and multidirectional reading. The essay traces the way in which the May Fourth cultural movement was first identified as a "Chinese Renaissance" by Hu Shi 胡適 and others, and then reinterpreted as a "Chinese Enlightenment" in the late 1930s, during which period Communist writers began to describe the May Fourth Movement in their own terms. Yu, however, proposes to discard analogies such as "Renaissance" and "Enlightenment," since "a great variety of Western ideas and values other than Renaissance and Enlightenment were also introduced into China during the same period."[1] The most important argument of Yu's essay is:

> The May Fourth intellectual world consisted of many communities of changing minds. Consequently, not only were there several May Fourth projects constantly undergoing changes and often conflicting with one another, but each project also had different versions. Perhaps the safest generalization one can make about May Fourth is that it must always be understood in terms of its multidimensionality and multidirectionality.[2]

Instead of merely focusing on the progressive writers associated with the magazine *New Youth*, Yu's essay highlights the variety of cultural discourses taking place in the May Fourth period. Of particular importance is that the essay aims to expand the May Fourth paradigm by including such cultural conservatives in the May Fourth period as Liang Shuming 梁漱溟, Wu Mi 吳宓, Mei Guangdi 梅光迪, Wang Guowei 王國維, and Chen Yinke 陳寅恪. From this perspective, one can certainly argue that Yu's essay is actually more inclusive than its title

---

[1] Yu Ying-shih, "Neither Renaissance nor Enlightenment: A Historian's Reflections on the May Fourth Movement," in *The Appropriation of Cultural Capital: China's May Fourth Project*, ed. Milena Dolezelova-Velingerova and Oldrich Kral (Cambridge, MA: Harvard University Press, 2001): 311.
[2] Ibid., 320.

might suggest. One is even tempted to rephrase the title of Yu's essay to make it more inclusive: perhaps "Both Renaissance and Enlightenment and Yet More."

A recently published book entitled *Why China did not have a Renaissance—and why that matters* also deserves some attention here. Just like Yu's essay, the book's title is rather misleading. If one reads the conclusion carefully one has every reason to rephrase the book title: perhaps *Did China Have a Renaissance—Conflicting Approaches to Periodization*. The book is designed to present an open-ended dialogue between a European historian and a Sinologist. Thomas Maissen, the European historian, concludes that the concept of *the* Renaissance has been defined in such a particular way that it is not useful to speak of Renaissance or renaissance in China or elsewhere. Barbara Mittler, the Sinologist, agrees that China did not have *this* particular Renaissance, but instead maintains that "China did have *a* Renaissance in the early twentieth century, as Chinese intellectuals were trying to make sense of their present by taking inspiration from what they read into *the* Renaissance as a chronotypical model."[3] Clearly these two parties disagree on whether or not China *had* a Renaissance. It is disappointing that the book title simply follows the European historian's argument while indicating none of the signs of this fundamental disagreement.

The real question behind this dialogue is also whether European periodization schemes can be used adequately in the writing of global history. While Thomas Maissen emphasizes the uniqueness of the European experience, Barbara Mittler questions this uniqueness by illustrating how other cultures such as Chinese have adopted terms such as "Renaissance" to live and describe their own historical experiences.[4] Indeed, I side with Mittler and her argument. In many ways, this essay demonstrates how "Renaissance" has been re-imagined and reinterpreted at critical historical junctures in various geo-political contexts far beyond Europe, including the May Fourth period in China. My discussion will focus on how the concept of "Renaissance" and the problem of the vernacular have intertwined in these different contexts.

---

3 Maissen, Thomas & Barbara Mittler, *Why China did not have a Renaissance—and why that matters* (De Gruyter, 2018): 161.
4 European historian Jack Goody has also successfully challenged the uniqueness of the European Renaissance. See Jack Goody, *Renaissances: The One or the Many* (Cambridge: Cambridge University Press, 2010).

1 Diglossia and the Triumph of the Vernacular

"Diglossia" is a term coined by Charles Ferguson in an important essay published in 1959. Ferguson defines "diglossia" as "two varieties of a language exist side by side throughout the community, with each having a definite role to play."[5] One is called the high language, associated with formal and official occasions, and the other serves as the low language, associated with informal and homey situations. With some appropriation, Ferguson's model is very instructive in delineating the social linguistic landscape in pre-modern China, which witnessed two written languages, *wenyan* 文言 (classical Chinese) and *baihua* 白話 (the vernacular), existing side by side, each having a clearly defined role to play.

In the history of China, the breakdown of this long-lasting diglossic situation took place at the beginning of the twentieth century. When Kang Youwei 康有為 wrote *The Book of Great Unity* 大同書, the Chinese language in his mind was without doubt "classical Chinese"—the language of Confucian Classics and the international language in East Asia. As he praised the "simplicity" of the Chinese language, "Chinese has one term for one thing, one character for one term, one sound for one character," (計語言之簡, 中國一物一名, 一名一字, 一字一音),[6] the "vernacular" must have been the last thing on his mind. But only a few years later, "classical Chinese" would be violently attacked by May Fourth progressive writers, while the "vernacular" would become the national language of modern China. Two decades after the publication of *The Book of Great Unity*, the "vernacular" would officially become the one and only right medium for Chinese literature.

The battles that the "vernacular" in modern China had to fight to triumph over "classical Chinese" were in some ways stylistic, but mainly, they were ideological. While the first modern Chinese vernacular writers had to exhibit the artistic capacities of the vernacular in various literary genres, especially in poetry (the most prestigious genre in Chinese literary tradition, which was reserved only for "classical Chinese"), the most important thing for the triumph of the vernacular in modern China was the triumph of the modernist ideology that rendered the vernacular as the one and only language for a progressive utopian future, and classical Chinese the language for a ghostly past.

While the vernacular has been perceived as the natural candidate for the "new language" according to the conventional scholarship of modern Chinese literature, it was indeed only one among several solutions suggested by

---

5 Charles Ferguson, "Diglossia," *Word* 15 (1959): 325–40.
6 Kang Youwei, *Da Tong Shu* 大同書 (Shanghai: Shanghai guji chubanshe, 2005), 101.

Chinese intellectuals at the early phase of the May Fourth literary revolution. In June 1918, Zhu Jingnong 朱經農, one of Hu Shi's overseas student friends, sent him a letter from the United States explaining his view of the ongoing literary revolution. Zhu wrote:

> These days there are four kinds of positions regarding the linguistic revolution: (first) reform classical Chinese, rather than abolishing classical Chinese; (second) discard classical Chinese and reform the vernacular; (third) preserve the vernacular, and adopt a phonetic system to replace the character script; (forth) abolish both classical Chinese and the vernacular, and adopt an alphabetic language as the national language.

> 現在講文字革命的大約可分四種: (第一種) 是 "改良文言," 並不 "廢止文言"; (第二種) "廢止文言" 而 "改良白話"; (第三種) "保存白話," 而以羅馬文拼音代漢字; (第四種) 是把 "文言," "白話" 一概廢了, 採用羅馬文字作為國語。[7]

Zhu's observation captured the plurality of the language proposals existing at the time. Qian Xuantong's 錢玄同 dramatic call for the adoption of Esperanto (English or French in the meantime) to replace the Chinese language made him the representative of the fourth position. Hu Shi was certainly the spokesperson for the second position: discarding classical Chinese and reforming the vernacular. But he and Chen Duxiu 陳獨秀 would have also been sympathetic to the third position, since both of them believed that in the future the Chinese script would be replaced by a phonetic system. Zhu Jingnong himself represented the first position, the most conservative of the four revolutionary proposals.

Shortly after the publication of Zhu Jingnong's letter, a consensus had been reached in the circle of *New Youth* that the vernacular should be the only medium for modern Chinese literature. Hu Shi's position (denounce classical Chinese, promote the vernacular) emerged as the dominant discourse of linguistic practice. At the center of Hu Shi's discourse of the vernacular was precisely the European Renaissance model, which captured Chinese intellectuals' imagination at that critical historical juncture.

---

7 Zhu Jingnong 朱經農, "Letter from Zhu Jingnong" in *Hu Shi xueshu wenji* 胡適學術文集 (Collected scholarly work of Hu Shi), ed. Jiang Yihua (Zhonghua shuju, 1993).

2   A Transcultural Reading of "Chinese Renaissance"

In June 1917, on his return trip to China from the United States, Hu Shi, who would soon become a major figure in the May Fourth literary movement, read a book, *The Renaissance*, by Edith Sichel (1862–1914). This book, commissioned by the Home University Library, was originally intended to educate general American audiences. Sichel would never have expected that her book on the European Renaissance would lead to a Chinese Renaissance.

Sichel's book follows the mainstream perception of the European Renaissance in 1910s America. Only toward the end of her book does Sichel mention the development of Europe's vernacular languages and their impact on the dominance of Latin as the European literary language. It was this story of the emergence of European vernacular languages, however, that captured Hu Shi's imagination.

As Hu Shi wrote in his diary on June 19, 1917, "we can see from Sichel's book that the national languages in Renaissance Europe all started as very small forces but ended up having a wide-reaching and powerful influence. Hence, we who advocate vernacular literature today ought to be confident about a promising future" (書中述歐洲各國國語之興起, 其作始皆極細微, 而其結果皆廣大無量. 今之提倡白話文學者可以興矣).[8] The problem of the vernacular was never highlighted by Burckhardt, nor by Sichel. But for Hu Shi, who had been occupied with the question of language reform in China for a few years, the rise of the vernacular became the central episode in the grand drama of the European Renaissance.

The word *Renaissance* (*la rinascita*), which means "the rebirth," was coined by a sixteenth-century Italian artist and critic, Giorgio Vasari (1511–1574). In his long introduction to the *Lives of the Great Painters, Sculptors, and Architects* (1550), Vasari labeled the art of his time *la rinascita*, suggesting that "these arts resemble nature as shown in our human bodies; and have their birth, growth, age, and death."

Vasari's declaration of a Renaissance thus can be perceived as a "speech-act" that describes and recreates the reality at the same time. It calls forth an understanding of Renaissance as both a period and an idea, thereby shaping the way that sixteenth-century Europe was imagined and understood by later generations. Since then, the idea of Renaissance has been repeatedly used and invoked in different geopolitical contexts for different purposes. When Hu Shi encountered the idea of Renaissance in his rumination on the

---

8   Hu Shi 胡適, *Hu Shi luxue riji*《胡適留學日記》(Hu Shi's diary while studying abroad) (Taipei: Commercial Press, 1959), 4: 1155.

problem of Chinese language, it was precisely the act of naming and claiming that led him to see the possibility of doing things with words, of promoting a Chinese renaissance that would transform the discourses of the vernacular in modern China.

Two of Hu Shi's essays, both crucial to the formation of the May Fourth literary revolution, may help us understand how the idea of Renaissance was received in the Chinese context.

"Wenxue gailiang chuyi" 文學改良芻議 (Some modest proposals for the reform of literature), published in 1917 in the *New Youth* 新青年, was often said to be the essay that inaugurated the May Fourth literary revolution. In this essay, Hu Shi challenges the conventional language hierarchy in China and champions vernacular literature as canonical, and highlights the link between May Fourth China and Renaissance Europe. Ironically, this essay is composed in classical Chinese, the very language that Hu Shi sought to overthrow. This fact is not surprising, however, because it was still the common literary language used among Chinese literati at the time. Even a progressive journal like *New Youth* would have to wait another year and a half before it began to publish vernacular literary works. It is thus clear that Hu Shi's essay was originally intended for the well-educated elites in China.[9]

Throughout the essay, Hu Shi explores the common ground between himself and his audience, citing books and writers from the Chinese literary tradition. Toward the end of the essay, he raises his provocative argument that vernacular literature should be considered canonical in the Chinese literary tradition, and he writes a brief passage on language transition in the European Renaissance. Interestingly, this passage is rendered in parentheses and is carefully built on his longer discussion on vernacular Chinese literary tradition. If there is a center and periphery in this essay, this small passage on European Renaissance, rendered in parentheses, is at the periphery. The author seems aware that some of his readers might be made uneasy by the association—some would be excited by it, some would be ambivalent, and some might find the analogy completely out of place. But it is precisely in this paragraph that we can reappraise Hu Shi's reception of Renaissance in his own terms. In any case, the idea of Renaissance was given a low-profile and modest debut in China and was associated with the Chinese vernacular movement in the May Fourth period.

The idea of Renaissance was mentioned again in another Hu Shi's essay, "Jianshe de wenxue geming lun" 建設的文學革命論 (Toward a constructive literary revolution), which was published in April 1918, which exhorts the May

---

9 Kirk Denton, ed., *Modern Chinese Literary Thought: Writings on Literature, 1893–1945* (Stanford, CA: Stanford University Press, 1996), 123.

Fourth literary revolution to advance to a new stage. The essay provides a systematic and constructive theoretical guideline for the May Fourth vernacular movement. At that time, Hu Shi was already a professor at Beijing University—the most prestigious university in China—and the most respected theorist in the literary circle of *New Youth*. The tone of the essay indicates that Hu Shi was more assertive in his propositions regarding a literary revolution.

This time, the discussion on the European Renaissance is given a central place in the essay, and it is recognized as a powerful model to be emulated. The story of the European Renaissance is told with more detail, and Hu Shi is also more confident in the symbolic value that the term "renaissance" embodies. According to Hu Shi, Italy was the first country to take the vernacular as the national language, and Dante was the first great master who elevated the Italian vernacular to replace Latin. Less than a century after Dante, Boccaccio and others wrote literary works in the vernacular, and the national language of Italy was firmly established. But a more detailed observation of the Italian vernacular movement would show that it took much longer for the Florentine vernacular to replace Latin as the dominant written language in the Italian peninsula. During this long transition, the relationship between Latin and the vernacular was complicated.[10] Perhaps it was Hu Shi's eagerness to see a sweeping victory of vernacular Chinese over classical Chinese that led him to oversimplify the rise of the modern Italian language. His assessment of the European Renaissance thus reflected his own vision of a Chinese literary movement.

Hu Shi's "misrepresentation" of the Renaissance can also be observed in the way in which he described Dante's attitude toward Latin. According to Hu Shi, Dante saw the vernacular as a language that was superior to Latin. But what is missing in Hu Shi's narrative is that, despite Dante's promotion of the vernacular, Dante would never have condemned Latin in the way Hu Shi and his fellow May Fourth writers did classical Chinese. Dante had great reverence for the Latin literary tradition. Virgil, after all, is chosen by Dante as the great

---

10   The vernacular gained considerable ground in the fourteenth century, although the main contributions to the development of the vulgar tongue were made by Dante, Petrarch, and Boccaccio, who drew strength from their knowledge of the classics in their efforts to give artistic nobility to Italian. In the early fifteenth century, the vernacular went through a crisis. The humanists' exaltation of Latin overshadowed the vernacular. However, in the last decades of the century, the humanists' search for a pure Latin only increased the use of the vernacular in practical spheres. Between 1470 and 1550, printing made a decisive contribution to the stability and uniformity of language in Italy. The final codification of a standard written language occurred in the sixteenth century. The national language of Italy that Hu Shi refers to did not even exist until the unification of Italy in the nineteenth century. See Bruno Migliorini, *The Italian Language* (Boston: Faber and Faber, 1984).

mentor to guide the pilgrim through the journey in *Inferno* and *Purgatory*. Moreover, Dante says very little about the Latin language in his famous defense of the vernacular, *De vulgari eloquentia*. Instead of denigrating Latin, Dante only separates the vernacular from Latin, endorsing the vernacular as a new authority to counterbalance the old one. By contrast, to Hu Shi and other May Fourth vernacular writers, the only way to establish the authority of vernacular Chinese was to abandon classical Chinese. Hu Shi's depiction of Dante as an anti-Latin hero therefore arises out of his desire to find an exemplar for the Chinese vernacular movement.

While the European literary context may have been oversimplified in the writings of Hu Shi, the idea of the Renaissance as a universal model inspired Hu Shi and other May Fourth writers. Along with the symbolic value that was accorded any idea from the West, Hu Shi has made "Renaissance" an indispensable term with which to describe the May Fourth cultural movement. The Renaissance narrative also consolidated Hu Shi's reputation as a great visionary leader and reaffirmed the vernacular movement as a grand project in pursuit of modernity and progress. Other May Fourth writers such as Fu Sinian 傅斯年 and Luo Jialun 羅家倫 all accepted this analogy when describing the nature of May Fourth literary movement.

The Renaissance narrative was also adopted a decade later when the writings of May Fourth intellectuals were canonized and institutionalized. The preface of the *Compendium of Modern Chinese Literature* published in the 1930s opens with the following paragraph:

> It has been nearly twenty years since Hu Shi and Chen Duxiu initiated the New Literature Movement in the *New Youth* in Beijing in 1917. Compared to the four-thousand years of Chinese civilization, two decades seem brief and unworthy of consideration. But the vision of this movement for the future of Chinese culture is similar to the European Renaissance; both point to a new era. Although what the movement had brought to the world may not be so miraculous and spectacular as the European Renaissance, the adventurous spirit of these pioneers provides a great model for our new youth, and the literary works they have created are invaluable treasures in the history of a new culture.

> 我國的新文學運動，自從民國六年在北京的《新青年》上由胡適陳獨秀等發動後，至今已經二十年. 這二十年時間，比起我國過去四千年的文化過程來，當然短促值不得一提，可是他對於未來中國文化史上的使命，正像歐洲的文藝復興一樣，是一切新的開始。他所結的果實，也許及不上歐洲文藝復興時代豐盛美滿，可是這一群先驅們開闢荒蕪的精神，至今

還可以當作我們年輕人的模範，而他們所產生的一點珍貴的作品，更是新文化史上的至寶。[11]

In this preface, readers are taught to associate the European Renaissance with the May Fourth literary movement as a way to understand it as well as envision the future development of a new Chinese literature. Here the term "Renaissance" is not merely a neologism that signifies a foreign period in a foreign culture, but a reinvented critical category used to legitimize and glorify certain literary values and practices.

While the idea of Renaissance had appealed to many May Fourth intellectuals, later scholars expressed doubts about this Western-imported analogy. For example, Chow Tse-tsung in his seminal book *The May Fourth Movement* gives a lengthy discussion on ways in which the May Fourth Movement bears little resemblance to the European Renaissance. Professor Yu Ying-shih's essay, for another example, argues that the intellectual diversity and complexity of the May Fourth Movement cannot be summarized by either the concept of Renaissance or that of Enlightenment. These scholars, whose works represented some of the best scholarship in May Fourth studies, had certainly reminded us of the cultural and historical specificity of the May Fourth Movement.

Nevertheless, I want to highlight the potential of "Renaissance" as a critical term that may continue to enable us to compare the Chinese with other cultures or regions. A loose analogy to the European Renaissance can be extremely helpful, if we can free ourselves from a mode of thinking that sees this term as a fixed Western "program" superimposed on the Chinese context. Hu Shi's idea of a Chinese Renaissance should be seen as one of many that free the concept of Renaissance from its European context and helps reshape this idea in cross-cultural imagining and communication.

3   Chinese Renaissance, Other Renaissances

In 1918, when Hu Shi (1891–1962) put the idea of Renaissance at the center of his literary theory, Sri Aurobindo Ghose (1872–1950), one of India's leading intellectuals, wrote four essays that were later published as *The Renaissance in India*. Aurobindo emphasized the difference between Indian Renaissance and

---

11   Zhao Jiabi 趙家璧, Preface to *Zhongguo xinwenxue daxi* 中國新文學大系 (Compendium of modern Chinese literature). 10 vols. Shanghai: Liangou tushu gongsi 上海：良友圖書公司, 1935.

European Renaissance. He considered the European Renaissance, which took place in the fifteenth and sixteenth centuries, as an overthrow of Christianized and feudalized Europe with the aid of the old Greco-Latin spirit, and said that this was radically different from what was happening in India. It was in the recent Celtic Revival in Ireland, which Aurobindo describes as "the attempt of a reawakened national spirit to find a new impulse of self-expression which shall give the spiritual force for a great reshaping and rebuilding,"[12] that Aurobindo found the closest analogy. In this sense, *The Renaissance in India* may be read as Aurobindo's attempt to define the "national spirit" that India was reawakening to as well as to map the scope and directions in which this "rebirth" would lead India.

In articulating an Indian Renaissance, Aurobindo identifies the three steps that should be taken in order to reach a true birth of Indian culture, i.e., a Renaissance in India:

> The first step was the reception of the European contact, a radical reconsideration of many of the prominent elements and some revolutionary denial of the very principles of the old culture. The second was a reaction of the Indian spirit upon the European influence, sometimes with a total denial of what it offered and a stressing both of the essential and the strict letter of the national past, which yet masked a movement of assimilation. The third, only now beginning or recently begun, is rather a process of new creation in which the spiritual power of the Indian mind remains supreme, recovers its truths, accepts whatever it finds sound or true, useful or inevitable of the modern idea and form, but so transmutes and indianises it, so absorbs and so transforms it entirely into itself that its foreign character disappears and it becomes another harmonious element in the characteristic working of the ancient goddess, the Shakti of India mastering and taking possession of the modern influence, no longer possessed or overcome by it.[13]

The third step that Aurobindo passionately elaborates reiterates what he had written earlier in the treatise, where he defines the most difficult task of the Indian Renaissance as "an original dealing with a modern problem in the light of Indian spirit and the endeavor to formulate a greater *synthesis* of a spiritualized society."[14] The key word here is "synthesis." Aurobindo not only believed in the revival of the Indian spiritual knowledge and experience in all its splendor,

---

12   Aurobindo Ghose, *The Renaissance in India*, 4th ed. (Sri Aurobindo Ashram Press, 1951), 3.
13   Ibid., 30–31.
14   Ibid., 27.

depth, and fullness, he also believed in the power and capacity of the Indian spirit to "accept" whatever it finds sound and true, to "transmute," to "indianise," to "absorb," and to "transform." This profound belief in "synthesis," in the possibility of harmoniously blending different linguistic and cultural elements marked Aurobindo's transcultural imagining of the Indian Renaissance.

Both Chinese and Indian literary modernization emerged from a breakdown of the conventional diglossic structure.[15] The results were, however, strikingly different. While Chinese intellectuals expressed hostility toward classical Chinese and Chinese script, Indian intellectuals like Aurobindo, encouraged by British Orientalists who admired the ancient Sanskrit language, retained a great sense of respect for their literary and cultural tradition. While the Chinese Renaissance championed by the May Fourth intellectuals took a radical stance on the use of modern vernacular and sought to eliminate classical Chinese altogether, the Indian Renaissance advocated by Aurobindo emphasized a more harmonious relationship with languages by highlighting the importance of "synthesis." In Aurobindo's paradigm, the revival of the Sanskrit tradition is not contradicted by the development of Bengali literature and the use of the English language.

In fact, the idea of "synthesis" played a significant role in early twentieth-century Indian intellectuals' pursuit of a national language. The candidates for the new national language were Urdu and Hindi, two languages often depicted as "identical twins [that] have chosen to dress as differently as possible."[16] The two languages are associated with different religious and cultural traditions: Urdu with Muslims, and Hindi with Hindus. They also had different scripts: Nastaliq for Urdu, and Nagari for Hindi. But the dream of a shared, syncretic

---

15   Pre-modern India was also a diglossic society, with Sanskrit as the high language and various regional vernaculars as the low language. The diglossic pattern changed in Northern India after the Muslim invasion, which resulted in a tri-glossic system, with Sanskrit, the vernacular, and Persian Arabic existing side by side. For a more detailed discussion, see Gang Zhou, *Placing the Modern Chinese Vernacular in Transnational Literature* (New York: Palgrave/McMillan, 2011).

16   Hu Shi's discourse on the vernacular had always been nationalistic. The Indian (Bengali) Renaissance was, in contrast, simultaneously regional and national. While Aurobindo imagined an all-"Indian" identity, the Bengali language was nevertheless regional. The leading North Indian vernacular had been Urdu, and then Hindi started to overthrow the hegemony of Urdu. See Harish Trivedi, "The Progress of Hindi, Part II: Hindi and the Nation" in *Literary Cultures in History*, edited by Sheldon Polock (Berkeley: University of California Press, 2003): 958–1022. Regarding the intriguing relationship among Urdu, Hindi, and Hindustani, see Christopher Shackle and Rupert Snell, *Hindi and Urdu since 1800: A Common Reader* (London: School of Oriental and African Studies, 1990); also see Madhumita Lahiri, "An Idiom for India: Hindustani and the Limits of the Language Concept," *Interventions: International Journal of Postcolonial Studies*, 18, no. 1 (January 2015): 60–85.

culture, an aspiration for Hindu-Muslim unity, drove Indian intellectuals and writers such as Nehru, Gandhi, and Premchand to promote the project of "Hindustani," which would produce a new national language legible to Indians from all religions and regions.

The most heated debate on the question of language in India took place in the 1920s and 1930s. In 1925 the Indian National Congress chose Hindustani, the synthesis of Urdu and Hindi, as the lingua franca of India. In his 1937 pamphlet "The Question of Language," Jawaharlal Nehru, the president of the Indian National Congress, who would later become the first prime minister of modern India, defined Hindustani as the "only possible all-India language." In 1934, Munshi Premchand, one of the most celebrated writers in modern India, wrote an essay titled "Urdu, Hindi, and Hindustani," in which he passionately supported Hindustani as the national language that can be used by Hindus, Muslims, Punjabis, Bengalis, and all ordinary people. This inclusive and syncretic dream was best reflected in Gandhi's speech in 1918 when he claims that a harmonious blend of Hindi and Urdu would be as beautiful as the confluence of the Ganga and the Yamuna and last forever.[17] In short, Hindustani became the language of Utopia in these writers' and intellectuals' imagining and creating of a modern India.

The idea of a Renaissance was also picked up by Arabic writers. *Al-Nahadah*, the Arab Renaissance in the nineteenth and early twentieth century, was another cultural movement that arose in response to this Western idea. The pre-modern Arab diglossic situation was similar to the Chinese situation, although the Arab intellectuals embarked on a completely different path for their linguistic and literary modernization. In contrast to the Chinese Renaissance, which radically condemned classical Chinese as the obstacle to China's modernization, the Arab Renaissance extolled classical Arabic and viewed it as Arabs' most enduring legacy, and as the key to the Arabs' successful revival in the modern era. As one Syrian writer claimed in the 1920s:

> The language is the most precious treasure our forefathers left us. It lived with our ancestors and outlived them. It had to contend with difficulties and proved to be stronger than they were.... It is the soul of the Arabs.... It is the homeland, nationalism, life and the *esprit de corps*. From the relationship between language and community, it appears to us quite evident that the regeneration of the community lies in the regeneration of the language in the same way that the soundness of the language is indicative of the soundness of the condition of the community that speaks it. It is

---

[17] See Trivedi, 979–980. Both Gandhi and Premchand later acknowledged that Hindustani was more a cherished dream than a hard fact.

so, because the language is the spirit of the vitality of the community and the sustenance of its nationalism. Can a body live without a soul, or can a soul hold on without a body?[18]

In other words, whereas the Chinese Renaissance and the Indian Renaissance witnessed the breakdown of a longstanding conventional diglossic structure, the Arabic Renaissance continued to uphold the traditional linguistic hierarchy. The Arabs still perceived the various forms of vernacular as vulgar, deficient, and devoid of literary merit. Like the Chinese, the Arabic Renaissance had initiated a monolingual language reform that excluded other cultural influences for their modernized society. Since the 1920s, vernacular Chinese has emerged as the only recognized written language in China. In the Arabic world, writers and linguists have expressed great passion for the "integrity" and "purity" of classical Arabic. In India, characterized by its multilingual social condition, English is designated as an "associate official language" that coexists with Hindi and other Indian vernaculars that represent various regional cultures and traditions.

In sum, a comparative study of the different cultural trajectories of a Renaissance in China, India, and Arabian countries demonstrates how the term Renaissance was circulated and appropriated in geopolitical contexts far beyond Europe, where the term originated. The juxtaposition of different Renaissances thus challenges the traditional nation-based framework of literary studies.

4 To Renaissance or Not to Renaissance

It is intriguing to notice that among today's five major civilizations as defined by Samuel Huntington in *The Clash of Civilizations and the Remaking of World Order*—Chinese, Japanese, Indian, Islamic, and Western—four of them, excepting Japan, had initiated a Renaissance at a significant historical juncture. Other Renaissances such as the Irish Renaissance, the Hebrew Renaissance, the Pan-African Renaissance, and the Maori Renaissance were all declared by a group of cultural elites who were proud of their unique and distinctive cultures and civilizations.[19]

---

18 Cited from Anwar Chejne, *The Arabic Language: Its Role in History* (Minneapolis: University of Minnesota Press, 1969), 20.

19 For more detailed discussion on these "Other Renaissances," see Brenda Schildgen, Gang Zhou, and Sander Gilman, eds., *Other Renaissances: A New Approach to World Literature* (New York: Palgrave/Macmillan, 2006). Also see Samuel Huntington, *The Clash of Civilizations and the Remaking of World Order* (New York: Simon & Schuster Paperbacks, 2011), 45.

In the case of Japan, the *genbun itchi* 言文一致 movement may be seen as Meiji Japan's counterpart of the Chinese May Fourth vernacular movement. The *genbun itchi* movement was an intriguing embodiment of the China–Japan–West triangular relationship. It originated with a petition in 1866, "Reasons for Abolishing Chinese Characters."[20] In the 1870s, there were multiple language reform proposals. In one of her article on the early Meiji language reform, Atsuko Ueda presents a "heterogeneous linguistic space in which many different views of language coexisted, competed, and influenced each other."[21] She discusses four reformers: Maejima Hisoka (1835–1919), Mori Arinori (1847–1889), Nanbu Yoshikazu (1840–1917) and Nishi Amane (1829–1897), who were arguing for the abolition of "useless Chinese" (referring to *kanji* and *kanbun*), the use of the Roman alphabet or *kana*, or even the adoption of English. However, it was the "unification of the spoken and written languages" that became the common name for the Meiji language movement, instead of the more confrontational proposal that sought to abolish Chinese characters. The result of this movement was the profound devaluation of Chinese writing, and the shift from the Chinese script to a Western phonocentric appreciation of language. In other words, the modernization of Japanese language was defined by its relation both to China and the West, rather than by a rediscovery of its own culture.

The Japanese attempt to de-Sinicize its writing system and shift towards Western phonocentrism clearly resembles Korea's linguistic and literary modernization. From the Gabbo Reform 甲午改革 in 1894 to the Japanese annexation of Korea in 1910, Korea underwent tremendous social and cultural upheaval. Up to that point, Korea had been a diglossic society with classical Chinese being the scholarly literary language and the Korean vernacular the vulgar language of daily use. Seeing China's humiliating defeat by Western powers, Korean intellectuals began to perceive Confucianism and classical Chinese as impediments to modernization. The first step in their linguistic modernization was therefore to dethrone classical Chinese.

Yet interestingly, such a goal was achieved by introducing a new Western lingua franca: English. The first vernacular newspaper in Korea was published in 1896, and it was provided with an English version. The English translation was initially published on the back page of the newspaper, and later as a separate four-page volume. The inclusion of the English language in this context served

---

20 See Kojin Karatani, *Origins of Modern Japanese Literature*, trans. Brett De Bary (Durham, NC, and London: Duke University Press, 1993), 45.

21 Atsuko Ueda, "Competing 'Languages': 'Sounds' in the Orthographic Reforms of Early Meiji Japan" in *Rethinking East Asian Languages, Vernaculars, and Literacies, 1000–1919*, edited by Benjamin Elman (Brill, 2014): 220.

several purposes.[22] First, the language that connects Korea to the outside world used to be classical Chinese, but the new vernacular newspaper replaced it with English. It was clearly a disavowal of the traditional image of China as the center of the world. Second, by emphasizing the Korean vernacular, this newspaper also reminded its Korean readers that classical Chinese is but one of the foreign languages, thereby raising the status of the Korean vernacular to that of a modern language. In this way, the long-standing hierarchical diglossic relationship between classical Chinese and Korean vernacular was irrevocably changed. Third, by using a phonetic language such as English, the newspaper also suggested the superiority of the Korean vernacular over classical Chinese, which by contrast was considered a pre-modern language based on the ideograph. By moving away from the Chinese script towards English, Korean intellectuals embarked on their path of linguistic modernization. Just like Japan, Korea's linguistic modernization was also defined by its relationship to China vis-à-vis the West. It is perhaps no surprise that a Renaissance was never adopted in Korea's discourses of modernization.

Another country that may also help shed light on the situation is Turkey, geographically located between East and West, between Asia and Europe. When the Ottoman Empire collapsed and gave way to the new republic, Mustafa Kemal Ataturk (1881–1938) created a homogeneous nation-state, modernizing all parts of life, including a language revolution that was carried out with lightning speed in the late 1920s. The Arabic script, which the Turks had used for a millennium, was replaced by the Latin alphabet; and the vast number of vocabulary borrowings from Arabic and Persian were purged. The transformation of the Turkish language was so radical and profound that Almet Hasim (1884–1933), one of the country's most influential poets, wrote in 1928:

> It is as if we are witnessing the reconstruction of old ruined streets with broken pavements, their opening up into boulevards. On these new streets, old words in nightcaps and bathrobes will not be able to walk without looking laughable. We await the pleasure of watching new ideas stroll back and forth on these modern avenues.[23]

The "catastrophic success" of the Turkish language modernization was defined by its relationship to the Arabic, Persian tradition vis-à-vis Western phonocentrism. Not coincidentally, the Turkish people never declared a Renaissance,

---

22   An Yelle, "Generality and Distinctiveness of Korean Language Modernization," Cambridge, MA: Harvard-Yenching Institute Working Paper Series.
23   Cited from Nergis Erturk, *Grammatology and Literary Modernity in Turkey* (New York: Oxford University Press, 2011), 3.

and we have every reason to consider Turkey an Islamic country rather than a separate civilization.

In their decisions whether to declare a Renaissance or not, all these civilizations (China, India, the Arab world) and nations (Japan, Korea, Turkey) were differentiated by their experiences of modernity under different historical circumstances. The modern literatures that emerged from these intralingual and translingual battles had transformed the landscape of world literature. By showing the different ways in which modern literatures emerged in these geopolitical contexts, one may question the "naturalness" and "inevitability" granted to certain ideas of linguistic modernity in any community. Perhaps the triumph (or defeat) of the vernacular, the pursuit of phonocentrism (or not), the declaration of a Renaissance (or not) was after all not a historical necessity but a political choice. Perhaps a careful study of all these different forms of language modernization can lead to a new understanding of world literature as a system of *variations*.

5 A Distant Reading of the May Fourth Movement

Franco Moretti's essay "Conjectures on World Literature" describes a division of labor between national and world literature: national literature for those who see trees; world literature for those who see waves. Trees and waves, of course, are metaphors. While the former describes the passage from unity to diversity, the latter shows how uniformity engulfed the initial diversity. The May Fourth Movement can be observed in this model. At the beginning of this chapter, I discuss Yu Ying-shih's essay "Neither Renaissance nor Enlightenment," which suggests abandoning the idea of "Renaissance" to take a closer look at the May Fourth period, bringing into view thus-far neglected thinkers and writers. But Moretti's model suggests a different approach to the study of May Fourth Movement.

Within the framework of world literature, a distant reading of "May Fourth" is only possible if we relate it to a broader category that can be perceived in different cultural contexts. This is why I propose a renewed interest in "Renaissance" as a critical term to describe and shed light on the May Fourth Movement. By comparing the Chinese Renaissance with other Renaissances, and by placing the Chinese literary modernity among other literary modernities, we can make new connections between the May Fourth Movement and other cultural movements in the world. As Moretti suggests, sometimes less is more, and distance is always *a condition of knowledge*.

Bibliography

Amritavalli, R., and K. A. Jayaseelan. "India." In *Language and National Identity in Asia*, ed. Andrew Simpson, 55–83. New York: Oxford University Press, 2007.

Burckhardt, Jacob. *The Civilization of the Renaissance in Italy*. Trans. S. G. C. Middlemore. New York: Penguin Books, 1990.

Chejne, Anwar G. *The Arabic Language: Its Role in History*. Minneapolis: University of Minnesota Press, 1969.

Chow, Tse-Tsung. *The May Fourth Movement: Intellectual Revolution in Modern China*. Cambridge, MA: Harvard University Press, 1960.

Dante. *Literature in the Vernacular* (De Vulgari Eloquentia). Trans. Sally Purcell. Manchester, Eng.: Carcanet New Press Limited, 1981.

Denton, Kirk, ed. *Modern Chinese Literary Thought: Writings on Literature 1893–1945*. Stanford, CA: Stanford University Press, 1998.

Dolezelova-Velingerova, Milena, and Oldrich Kral, eds. *The Appropriation of Cultural Capital: China's May Fourth Project*. Cambridge, MA: Harvard University Press, 2001.

Erturk, Nergis. *Grammatology and Literary Modernity in Turkey*. New York: Oxford University Press, 2011.

Ferguson, Charles. "Diglossia," *Word* 15 (1959).

Ghose, Aurobindo. *The Renaissance in India*. Pondicherry, India: Sri Aurobindo Ashram Press, 1951.

Goody, Jack. *Renaissances: The One or the Many* (Cambridge: Cambridge University Press, 2010).

Hu Shi 胡适. *Hu Shi wenchun* 胡適文存 (Collected works of Hu Shi). 4 vols. Shanghai: Yadong Tushuguan (Yadong Library), 1924.

Hu Shi 胡适. *Hu Shi liuxue riji* 胡適留學日記 (Hu Shi's diary while studying abroad). 4 vols. Taipei: Taipei Commercial Press, 1959.

Huntington, Samuel. *The Clash of Civilizations and the Remaking of World Order*. New York: Simon & Schuster Paperbacks, 2011.

Kang Youwei 康有為. *Da Tong Shu* 大同書 (The Book of Great Unity). Shanghai: Shanghai guji chubanshe, 2005.

Karatani, Kojin. *Origins of Modern Japanese Literature*. Trans. Brett De Bary. Durham, NC, and London: Duke University Press, 1993.

Kopf, David. *British Orientalism and the Bengal Renaissance: The Dynamics of Indian Modernization 1773–1885*. Berkeley: University of California Press, 1969.

Lahiri, Madhumita. "An Idiom for India: Hindustani and the Limits of the Language Concept," *Interventions: International Journal of Postcolonial Studies*, 18, no. 1 (Jan. 2015): 60–85.

Lee, Leo Ou-fan. *The Romantic Generation of Modern Chinese Writers*. Cambridge, MA: Harvard University Press, 1973.

Lewis, Geoffrey. *The Turkish Language Reform: A Catastrophic Success*. New York: Oxford University Press, 1999.

Maissen, Thomas & Barbara Mittler. *Why China did not have a Renaissance—and why that matters*. De Gruyter, 2018.

Migliorini, Bruno. *The Italian Language*. Boston: Faber and Faber, 1984.

Moretti, Franco. "Conjectures on World Literature." In *Debating World Literature*, ed. Christopher Prendergast, 148–162. New York: Verso, 2004.

Prendergast, Christopher, ed. *Debating World Literature*. New York: Verso, 2004.

Sachsenmaier, Dominic, Jens Riedel, and Shmuel N. Eisenstadt, eds. *Reflections on Multiple Modernities: European, Chinese and Other Interpretations*. Leiden, NL: Brill, 2002.

Schildgen, Brenda, Gang Zhou, and Sander Gilman, eds. *Other Renaissances: A New Approach to World Literature*. New York: Palgrave/Macmillan, 2006.

Shackle, Christopher, and Rupert Snell. *Hindi and Urdu since 1800: A Common Reader*. London: School of Oriental and African Studies, 1990.

Sichel, Edith. *The Renaissance*. New York: Henry Holt, 1914.

Simpson, Andrew, ed. *Language and National Identity in Asia*. New York: Oxford University Press, 2007.

Trivedi, Harish. "The Progress of Hindi, Part II: Hindi and the Nation." In *Literary Cultures in History*, ed. Sheldon Polock, 958–1022. Berkeley: University of California Press, 2003.

Ueda, Atsuko. "Competing 'Languages': 'Sound' in the Orthographic Reforms of Early Meiji Japan." In *Rethinking East Asian Languages, Vernaculars, and Literacies, 1000–1919*, ed. Benjamin A. Elman, 220–253. Brill, 2014.

Vasari, Giorgio. *The Lives of the Artists*. Trans. Julia Conaway Bondanella and Peter Bondanella. New York: Oxford University Press, 1998.

Yu, Ying-shih. "Neither Renaissance nor Enlightenment: A Historian's Reflections on the May Fourth Movement." In *The Appropriation of Cultural Capital: China's May Fourth Project*, 299–320.

Zhao, Jiabi, ed. *Zhongguo xinwenxue daxi* 中國新文學大系 (Compendium of Modern Chinese Literature) 10 vols. Shanghai: liangyou tushu gongsi, 1995.

Zhou, Gang. *Placing the Modern Chinese Vernacular in Transnational Literature*. New York: Palgrave/Macmillan, 2011.

CHAPTER 5

Hu Shi and the May Fourth Legacy

Yung-chen Chiang

Among the leaders of the May Fourth Movement, Hu Shi was the one who was most aware of the movement's historical significance. He was the only one among them who persisted throughout his life to stake his claim on the meaning as well as the legacy of the "May Fourth." His emphasis, moreover, was not just on China, but the modern world led by the West, in which China was a junior but avid member. At his brief radical swing to the right in 1926 and 1927, he rhapsodized on the May Fourth Movement's turn to politics and party discipline under the aegis of the Soviet Union and the Third International. As he turned conservative in the early 1930s, he reverted to his earlier position by emphasizing individualism and referred to the movement as a watershed that separates China's "Victorian Age" from its "Age of Collectivism." Toward the end of his life, he lamented that the meaning of this movement was hijacked by cunning and ruthless political parties. The fact that Hu Shi had always sought to situate the May Fourth Movement in a global, albeit Eurocentric, contexts—even when his political positions shifted—should lead us to follow his example and continue to (re)interpret the May Fourth Movement in its various historical and political contexts.

Hu Shi began to lay claims on the "correct" interpretation of the significance of the May Fourth Movement as early as 1919, when it had just begun to gain its momentum. He asserted that the defining feature of the May Fourth Movement, which manifested itself in the introduction of various schools of thoughts from the West, was a critical spirit. Quoting Friedrich Nietzsche (1844–1900), he characterized this common spirit as the "transvaluation of values" (重新估定一切價值), that is, to apply modern Western ideas to study and reevaluate all pressing issues in China, such as Confucianism, literary reforms, the emancipation of women, ethical norms, educational reforms, the marriage institution, and the family system.

By portraying ideas from the West as instruments for studying problems and finding solutions, Hu Shi at once privileged pragmatism he championed and disparaged the ideas on the right and the left of the ideological spectrum:

> Studying problems is the best way to develop a critical attitude, an interest in research, and a habit of independent thinking. Reading ten volumes of *The Critique of Pure Reason* or its equivalent is no better than having

a critical attitude; reading ten volumes of *Theories of Surplus Value* or its equivalent is no better than having an interest in research; reading ten volumes of the *Government by All the People* or its equivalent is no better than inculcating a habit of independent thinking.

研究問題最能使讀者漸漸的養成一種批評的態度, 研究的興趣, 獨立思想的習慣. 十部《純粹理性的評判》, 不如一點評判的態度; 十部《贏餘價值論》, 不如一點研究的興趣; 十種《全民政治論》, 不如一點獨立思想的習慣.[1]

A few months before he penned this essay on the need to inculcate a critical attitude, an interest in research, and an independent thinking, Hu Shi had already launched his critique of those to his right and left. In his famous debates with Li Dazhao 李大釗 (1888–1927) and Lan Gongwu 藍公武 (1887–1957) on the issue of "problems and isms" (問題與主義), he chastised them for treating Western philosophical doctrines as if they were the panacea for China's problems. He lectured them that all "isms" were originally concrete solutions proposed for specific problems and that no social reforms could be accomplished overnight, but through painstaking work one step at a time.[2]

1 Hu Shi's Interpretation of the May Fourth Movement in the 1920s

By the early 1920s, Hu Shi believed that his legacy in the May Fourth Movement was assured. His advocacy of the use of vernacular Chinese, which he had anticipated to be a bitter and protracted battle, turned out to be a quick victory. In 1920, the Ministry of Education had decreed that in three years all elementary schools in China should adopt vernacular textbooks. The vernacular Chinese, which had still been derided as the language of the hawkers and peddlers a few years earlier, had assumed the status of a national language in the early 1920s. As he described it to his American friend Edith "Clifford" Williams (1885–1971):

> When we began in 1917, we expected it to have a hearing in ten years and to succeed in 20 years. But the time had long been ripe, thanks to the numerous nameless vulgate writers of the past 1,000 years! And we routed

---

[1] Hu Shi, "*Xinsichao de yiyi* 新思潮的意義 (The meaning of the new thought)," *Hu Shi quanji* (The complete works of Hu Shi; hereafter *HSQJ*), 1: 691–700.
[2] Hu Shi, "*Wenti yu zhuyi* 問題與主義 (Problems and isms)," *HSQJ*, 1: 324–328.

the opposition in a little over a year, and won the battle in less than five years.[3]

The victory of the vernacular movement emboldened Hu Shi. In a talk given to a literary society organized by expatriate Westerners in Beijing in 1921, Hu Shi maintained that vernacular Chinese, after freeing itself from the influence of classical Chinese, was the most progressive and democratic language in the world. He argued that English did not have the same good fortune as did vernacular Chinese, which had been used by the commoners for centuries. The fact that modern English had been developed and dominated by the cultural elites had prevented it from evolving into a language of the common people. This led to the retention of unnecessarily complicated grammatical features such as cases and inflections, when a more simplified conjugation such as "I ain't, you ain't, he ain't" could have conveyed the same meaning.[4]

Hu Shi's victory in the "Debate on Science and the Philosophy of Life" (科學與人生觀論戰)—a debate that took place in 1923 on the question of whether science can solve all human problems and explicate the meaning and beauty of life[5]—made him believe for a while that China might overtake the West in humanity's march toward a worldview thoroughly informed by science. He wrote to Clifford Williams:

> My hope is that intellectual China which has not been burdened down with any form of supernatural religion, may in the long run carry out the scientific views of the universe and of life to their logical conclusions more consistently and more courageously than they have been in Europe and America. We are here living over the days of Huxley and W. K. Clifford. "Produce your evidences, and I'll believe" is again the war-cry of my friends today.[6]

Hu believed that he and his coterie of friends were poised to vicariously carry Huxley's fight against religion to its logical conclusions in China. So much so that when he traveled to Europe in 1926 he assumed the role of a reverse

---

3 Hu Shi to Edith Clifford Williams, 12 March 1923, *HSQJ*, 40: 217.
4 Hu Shi, "The Evolution of the Chinese Grammar," *HSQJ*, 36: 140–155.
5 The debate on science and the philosophy of life took place in 1923 between the believers in the omnipotence of science and the conservatives who contended that scientific analyses could not exhaust the meaning and beauty of life. See Charlotte Furth's "May Fourth in History," in *Reflections on the May Fourth Movement: A Symposium* (Cambridge, MA: Harvard University Press, 1972), 61–66. Also see Furth's *Ting Wen-Chiang: Science and China's New Culture* (Cambridge, MA: Harvard University Press, 1970), 94–135.
6 Hu Shi to Edith Clifford Williams, 4 January 1924, *HSQJ*, 40: 225.

missionary bringing the gospel of modern civilization back to the Europeans and Americans, who had lost faith in Western civilization in the aftermath of the WWI and who looked for solace and truth in the older civilizations of the East. The modern civilization, Hu Shi maintained, was in its spirit "a new religion, which in the absence of a better name, I shall term the religion of Democracy":

> This religion of Democracy which not only guarantees one's own liberty, nor merely limits one's liberty by respecting the liberty of other people, but endeavors to make it possible, for every man and every woman to live a free life; which not only succeeds through science and machinery in greatly enhancing the happiness and comfort of the individual but also seeks through organization and legislation to extend the goods of life to the greatest number—this is the greatest spiritual heritage of the Western civilization.[7]

This eulogy is not based on a blind faith, Hu Shi insisted, but a careful appraisal of modern Western civilization.

In his lecture on "The Chinese Renaissance" given at Liverpool University on November 25, 1926, he said that he and his fellow Chinese thinkers were aware of the problems of modern Western civilization, the most glaring of which were manslaughter machines in wars and the brutalities of the industrial system. Nevertheless, from the perspective of an outsider, Hu Shi pointed out, the modern scientific and democratic civilization that originated from the West contains spiritual potentialities that many Europeans and Americans were not aware of:

> If the East is to make any contribution to the new civilization of the future world, it is not to come in the form of a return to Eastern spirituality, but in helping the West to realize those spiritualities. There should be co-operation to bring those potentialities into reality. The West, which is becoming sick of its materialism, has been yearning for certain spiritual messages. You find fundamentalist revivals, phases of faddism for Hindoo religion, and all sorts of theosophism and spiritualism. We modern Chinese have come to the conclusion that if Western civilization is to

---

7 Hu Shi, "The Civilizations of the East and the West," *HSQJ*, 36: 342, 345–346.

save itself it cannot go back to the old ways that are past, but must seek its own salvation in the direction of realizing its spiritual potentialities.[8]

It may seem preposterous for Hu Shi to proselytize to the Europeans and Americans the gospel of modern Western civilization. Yet, as he pointed out repeatedly, he was merely fleshing out and pushing to its logical conclusion the scientific and democratic outlook of the world that had inspired the May Fourth Movement.

Ironically, just as Hu Shi was seeking to place the May Fourth Movement at the forefront of humanity's march toward the realization of "the religion of Democracy," he introduced a dramatic new twist to his interpretation of the movement itself. In the mid-1920s, after the May Thirtieth Massacre, a labor and anti-imperialist movement that took place in Shanghai in 1925, Hu Shi's political view began to swing to the right.[9] When he left for Europe in mid-July 1926, the Northern Expedition launched by the Nationalist Party (KMT), trained and equipped by the Soviets, under the leadership of Chiang Kai-shek, had just started. By October of the same year, Chiang's Northern Expedition army had taken Wuhan. Elated by the victory of the expedition, which he predicted would unify the country in a few months, Hu began to see the victorious Nationalist Party as the embodiment of the spirit of the latest phase of the May Fourth Movement.

In "The Renaissance in China,"[10] a speech he delivered at the Royal Institute of International Affairs on November 19, 1926, Hu used the word "Renaissance" to refer to the May Fourth Movement, which, according to his interpretation, had begun as a literary revolution. This revolution was then followed by student demonstrations and culminated in the victory of the Nationalist Party. Although the concept of "Renaissance" originated from the West, Hu Shi used this word as a general term to refer to any form of cultural renewal or rebirth. While Hu presented throughout his life many different versions of the many "Renaissances" that had taken place in the Chinese history, this speech in

---

8   Hu Shi, "The Chinese Renaissance," report of lecture delivered by Dr. Hu Shih at Liverpool University on November 25, 1926, *The Promotion of Closer Cultural Relations between China and Great Britain* (London: The Universities China Committee [1926]), 11.
9   For a detailed analysis of Hu's swing to the right, see Chiang Yung-chen 江勇振, *Shewo qishei: Hu Shi, Di'erbu: Rizheng dangzhong, 1917–1927* 舍我其誰: 胡適, 第二部, 日正當中 1917–1927 (The titan: Hu Shi, vol. 2: The midday sun, 1917–1927) (Taipei: Linking Publishing Company, 2013; Hangzhou: Zhejiang People's Press, 2013), 828–909; 330–400.
10 The following analysis of "The Renaissance in China," unless otherwise noted, is based on this speech by Hu Shi in *HSQJ*, 36: 156–190.

1926 was unique in that not only did he focus exclusively on the May Fourth Movement as modern China's Renaissance, but he saw it as culminating in the Leninist party organization of the KMT under the aegis of the Soviet Union.

This speech in England represents Hu Shi's first attempt to expound the historical significance of the May Fourth Movement. The way he described the literary revolution in this speech, which he termed as the first stage of the Chinese "Renaissance," would become his standard interpretation of the May Fourth Movement.[11]

Hu Shi's justification of the student demonstration, which he considered the second stage of the Chinese "Renaissance," also became part of his standard interpretation of the May Fourth Movement until the late 1940s. Contrary to the common misconception about Hu's alleged aversion to politics,[12] he was active in political activities when he was a student in the United States. Disheartened by the political chaos he witnessed upon his return to China, he vowed that he would not participate in politics for twenty years and would only focus on the intellectual transformation of China through educational reforms. However, not only did he begin discussing politics a few years later, he also maintained that throughout his life he had taken a "disinterested interest in politics as a civic duty of an educated man."[13] While Hu Shi always urged students to focus on studying instead of politics, he believed that student demonstrations took place because the adults had forsaken their responsibility. In his speech in England, he said:

> The constant interference of students in politics is regarded as strange in foreign countries, but when you come to think of it, it is quite a usual phenomenon in the history of mankind. It is almost a universal rule that whenever abnormal conditions of society exist, whenever there is lacking a regular channel for the expression of popular wishes and ideas, whenever the older generation fails to satisfy the desires of the people,

---

11 Hu Shi's standard narrative of this literary revolution is that it actually started as a conversation between himself and his friends in the United States, and that while vernacular Chinese literature had been produced for thousands of years, it would require a conscious effort to make it a movement. See Hu Shi, "*Bishang Liangshan—wenxue geming de kaishi* 逼上梁山: 文學革命的開始 (Forced to rebel: The beginning of the literary revolution)," *HSQJ*, 18: 99–132, and "Dr. Hu Shih's Personal Reminiscences." In "Chinese Oral History Project" (Columbia University, 1958), 128–176.

12 Grieder, *Hu Shih and the Chinese Renaissance* (Cambridge, MA: Harvard University Press, 1970), 54, 175–176. Also see Chou Ming-chih, *Hu Shih and Intellectual Choice in Modern China* (Ann Arbor: University of Michigan Press, 1984), 16–18, 107–109.

13 "Dr. Hu Shih's Personal Reminiscences," 42.

the burden of political interference almost invariably falls upon the shoulders of the younger generation of intellectuals—the students.[14]

History abounds with examples in which student movements change the course of history. Hu Shi cited as examples political protests in Chinese history, the revolution of 1848 in Europe, and contemporary student protests in India, Korea, Turkey, and Russia. Nonetheless, no matter how formidable these student movements appeared, such movements lacked organization and were transitory by nature. Once the issues in question were resolved, student movements disappeared. Hu Shi believed that the May Fourth student movement in 1919 could have suffered the same fate. In its first stage, the movement was spontaneous and did not have any organization. But after that it had revealed its power and usefulness, it attracted the attention of leaders of political parties, who began to organize the students, and this led to the second stage of the movement. Hu Shi wrote:

> Then in 1924 the Kwo-min-Tang [Nationalist Party; KMT]—probably the only Chinese party that deserves the name of a political party—officially adopted the policy of enlisting students among its members. From that time onward party organizations have existed in the colleges and universities throughout the country, and wherever you find an educational center you will find a party organization of some kind.[15]

After the second stage of the movement came the third stage, in which "the students were no longer a loose organization, but a highly organized body under the influence of Soviet Russia and of the Third International."[16] This Soviet influence was truly revolutionary, exclaimed Hu, for "[t]he Chinese as a race have always shown a lack of organization. Even in literature we find in the whole literary harvest of 2,500 years no single book written with a plot, with an organization, with a desire for architectonic structure. Even the novels and dramas show a lack of plot, of organization."[17] The result was to transform the Nationalist Party into a Leninist party:

> The new Kwo-min-Tang, or National[ist] Party, has adopted a highly developed organization, a new army, a new discipline. The army became

---

14   Hu Shi, "The Renaissance in China," *HSQJ*, 36:177.
15   Hu Shi, "The Renaissance in China," *HSQJ*, 36:178–179.
16   Hu Shi, "The Renaissance in China," *HSQJ*, 36:179.
17   Hu Shi, "The Renaissance in China," *HSQJ*, 36:179.

a part of the party, and the party became the directorate, the teacher, the soul, the brain of the army. The whole organization of the military arm and of the party itself is practically identical, at least interlocked. There is a party representative in every unit of the army. At the same time, the whole party is more or less under a military type of discipline.[18]

In his praise for the success of the Nationalist Party, Hu acknowledged that he had been wrong in considering an intellectual revolution more important than a political revolution. He argued:

Thus the movement of Chinese Renaissance swings back to politics. This is, perhaps, inevitable. The political anarchy had become intolerable and the outside world, as well as Young China, has grown quite impatient. It may be that the new political movement was after all not so premature as it had once seemed to us. Recent events seem to point to the possibility of an early success of the new political revolution under the leadership of the Nationalist Party. The old forces set loose by the revolution of 1911 have gradually exhausted themselves and are offering no serious resistance to the new forces which have the advantage of organization and the inspiration of political ideals. As an impartial and non-partisan liberal, I wish them success and welcome it.[19]

Even though Hu praised the Soviet Union and the Third International in "The Renaissance in China," what he eulogized was party organization and discipline that they injected into the KMT and the student organizations. That it was not the Soviet ideology, but party organization and discipline, that interested Hu can be testified to by a conversation he had with the Y.M.C.A. secretary Wilson Mills in Beijing on March 24, 1928: "He said that what China needs today is a Michael Borodin of the Anglo-American type. I said it is really a pity that England and the United States cannot produce a Borodin" (他說, 此時中國需要一個英美式的鮑洛庭. 我說, 可惜英美國家就產生不出一個鮑洛庭!)[20]

Contrary to the claims made in recent Chinese scholarship, Hu Shi's approval of the Soviet Union's Five-Year Plan represented not a fling with

---

18   Hu Shi, "The Renaissance in China," *HSQJ*, 36:179–180.
19   Hu Shi, "The Renaissance in China," *HSQJ*, 36:180.
20   Hu Shi, diary entry of 24 March 1928, *Hu Shi riji quanji*, 5: 5.

socialism or communism.[21] His endorsement of the Soviet Union's economic plan only reflected his fascination with economic planning, which he considered to be the latest development of the modern Western civilization. While he preferred the American model, he defended the Soviets for their right to experiment with an alternative approach.[22] Even if one disliked their ideology, one had to admire their determination to "catch up with the United States on productivity."[23]

That there was never a swing to the left, but rather a swing to the right, when Hu Shi hailed the KMT for acquiring the Leninist party organization and discipline, can further be attested by his reaction to its purge of the Communists in April 1927, which occurred while he was on a homeward steamship from Seattle. He applauded the KMT's massacre of the Communists in Shanghai. As he told his American journalist friend Lewis Gannett: "The coup d'état in China took place while I was on the ocean. It looked as if the Kuomintang is coming to itself."[24]

2   Hu Shi's Interpretation of the May Fourth Movement in the 1930s and 1940s

Inasmuch as Hu's swing to the right in 1926 presaged his becoming a Cold War liberal during the last phase of his life,[25] this earlier move to the right turned out to be short-lived, however. Following the advice of his friends, Hu stayed in Japan waiting for the dust to settle. After 23 days, he lost patience. Declaring that his heart was "in [with] the South [the KMT]" and believing that "his

---

21   See, for example, Luo Zhitian 羅志田, *Zaizao wenming de changshi: Hu Shi Zhuan, 1891–1929* 再造文明的嘗試: 胡適傳 1891–1929 (The endeavor to reconstruct civilization: A biography of Hu Shi, 1891–1929), 2006, 252, and Shao Jian 邵建, *Qiao, Zhe ren: Riji, shuxin, nianpu zhong de Hu Shi (1891–1927)* 瞧, 這人: 日記、書信、年譜中的胡適 (1891–1927) (Ecce homo: The Hu Shi appeared in his diaries, correspondence, and autobiographic sketches, 1891–1927), 355–383.

22   Yung-chen Chiang, *Shewo qishei: Hu Shi, Di'erbu: Rizheng dangzhong*, Taipei edition, 828–854; Hangzhou edition, 2:330–352.

23   Hu Shi to Xu Zhimo, 4 October 1926, *HSQJ*, 3:56–57.

24   Hu Shi to Lewis Gannett, 17 May 1927, Lewis Gannett Papers, 1900–1965 (bulk), MS Am 1888 (586), Houghton Library, Harvard University.

25   For a book-length analysis of Hu as a Cold War liberal, see Chiang Yung-chen, *Shewo qishei: Hu Shi, Disibu: Guoshi ceshi, 1932–1962* 舍我其誰: 胡適, 第四部: 國師策士, 1932–1962 (The titan: Hu Shi, vol. 4: The cold warrior, 1932–1962), Taipei: Linking Publishing Company, 2018.

friends in Shanghai do not look at things in proper perspective,"[26] he set sail and, upon arriving in Shanghai, dropped everything and rushed to Nanjing, the new capital of the victorious KMT.

It was an anticlimax. Hu's disillusionment with the KMT was instant. He discovered that it had no visions, no plans, and no technocrats to launch China onto the path of modernization. Worse, it ruled the country by the authoritarian Chiang Kai-shek at the top down to the party lackeys at the local level. Two years later, Hu would launch his celebrated attacks on the KMT for its procrastination to establish a rule of law, which required the adoption of a constitution and, by extension, of a bill of rights.[27]

As late as 1929 after he had excoriated the KMT for not establishing a system of laws, Hu Shi was still nostalgic about the vitality that the Nationalist Party once had. In an essay entitled "The New Culture Movement and the Goumindang," he praised Sun Yat-sen for his astute grasp of the instrumental value of the May Fourth Movement for revolution. Sun Yat-sen wrote: "If our Party would like to see the revolution succeed, we will have to rely on the transformation in the realm of ideas" (吾黨欲收革命之功, 必有賴於思想之變化).[28]

As Hu propounded only in English his three-stage trajectory of the May Fourth Movement that culminated in the KMT's becoming a Leninist party, no one in China then and later knew about it. As a result, not only did it not tarnish his reputation at home, but it also spared him of the embarrassment of having to correct or chastise himself.

Hu had learned his lesson, however. He returned to his earlier position to refrain from involving in politics and to concentrate on the intellectual transformation of the nation. It should be pointed out that even though Hu Shi always believed that intellectual transformation is a prerequisite for any real social and political reform, he remained positive about the student movement. As late as the 1940s, Hu Shi continued to argue, as he did in "The Renaissance in China," that the student movement would remain a persistent feature in any societies that lack regular channels for expressing public opinions. His most positive comment about the student movement was the article he coauthored with Jiang Menglin 蔣夢麟 (1886–1964) on the first anniversary of the May Fourth Movement:

---

26 Hu Shi to Lewis Gannett, 17 May 1927, Lewis Gannett Papers.
27 Chiang Yung-chen, *Shewo qishei: Hu Shi, Disanbu: Weixue lunzheng, 1927–1932* 舍我其誰: 胡適, 第三部: 為學論政, 1927–1932 (The titan: Hu Shi, vol. 3: The public intellectual, 1927–1932), (Taipei: Linking Publishing Company, 2018), 117–173.
28 Hu Shi, "*Xinwenhua yundong yu Guomindang* 新文化運動與國民黨 (The New Culture Movement and the Guomindang)," *HSQJ*, 21:448–449.

The student movement that has happened is a manifestation of the vitality of the youth. It is a fine thing. We should not suppress it. We should not even try to. Our advice to the educators is: "Don't even dream of suppressing the student movement. There is only one way to deal with student demonstrations, which is to steer their energy to fruitful and productive activities."

學生運動已發生了, 是青年一種活動力的表現. 是一種好現象, 決不能壓下去的, 也決不可把他壓下去的. 我們對於辦教育的人的忠告是 "不要夢想壓制學生運動: 學潮的救濟只有一個法子, 就是引導學生向有益有用的路上去活動".[29]

On May 4, 1928, Hu Shi gave a speech at a university in Shanghai, in which he repeated what he argued in "The Renaissance in China," that the student movement was a normal phenomenon in an abnormal society:

The May Fourth Movement proves a universal historical law: Wherever there is an abnormal society or country where politics is corrupt and where no representative institutions exist, then the task of intervening in politics would necessarily fall on the shoulders of young students.

五四運動可證明歷史上古今中外的原則: 就是少年干政. 在變態社會與國家裡面, 政府非常腐敗, 沒有代表民意的機關, 干涉政治及參與政事的責任, 是落在青年學生的肩上.[30]

He pointed out the Nationalist Party's attempt to defy this historical law:

Lately many people have expressed their disapproval of students' involvement in politics because of the cost of sacrifice the latter made. Fully ninety percent of those who lost their lives for their actions are under 25. The more than two hundred people who were executed in Wuhan last year were mostly students of this age. Thus efforts have been made to prohibit it. The KMT in the Fourth Session of the Second Congress of the Central Executive Committee passed a resolution that states that

---

29 Hu Shi and Jiang Menglin, "*Women duiyu xuesheng yundong de xiwang* 我們對於學生運動的希望 (Our hopes for the student movement)," *HSQJ*, 21:227.

30 Hu Shi, "*Wusi yundong zhi qianyinhouguo*" 五四運動之前因後果 (The causes and effects of the May Fourth movement), *Guanghua Weekly*, 3.9 (1928), p. 5. Note that I consider this transcript more accurate than "*Wusi yundong jinian*" (Commemorating the May Fourth movement), *HSQJ*, 21:372–373.

young students—whose physique is not yet fully developed, knowledge base not yet firmed, and mental faculty not yet matured—are prone to be led astray that ended in their making a pointless sacrifice and, therefore, should not be involved in politics.

> 近來很多人覺得學生干政犧牲太大. 所犧牲者, 在二十五歲以下, 有百分之九十. 二十歲以下者, 亦不少. 去年武漢殺二百多人, 大都是這樣年紀的青年學生. 所以常有人設法禁止. 此次第四次中央會議宣言裡也說到學生體力未強、智識不足、經驗不富, 易受人惑, 作無謂的犧牲, 所以不應當干政.[31]

While Hu Shi partially agreed with the Nationalist Party's policy, he did not believe that it would succeed because it failed to address the root cause:

> If we would like to prevent students from involving in politics, there are only two solutions: first, let people of mature age restore normalcy to politics; two, let people of mature age—who are physically fit, intellectually accomplished, and experienced—enter politics.

> 若要免除學生干政, 我們只有這兩個希望: 第一、希望中年人使政治早上軌道; 第二、希望體力強健、智識高深、經驗豐富的中年, 出來把政治幹好.[32]

On December 9, 1935, a new student demonstration took place that was provoked by the Japanese scheme to create an "autonomous" region in north China. In an essay published a week after the demonstration, Hu Shi lamented that the student movement had ebbed in recent years, which he attributed to political repression, and said he was overjoyed to see students were finally marching on the street again.[33] In his diary, however, he revealed a completely different attitude toward this student demonstration. Initially, he was relieved to learn that the Peking University students did not participate in this demonstration. He was startled and expressed his anger later when he discovered that some Peking University students joined the demonstration.

While Hu Shi adopted diametrically different postures in public and private toward the 1935 student demonstration, he was consistent in his position on

---

31   Hu Shi, "*Wusi yundong zhi qianyinhouguo*," *Guanghua Weekly*, 3.9 (1928), pp. 5–6.
32   Hu Shi, "*Wusi yundong zhi qianyinhouguo*," *Guanghua Weekly*, 3.9 (1928), p. 6.
33   Hu Shi, "*Wei xuesheng yundong jin yiyan*" 為學生運動進一言 (An advice to the student movement), *HSQJ*, 22: 412.

how students should concentrate on study. In his essay on the December 9 movement, he gave four reasons why boycotting classes was the most useless and ill-advised tactic: first, the only legitimate goal for the students is to make their voices heard, but not direct action; second, students should abide by the law and not transgress it; third, students should cultivate independent thinking and not be led by others by the nose; fourth, students should know their task is to acquire knowledge and skills for future service to the nation.[34]

Throughout his life, Hu Shi loved to quote Henrik Ibsen's (1828–1906) two lines to Georg Brandes (1842–1927): "There is no way in which you can benefit society more than by coining the metal you have in yourself ... There are actually moments when the whole history of the world appears to me like one great shipwreck, and the only important thing seems to be to save one's self." (真正的個人主義在於把你自己這塊材料鑄造成個東西 ... 有時候我覺得這個世界就好像大海上翻了船, 最要緊的是救出我自己.) He would eventually conflate these two lines of Ibsen's and turn Ibsen, whom he characterized as an anarchist, into a nationalist: "Ibsen's 'genuine, full-blooded egoism' is the one and only road to nationalism." (易卜生說的 "真正的個人主義" 正是到國家主義的唯一大路).[35]

In his essay on the December 9, 1935, movement, for the first time Hu Shi assigned a very limited function for students to play politically:

> Under an abnormal political situation, the bare-fisted student movement can only have one objective, that is, to use the voice of protest to monitor or remonstrate with the government. Such a voice represents the public opinion and an expression of public will. If a protest is held appropriately, it can be effective and will make an amenable government readjust itself, and an unamenable one fearful. Once they recognize this, they will understand that any direct action that transgresses the boundary of such a protest (the function of public opinion) should not be the proper objective of a student movement.

---

34 Hu Shi, "*Wei xuesheng yundong jin yiyan*" (A word to student movement), *HSQJ*, 22: 413–414.
35 Hu Shi, "*Aiguo yundong yu qiuxue* 愛國運動與求學 (Patriotism and studying)," *HSQJ*, 3: 823. Hu Shi's paraphrase of Ibsen's words derived from Ibsen's letter to George Brandes (1842–1927): "There is no way in which you can benefit society more than by coining the metal you have in yourself.... There are actually moments when the whole history of the world appears to me like one great shipwreck, and the only important thing seems to be to save one's self." See "Henrik Ibsen to George Brandes" (September 24, 1871), *The Correspondence of Henrik Ibsen*, 218.

在這樣的變態政治之下，赤手空拳的，學生運動只能有一個目標，就是用抗議的喊聲來監督或糾正政府的措施。他們的喊聲是輿論，是民意的一種表現。用在適當的時機，這種抗議是有力量的，可以使愛好的政府改過遷善，可以使不愛好的政府有所畏懼。認清了這一點，他們就可以明白一切超過這種抗議(輿論作用)的直接行動，都不是學生集團運動的目標。[36]

Hu Shi served as Chiang Kai-shek's ambassador to Washington from 1938 to 1942. After he was relieved from ambassadorship, he resided in New York until he accepted the presidency of Peking University in 1946. Hu now threw himself completely behind Chiang Kai-shek. In 1947, Chiang pressured him to join the Council of National Government, the highest government organ of the nation. Hu knew that Chiang was only using him to win the support of George Marshall (1880–1959), who had become the U.S. Secretary of State upon his return from the failed mission to avert the civil war between the Nationalist Party and the Communists. As Hu told Fu Sinian 傅斯年 (1896–1950), his long-time comrade and confidant, that he and three others appointed to the Council were "the so-called 'Chinese liberals' in Marshall's eye ... and were all sham tokens to show the Americans. For me personally, it offers no benefit, but great harm; for the country, it serves as a sham token, but nothing else." (馬歇爾心目中所謂"中國自由主義者"也 ... 皆是對美國人的幌子 ... 此事於我個人絕無益而有大損失，於國家除了 "充幌子" 之外亦無其他用處).[37] It was only after Fu strenuously opposed it did he decline Chiang's summons.

When Hu was serving as Chiang's ambassador in Washington, he loved to liken himself figuratively to the "soldier" (equivalent of the "pawn" in the Western board game) in the Chinese chess by saying that "having crossed the river (過河卒子), he can only push ahead." Upon his return to China in 1946, the "soldier" had literally turned into Chiang Kai-shek's pawn.

3   Hu Shi's Interpretation of the May Fourth Movement after 1949

After the Communists won the civil war, Hu Shi would never again say that an abnormal political situation would necessarily beget student movements. After 1949, he saw the Russian conspiracy in all demonstrations since the mid-1920s. For example, in "China in Stalin's Grand Strategy," he wrote:

---

36   Hu Shi, "*Wei xuesheng yundong jin yiyan*" (A word to student movement), *HSQJ*, 22: 413.
37   Hu Shi to Fu Sinian, 22 March 1947, Wang Fan-sen 王汎森 comp., "*Shiyuso cang Hu Shi yu Fu Sinian laiwang hanzha*" 史語所藏胡適與傅斯年來往函札 (Correspondence between Hu Shi and Fu Sinian deposited at the Institute of History and Philology), *Dalu zazhi*, 93, No. 3, 18–19.

As we now look back, the Nanking incident seems to be the last of a series of deliberate anti-foreign moves designed to force the foreign Powers to resort to armed intervention and thereby to create a situation of a real "imperialist war"—which, we must remember, Stalin and the Comintern regard as the necessary "objective condition" for the victory of the revolution.[38]

It was British restraint and Chiang Kai-shek's prescience that foiled the Russian plots in instigating the anti-British strikes and boycotts in the aftermath of the May Thirtieth Massacre of 1925 and the anti-foreign riot in 1927 when the Northern Expedition army reached Nanjing. Hu lamented that the purge of 1927 averted an imminent Communist revolution, but did not eliminate the root cause of the scourge. The Chinese Communists under the aegis of the Russians continued to instigate various demonstrations, particularly student demonstrations, to undermine the government. In order to save the remnant Red Army after the Long March from being exterminated by Chiang Kai-shek, Stalin ushered in a new "United Front" policy to force the government to turn its attention to Japan:

Under this new party line, the Chinese Communist Party was organizing all kinds of front organizations such as "The Association for National Salvation and Resistance to Japan," "The People's United Association against Japan," and so on. These associations were carrying on antigovernmental agitation under the cloak of anti-Japanism.... Throughout the winter of 1935–36, student strikes and student demonstrations broke out in Peiping and other metropolitan centers of education. Hundreds and even thousands of young students, boys and girls, would often block railway transportation by lying down on railway tracks and demanding free passage to Nanking to petition the Government to fight Japan.[39]

Hu Shi acknowledged that the sinister use of students as agents to subvert the government was only a tiny part of the larger strategy that he attributed to Stalin, an analysis of which lies beyond the scope of this essay. According to Hu, the victory of Communism in China in 1949, far from being a result of the collapse of a corrupt and authoritarian regime led by Chiang, which Hu refuted vigorously, was a major victory of Stalin's global strategy of world conquest. Hu would spend the rest of his life advocating a counter global strategy

---

38   Hu Shih, "China in Stalin's Grand Strategy," *Foreign Affairs* 29.1 (October 1950): 19.
39   Hu Shih, "China in Stalin's Grand Strategy," *Foreign Affairs* 29.1 (October 1950): 19–20, 27.

under U.S. leadership that would not only help Chiang Kai-shek reconquer China, but also liberate the Russian people under the yoke of Communism.[40]

Just as the fervent Cold warrior was busy assigning historical culpability for the loss of China and in advocating his own global anti-Communist strategy, he discovered to his dismay that he was in danger of losing altogether his claim on the "correct" interpretation of May Fourth Movement, together with his own legacy in it.

As Vera Schwarcz pointed out, the legacy of the May Fourth Movement had not only been appropriated by the Communists and the KMT, it had also been reclaimed by its participants as well as adherents. In fact, the legacy of this movement was reinvoked time and again in various social and political contexts and hence constituted a kind of collective memory for the Chinese.[41] Schwarcz errs, however, in asserting that the movement was defined narrowly by Hu Shi as a language Renaissance.[42] Hu himself made it clear in his memoir, "Dr. Hu Shih's Personal Reminiscences" (hereafter: "Reminiscences"), that the "linguistic reform was only the earlier, more important, and probably more successful aspect of a larger cultural movement".[43]

That Schwarcz should err in misattributing a narrow definition of the May Fourth Movement to Hu is understandable, for Hu in his old age was extremely wary of revealing his political alignment with Chiang Kai-shek. Tong Te-kong 唐德剛 (1920–2009), the collaborator for Hu's "Reminiscences," put it bluntly that "there is nothing that is new in his 'Reminiscences'."[44] Take for example Hu's characterization of the May Fourth Movement. The four-fold meaning of the movement that he articulated in his "Reminiscences" was simply a recapitulation of what he said in 1919.[45] Even when he expressed his lament about how the May Fourth project was derailed by political movement, his comments were laconic at best: "From the point of view of the cultural movement which we call the Chinese Renaissance, the May 4th Movement of 1919 ... was

---

40 For detailed analyses of Hu's Stalinisque strategy, see my *Shewo qishei: Hu Shi, Disibu: Guoshi ceshi*.

41 Schwarcz, *The Chinese Enlightenment: Intellectuals and the Legacy of the May Fourth Movement of 1919* (Berkeley: University of California Press, 1986), 240–282.

42 Schwarcz, *The Chinese Enlightenment*, 257, 267.

43 "Dr. Hu Shih's Personal Reminiscences," 177.

44 Tong Te-kong 唐德剛, "*Hu Shi koushu zizhuan: xiezai shuqian de yihougan*" 胡適口述自傳: 寫在書前的譯後感 (Preface to the Chinese translation of Hu Shih's personal reminiscences), *HSQJ*, 18:135.

45 Some of Hu Shi's earlier definitions of the May Fourth Movement include the transvaluation of traditional values, the introduction of Western theories and ideas, and a systematic study of China's cultural heritage.

really an historical interruption and obstacle which cut into the whole cultural movement and converted it into a political movement."[46]

This memoir, however, still does not represent Hu Shi's final view on the May Fourth Movement. There are in his archives two sets of manuscript fragments, one in Chinese and the other in English, in which he disclosed his more candid thoughts on the legacy of the May Fourth Movement. These documents were written in 1955 and were delivered as lectures to the Chinese and American audiences in the United States in 1956. They constituted his response to the massive anti-Hu Shi campaign launched by the Communist regime in 1954–55. Of these two versions, the English version is more candid and incisive, for he knew that these documents will be less likely read by the Chinese readers. To date only the Chinese version has been published and posthumously.[47]

Hu Shi probably would not have stated his claim on the May Fourth Movement as forcefully as he did if the Communist regime had not launched a ferocious campaign against him:

> After carefully analyzing the vast amount of documents related to the whole comico-tragedy of the persecution of Yü P'ing-po and the ghost of Hu Shih, and the purge and liquidation of Hu Feng and his friends, I cannot help interpreting the whole affair as a struggle on the part of the Chinese Communist dictatorship to overcome and destroy the strong power of resistance which the Chinese Renaissance of the last four decades has built up and had left behind.[48]

That the Communists had won the civil war was a fact that Hu Shi could never accept. With the anti-Hu Shi campaign, he was convinced that the Communists had sought to obliterate his legacy in this movement. He declared that the legacy of the movement was hijacked by the Communists; Mao Zedong had stolen it as early as 1940 when he pronounced: "The May Fourth Movement came into being at the call of the world revolution, of the Russian Revolution

---

46   "Dr. Hu Shih's Personal Reminiscences," 188.
47   See Hu Shi, "Sishinianlai Zhongguo wenyifuxing yundong liuxia de kangbao xiaodu liliang—Zhongguo gongchandang qingsuan Hu Shi sixiang de lishi yiyi" 四十年來中國文藝復興運動留下的抗暴消毒力量—中國共產黨清算胡適思想的歷史意義 (The power of resistance to violent repression and of antivenin bequeathed by the Chinese Renaissance of the past forty years—The historical significance of the campaign against Hu Shi's thought launched by the Chinese communist party), *Hu Shi Manuscripts* (Taipei: the Hu Shih Memorial, 1970), 9: 489–512, 513–519, 520–544, 545–557.
48   Hu Shi, "Untitled manuscript fragment," the Hu Shi Archives, HS-US01-039-010, the Hu Shih Memorial, Taipei, Taiwan.

and of Lenin. It was part of the world proletarian revolution of the time" (五四運動是在當時世界革命號召之下, 是在俄國革命號召之下, 是在列寧號召之下發生的. 五四運動是當時無產階級世界革命的一部分).[49]

> The New Literature Movement, or the Literary Revolution or Renaissance, was started among my friends in the American universities as early as 1915–1916, long before the Bolshevik Revolution of 1917—and its first statements of principles by Hu Shih and Ch'en Tu-hsiu were published in January and February of 1917, respectively—also before the Bolshevik Revolution.[50]

In addition, far from being inspired by the Bolshevik Revolution, the May Fourth Movement was originally a political protest led by students that facilitated the rise of the vernacular movement:

> [It] was a student movement—in protest to the Paris Peace Conference's yielding to Japan's demands on the question of former German possessions in Shantung—led by the Peking students and responded to by students and teachers and chambers of commerce in many other cities. The student movement of 1919 has often been regarded as a political expression of the Literary Renaissance, and, in fact, has given a tremendous impetus to the spread of the use of the spoken tongue (*pai-hua*) in writing and publication.... In that sense, the May 4th student movement helped to place the New Literature movement on a nationwide scale, and thereby gave it a political tint.[51]

In order to disassociate the link between the May Fourth Movement and the Bolshevik revolution, Hu Shi traced the origin of the movement to the late Qing reformers, calling them the pioneers of the Chinese Renaissance in the modern era:

> The generation of the Reformers of 1898 dreamed vaguely of Science and Democracy, of which they knew little. Their political reforms disappeared

---

49 Mao Zedong, "On New Democracy," *Selected Works of Mao Tse-tung* (Peking: Foreign Languages Press, 1965), 2: 373.
50 Hu Shi, "untitled manuscript fragment," n.p., the Hu Shi Archives, HS-US01-110-007, the Hu Shih Memorial.
51 Hu Shi, "untitled manuscript fragment," the Hu Shi Archives, HS-US01-110-007.

in a "hundred days." Even their intellectual achievements did not last long. But they left something of more permanent value, namely, a spirit of doubt and free thinking. T'an Ssu-t'ung practically doubted every institution of the old tradition. K'ang Yu-wei, in his young and most creative days, cast doubt and suspicion on nearly all the major scriptures of the Confucian Canon. Liang Ch'i-ch'ao set the example of free thought and intellectual tolerance by his historical studies and by his warm and sincere admiration of the modern Western civilization, and, in particular, the virtues of the Victorian Age.[52]

This was not the first time that Hu invoked the term, "the Victorian Age," to characterize the ethos of modern China. In his diary dated December 22, 1933, he wrote:

> If we want to periodize the development of modern Chinese thought, I think we can see two periods:
> 1, The Victorian Age: from Liang Qichao to the *New Youth*, emphasizing the emancipation of the individual;
> 2, The Age of Collectivism: All the ethos since 1923 exhibited an anti-individualistic tendency, whether the nationalist or the Communist movement.
>
> [中國現代思想] 如必須劃分, 我想可分兩期: 一、維多利亞思想時代, 從梁任公到《新青年》, 多是側重個人的解放; 二、集團主義時代, 1923年以後, 無論為民族主義運動, 或共產革命運動, 皆屬於這個反個人主義的傾向.[53]

Hu Shi touted this individualism of modern China's Victorian Age in glowing terms in an earlier piece written in 1930:

> This individualistic philosophy of life teaches us to learn from [Ibsen's] Nora by coining the metal we have in ourselves, and to learn from Dr. Stockmann in being independent, daring to speak the truth, and staring down the evil forces in society. Young friends! Do not laugh at this as a fossilized idea of the Victorian Age of the 19th-Century! We are still far from reaching the stage of the Victorian Age. The civilized world we have today is indebted to the individualism of the 18th and 19th centuries in

---

52 Hu Shi, "untitled manuscript fragment," the Hu Shi Archives, HS-US01-110-007.
53 Hu Shi, diary entry of 22 December 1933, *Hu Shi riji quanji*, 6:730.

Europe that produced countless indomitable and independent souls who treasured freedom more than bread and loved truth more than life.

這個個人主義的人生觀一面教我們學娜拉，要努力把自己鑄造成個人；一面教我們學斯鐸曼醫生，要特立獨行，敢說老實話，敢向惡勢力作戰. 少年的朋友們，不要笑這是十九世紀維多利亞時代的陳腐思想！我們去維多利亞時代還老遠哩. 歐洲有了十八九世紀的個人主義，造出了無數愛自由過於麵包、愛真理過於生命的特立獨行之士，方才有今日的文明世界.[54]

In his old age seeing the Communists bent on obliterating his legacy in the May Fourth Movement, Hu Shi reached further back in the Chinese tradition to find parallels to the individualism in the Victorian Age in the West. He evoked Mencius, Wang Yangming, and even Zhuangzi, whom he otherwise loathed. For example, he cited Mencius's famous sayings such as: "The nature of man is good," "All things are complete within one's self," and "The great man is he who is 'not tempted by honor and riches, nor budged by poverty or lowliness, nor bent by power and authority.'" He also cited Wang Yangming's claim that "Every man has his own moral conscience, which is his own measure of judgment and which sees right to be right, and wrong to be wrong"; and from Zhuangzi: "Even if the whole world praises me, I am not for that reason more persuaded. Even if the whole world condemns me, I am not for that reason more dissuaded". He then drew the conclusion:

> It is that fighting individualistic tradition of China which has made the Chinese intellectuals warmly welcome the new individualism of John Stuart Mill, Henrik Ibsen, John Morley, and John Dewey. The Chinese intellectuals read Mencius and Chuang Tzu out of the fighting character of Dr. Stockmann in "An Enemy of the People," which declares: "The strongest man in the world is he who stands alone."[55]

Hu Shi not only traced the origin of the May Fourth Movement to the late Qing period, but also regarded it as an on-going project. He claimed that the ideological campaign directed against him was "a struggle on the part of the Chinese Communist dictatorship to overcome and destroy the strong

---

54 Hu Shi, *"Jieshao wo ziji de sixiang"* 介紹我自己的思想 (Introducing my own thought), HSQJ, 4:663.
55 Hu Shi, "untitled manuscript fragment," n.p., the Hu Shi Archives, HS-US01-039-010.

power of resistance which the Chinese Renaissance of the last four decades has built up and has left behind."[56]

In other words, even though political movements to the left and the right had increasingly constricted the space for freedom and individualism, the spirit of the May Fourth Movement lived on:

> The narrow nationalism of the Kuomintang did not succeed in killing that power of resistance. A decade of devastating and impoverishing war did not kill it. And decades of dogmatic Marxism-Leninism and six years of ruthless Communist totalitarian rule are now clearly meeting strong resistance in the spirit of reason, of doubt, of free and critical thinking.[57]

Notwithstanding his feisty language, Hu knew he was fighting a losing battle. What irked him the most was that some scholars in the West had followed the Communist periodization of the May Fourth Movement:

> Superficial Sinologists like Professor [sic] John K. Fairbank and Ssu-yü Teng assigned to the Chinese Renaissance (which they, following the usage of the Communists, called "The May Fourth Movement"!) only the years 1912–1923 as its period of life and activities. As a matter of record, the Chinese Renaissance has been going all these decades in spite of what they term as "the impact of Marxism-Leninism on Chinese Thought and politics."
> TENG AND FAIRBANK, [*China's Response to the West*], pp. 231–276[58]

No one was more vigilant in safeguarding the legacy of the May Fourth Movement than Hu Shi himself. As he was the most celebrated leader of this movement, the Communist regime launched a massive anti-Hu Shi campaign to purge his influences in the mid-1950s. A case can be made that Hu may have won the war after all, even if only posthumously. The argument he presented in 1933 and reiterated in 1955 that the May Fourth Movement commenced in the late Qing anticipated similar argument made by China scholars in the past forty years.[59]

---

56 Hu Shi, "untitled manuscript fragment," n.p., the Hu Shi Archives, HS-US01-039-010.
57 Hu Shi, "untitled manuscript fragment," n.p., the Hu Shi Archives, HS-US01-110-007.
58 Hu Shi, "untitled manuscript fragment," the Hu Shi Archives, HS-US01-039-010.
59 See, for example, Hao Chang, *Liang Ch'i-ch'ao and Intellectual Transition in China, 1890–1907* (Cambridge, MA: Harvard University Press, 1971), 296–307 and David Der-wei Wang, *Fin-de-siècle Splendor: Repressed Modernities of Late Qing Fiction, 1849–1911* (Stanford, CA: Stanford University Press, 1997), 1–9.

Notwithstanding Hu Shi's injunction that we understand correctly the meaning of the May Fourth Movement, he offered multiple and contrary versions of it throughout his life, each of which reflected his assessment of China in the global historical context at the time. At his most optimistic in the early 1920s after the victory in the "Debate on Science and the Philosophy of Life," he waxed lyrical about how China was poised to overtake the West in humanity's march toward a worldview informed by science. Most dramatic was his turn to the right in 1926 in England, when he applauded the incorporation of the May Fourth Movement into the KMT party organization under the tutelage of the Soviet Union and the Third International. The triumph of the Chinese Communists and the ensuing Cold War impelled him to shift yet again. In this last attempt to get history right, he refused to accept the Chinese Communist Party's conflation of the May Fourth Movement with the New Culture Movement, thereby allowing it to claim its leadership role in it. Hu Shi, however, had completely delinked these two movements. In this last iteration in his life, the May Fourth Movement no longer constituted the third stage of the New Culture Movement that culminated in its incorporation into the Leninist organization of the KMT, as he eulogized in 1926. Instead, it amounted to a tragic interruption, as he lamented in his "Reminiscences," that politicized and sidetracked the cultural mission of an intellectual movement that he insisted on calling the "Chinese Renaissance."

It is true that Hu differed from recent revisionist scholarship in that what he celebrated was a triumphant May Fourth discourse. It was at the same time unabashedly Eurocentric, as manifested in his characterization of the whole period as China's "Victorian Age" and in his penchant to use the trajectory of Western history as the yardstick to measure China's development.[60] He was nevertheless true to his conviction that what happened in the May Fourth represented China's joining the ranks at the most opportune moment just as the modern West was marching toward the blessed new world of science and democracy.

---

60 For more examples, see my *Shewo qishei: Hu Shi, Disanbu: Weixue lunzheng, 1927–1932*, 548–549.

Bibliography

Chang, Hao. *Liang Ch'i-ch'ao and Intellectual Transition in China, 1890–1907*. Cambridge, MA: Harvard University Press, 1971.

Chiang, Yung-chen 江勇振. *Shewo qishei: Hu Shi, Di'erbu: Rizheng dangzhong, 1917–1927* 舍我其誰: 胡適, 第二部, 日正當中 1917–1927 [The Titan: Hu Shi, Vol. 2: The Midday Sun, 1917–1927]. Taipei: Linking Publishing Company, 2013; Hangzhou: Zhejiang People's Press, 2013.

Chiang, Yung-chen 江勇振. *Shewo qishei: Hu Shi, Disanbu: Weixue lunzheng, 1927–1932* 舍我其誰: 胡適, 第三部: 為學論政, 1927–1932 [The Titan: Hu Shi, Vol. 3: The Public Intellectual, 1927–1932]. Taipei: Linking Publishing Company, 2018.

Chiang, Yung-chen 江勇振. *Shewo qishei: Hu Shi, Disibu: Guoshi ceshi, 1932–1962* 舍我其誰: 胡適, 第四部: 國師策士, 1932–1962 [The Titan: Hu Shi, Vol. 4: The Cold Warrior, 1932–1962]. Taipei: Linking Publishing Company, 2018.

Chou, Ming-chih. *Hu Shih and Intellectual Choice in Modern China*. Ann Arbor: University of Michigan Press, 1984.

Furth, Charlotte. *Ting Wen-Chiang: Science and China's New Culture*. Cambridge, MA: Harvard University Press, 1970.

Furth, Charlotte. "May Fourth in History." In *Reflections on the May Fourth Movement: A Symposium*, ed. Benjamin Schwartz, 59–68. Cambridge, MA: Harvard University Press, 1972.

Grieder, Jerome. *Hu Shih and the Chinese Renaissance*. Cambridge, Mass.: Harvard University Press, 1970.

Hu Shi 胡適. *Hu Shi quanji* 胡適全集. Anhui: Anhui jiaoyu chubanshe, 2003.

Hu Shi 胡適. *Hu Shi riji quanji* 胡適日記全集. Taipei: Linking Publishing Company, 2004.

Hu Shi 胡適. Letter to Lewis Gannett, 17 May 1927, Lewis Gannett Papers, 1900–1965 (bulk), MS Am 1888 (586), Houghton Library, Harvard University.

Hu Shi 胡適. Letter to Fu Sinian, 22 March 1947. In "*Shiyuso cang Hu Shi yu Fu Sinian laiwang hanzha*" 史語所藏胡適與傅斯年來往函札, compiled by Wang Fan-sen, *Dalu zazhi* 93, 3: 1–23.

Hu Shi 胡適. "*Sishinianlai Zhongguo wenyifuxing yundong liuxia de kangbao xiaodu liliang—Zhongguo gongchandang qingsuan Hu Shi sixiang de lishi yiyi*" 四十年來中國文藝復興運動留下的抗暴消毒力量—中國共產黨清算胡適思想的歷史意義. *Hu Shi Manuscripts*. Taipei: Hu Shih Memorial, 1970.

Hu Shi 胡適. Untitled manuscript fragment, HS-US01-110-007, HS-US01-039-010, Hu Shi Archives, the Hu Shih Memorial, Taipei, Taiwan.

Hu Shi 胡適. "*Wusi yundong zhi qianyinhouguo*" 五四運動之前因後果, *Guanghua Weekly*, 3.9 (1928): 2–6.

Ibsen, Henrik. Letter to George Brandes, 24 September 1871. In *The Correspondence of Henrik Ibsen*, trans. and ed. Mary Morison, 217–219. New York: Haskell House Publishers Ltd., 1970.

Kagawa, Toyohiko. "Kagawa and Hu Shih: Interview between Dr. Kagawa and Prof. Hu Shih," August 1927, Kagawa Archives and Resource Center.

Luo Zhitian 羅志田. *Zaizao wenming de changshi: Hu Shi Zhuan, 1891–1929* 再造文明的嘗試: 胡適傳 1891–1929 [The Endeavor to Reconstruct Civilization: A Biography of Hu Shi, 1891–1929]. Beijing: Zhonghua shuju, 2006.

Mao, Tse-tung 毛澤東. "On New Democracy," *Selected Works of Mao Tse-tung*, Vol. 2. Peking: Foreign Languages Press, 1965.

Schwarcz, Vera. *The Chinese Enlightenment: Intellectuals and the Legacy of the May Fourth Movement of 1919*. Berkeley: University of California Press, 1986.

Shao Jian 邵建. *Qiao, Zhe ren: Riji, shuxin, nianpu zhong de Hu Shi (1891–1927)* 瞧, 這人: 日記、書信、年譜中的胡適 (1891–1927) [Ecce Homo: The Hu Shi Appeared in His Diaries, Correspondence, and Autobiographic Sketches, 1891–1927]. Guilin, Guangxi: Guangxi shifadaxue chubanshe, 2007.

Sokolsky, George. Letter to Lewis Gannett, 23 May 1928, Lewis Gannett Papers, 1900–1965 (bulk), MS Am 1888 (586), Houghton Library, Harvard University.

Wang, David Der-wei. *Fin-de-siècle Splendor: Repressed Modernities of Late Qing Fiction, 1849–1911*. Stanford, CA: Stanford University Press, 1997.

CHAPTER 6

Theory and Practice in the May Fourth Period

Shakhar Rahav

> *I think our Study Society should not merely be a gathering of people, bound by sentiment; it must become a group of people bound together by an ism. An ism is like a banner; only when it is raised will the people have something to hope for and know in what direction to go. What do you think?*[1]

∴

Should a cultural movement be studied in terms of its ideas? How else might we approach studies of thinkers and figures that historiography has enshrined for their perceived intellectual influence? The above words written by twenty-seven-year-old Mao Zedong in November 1920 raise thorny questions of the relationship between ideas, ideology, and practice. Moreover, they show how these questions trouble not only researchers in retrospect, but rather that they drove some of the historical actors who are the subject of this research. In this case Mao exhorts his readers, and by extension researchers, to turn to ideology—what he calls here "isms." But to what extent does a cultural movement coalesce around such "isms"? What of the gaps between isms and practice? Are gaps between theory and practice obstacles to success? This paper addresses such questions by examining the relation between ideology and practice in China's May Fourth movement (1915–1923), widely viewed as a cultural and political watershed in China's modern history.

I wish to demonstrate that although May Fourth is largely seen as an intellectual movement, studying the everyday life of May Fourth activists can reveal information about the movement that changes our assessment of its character and significance. I argue, first, that the relationship of theory to practice was a topic of concern in Chinese political discourse during the May Fourth period and beyond. Second, that since activists themselves viewed the relationship of theory to practice as an issue deserving of attention, scholars researching the movement should pay attention to this problematic as well. Consequently,

---

1 Mao Zedong, "Letter to Luo Aojie," in *Mao's Road to Power*, vol. 1 (Armonk: M. E. Sharpe, 1992), 600.

the second half of the article demonstrates this approach by examining the early political career of Yun Daiying (恽代英), an educator, journalist, and activist during the time of May Fourth in central China's most important urban center—Wuhan. Most studies of Yun portray him as an intellectual driven by an interest in anarchism and socialism that made him a prominent activist of the Chinese Communist Party (CCP) in the 1920s, until he was martyred by the Nationalist (Guomindang, GMD) government in 1931. I will try to show how examining practice and daily comportment can reveal unexpected sources of inspiration that belie Yun's image as an ideologically-driven party operative.

I wish to demonstrate that, contrary to the iconoclastic and anti-religious position Yun articulated, Yun's early activism was inspired among other things by a profound attraction to spiritual matters, and was influenced by the techniques, and arguably theology, of Christian missionaries, as well as a traditional neo-Confucian moral ethos. Since May Fourth is associated with a turn toward science and ideology and away from religion, superstition, and Confucian ethics, demonstrating such interests in a prominent figure like Yun suggests that the embrace of foreign ideologies did not necessarily entail a rejection of traditional ways of interpreting the world but rather a reworking of their meaning. Illuminating such sources of inspiration does not negate the importance of ideologies like socialism or anarchism in the political work of Yun and his compatriots, yet it provides a more nuanced understanding of the affective significance of these political ideas for their proponents. In other words, this approach offers insight into the lived meaning of cerebrally articulated ideas.

1   The Historiography of May Fourth

Much of the historiography of May Fourth has been marked by an emphasis on intellectual change and a focus on the emergence of Chinese Communism. To be sure, there is much to justify these approaches, but characterizing the movement mainly in these terms limits our grasp of it. The movement was spear-headed by educated elites—students, teachers, and the intelligentsia—and many of the movement's participants explicitly advocated changing people's consciousness through ventures such as the pioneering of a new literature. These elites conceived of the change they sought as one guided by knowledge, rationality, and intent. This cerebral emphasis was eventually reified by studies of the movement, as evinced by the titles of Chow

Tse-tsung's foundational book *The May Fourth Movement: Intellectual Revolution in Modern China*, or the later study by Vera Schwarcz, *The Chinese Enlightenment*.[2]

The CCP interpretation of the movement as sowing the seeds for the rise of Communism and the party—an interpretation put forth by Mao Zedong himself—contributed to the scholarly emphasis on intellectual change during May Fourth.[3] While this interpretation has come under criticism since the 1990s[4] there is much to support it. For CCP leaders born in the 1890s such as Mao Zedong, Zhou Enlai, and Liu Shaoqi, as well as for their opponents, the May Fourth period was truly a formative time in which they came of age. For many of this generation, intellectual awakening and maturation of personality became intertwined with politics, thus the subsequent narratives they told of personal development and national liberation overlapped.[5] For early Communists the meaning of May Fourth has therefore resided in turning Chinese intellectuals toward Marxism, as was true for themselves. Much of the subsequent historiography written in China under the aegis of the CCP adopted such an interpretation. Correspondingly, post-World War II Anglo-American historiography, shaped by cold-war rivalries, similarly interpreted May Fourth as an intellectual revolution that led to the adoption of Communism in China.[6]

---

2 Chow Tse-tsung, *The May Fourth Movement: Intellectual Revolution in Modern China* (Stanford, CA: Stanford University Press, 1967); Vera Schwarcz, *The Chinese Enlightenment: Intellectuals and the Legacy of the May Fourth Movement of 1919* (University of California Press, 1986).

3 Mao Zedong, "Speech at the Meeting in Yan'an in Commemoration of the Twentieth Anniversary of the May Fourth Movement (May 4, 1939)," in *Mao's Road to Power: Revolutionary Writings 1912–1949* (Armonk, NY: M. E. Sharpe, 2005) 7: 69–79.

4 See, e.g.: Milena Doleželová-Velingerová and Oldřich Král, *The Appropriation of Cultural Capital: China's May Fourth Project* (Cambridge, MA: Harvard University Press, 2001); Kai-Wing Chow et al., eds., *Beyond the May Fourth Paradigm: In Search of Chinese Modernity* (Lanham, MD: Lexington Books, 2008).

5 For the application of generational theory developed by sociologist Karl Mannheim to the case of May Fourth, see Schwarcz, *The Chinese Enlightenment*, 23–28.

6 Seminal works of the 1950s and 1960s that shaped much of the subsequent scholarship are Joseph R. Levenson, *Confucian China and Its Modern Fate: A Trilogy*, 3 vols. (Berkeley: University of California Press, 1968); Maurice Meisner, *Li Ta-Chao and the Origins of Chinese Marxism* (New York: Atheneum, 1974); Benjamin Schwartz, *Chinese Communism and the Rise of Mao* (Cambridge, MA: Harvard University Press, 1958).

In this essay I hope to demonstrate the way in which examining the everyday practices of individuals—in this case Yun Daiying—can shed new light on a movement such as May Fourth, taken to be primarily an intellectual movement.[7] I begin by arguing that the relationship of ideas with practice, knowing to doing, was important to May Fourth activists.

2 *Theoria* and *Praxis*: Knowing and Doing

The relationship of theory to practice is the subject of discussion in different intellectual traditions. In China, the relationship between action and knowing has been a long-standing theme harking back to the *Book of History* (尚書 Shang shu), which states "It is not the knowing that is difficult, but the doing" (非知之艱, 行之惟艱).[8] This relationship is seen as constituting the essence of the *Doctrine of the Mean* 中庸 (which one translator has consequently rendered as *The Practice of the Mean*).[9] The Ming dynasty philosopher Wang Yangming 王陽明 discussed at length the relationship between knowing and doing and argued for a "unity of knowledge and action" (知行合一).[10] Indeed, one might read Confucian classics such as the *Analects* or *Mencius* as entirely preoccupied with questions of personal conduct and social relations that are by necessity questions of practice rather than theory. Given that these books

---

[7] Since the 1990s histories of the early republican era have grown in sophistication, analyzing institutions, political culture, the construction of knowledge, and aspects of everyday life. E.g.: Wen-hsin Yeh, *Provincial Passages: Culture, Space, and the Origins of Chinese Communism* (Berkeley: University of California Press, 1996); Henrietta Harrison, *The Making of the Republican Citizen: Political Ceremonies and Symbols in China 1911–1929* (Oxford, 2000); John Fitzgerald, *Awakening China: Politics, Culture, and Class in the Nationalist Revolution* (Stanford: Stanford University Press, 1996); Timothy Weston, *The Power of Position: Beijing University, Intellectuals and Chinese Political Culture, 1898–1929* (Berkeley: University of California Press, 2004); Fabio Lanza, *Behind the Gate: Inventing Students in Beijing* (New York: Columbia University Press, 2010). Recent studies of the People's Republic of China similarly explore the Maoist years not by means of political statements but as experienced by citizens, see e.g. Gail Hershatter, *The Gender of Memory: Rural Women and China's Collective Past* (Berkeley: University of California Press, 2011); Jeremy Brown and Matthew D. Johnson, eds., *Maoism at the Grassroots: Everyday Life in China's Era of High Socialism* (Cambridge, MA: Harvard University Press, 2015).

[8] "*Shang Shu* (Book of documents)," Chinese Text Project, n.d., http://ctext.org/shang-shu/charge-to-yue-ii.

[9] Andrew Plaks, trans., *Ta Hsueh and Chung Yung* (The highest order of cultivation and the practice of the mean) (London: Penguin, 2003). For a discussion of these two books and of their place in Chinese culture see the translator's introduction.

[10] Wing-tsit Chan, *A Source Book in Chinese Philosophy* (Princeton, NJ: Princeton University Press, 1963), 558–559, 657–657, 668–671.

were at the core of literate education at least until the early twentieth century, their influence cannot be overestimated.

The tension between theory and practice troubled thinkers in the European tradition as well. The Greek term *praxis*—often taken to mean theoretically-informed doing—has been the subject of discussion since Aristotle, who distinguished *praxis* from *theoria*—knowledge for the sake of knowledge.[11] In modern political thought Marx called attention to the difference between theory and action, arguing, "Social life is essentially *practical*" and that "The philosophers have only *interpreted* the world, in various ways; the point, however, is to *change* it."[12] Subsequently, theorists and scholars influenced by the German philosophical tradition and Marx in particular have often used the concepts of "theory" and "praxis" as tools of analysis. Lenin (following Engels) emphasized the importance of a correct balance between theory and practice stating that "Without revolutionary theory there can be no revolutionary movement."[13]

The relationship of knowledge to action might be seen as a theoretical problem but at a time of national crisis it assumed a concrete urgency. In the first decade of the twentieth century the weakening Qing dynasty attempted to prop up its rule by adopting radical reforms that had far-reaching implications for the occupations and livelihoods of the educated elites and growing urban classes. Questions of what type of knowledge might provide livelihood in a rapidly changing environment were not theoretical, but deeply personal, at the same time as they concerned what direction the entire nation might take. These questions yet more pressing after the demise of the Qing and the foundation of the Republic in 1912. In this context, political activists and intellectuals reflected once more on the relationship of knowledge and action. Thus, the revolutionary leader Sun Yat-sen resorted to earlier formulations of the relationship of theory and practice, and argued that, although knowing is difficult, action is easy (知難行易). Sun wished to convince his audience that "China's lack of strength was not because our people could not act but because they lacked knowledge." In one speech Sun exhorted his countrymen to "happily take action without fear." Sun began his speech stressing the importance of knowledge; he then however proceeded to argue that even "without knowledge one can still act" for "human progress originates in men not knowing and yet

---

11 Richard J. Bernstein, *Praxis and Action* (University of Pennsylvania Press, 2011); Stephen G. Salkever, *Finding the Mean: Theory and Practice in Aristotelian Political Philosophy* (Princeton: Princeton University Press, 1990).
12 Richard J. Bernstein, *Praxis and Action*, 2011; Stephen G. Salkever, *Finding the Mean*; Karl Marx, "Theses on Feuerbach," in *The Marx–Engels Reader* 2nd ed. (New York: Norton, 1978), 144–145. Original emphasis.
13 Vladimir Ilych Lenin, *The Lenin Anthology*, ed. Robert C. Tucker (New York: Norton, 1975).

acting." Wishing to recruit support, Sun was thereby arguing that experimentation and trial and error—as was the case with some of his policies—were necessary to lead the nation forward.[14]

Sun's formulation was adopted by his successor as leader of the Nationalist party (Guomindang), Chiang Kai-shek, who even named his quasi-military political organization the Society for Vigorous Practice (*Lixingshe* 力行社).[15] Chiang's application of the phrase became the subject of criticism and debate by such intellectuals as Hu Shi and Lu Xun who wrote essays with titles such as "To Know Is Difficult, To Act Is Difficult" (知難行難).[16] The terms "knowledge" and "practice" persevered therefore as categories of thought that shaped political and cultural discourse.

3   Theory and Practice among May Fourth Activists

Sun Yat-Sen's concern with the tension between knowledge and action was shared by activist youths. In the wake of the 1911 revolution schools and education emphasized new practices meant to embody new ideals. At Zhejiang First Normal School, for instance, the principal considered the school a site where the new society would first be realized, and the original emphasis was that students strive to live up to the motto of the school: diligence, prudence, sincerity, forbearance, and composure.[17] At Hunan First Normal, whose students between from 1914 to 1918 included Mao Zedong, the statement of school goals emphasized "real practice" and called for teaching students to investigate social realities and seek truth from facts.[18]

Educator Tao Xingzhi 陶行知 (1891–1946) attributed such importance to the relationship of thought and action that he twice changed his name in accordance with it. Named at birth Wenjun, in 1913 he changed his name to Zhixing 知行—knowledge and action—in order to inscribe his very identity with Wang

---

14   Speech given December 3, 1918. Yat-sen Sun, *Prescriptions for Saving China: Selected Writings of Sun Yat-Sen*, ed. Julie Lee Wei, Ramon H. Myers, and Donald G. Gillin (Stanford, CA: Hoover Institution Press, 1994). The quotations are taken from pp. 200 and 215. See also Antonio S. Cua, ed., *Encyclopedia of Chinese Philosophy* (Routledge, 2002), 50.
15   Frederic Wakeman, "A Revisionist View of the Nanjing Decade: Confucian Fascism," *The China Quarterly*, no. 150 (June 1997): 395–432.
16   Lu Xun 魯迅, "Zhi Nan Xing Nan" 知難行難 (To know is difficult, to act is difficult) in *Lu Xun Xuanji* 魯迅選集 (Selected works of Lu Xun) 4 vols. (Beijing: Renmin wenxue chubanshe, 1992), vol. 3: 103–105.
17   Yeh, *Provincial Passages*, 87–88.
18   Cited in Liyan Liu, *Red Genesis: The Hunan Normal School and the Creation of Chinese Communism, 1903–1921* (Albany: State University of New York Press, 2012), 46.

Yangming's view of the unity of thought and action. In the following decade, Tao altered the sequence of the words in his name to Xingzhi 行知—action and knowledge—to reflect the primacy he now gave to action and scientific, empirical knowledge.[19]

The tension between knowing and doing, speech and deed, marked the relationship of Wuhan educator and activist Yun Daiying (1895–1931) with Wang Guangqi 王光祈 (1892–1936), who was a co-founder of the Young China Association 少年中國學會. Initially Yun was attracted to the Association because of its emphasis on practice. "I very much like reading *New Youth* and *New Tide* because they spread the gospel of liberty, equality, universal love, mutual aid, and labor. But I enjoy even better reading your association's reports, for you diligently practice what you preach." (我很喜歡看見《新青年》,《新潮》, 因為他們是傳播自由, 平等, 博愛, 互助, 勞動 的福音. 但是我更喜歡看見你們的會務報告, 因為你們是身體力行的). This was a point that Yun referred to throughout the letter. "I believe that so long as one puts into practice the truths of liberty, equality, universal love, labor, and mutual aid one by one, makes an effort to do so oneself, but not to make others do so, others will then naturally be moved, society will naturally change ..." (我信只要自己將自由, 平等, 博愛, 勞動, 互助的真理, 一一實踐起來, 勉強自己摸勉強人家, 自然人家要感動的, 自然社會要改變的) and concluded the letter saying, "An advocate of new thought who diligently practices can stand his ground against ten thousand Confucians. As things stand, if we wish to triumph we have no other way but to diligently practice what we preach." (一個身體力行的新思想家, 亦可以抵得住一萬個只知說話的空教徒).[20]

An impulse to address the relationship between theory and practice was at the heart of the Work Study Mutual Aid Corps (*gongdu huzhu tuan* 工讀互助團)—small egalitarian communes that Wang Guangqi had initiated, whose members were to study and support themselves by labor. The corps was viewed as a way to realize an ideal. As Wang wrote: "If the Work Study Mutual Aid Corps is as successful as we expect, and gradually expands, our ideal of 'from each according to his ability and to each according to his need' will gradually

---

19 Yusheng Yao, "Rediscovering Tao Xingzhi as an Educational and Social Revolutionary," *Twentieth-Century China* 27, no. 2 (2002): 90–91.
20 Yun Daiying, 惲代英 *Yun Daiying Riji* 惲代英日記 (The diary of Yun Daiying), ed. Zhongyang danganguan, Zhongguo ge ming bowuguan, Zhonggong zhongyang dangxiao chubanshe (Beijing: Zhongyang danganguan, Zhongguo ge ming bowuguan, Zhonggong zhongyang dangxiao chubanshe, 1981), 624–25.

be realized.'" (若是工讀互助團果然成功, 逐漸推廣, 我們'各盡所能, 各取所需' 的理想漸漸實現).[21]

In the period 1920–1921 several such groups were attempted in China's big cities. Although most of these attempts eventually failed after a short time, the endeavor received wide coverage in the radical periodical press of the time.[22] Much of this attention was due to the way in which the corps attempted to realize an ideal here and now. It was the promise of such realization of ideals that impelled one supporter to write a letter to the progressive newspaper supplement *Awakening* (覺悟) to complain of peers who intended to "realize work-study-ism" (來實行工讀主義). The writer assumed that it was "necessary that name and reality correspond with one another" (必須名實相符) and therefore complained that the members of the Yangzhou group were not living up to their proclaimed ideal of labor (工 *gong*) since their income was based on peddling food. The editor of *Awakening* responded by harking back to Sun Yat-sen's formulation: "The phrase 'knowledge is difficult, doing is easy' has much value" ('知難行易' 的話, 是很有價值的).[23]

Precisely because Yun had earlier been attracted to Wang's implementation of ideals, he was eventually disappointed with Wang's conduct. Wang, who had promoted the corps and pushed for similar ones to be set up across China, never joined it, and according to Yun did not even wish for his friends to join the commune. Moreover, in spring 1920, as the corps was dispersing, Wang left China to study in Europe. Yun accused Wang of behaving like an outsider, and called on Wang to quite simply try to do what he exhorted others to: "I simply hope that you will note that if you wish to organize a work study mutual aid corps you must join it yourself, you cannot merely be an endorser [of the project]" (只盼望你注意組織工讀互助團便要自己加入, 不可只做個發起人).[24]

For activists of this generation who became Communists, practice assumed special importance due to the Marxist emphasis on fostering social change noted above. In a 1937 lecture titled "On Practice" Mao suggested that a correct

---

21   Wang Guangqi 王光祈, "Gongdu Huzhu Tuan," 工讀互助團 (Work study mutual aid corps) *Shaonian Zhongguo* 少年中國 (Young China) 1, no. 7 (January 15, 1920): Reprinted in *Wusi shiqi de shetuan* 五四時期的社團 (Associations of the May Fourth period), 2: 369–372.

22   Shakhar Rahav, "A May Fourth 'Peach Blossom Garden': The Number One Work Study Mutual Aid Corps in Beijing," *Twentieth Century China* 33, no. 1 (2007): 81–103.

23   Zhang Xiaochen 張嘯尘 and Shao Lizi 邵力子, "Yangzhou Di Ba Zhongxue Gongdu Huzhu Tuan" 揚州第八中學工讀互助團 (The eighth high school work study mutual aid corps in Yangzhou) in *Wusi Shiqi de Shetuan* (Beijing: Sanlian, 1979) (4 vols.), 2: 491–492.

24   Yun Daiying, "Zhi Wang Guangqi," 至王光祈 (Letter to Wang Guangqi) in *Yun Daiying Wenji* 惲代英文集 (Collected works of Yun Daiying), (2 vols.) (Beijing: Renmin chubanshe, 1984) 1: 305–315.

understanding of the relationship between knowledge and practice could lead to transcendental ideals of perfection:

> Produce the truth through practice, and again through practice verify and develop the truth.... Practice, knowledge; again practice, and again knowledge. This form develops in endless cycles and with each cycle the content of practice and knowledge rises to a higher level. Such is the whole of the dialectical materials theory of knowledge, and such is the dialectical materials theory of the unity of knowing and doing.[25]

Mao's emphasis on the relationship of theory to practice led him to advocate the "Sinification of Marxism"; "practice" and "sinification" both became key features of the theoretical writings that were later enshrined as Mao Zedong Thought.[26]

Mao's views on the importance of practice were repeated in Liu Shaoqi's tract "How to Be a Good Communist" (1939): "First of all, we must oppose and resolutely eliminate one of the biggest evils bequeathed to us by the education and learning in the old society—the separation of theory from practice." While Mao wrote in conceptual abstractions in order to provide a theoretical basis for social revolution, Liu grounded them in the neo-Confucian practice of self-cultivation, thereby defining the individual as a site of revolutionary struggle. Liu used Marxist-Leninist terminology to argue that "We are materialists, and our cultivation cannot be separated from practice." At the same time Liu referred several times to examples taken from classical texts, such as citing Confucius's disciple Zengzi, who said "I examine myself three times a day."[27] Liu criticized the class-standing of the ancient scholars, but upheld their efforts at self-cultivation and moral conduct. In this way he drew a line of continuity with the past even as he called for revolution. Liu and Mao thus presented theory and practice as complementary—correct views would promote revolution, and correct views were the result of self-cultivation; correct self-cultivation then would lead to social revolution. This view of ideology as a tool shaped by practice and of everyday life as a measure of ideological commitment guided Communist policies in their base areas during the long years

---

25 Mao Zedong, "On Practice," in *Mao's Road to Power* (Armonk, NY: M. E. Sharpe, 2004), 6: 603, 614–615.
26 Stuart R. Schram, "Mao Tse-Tung's Thought to 1949," in *An Intellectual History of Modern China* (Cambridge: Cambridge University Press, 2002), 322; Nick Knight, "Mao Zedong and the 'Sinification of Marxism,'" in *Marxism in Asia* (London and Sydney: Croom Helm, 1985), 83–90.
27 Liu Shaoqi, "How to Be a Good Communist," in *Sources of Chinese Tradition* (2 vols.) (New York: Columbia University Press, 2000), 2: 428.

of war with the Nationalists and the Japanese. It eventually was employed to police the lives of the citizens of the People's Republic of China.

4 Radical Practice between Spirituality and Socialism

If practice, or praxis, was so important for May Fourth activists, might investigating their praxis affect how we see the movement? I tackle this question by focusing on Yun Daiying and members of his social circle. English-language scholarship has for the most part portrayed Yun as a prominent radical in central China during May Fourth and as an important CCP operative in Shanghai during the 1920s. Since most of these studies have taken as their focus the advent of Marxism in China, they emphasize Yun's contribution to the founding of a Communist cell in Wuhan, and his subsequent career in the service of the CCP.[28] Chinese scholars have written more extensively about Yun but the *telos* of their interpretations too is his gravitation toward Marxism and his role in the party politics of the 1920s. In what follows I will show how reading the sources for information about the everyday illuminates Yun Daiying in a different light; it suggests that Yun's political career was impelled by an interest in the sublime, and a desire to manifest it in everyday life.

Such an emphatic attraction to the sublime runs counter to earlier views of May Fourth that associated the movement and modern Chinese nationalism with a turn against religion. Although Christian missionary schools and organizations were important agents for the introduction of modern Western knowledge, one of the hallmarks of modernity that was strongly associated with the newly venerated scientific thought was secularism. Cai Yuanpei, who had served as the republic's first Minister of Education and under whose tenure Beijing University became an influential center of iconoclastic ideas, promoted culture and "aesthetic education" as alternatives to religion.[29] Not all advocates of reform repudiated religion—many Chinese Christians were also activists for social change, and for a short time even Chen Duxiu extolled

---

28 E.g.: Hans J. Van de Ven, *From Friend To Comrade: The Founding of the Chinese Communist Party, 1920–1927* (Berkeley: University of California Press, 1991); Arif Dirlik, *The Origins of Chinese Communism* (Oxford: Oxford University Press, 1989). Recent exceptions are Guo Wu, "From Private Library and Bookstore to Communist Party: Yun Daiying's Social Engagement and Political Transformation, 1917–1921," *Journal of Modern Chinese History* 5, no. 2 (2011): 129–150; Shakhar Rahav, *The Rise of Political Intellectuals in Modern China: May Fourth Societies and the Roots of Mass-Party Politics* (New York: Oxford University Press, 2015).

29 Timothy Weston, *The Power of Position: Beijing University, Intellectuals and Chinese Political Culture, 1898–1929* (Berkeley: University of California Press, 2004), 81–83.

Christian ideals of uplifting the poor—but for the most part reformers were wary of Chinese religion, superstition and folk beliefs, and of Christianity as well.[30] Debates about religion became particularly heated in 1920–1922, giving rise to the formation of an anti-Christian organization, but also led to what some have called an "anti-religious movement." Among many members of the radical intelligentsia, religion, even when tolerated, was not viewed as positive.[31]

What, then, was the role of religion in the case of a radical activist like Yun Daiying? Accounts that portray Yun as a devoted member of the Chinese Communist Party certainly give us cause to believe that he was interested in socialism and anarchism from an early stage.[32] At the same time, as early as 1915, Yun published in his school journal an essay rejecting beliefs in spirits and proclaiming that, thanks to the advancement of knowledge, religion was waning.[33] After joining the Communist Party and becoming part of its propaganda apparatus in the early 1920s, Yun referred to Christianity as "a school of superstitious nonsense" (迷信的一派鬼話) and attacked the YMCA. Yun opposed Christianity in large part due to its association with foreign imperialist powers whose protection it enjoyed, but also because of a skepticism about religious faith itself. Yun did not view Christianity as worse than other religions, but he saw them all rather dismally: "Christianity and other teachings are the same, in that they do not help people cultivate character" (基督教與別的教一樣, 不配使人有人格).[34]

Given these statements, it comes as something of a surprise to discover evidence of active interest in spirituality and religious thought in his earlier years, including in Christianity. Yun's diary indicates that he studied philosophy and read about spiritual matters regularly in 1917–1919. For example, Yun studied Indian philosophy on his own, read an English language publication titled *Young Hindu*, and corresponded extensively with one of his teachers about philosophical subjects, especially about Buddhism. At the same time, Yun's diary suggests that he was familiar with the Christian devotional classic *The Pilgrim's Progress*, to which he alludes. In 1917 Yun also contributed several

30   Germaine A. Hoston, "A 'Theology' of Liberation? Socialist Revolution and Spiritual Regeneration in Chinese and Japanese Marxism," in *Ideas Across Cultures: Essays in Honor of Benjamin I. Schwartz* (Cambridge, MA.: Harvard University Asia Center, 1990), 165–98.
31   Chow, *The May Fourth Movement*, 320–26; Chen Yiyi, "Peking University's Role in China's Anti-Christian Movement in 1922–1927," *Social Sciences in China* 31, no. 1 (February 2010): 184–97, https://doi.org/10.1080/02529200903565160.
32   Yun, *Yun Daiying Riji*, 624.
33   Yun Daiying, "Lun Xinyang," 論信仰 (On faith) in *Yun Daiying Wenji*, vol. 1, 2 vols. (Beijing: Renmin chubanshe, 1984), 44–47.
34   Yun Daiying, "Jidujiao Yu Renge Jiuguo," 基督教與人格救國 (Christianity, personal integerity, and saving the nation) in *Yun Daiying Wenji*, vol. 1, 2 vols., 1984, 371–73.

articles to the YMCA publication *Youthful Progress* (青年進步 Qingnian jinbu). Such was his interest in the missionary enterprise that in the summer of that year Yun and two friends set off from their hometown of Wuchang to attend a camp for young men organized by the YMCA at the resort town of Guling (Kuling) 牯嶺 on Mount Lu (Lushan 廬山)—a site for religious and spiritual reflection for centuries. There they spent over a week attending lectures and taking part in discussions on questions of faith and religious practice. Yun's experience was so favorable that he organized a group to attend the camp the following year as well.[35]

Why did Yun decide to commit time and money to attending a missionary camp? Yun hoped to observe techniques that would help him realize his own goals, which included setting up a youth organization that would contribute to national salvation—this is a point he makes several times in his diary entries. Chinese reformers such as Kang Youwei attributed missionary success in gaining converts to their superior methods of proselytization, but Yun went further than most when he considered applying such methods for cultural and even political change.[36] It was the YMCA camp that provided Yun with the inspiration to establish his first truly successful political-cultural organization, the Mutual Aid Society (互助社). Yun conceived the society during the camp and took the first steps towards its establishment shortly after the camp ended.

Yun, however, was drawn to the camp not solely for such utilitarian purposes. Although Yun states repeatedly in his diary that his interest in the YMCA is purely organizational, and he certainly seems to have emerged from the camp a non-believer, his original interest seems to have contained a spiritual component as well. Yun states as his first reason for attending the camp "examining the true meaning of Christianity."[37] This spiritual interest is suggested by a passage in which Yun describes his climb to the camp in terms that echo the Chinese tradition of mountain ascent as a spiritual experience, the Daoist sage Laozi, and the "Peach Blossom Spring" as a form of paradise; at the same time he invokes the Judeo-Christian name Jehovah:

> While climbing the mountain I thought constantly of Bunyan's *The Pilgrim's Progress*. When we arrived at the middle of the mountain it was like entering paradise (*taoyuan*); such must be the joy of a hermit's life! As the Catholic minister said, Laozi says, "We look at it but do not see,

---

[35] Yun, *Yun Daiying Riji*, 40, 132–141, 258–275.
[36] Y.-p. Kuo, "'Christian Civilization' and the Confucian Church: The Origin of Secularist Politics in Modern China," *Past & Present* 218, no. 1 (February 1, 2013): 235–264.
[37] Yun, *Yun Daiying Riji*, 132.

we name this 'the elusive'; we listen to it but do not hear, we call it 'the rarefied'; we feel for it but cannot grasp it, this is called 'the infinitesimal' (*wei*). Elusive, rarefied, infinitesimal, this is Jehovah."[38]

登山時, 每想及奔楊《天路歷程》一書, 及至山中, 則入 桃源; 隱居之樂 蓋如此夫! 羅馬教牧某言, 老子所雲視之不見, 謂之夷; 聽之不聞, 謂之希; 搏之不得, 謂之微. 希, 夷, 微, 即耶和華也.

Yun, as we saw earlier, was attuned to the tension between theory and practice, knowing and doing. It was for this reason that he was particularly impressed with the daily practices of the missionaries and the ways in which they seemed to combine belief with personal conduct. "I have observed their prayers and the efficacy of their bible-study and have realized the necessity of 'examining oneself three times a day'" (觀彼中祈禱, 查經之效, 而悟一日三省之必要).[39] Yun here expressed his admiration of missionary comportment by citing the same Confucian phrase that Liu Shaoqi later referred to as a guideline for personal conduct for Communists.

Others in Yun's social circles shared his interest in spirituality and the sublime. Yun's friend Huang Fusheng also planned to study Buddhism with Liu Zitong, and one of the friends who attended the YMCA camp with Yun—Liang Shaowen—declared his intention to pray three times a day. Members of Yun's newly formed Mutual Aid Society (互助社 *Huzhushe*) decided to open meetings with a form of meditation (靜坐 *jingzuo*).[40] Meditation was a practice advocated by neo-Confucians as a method of moral improvement but was also associated with Buddhism.

A similar ambiguous relationship to the sublime is evident in the writings of Yun Daiying's friend, Zuo Shunsheng. Like Yun, Zuo went on in the early 1920s to write articles that attacked missionary education and exhibited an antipathy toward religion, and he thus helped start the anti-religious movement of 1920–1922.[41] However, in 1917, at roughly the same time that Yun was attracted to the YMCA, Zuo, in his own words, "was suddenly drawn toward religion and resorted to prayers." As in the case of Yun and many others, Zuo's short-lived

---

38   Yun, 134. For an alternative view of Lushan at that same time, yet one also associated with climbing as spiritual revelation, see Grace S. Fong, "Reconfiguring Time, Space, and Subjectivity: Lu Bicheng's Travel Writing on Mount Lu," in *Different Worlds of Discourse: Transformations of Gender and Genre in Late Qing and Republican China* (Leiden: Brill, 2008), 87–114.
39   Yun, *Yun Daiying Riji*, 139, 142.
40   Yun, 162.
41   Zuo Shunsheng and Julie Lien-ying How, "The Reminiscences of Tso Shun-Sheng" (New York: East Asian Institute of Columbia University, 1965), 18–19.

religiosity was not orthodox, and it combined the allure of Christianity with indigenous concepts he had imbibed earlier, as he recalls:

> To whom did I pray? God. Which God? I guess the Chinese concept of Heaven; I had faith in Heaven. Although he was a devout Protestant, Mr. Liu [Liu Bomin, Dean at the Methodist Nanjing University] advised me not to pray. He considered prayers as negative; he stressed positive living. I found his arguments convincing. In any case, my interest in religion was born of emotional stress and lasted no more than three months.[42]

Although his interest in religion and its practices was brief, the intellectual and spiritual impetus that underlay this interest persisted into later years. Zuo characterizes his years in Nanjing (roughly 1917 to 1923) as being a "spiritually" active period. At this time Zuo was an active member of the Young China Association, which he describes as neither a political party nor a scholarly society, but rather a loose organization that held few formal meetings, and these were not well attended. Nonetheless, Zuo was attracted to the society because "Emphasis was placed on the spirit ... I thought highly of the association's spirit. Its principle was: 'work for society in accordance with the scientific spirit in order to build a Young China.' Its slogan was: 'Do not rely on established influence; do not depend on past personages.' This made a deep impression on me."[43]

One might attribute the turning to spiritual practices at this time to the personal difficulties experienced by the activists of the time: Yun Daiying was often concerned with his future, and in early 1918 his wife died during childbirth; Zuo Shunsheng complained of great difficulty with his family. Yet the fact remains that regardless of the motives they were attracted to spiritual teaching in a manner not reflected in their public writings.

At the camps Yun attended, he was much impressed by the missionaries—both Chinese and foreign—with whom he held lengthy conversations and debates about religion and faith, a recurring point being whether faith was necessary in order to attain goals such as social reform and personal moral improvement. Missionaries who particularly impressed Yun were Zhang Fuliang, Frank W. Price, and Frank Buchman. Zhang had studied at Yale and returned to China as part of the Yale-in-China missionary group.[44] Price had grown up in China as the son of missionaries, was fluent in Chinese, and would

---

42 Zuo Shunsheng and How, 9.
43 Zuo and How, 21.
44 Charles W. Hayford, *To the People: James Yen and Village China* (New York: Columbia University Press, 1990), 22.

eventually translate Sun Yat-sen's *Three Principles of the People* into English and become close to Generalissimo Chiang Kai-shek. Both Zhang and Price became active in the Rural Reconstruction movement in the 1930s.[45] Buchman would become a highly influential if controversial evangelical and founded the "Oxford Group" or "Moral Rearmament" Christian organization, which eventually influenced Alcoholics Anonymous as well. Buchman had attended the Guling conference in the previous two years as well and by 1918 was one of its main organizers. It was in talks at Guling that he developed his particular vision of personal transformation that emphasized the importance of personal contact and intimate conversations as a means to conversion and salvation—a vision that fed into his later evangelism. Judging from Yun's diary, Yun was one interlocutor with whom Buchman practiced this method. Despite such missionary appeals, Yun remained firm in his lack of faith, but it seems that these experiences and messages combined with Yun's earlier neo-Confucian precepts to affect Yun's emphasis on personal rectification not only by self-reflection, but also by conversation and confession with one's peers.[46]

This striving for moral improvement shaped another important activity of the Mutual Aid Society in its early months. In daily meetings members would report their everyday experiences—often involving school work and encounters with friends, family, and passersby—to their peers and evaluate to what degree they accorded with, or diverged from, their moral views. Such practices had roots in neo-Confucian practices of self-cultivation, however, it seems that in Yun's case they were reinforced by his exposure to the evangelical practices at the YMCA camp.[47]

May Fourth activists were of course influenced by foreign scholars, and some (for example James Yen) adopted Christianity and became missionaries themselves. Our examination of the everyday practices of Yun Daiying during the May Fourth period suggests that foreign missionaries might have been agents of social change even among figures not associated with Christianity or who had not studied abroad. Indeed, it seems likely that it was precisely Yun's early association with missionaries that caused him a few years later to criticize them so virulently, as he sought to distance himself from his earlier

---

45   Samuel Hsueh-chin Chiow, "Religious Education and Reform in Chinese Missions: The Life and Work of Francis Wilson Price" (Ph.D. Dissertation, Saint Louis University, 1988).
46   Yun, *Yun Daiying Riji*, 428–32; Philip Boobbyer, *The Spiritual Vision of Frank Buchman* (University Park: Penn State University Press, 2013), 23–31. Yun spells this as "Bookman" but I assume that he is referring to Buchman.
47   Barry C. Keenan, *Neo-Confucian Self-Cultivation* (Honolulu: University of Hawai'i Press, 2011); See also Henrietta Harrison, *The Man Awakened from Dreams* (Stanford: Stanford University Press, 2005).

religious interest, even as he deployed methods and practices he learned from them.

Another associate of Yun who expressed strong anti-religious sentiments in the ideological debates of the 1920s is Deng Zhongxia (鄧中夏). Like Yun, Deng too seems to have harbored some interest in religion, albeit not explicitly. Upon graduating from Peking University, Deng traveled with his friend Ma Yuancai (馬元材) to Mount Tai in Shandong—an important site in popular religion and state ritual. There, Deng was inspired to write extensively in his journal and attempt a poem; and both Deng and Ma seem to have been alternately fascinated and repelled by the Buddhist nuns they met on their trip.[48]

While the spirit of the times may have been one of secularization, associated with modernity, harbingers of these secular tides still bore the integuments of traditional Chinese religion. A yearning for the sublime, expressed both in traditional Chinese idioms and modern imported ones, can be detected in the writings and actions of these young activists; indeed, it seems to have affected the way they ascribed meaning to foreign ideologies and were attracted to them.

5 Conclusion

May Fourth has been remembered for its political and cultural iconoclasm, but this should be seen together with aspirations for liberation in many aspects of life—physical, sexual, martial, but also spiritual, religious, and physical. To a large extent all of these expressed a deepening sense of individualism and subjectivity, but at the same time this sense of self was also inseparable from a growing sense of belonging to the nation. May Fourth activists attempted to make sense of their own lives at a time of momentous change, and consequently they envisaged a just and desirable social order.

Reading sources with an eye to practices reveals ambiguities, which do not surface in doctrinal texts such as the articles May Fourth activists published on the burning issues of the day. While scholarship since the turn of the current century has investigated changes in everyday life in the May Fourth period, sources like Yun Daiying's diary reveal how these changes were part and parcel of the intellectual ferment and political interests of the time. In the case of Yun Daiying we find practices that do not conform to interpretations of May Fourth as a wholesale adoption of foreign views, or as a transitional stage leading to Marxist socialism. Rather, examining the everyday practices of political

---

[48] Ma Yuancai 馬元材, "Xiyuan Huiyilu," 曦園回憶錄 (Recollections of the garden of morning light), part 10 *Tuanjie Bao*, no. 586 (1982).

activists like Yun reminds us that there was no division of labor—with some radicals acting in the sphere of politics, others in culture, fashion, or sports. The conflicting impulses in May Fourth created a synergy greater than the sum of its parts that transformed culture, society, and politics. Studying the daily practices of political and intellectual figures allows us to see how political activism was imbricated with global modernity.

Studies of the May Fourth movement have emphasized rising nationalist sentiments and the ideological and cultural fermentation that characterized the movement. One wonders, however, if these aspects have not been overemphasized at the expense of the overall experience of the life of which they were part. All the more so if we take into account the emphasis Chinese thinkers, politicians, and activists of this time put on bringing into accord views and everyday experiences. A reading of sources that emphasizes practices does not marginalize ideology or systems of belief, but rather it gives them a fine-grained meaning.

The case of Yun Daiying suggests that we should re-examine the role of foreign missionaries as well as the role of indigenous practices of moral cultivation in inspiring the revolutionary ideas and practices of the May Fourth period. We should thus be circumspect about ascribing to the movement labels—the "isms" upheld by Mao in the quotation with which this essay opened—that elide the complexity of the people we study and the significance of their actions as they appeared at the time. The challenge of our practice as scholars is to simultaneously present the significance of the phenomena we study as it seemed at the time they occurred, and as part of a larger arc of history that reaches to our own era and beyond. Can we combine our knowledge of historical outcomes with the view on the ground at the time?

Bibliography

Bernstein, Richard J. *Praxis and Action*. Philadelphia: University of Pennsylvania Press, 2011.

Boobbyer, Philip. *The Spiritual Vision of Frank Buchman*. University Park, PA: Pennsylvania State University Press, 2013.

Brown, Jeremy, and Matthew D. Johnson, eds. *Maoism at the Grassroots: Everyday Life in China's Era of High Socialism*. Cambridge, MA: Harvard University Press, 2015.

Chan, Wing-tsit. *A Source Book in Chinese Philosophy*. Princeton, NJ: Princeton University Press, 1963.

Chiow, Samuel Hsueh-chin. "Religious Education and Reform in Chinese Missions: The Life and Work of Francis Wilson Price." Ph.D. Dissertation, Saint Louis University, 1988.

Chow, Kai-Wing, Tze-ki Hon, Hung-yok Ip, and Don C. Price, eds. *Beyond the May Fourth Paradigm: In Search of Chinese Modernity*. Lanham, MD: Lexington Books, 2008.

Chow, Tse-tsung. *The May Fourth Movement: Intellectual Revolution in Modern China*. Stanford, CA: Stanford University Press, 1967.

Cua, Antonio S., ed. *Encyclopedia of Chinese Philosophy*. London: Routledge, 2002.

Culp, Robert. *Articulating Citizenship: Civic Education and Student Politics in Southeastern China, 1912–1940*. Cambridge, MA: Harvard University Asia Center, 2007.

Dirlik, Arif. *The Origins of Chinese Communism*. Oxford: Oxford University Press, 1989.

Doleželová-Velingerová, Milena, and Oldřich Král. *The Appropriation of Cultural Capital: China's May Fourth Project*. Cambridge, MA: Harvard University Press, 2001.

Fitzgerald, John. *Awakening China: Politics, Culture, and Class in the Nationalist Revolution*. Stanford, CA: Stanford University Press, 1996.

Fong, Grace S. "Reconfiguring Time, Space, and Subjectivity: Lu Bicheng's Travel Writing on Mount Lu." In *Different Worlds of Discourse: Transformations of Gender and Genre in Late Qing and Republican China*, 87–114. Leiden: Brill, 2008.

Harrison, Henrietta. *The Making of the Republican Citizen: Political Ceremonies and Symbols in China 1911–1929*. Oxford: Oxford University Press, 2000.

Harrison, Henrietta. *The Man Awakened from Dreams*. Stanford: Stanford University Press. 2005.

Hayford, Charles W. *To the People: James Yen and Village China*. New York: Columbia University Press, 1990.

Hershatter, Gail. *The Gender of Memory: Rural Women and China's Collective Past*. Berkeley: University of California Press, 2011.

Keenan, Barry C. *Neo-Confucian Self-Cultivation*. Honolulu: University of Hawai'i Press, 2011.

Knight, Nick. "Mao Zedong and the 'Sinification of Marxism,'" in *Marxism in Asia*, 62–93. London & Sydney: Croom Helm, 1985.

Kuo, Ya-pei. "'Christian Civilization' and the Confucian Church: The Origin of Secularist Politics in Modern China," *Past & Present* 218, no. 1 (February 1, 2013): 235–264. https://doi.org/10.1093/pastj/gts030.

Lanza, Fabio. *Behind the Gate: Inventing Students in Beijing*. New York: Columbia University Press, 2010.

Levenson, Joseph R. *Confucian China and Its Modern Fate: A Trilogy*. 3 vols. Berkeley: University of California Press, 1968.

Li Liangming 李良明. *Yun Daiying Nianpu* 恽代英年谱 (A Chronological Record of Yun Daiying). Wuhan: Huazhong shifan daxue, 2008.

Liu, Liyan. *Red Genesis: The Hunan Normal School and the Creation of Chinese Communism, 1903–1921*. Albany: State University of New York Press, 2012.

Liu Shaoqi. "How to Be a Good Communist." In *Sources of Chinese Tradition*, 2: 427–342. New York: Columbia University Press, 2000.

Lu Xun 魯迅. "Zhi Nan Xing Nan." In *Lu Xun Xuanji* 魯迅選集, 3: 103–105. Beijing: Renmin wenxue chubanshe, 1992.

Ma Yuancai 马元材. "Xiyuan Huiyilu" 曦园回忆录 (Recollections of the Garden of Morning Light), *Tuanjie Bao*, October 16, 1982.

Mao, Zedong. "Letter to Luo Aojie." In *Mao's Road to Power*, 1: 599–601. Armonk, NY: M. E. Sharpe, 1992.

Mao, Zedong. "On Practice." In *Mao's Road to Power*, 6: 601–615. Armonk, NY: M. E. Sharpe, 2004.

Mao, Zedong. "Speech at the Meeting in Yan'an in Commemoration of the Twentieth Anniversary of the May Fourth Movement (May 4, 1939)." In *Mao's Road to Power: Revolutionary Writings 1912–1949*, 7: 69–79. Armonk, NY: M. E. Sharpe, 2005.

Marx, Karl. "Theses on Feuerbach." In *The Marx–Engels Reader*, 2nd ed., 144–145. New York: Norton, 1978.

Meisner, Maurice. *Li Ta-Chao and the Origins of Chinese Marxism*. New York: Atheneum, 1974.

Plaks, Andrew, trans. *Ta Hsueh and Chung Yung* (The Highest Order of Cultivation and On the Practice of the Mean). London: Penguin, 2003.

Rahav, Shakhar. "A May Fourth 'Peach Blossom Garden': The Number One Work Study Mutual Aid Corps in Beijing," *Twentieth Century China* 33, no. 1 (2007): 81–103.

Rahav, Shakhar. *The Rise of Political Intellectuals in Modern China: May Fourth Societies and the Roots of Mass-Party Politics*. New York: Oxford University Press, 2015.

Salkever, Stephen G. *Finding the Mean: Theory and Practice in Aristotelian Political Philosophy*. Princeton: Princeton University Press, 1990.

Schram, Stuart R. "Mao Tse-Tung's Thought to 1949." In *An Intellectual History of Modern China*, 267–348. Cambridge: Cambridge University Press, 2002.

Schwarcz, Vera. *The Chinese Enlightenment: Intellectuals and the Legacy of the May Fourth Movement of 1919*. University of California Press, 1986.

Schwartz, Benjamin. *Chinese Communism and the Rise of Mao*. Cambridge, MA: Harvard University Press, 1958.

"Shang Shu (Book of Documents)." Chinese Text Project, n.d. http://ctext.org/shang-shu/charge-to-yue-ii.

Sun, Yat-sen. "The Doctrine of Sun Yat-Sen: To Act Is Easy, to Know Is Difficult." In *Prescriptions for Saving China*, 199–222. Stanford, CA: Hoover Institution Press, 1994.

Tian Ziyu 田子渝. *Wuhan Wusi Yundong Shi* 武漢五四運動史 (A History of Wuhan during the May Fourth Movement). Wuhan: Hubei renmin chuban she, 1999.

Tian Ziyu 田子渝, Ren Wuxiong 任武雄, and Li Liangming 李良明. *Yun Daiying Zhuanji* 惲代英傳記 (The Biography of Yun Daiying). Wuhan: Hubei Renmin Chubanshe, 1984.

Van de Ven, Hans J. *From Friend to Comrade: The Founding of the Chinese Communist Party, 1920–1927*. Berkeley: University of California Press, 1991.

Wakeman, Frederic. "A Revisionist View of the Nanjing Decade: Confucian Fascism," *The China Quarterly*, no. 150 (June 1997): 395–432.

Wang Guangqi 王光祈. "Gongdu Huzhu Tuan" 工讀互助團 (The Work-Study Mutual Aid Corps), *Shaonian Zhongguo* 少年中國 (Young China) 1, no. 7 (January 15, 1920); reprinted in *Wusi Shiqi de Shetuan* 五四時期的社團 2: 369–372.

Weston, Timothy. *The Power of Position: Beijing University, Intellectuals and Chinese Political Culture, 1898–1929*. Berkeley: University of California Press, 2004.

Yao, Yusheng. "Rediscovering Tao Xingzhi as an Educational and Social Revolutionary," *Twentieth-Century China* 27, no. 2 (2002): 79–120.

Yeh, Wen-hsin. *Provincial Passages: Culture, Space, and the Origins of Chinese Communism*. Berkeley: University of California Press, 1996.

Yiyi, Chen. "Peking University's Role in China's Anti-Christian Movement in 1922–1927," *Social Sciences in China* 31, no. 1 (February 2010): 184–197. https://doi.org/10.1080/02529200903565160.

Yun Daiying 惲代英. "Jidujiao yu renge jiuguo." (Christianity, Personal Integrity, and Saving the Nation) In *Yun Daiying Wenji* (The Collected Works of Yun Daiying), 1: 371–373, 1984.

Yun, Daiying. "Lun Xinyang." (On Faith) In *Yun Daiying Wenji* (The Collected Works of Yun Daiying), 1: 44–47. Beijing: Renmin chubanshe, 1984.

Yun, Daiying. *Yun Daiying Riji*, ed. Zhongyang danganguan, Zhongguo ge ming bowuguan, Zhonggong zhongyang dangxiao chubanshe. Beijing: Zhongyang danganguan, Zhongguo ge ming bowuguan, Zhonggong zhongyang dangxiao chubanshe, 1981.

Yun, Daiying. "Zhi Wang Guangqi." (Letter to Wang Guangqi) In *Yun Daiying Wenji* (The Collected Works of Yun Daiying), 1: 305–315. Beijing: Renmin chubanshe, 1984.

Zhang Xiaochen and Shao Lizi. "Yangzhou Di Ba Zhongxue Gongdu Huzhu Tuan," (The Eighth High School Work Study Mutual Aid Corps in Yangzhou) in *Wusi Shiqi de Shetuan*, vol. 2, 4 vols. Beijing: Sanlian, 1979, 491–92.

Zuo, Shunsheng, and Julie Lien-ying How. "The Reminiscences of Tso Shun-Sheng." New York: East Asian Institute of Columbia University, 1965.

PART 2

Literature and Languages

CHAPTER 7

Nature and Critique of Modernity in Shen Congwen: an Eco-Critical Reading

Ban Wang

Reprint by permission of Duke University Press of Ban Wang, "Nature and Critique of Modernity in Shen Congwen," in *Prism*, volume 16, no. 1, pp. 115-135. Copyright 2019, Lingnan University.

Eco-criticism has targeted anthropocentrism as the intellectual culprit in the human domination of nature. Seen as the root cause for contemporary ecological crises and environmental degradation, anthropocentrism takes the human as the center of reference in apprehending human–nature relations and holds human reason to be an instrument to treat nature as a set of economic resources and a means for human construction. An anthropocentric view also undergirds modern literature with its humanist agenda.

Consider, for example, the familiar authorial stance in realist fiction. As a dominant legacy of China's May Fourth literature, realism, according to Marston Anderson, is "anchored in the capacity of human beings to free themselves from superstition and prejudice through the exercise of their faculty of reason."[1] In approaching human reality and non-human nature, "the mind assimilates external reality to the linguistic structures."[2] These linguistic codes authorize the observing mind and enable it to aspire to a privileged platform from which to register and document slices of reality—with an objective distance. In doing so the mind discovers its independence and freedom, yet its exercise of freedom is made possible "only when it sets itself in opposition to tradition."[3]

Anderson's insight suggests the underlying link between anthropocentricism and literary realism. Rooted in the Enlightenment and secular belief in the power of human reason, both discourses take a critical stance and seek

---

1 Marston Anderson, *The Limits of Realism: Chinese Fiction in the Revolutionary Period* (Berkeley: University of California Press, 1990), 11.
2 Anderson, 11.
3 Anderson, 11.

freedom from superstition and prejudice, and from limits set by nature, biology, and ecosystems. A product of liberal humanism, the writing self, as Timothy Clark puts it, is endowed with a "seemingly pre-given, personal, unique identity, a realm of unshakable privacy, center of its own world of values, perceptions, beliefs, commitments and feelings."[4] Realist writing may register and document disturbances of historical reality and natural disasters to shake up the existing cultural and linguistic norms, but it is the mind that wields the objectifying power. The realist author arrogates to himself an idealistic, disembodied spirit, "an ahistorical higher consciousness."[5] This stripped-down subjectivity overshoots not only the biological body but also the body writ large in entrenched, long-enduring traditions, customs, and rituals, which are more intimately embedded in humans' biological, primordial, and evolutionary existence. Yet, as Anderson notes in his critique of May Fourth realism, this disembodied stance runs into the limits set by the tenacious natural environment.

Eco-criticism in Chinese studies has focused on contemporary environmental despoliation, environmental injustice linked to social injustice, public policy, neoliberal economic production and consumerism, and romantic traditions of human–nature bonds. Faced with looming calamities, eco-critics tend to focus on recent works of literature and film that grapple explicitly with environmental crises.[6] The May Fourth literary canon, with its express goals of humanism, modernity, and science, seems quite contrary to ecological consciousness and has not been adequately tapped for eco-criticism.

Though a product of May Fourth culture, Shen Congwen found roots of his inspiration from folk traditions, supernatural beliefs, and regional lifeworlds, which were discredited by May Fourth. This chapter will explore Shen Congwen's ecological imagination that throws a critical light on May Fourth ideas and related modern narratives. Scholars are beginning to rethink Shen Congwen's ecological consciousness, but few works appear in English.[7]

---

4 Timothy Clark, *The Cambridge Introduction to Literature and Environment* (Cambridge, UK: Cambridge University Press, 2011), 65.
5 Anderson, 11.
6 See Scott Berman, "Chinese Ecocriticism: A Survey of the Landscape," *Literary Compass* 8 (2015): 396–403; Sheldon Lu and Jiayan Mi, eds., *Chinese Ecocinema in the Age of Environmental Challenge* (Hong Kong: Hong Kong University Press, 2009).
7 Studies on Shen's ecological perspectives are few and far between. Karen Thornber writes that May Fourth writers like Lu Xun and Shen Congwen address "environments that are not grievously harmed by human behaviors." Karen Thornber, *Ecoambiguity: Environmental Crises and East Asian Literatures* (Ann Arbor, MI: The University of Michigan Press, 2012), 49. Thornber's initial suggestion of this topic was gaining momentum in China. By my rough estimate, since 2005, a dozen or so students have written MA or doctoral dissertations from

Unaware of the intensity of today's environmental problems, Shen Congwen is nevertheless prescient about modernity's menace to traditional life, which is premised on the organic intertwinement of human life and nature. He was able to discern the seeds of crisis by critiquing the way in which modern civilization severs humanity's ecological roots in nature. Despite being a May Fourth writer, Shen offers the conviction that human life on earth remains part and parcel of ecosystems, and that humans can never pull themselves up by their own bootstraps from planet Earth.

Studies have portrayed Shen Congwen as a writer deeply rooted in the rural soil, embedded in a life-world and the idea of labor entwined with nature, in primordial strata of folk traditions, and in the relationship between people and the ecosystem of climate, rivers, mountains, trees, and animals. Jeffrey Kinkley has appraised in Shen's writing the raw vitality of the people of Western Hunan and the Miao minority, and their uninhibited sensuality. David Wang's comprehensive and insightful study of Shen Congwen identifies a lyrical vision with the power to bring forth primeval energy and imagination that has been inhibited by modern civilization. Rather than subordinate "the subject of passion to the rhetoric of hard-core realism,"[8] the lyrical vision allows hidden passions, desire, and vitality to burst through the established moral codes and social norms imposed by modern transformations. By preserving a place for the supernatural and the uncanny, David Wang writes, Shen Congwen held that the "moral codes of a community should not be predicated on pre-established grounds but should evolve as a result of the harmonious associations of things in their phenomenal state."[9] That "phenomenal state" gestures toward an aesthetic of poetic language linked to the ecological sensibility. This sensibility entails a deeply resonant and intertwined relationship between humans and the natural world. The term "phenomenal" recalls phenomenology, which is an aesthetic inquiry into humans' experiential, sensuous, and vital affinity with the world. "Aesthetics" probes into how "the world strikes the body on is sensory surfaces, of that which takes root in the gaze and the guts and all that

---

the ecological perspective on Shen Congwen since 2005. She Aichun's 佘愛春 MA thesis *A Study of Shen Congwen from the Eco-Critical Perspective* in Guangxi Normal University was probably the first one. A 2018 MA thesis by Luo Lin entitled "Landscape of Lost and Found: Nature in Shen Congwen and Gao Xingjian" in Hong Kong University is a more recent work. This chapter looks at the issues of Shen's animistic language, the long duration of time vs. modern history, and ecological and amoral treatment of sexuality.

8 David Der-wei Wang, *Fictional Realism in Twentieth-Century China: Mao Dun, Lao She, Shen Congwen* (New York: Columbia University Press, 1992), 242.
9 Wang, *Fictional Realism*, 242.

arises from our most banal, biological insertion into the world."[10] In focusing on human sensuality in conviviality with myriad living things, Shen Congwen marks a departure from the disembodied, realistic subject of modern literature. Shen's writing evinces a refusal to elevate the human subject above animals, plants, landscapes, and climate.

In this chapter I explore the question of the human–nature relationship and seek to extend the study of Shen Congwen in an ecological direction. I will go beyond the portrayals of Shen as a nature writer, a painter of rural folk manners, and a curator of West Hunan local colors. Natural and ecological motifs in Shen's work are taking on renewed significance in the current worldwide critique of anthropocentrism.

As a prominent writer of the May Fourth culture, Shen Congwen drew inspiration and resources from romanticism, modernism, Freudianism, and anthropology. While he contributed to the formation of the humanist subject in search of freedom and modernity, Shen did as much to disperse the primacy of the human self by grounding it in an ecological context and by recovering human roots in the nonhuman environment. Chinese traditions of thought also fed into Shen's proto-ecological thinking. Shen's favorite classics include essays by Liu Zongyuan 柳宗元, who pondered humans' resonance with the heavens and earth. Karen Thornber has referenced Liu Zhongyuan's *Tian shuo* 天說 (Theory of Heaven) to advance the theory of ecoambiguity.[11] Li Daoyuan 酈道元's *Shuijing zhu* 水經注 (A Commentary on the *Classic of the Waterways*), and Taoist writer Zhuangzi 莊子 might have shaped Shen's thoughts about humans in the cosmos. A rich repertoire of ideas about humans' relationship with nature, these references converge into a critical resource for rethinking how modern civilization rationalizes, represses, and reifies nature as well as human inner nature.

The modern conception of environmental crises has its cultural and philosophical origin in the Enlightenment view that humanity is separable from and superior to the natural world. By reading Shen's essays and stories, I argue that Shen affirms an ecological "understanding of life in which the thinking of the self must already include other organisms" and all that sustain them, entailing "an ever-widening circle of identification with other living things."[12]

---

10   Terry Eagleton, *The Ideology of the Aesthetic* (Oxford, UK: Blackwell, 1990), 13.
11   Thornber, *Ecoambiguity*, 32.
12   Clark, *Literature and Environment*, 23.

1 Natural Beauty, Language, and Modern Civilization

Invocations of nature are problematic in this age of built environments and digitalized, engineered nature. David Wang has claimed that natural landscapes in Shen Congwen appeal to an imaginary nostalgia for a lost home in terms of a trans-historical overview.[13] Eco-critics fret that natural images and landscapes often serve as spectacles for aesthetic and tourist consumption by jaded urbanites.[14] I contend that natural images in Shen prompt us to rethink the relations between humans and their deep ties to nonhuman nature. I will elaborate on Kinkley's point that Shen Congwen "loved nature above artificiality."[15]

The place of nature in modern civilization has been on the wane in the midst of accelerated technological advances. Alert to the way modern civilization assaults the intimate relations between rural people and the natural environment, Shen inquires into how urban consumerism, print technology, politics, and fashions inflict harm on nature. He probes into how human imagination and artifice relate to the idea of natural beauty, and searches for a natural vision not yet codified and reified as second nature. In his writing, descriptions of nature—trees, rivers, mountains, and animals—are a powerful and ubiquitous presence. Shen's fictional characters live in the midst of nature and make a living out of it. We may cite an oft-quoted scene in *Bian Cheng* 邊城 (*Border Town*). Describing human abodes along the river Yuan, the narrator dilates on the high mountains close to the river bank, which are "covered with delicate, thin bamboo"[16] and display "in all seasons such a deep emerald color as to transfix the eyes. Households near the water appeared among peach and apricot blossoms … whenever there were peach blossoms there was sure to be a home, and wherever there were people, one could stop for a drink."[17] The cottages, on the cliffs and the riverbanks, are in harmonious order and in tune with their surroundings. A poetic feeling arises from this panorama, inducing marvel at the bold craftsmanship of nature. This landscape intimates a deep ecological sensibility, suggesting that human dwellings, rather than being constructed, seem to rise organically from the soil, the rivers, and the

---

13 Wang, *Fictional Realism*, 253.
14 Clark, *Literature and the Environment*, 39.
15 Jeffrey Kinkley, *The Odyssey of Shen Congwen* (Stanford, CA: Stanford University Press, 1987), 113.
16 Shen Congwen. 沈從文 *Border Town*, trans. Jeffrey Kinkley (New York: HarperCollins, 2009), 11.
17 Shen, *Border Town*, 11.

mountains. Human activity, while centered on human interest and survival, cannot cut itself off from nature; it blends into vegetation, plants, and natural terrains. The novel's protagonist Cuicui is evidently a child of nature:

> Cuicui grew up under the sun and the wind, which turned her skin black as could be. The azure mountains and green brooks that met her eyes turned them clear and bright as crystal. Nature had brought her up and educated her, making her innocent and spirited, in every way like a little wild animal. Yet she was as docile and unspoiled as a mountain fawn, wholly unacquainted with cruelty, never worried, and never angry.[18]

Images of human abodes on the river pervade Shen's narratives. At the ecological level, this signals a fluid interflow and interdependence between humans and nature. Eco-critics have used the motif of water to describe this intimacy and unity. Freud's notion of the child's oceanic immersion in the primordial surroundings of the maternal presence marks a world where, in the words of Georges Bataille, "the animal is in the world like water in water."[19] Shen's favorite natural image, water—rain, waterway, stream, and river—flows into his writing as a significant stream of his creativity. In the essay entitled "Wode xiezuo yu shui de guanxi" 我的寫作雨水的關係 (The Relation of My Writing to Water), Shen writes, "That I can think at all with my little brain depends on water. If I have a deeper understanding of the cosmos, it is thanks to water."[20] The local waters never cease to inspire him, and they form the setting of many of his stories. To him, the sea, the rivers, and the rains inform human moods and nurture human life. Readily associated with living natural forms such as trees, vegetation, clouds, and sunshine, the waters are more than a physical setting for human action; they embody a lifeline linking nature to human desires and hopes, and sensuous affinity with other organisms. The mirage between the sky and the sea, veiled in watery mist, gives a feeling of light-heartedness, softness, music, and eroticism. The blue sky is a "magic picture, evocative of youthful signs, triggering fantasies and dreams."[21]

---

18 Shen, *Border Town*, 5.
19 Quoted in Colin Campbell, "From 'Unity of Life' to the Critique of Domination," in *Critical Ecologies: The Frankfurt School and Contemporary Environmental Crises*, edited by Andrew Biro (Toronto and London: University of Toronto Press, 2011), 144.
20 Shen Congwen, *Shen Congwen piping wenji* 沈從文批評文集 (A collection of critical essays by Shen Congwen), ed. Liu Hongtao (Zhuhai, Guangdong: Zhuhai chubanshe, 1998), 277.
21 Shen, *Piping wenji*, 284.

By locating origins of creativity in vibrant, fluid nonhuman elements, Shen Congwen addresses the natural foundation for the ideal of the beautiful in human artworks. Aesthetic thinkers Cai Yuanpei 蔡元培 and Zhu Guanqian 朱光潛, writing around the same time as Shen, believed that the beauty of artworks originated from the primitive conditions of hunters and gatherers living in and engaging closely with nature.[22] Comparing Chinese aesthetics with Western ideas, Zhu wrote that Western thinkers tend to "view nature as something in opposition to humans" and treat the whole nonhuman realm as nature.[23] The Chinese veneration of nature seems different but is actually a late development: the nature cult did not become a dominant motif until the Jin and Tang dynasties—under the influence of Daoism and Buddhism. The poems of *Shijing* 詩經 (Book of Songs) treat nature as a backdrop that provokes the inner feelings of the poet, who deploys nature for expressive purposes. What sets the Chinese attitude apart from the anthropocentric view, according to Zhu, is that Chinese seem to be content with Heaven and Earth (*letian zhizu* 樂天知足) and are inclined to "immerse themselves in nature, believing in the intimacy and cozy coexistence of humans and nature."[24]

Human–nature intimacy is not just a Chinese characteristic, of course, but is also a strong motif in Western aesthetics. Theodor Adorno gives primacy to nature as the genuine source of beauty, over human reason and artifice. The aesthetics of the Enlightenment, represented by Hegel and Kant, privileges manmade artworks and artifice as the source of the beautiful, thus privileging rational design over the nonhuman world of nature. As human artifice expunges the rawness of nature and transcends its otherness, a human-centered aesthetic took hold and evolved in the modern age, signaling the triumph of the idealist, rational subject setting itself as separate from the object. A sign of the human domination of nature, the human-centered aesthetic is, Adorno wrote, "culpable of elevating the human animal above the animal."[25] Destructive and violent, this aesthetic runs roughshod over everything that does not fit into an identity with the anthropocentric subject.

Looking for an alternative notion of natural beauty, Adorno seeks to restore nature to its rightful place in aesthetic thought. Evoking the hawthorn hedge in Marcel Proust, he sees the natural image as a sign of the urge to step out of the stuffy house in order to seek a breath of fresh air. A genuine aesthetic

---

22   Cai Yuanpei 蔡元培, *Cai Yuanpei meixue wenlun* 蔡元培美學文論 (Aesthetic essays by Cai Yuanpei) (Beijing: Peking University Press, 1983), 86.
23   Zhu Guangqian 朱光潛, *Zhu Guangqian meixue wenji* 朱光潛美學文集 (Collected essays by Zhu Guangqian) (Shanghai: Shanghai wenyi, 1982), 1: 132.
24   Zhu, *Meixue wenji*, 133.
25   Theodor Adorno, *Aesthetic Theory* (Minneapolis: University of Minnesota Press, 1997), 62.

experience is to be had by fleeing the house of our secondary nature in order to embrace primal nature, brimming with health and vitality. Citing Rousseau, Adorno observes that even the individual with refined taste and aesthetic judgment may find tremendous relief when he or she steps into the open air out of a gallery packed with beautiful paintings and artifacts. Moving away from those artworks that "minister to vanity and social joys," the viewer would fall in love with "the beautiful in nature" and appreciate "a voluptuousness for the mind in a train of thought that he can never unravel."[26]

Adorno's insight is helpful for understanding Shen Congwen's critique of the erosion of nature, alienation of inner nature, and destruction of rural communities in China's drive for modernity. This reading, however, should not lead to a leveling of humans and nonhumans. Cognizant of nature's menace to humans, Shen recognizes human agency and courage in the conflicted attempt to maintain a fragile equilibrium between humans and nature. Because works of beauty result from human design, humans, though not the sole maker, are the prime agent. On the ecological level, humans are one organism involved and bound up with all other organisms. But on the aesthetic level, the artists take the lead in creating beauty. Treating humans as a prime agent in maintaining ecological balance is not anthropocentricism, but a process of give-and-take. Shen wrote, "all flowers and fruits receive from the sun their life and fragrance. In the order of nature, humans are also one life-form and need to receive nourishment and wisdom from the sun." But while "the sky, trees, and sea merge into my solitary soul … I feel the robust wisdom of life. From the rhythmic beat of my heart arises a refreshing and graceful poem and crooning songs honoring youthful energy."[27]

Kinkley observes that Shen often conveys the romantic lovers' conversation in a metaphoric language that "resonated with the climate and nature scene."[28] I suggest that Shen's language is animistic rather than metaphoric. The metaphor assumes that the sign system treats natural imagery as an external means of representing human feelings and intent, deploying nature as lengthened shadows of humanity. In contrast, Shen's writing makes sense in terms of animistic language. His nature imagery does not treat natural scenes, sights, and sounds solely in a attempt to articulate human desire, emotion, and intent, and much less to impose human schemes and categories. It is a stream of signals, sounds, and gesture that organically arises from yet remains embedded in nature, as if it were the voice of nature. His style does not define and shape

---

26   Adorno, 63.
27   Shen Congwen, *Piping wenji*, 280, 282.
28   Kinkley, *Odyssey*, 139.

human characters' experience of nature, but is open-ended and co-exists with other "languages of nature."

Defining animistic language in his influential ecological work *The Spell of the Sensuous*, David Abram claims that the sources of animistic language lie in a realm that knows no distinction between human and nonhuman.[29] Animistic language reveals the deeper conditions of language that allows humans to experience and access the world directly in a bodily and incarnate medium.[30] Instead of setting the human apart from nature, it allows human bodies to experience immediate sensations, sights, and sounds from nature. More than a means to human ends, the sensuous medium involves humans, plants, rocks, and all animate forms in a ceaseless conversation, in constant beckoning and responding, forging a wordless conversation in the "common field of our lives and other lives, with which ours are entwined."[31] Animistic language allows humans to have a delicate reciprocity with the myriad textures, sounds, and shapes of the earth and to carry on "a sort of silent conversation," a continuous dialogue that unfolds far below human linguistic and conceptual awareness.[32]

The folk characters in Shen seem to be equipped with this animistic language. As Kinkley rightly observes, the country folks in Shen's works "are able to communicate their moods and feelings without much recourse to speech. In communication, their intuitions, sensitivity, and sensuous alertness to gestures and remarks, and their ability to enter each other's mind, are sufficient."[33] This sensuous language can be a folk erotic song for flirtation and courting, or a natural atmosphere complete with botanical, animal, and cosmic images.

The short story "Yu Hou" 雨後 (After Rain) illustrates the gap between elegant poetry and animistic language. Set in a mountainous enclave after a rain shower, the male character Fourth Dog seduces a girl and has sex with her. They approach each other as if driven by the most auspicious and compelling forces of nature. The bucolic setting extends to a cosmic space between Heaven and Earth: the re-emergence of the sun after the rain, the clouds that rush like wild hogs, and the ceaseless humming of insects. The boy makes an attempt to caress the girl and feel her breast while singing a customary courting song. The girl is coy at first. Schooled in classical poetry, she warns that she will soon fade away, for classical poems of nature always lament the transience of female beauty like the withering of flowers. When her recitation of poetic

---

29   David Abrams, *The Spell of the Sensuous* (New York: Vintage Books, 1997), 66–67.
30   Abrams, 89.
31   Abrams, 40.
32   Abrams, 52–53.
33   Kinkley, *Odyssey*, 180.

lines threatens to block the spontaneous outburst of love, the narrator complains that poetic literacy is to blame for the girl's hesitancy. The poetic canon laments the transience of floral bloom and ignores bodily, sensuous spontaneity, blocking the moment of pleasure as incomplete and unsatisfactory. Fortunately, Fourth Dog is illiterate and immune to the cliché poetic foreboding of the fading of girls/flowers. He simply follows his natural instinct, which is "his poetry."[34] His plunge into passion suggests an animistic poem, invocative of the sensuous and spontaneous outburst of libido in conjunction with nature. The sounds of big and small insects, the grasshoppers flying around the lovers, the raindrops falling from the trees and leaping around on the ground, and the audible heartbeat of the girl next to him—all these converge into a polyphonic chorus, which is exquisite poetry to this illiterate country boy. He feels that "maple leaves are her bedding, and he her quilt, and he will frolic with her like a dog" in a way that "cannot be explained by any language."[35]

Instead of imitating nature and deploying natural images from the anthropocentric height, Shen's animistic language immerses bodily sensations, pleasure, and feelings in nature. Human language is not a construct deemed more expressive than sounds, cries, buzzes, and a wide spectrum of sensations, perceptions, and shapes from nature. Engulfing subject and object, animistic language is one voice in a web of sounds and signals in communication, reciprocity, and circulation with other living organisms. Birds have their chirping languages, and the trees beckon and answer with their own signals, just as humans communicate with other living bodies and forms.

The story "Sange nüxing" 三個女性 (Three Girls) contrasts literary language, of both classical and modern traditions, with the language of nature. As three girls go sightseeing on the seashore during a summer vacation, two younger girls, overwhelmed by the blue sky, clouds, pine trees, and the ocean, rack their brains for lines of poetry in response to the intoxicating natural environs. But Pu Jing, the mature one among them, deems it silly to search for poetic lines and romantic aura when one is enveloped, body and soul, by a refreshing ambiance. Waxing poetic and rhetorical, the two other girls lose their way in the winding path. To correct this habit of imposing lines of poetry on such a rich and diverse scene, Pu Jing urges the girls to lie flat on the rocks and feel their residual warmth. "If you want to be poet, you should get closer to nature,

---

34 Shen, "Yu hou," in *Shen Congwen wenji* 沈從文文集 (Collected essays) (Hong Kong: Sanlian, 1982) 2: 93.
35 Shen, *Wenji*, 93–95.

to lie down in the embrace of nature."[36] As all three proceed to lie down on a big slab of rock on the cliff overlooking the ocean, one girl exclaims in an epiphany: the sky is right over my head! When asked for a song to sing of their being in thrall to nature, this girl, now converted to animistic faith, remarks that songs, like poetry, are ineffective and inadequate. "Can we string together sounds and language to identify and capture what we are feeling?"[37] Silence, she concludes, is the only appropriate response. Songs crafted by humans, like poetry, are all very simplistic and poor; they sing of superficial gain and loss, happiness and sadness. Pu Jing, the theorist of natural beauty, claims that it is not enough to preserve our amazing experience of nature by means of song or poetry. Instead, the main point of poetry is to "forget ourselves," to have "our soul melt into intricate lights and subtle colors of nature."[38] Thus, if we approach nature through the educated poetic sensibility, we will fail to appreciate what is naturally beautiful. She goes on to philosophize: "The beautiful is ubiquitous and fluid. The fewer poets we have, the more likely it would be for humans to access and enjoy beauty."[39] Human-centered literature stands in the way of natural beauty, and lettered poetry, instead of making people wiser and more perceptive, only makes for decoration, vanity, and the social status of the philistines.[40]

Shen Congwen pits the image of nature against ideas of progress in urbanization, industrialization, and consumerism. His valorization of nature targets the way human construction in the city erodes the simplicity, multiplicity, and vitality of rural life. The story "Deng" 燈 (The Lamp) explores the tension between an authentic way of life and the alienating environment of the modern university in Shanghai. Urban life appears to be one of uncertainty and spiritual hollowness for the narrator/professor, who is obviously Shen's alter ego. The supply of electricity is unreliable; the professor is constantly stressed out about his meaningless teaching duties; his housekeeper is dishonest and deceptive; students write about love in the melodramatic style of "love has broken my heart" five times in the first paragraph of their essays. Conversations with colleagues are "idle chatter": knowledge of literature is little more than a display of vanity and gossip about a writer's private romance. As a "village product," the narrator feels wronged and becomes weary of city life, and weary of life itself. In spite of all urban amenities, he yearns to return to the home

---

36 Shen, *Shen Congwen quanji* 沈從文全集 (Complete works) (Taiyuan, Shanxi: Beiyue wenyi, 2002) 7: 362.
37 Shen, *Shen Congwen quanji*, 7: 363.
38 Shen, *Shen Congwen quanji*, 7: 363.
39 Shen, *Shen Congwen quanji*, 7: 365.
40 Shen, *Shen Congwen quanji*, 7: 365.

village and to do a simple job. There he would enjoy a simple life by listening to the "frogs croaking in the rainwater puddles in the yard, and practicing calligraphy."[41] Under the misty lamplight, this romantic nostalgia points to a divide between Western modernity and the traditional, natural life-world unique to "the Eastern race." In the old soldier, the story's main protagonist, the narrator discerns a paragon of rural and natural virtue. The soldier has echoes of "so many of his rural fellow-countrymen, all uneducated, but at the same time all so good and honest."[42] Modern times "have uprooted the peace-loving soul of an old eastern race, and thrust it into a world of wars with which it had no empathy."[43]

Tearful and melancholy, the narrator yearns for the lost rural life, and this reveals the gap between natural beauty and the artwork's attempt to heal the wounded soul of the "village product." Urban life suffocates spontaneous life, inflicts wounds on nature and inner life. "The concept of natural beauty rubs on a wound," Adorno wrote.[44] The primacy of artificiality in aesthetics and the instrumental rationality of modern civilization inflict wounds on nature. Modernity, along with its bureaucracy, markets, technology, consumerism, and a whole slew of alienating mechanisms, represses the spontaneity, multiplicity, and naturalness of the rural life-world. Unlike the sunny images of natural beauty we saw earlier, "The Lamp" conjures up a form of beauty derived from nature but scarred with wounds and losses.

Offering a similar critique of modern alienation, Shen Congwen formulates a more nuanced theory of natural beauty in the essay "Shui Yun" 水雲 (Water and Clouds). Positing water and clouds as the ultimate fountainhead, Shen repeats his insight that all artistic originality and creativity stem from the obsessive image of water. Beautiful works of art draw energy and inspiration from nature and from deep engagement with all living organisms. When artificial conventions, consumerist taste, and fashions hold sway, images of nature become infrequent and flash up only by chance (*ouran* 偶然). Impulses of nature are always awaiting the wing to burst forth with sparks and flourishes. What goes by the name "society," with its new trends, cultural industry, technologies of writing, media, fashions, and consumerism, amounts to the narrow "hypocritical manners and behavior that distort and repress human nature."[45] The alienation suppresses the spontaneous desires of boys and girls,

---

41 Joseph Lau, C. T. Hsia, and Leo Lee, eds. *Modern Chinese Stories and Novellas: 1919–1949* (New York: Columbia University Press, 1981), 239.
42 Lau et al., 240.
43 Lau et al., 240.
44 Adorno, *Aesthetic Theory*, 62.
45 Shen, *Piping wen ji*, 283.

locks middle-age individuals into anxiety about the loss of power, and confines the elderly to declining health.[46] Urban dwellers busily and mindlessly throng in and out of stores and banks, and everything is driven by money. The iconic modern buildings, such as the city hall and churches, only remind one of the power struggles and conflict of the past—a record of bygone victories and defeats, successes and failures. Modern culture has created the orthodox canons of literature and art and used bricks and wood to build ugly buildings. These material and cultural constructions serve only to perpetuate the received opinions of some authorities, and routinely provide a means of livelihood for later docile generations. The ossified superstructures are becoming "cartoonist, shadowy, sham and vulgar." Humans are reified: we get much from things, but we lose ourselves.[47] The essay echoes William Wordsworth's famous lines:

> The world is too much with us; late and soon,
> Getting and spending, we lay waste our powers;—
> Little we see in Nature that is ours;
> We have given our hearts away, a sordid boon!
> This Sea that bares her bosom to the moon;
> The winds that will be howling at all hours,
> And are up-gathered now like sleeping flowers;
> For this, for everything, we are out of tune ...[48]

Yet for all the seamless human, artificial constructs, natural beauty may crop up by chance through the cracks. Shen registers an epiphany at the dawning of such beauty. When he sees how delicately dressmakers and hair dressers wield the beautifiers' skills on young female bodies, he comments that these skills do little more than enhance the stylistic effects and the looks of an average person. But penetrating through the artificialities one is able to discern, by default and by contrast, the perfection and exquisiteness that nature has conferred on a young and healthy female body. The irruption of lost natural beauty, glaringly absent from the stylized female body—a mere mannequin—entails genuine artistic imagination and penetrating insight linked to primeval nature. "I am entirely in the position of art connoisseur," Shen notes. By seeing through artificiality, Shen is able to detect a natural life form that blends into art, one that

---

46 Shen, *Piping wen ji*, 283.
47 Shen, *Piping wen ji*, 290.
48 www.poetryfoundation.org. Accessed March 31, 2018.

projects a broader natural moral vision and that transcends fissures between aesthetic form and natural body.[49]

2 Sexuality, Biology, and Nature

Shen Congwen attempts to find a way to bridge inner and outer nature by addressing the gap between culture and nature. The gap drives a wedge between human norms, which are time-specific, as the *Zeitgeist*, and the *longue durée* of biology and evolution. The advent of modernity, dominated by the *Zeitgeist* of the Anthropocene, has widened the gap between the two time spans. On the surface runs a fast human-centered narrative—one that makes epoch-making changes in the human mind and on the earth. Lagging behind and submerged flows a long evolutionary stream, with humans enmeshed with nonhuman eco-systems and embedded in naturally evolved habits, customs, myth, and folklore. This evolutionary process testifies to a sense of temporality so slow and imperceptible that it takes on the quality of timelessness. The *longue durée* intimates a close affinity and entwinement between the human and nonhuman worlds, implying the idea of social ecology embedded in natural ecology.

Romantic critics tend to favor this "timeless" nature, and forget what David Wang calls "naturalization," referring to a writing strategy to remove "things and ideas from historical contingencies" by "fitting them into an ideology of Nature."[50] But rather than viewing nature as a retreat to Nature, we may identify in Shen's work an ecological pace of change involving landscapes, climate, customs, and pre-historical life-worlds—changes that have never cut humans' umbilical cord from Mother Earth. This subterranean, ecological stratum exerts a shaping force on the human world. Sensitive to this ecological temporality, Shen Congwen probes into a "timeless nature" beneath the vicissitudes of human fate, political change, and social transformation—swift mutations under the teleology of modern history.

The telling "Humans and Soil" 人與地 chapter opens the novel *Changhe* 長河 (The Long River). A long-range view and the slow description of landscape draw us into a geological timeline. The narrator delves into a submerged natural history entwined with the living conditions of the local folk. Thanks to the fertility of the soil and proper climate, there has been an overproduction of oranges along the Yuan River in West Hunan. The oranges hark back to the

---

49 Shen, *Piping wenji*, 300–301.
50 Wang, *Fictional Realism*, 239.

deep and long kinship between human inhabitants and natural conditions. Two thousand years ago, when Qu Yuan 屈原, the exiled official of the Chu state, took a boat upstream, he must have been struck by these brilliant orange groves. The natural elegance and colors inspired him to write the "Ju Song" 橘頌 (Ode to Oranges). Over two millenniums, while things have changed somewhat, the same people still live in the area, and the trees still draw nourishment from the soil on the riverbanks. Throughout the sun, rains, and snows; throughout all the climate changes, the old passed away; the young grew up, as if springing up from the soil.[51]

This image of the perennially flowing river provokes a critique of historical and anthropocentric constructs as fleeting bubbles on the surface:

> Written history, besides telling us stories of mutual killing among certain groups of people in certain places on earth, will never sufficiently tell us what we should know. But this river has told me the sadness and happiness of some people in an era of time. The little gay fishing boats ... the half-naked, bending boat-pullers, walking on the pebble beach. These things have nothing to do with history, and they remain the same, in the last or next hundred years.[52]

This "unwritten life" sinks its roots in the millennial entwinement of the local folks' archaic ways of living with the soil, landscape, and the earth. Human labor and behavior, instead of transcending the biological needs of survival, are deeply in tune with and embedded in the nonhuman world of climate, clouds, plants, animals, rivers, and mountains. Human characters are portrayed as not yet weaned from an all-encompassing Mother Nature.

Speaking of human constructs in art, literature, and philosophy, Shen cautions that our rational examinations of life require a distancing from our true self and our body. Detached from the biological life as an integral part of nature, our reflection entails an estrangement from "human nature as inherent in biological nature" (*shengwu zhong ren de benxing* 生物中人的本性).[53] Rather than shedding the animal traits and roots, the sense of human biology ensures that the species and blood ties persist and continue to survive by connecting with other organisms. Compared with this deeper ecosystem, pains and joys in human-centered life and society seem petty, and human efforts are motivated mostly from the pursuit of trivial gains and losses, from paybacks

---

51 Shen, *Shen Congwen quanji*, 10: 12.
52 Quoted in Wang, *Fictional Realism*, 226.
53 *Shen Congwen quanji*, 12: 42–43.

and adjustments. When philosophers and artists busily search for abstract designs, they tend to alienate humans from nature, even if they do not inflict wounds upon it. But human abstractions neglect and repress the complexity, richness, and life-shaping forces of nature.[54]

Nature has far broader horizons than human-centered schemes. Nature's timeline is much longer than the anthropocentric subject—the agent of history. As we saw earlier, beautiful things created by human beings cannot be attributed to humans' unique endeavors, but reflect an ecological relationship in which "humans submit to nature's order with joy" and yield to its disciplines. All human wisdom draws inspiration and substance from nature's influence.[55]

Bound up with natural ecology, the biological concept of human nature accounts for Shen's sympathetic and non-judgmental depictions of sensuality and sexuality. Kinkley observes that among Shen's mountain folk, sensuous love is innocent and naïve, and their passionate nature knows "no tormented desires and affects expressible through simple nature metaphors."[56] Although he sees the depiction of innocent sexuality as more a product of a mediating work rather than a spontaneous outpouring of libido, David Wang has drawn attention to the childlike innocence and indulgence regarding sexual transgression.[57] In sexual acts, lovers in Shen's stories evince a naïve life force unconstrained by moral qualms.

Let us look at the famous story "Xiaoxiao" 蕭蕭. A child bride engaged at age twelve to a two-year-old boy, Xiaoxiao has a sexual affair with a farmhand and becomes pregnant. Instead of being condemned and punished, she is absolved from her transgression. Her becoming a child bride and laboring as a little nanny for the in-law family would have been the prime subject matter for the May Fourth attack on the oppression of women in traditional China. Xiang Lin's Wife in Lu Xun's "Zhufu" 祝福 (New Year's Sacrifice) is a well-known example of a woman victimized by the patriarchal family. Yet far from deploring Xiaoxiao's servitude and hardship, the narrative takes on a sympathetic tone and even cheers her on. The child bride appears to take great strides in her hard life. She enjoys playing with her child husband; she dreams the dreams of a girl of her age and embraces whatever life has to offer. A vibrant and irresistible force of nature is throbbing within her, which the hard labor can barely dampen. After a sleepless night due to the exhausting care of the baby husband, she would "flick her eyes open and shut to see the yellow-and-purple sunflowers

---

54   Shen, *Congwen quanji*, 12: 42–43.
55   Shen, *Congwen quanji*, 12: 23.
56   Kinkley, *Odyssey*, 139.
57   Wang, *Fictional Realism*, 243.

outdoors shifting forms before her very eyes."[58] Growing a little older, the little wife "is not the worse for wear"; one look at her figure shows that "she was like an unnoticed sapling at a corner of the garden, sprouting forth big leaves and branches after days of wind and rain" (228). "She grew and blossomed" and "flourished in the clean country air, undaunted by any trial and ordeal" (232).

The climatic moments fall on the seduction scene, her sexual transgression, and the resolution. As the farm hand Motley is seducing her, the attraction is mutual and reciprocal. The impartial narrator conveys a sense that Xiaoxiao yields willingly and naturally to the charms of Motley's male body: she cannot help looking at his brawny arms and is drawn to his erotic folk songs, with which Motley sings his way into her heart. Like many love scenes in Shen Congwen, the sexual act happens in the mountains, amid lush foliage and among wild fruits and trees, adding a pastoral, innocent flavor to the lovemaking.

Although Xiaoxiao's sexual activity and resulting pregnancy are a transgression that dishonors the family, the lack of Confucian education among the family elders spares her from the potentially harsh penalty. "By rights, she should have been drowned, but only heads of families who have read their Confucius would do such a thing to serve the family's honor" (235). Xiaoxiao's "sin" is thus absolved, not on moral grounds but through an appeal to economic benefits and compensation. The in-law family tries to sell her, but there are no takers. Meanwhile the affectionate bond between Xiaoxiao and her baby-husband keeps her at home. In time, the birth of the illicit baby turns out to be a blessing. Promising added labor power, the child gives Xiaoxiao a legitimate place in the family.

In a departure from Confucian moral strictures, "Xiaoxiao" points to a practical consideration premised on economic necessity and species survival. By depicting Xiaoxiao's vitality and sexuality, the libidinal impulses of puberty, the urges of inner nature enveloped by a lush landscape, the courting ritual through erotic songs, and finally the economic gain in labor power, the author not only mitigates and pardons the "sin" of Xiaoxiao, but more importantly, gives her experience a force of justification and legitimacy, affirming the principles of biological nature and species survival.

Shen Congwen portrays sexuality as an unbridled and non-ethical expression of an inner nature consonant with primal natural environments. Both inner and outer natures are charged with restless impulses, vigor, and conviviality, with human libidinal drives blending with the fluid vitality of trees, plants, and animals.

---

58   Lau et al., *Modern Chinese Stories*, 228. References to "Xiaoxiao" and other stories below will be indicated by the page number in parentheses in the text.

The claims of nature and biological survival also account for Shen's descriptions of prostitution, which are disturbing to moralistic and ideological readers. These episodes evince a consistent refusal to raise any moral concerns regarding the female body. The female body was a major bone of contention in the May Fourth culture between progressives and conservatives. The New Culture embraced the modern ideas of woman's self-consciousness and autonomy, and decried the treatment of women as commodity and property by the traditional mores and family. By contrast, the Confucian moralists condemned the sin of prostitution while many of them indulged in sexual license. Shen's view of sex work gestures toward the biological realm beyond the scrim of humanist or Confucian morality. Sexual intercourse, as Kinkley rightly puts it, "is described with surprising moral neutrality."[59] But the neutral tone, found throughout Shen's stories, is not so surprising. It implies an understanding of the organic unity of human biological nature and the world's own nature.

The story "Zhangfu" 丈夫 (The Husband) illustrates the same justification of sexual behavior on the same practical and amoral grounds as in "Xiaoxiao." In the story, the peasant women leave their husbands behind in the village and go to work as prostitutes on the boats in a small town. These women and their husbands "call this activity by the same name as it is known elsewhere: *business*. Business is what they've all come for. It holds the same status as any other work, being neither offensive to morality nor harmful to health" (30). There is little hint of immorality, infidelity, and depravity. The peasant women turned prostitutes remit their earnings to their husbands and provide their families with a better life. The husband "keeps the rights to his wife and the profits, too" (30). So the couple does business, one in the field and the other in the city. This, the narrator comments, matter-of-factly and without irony, is "all so simple" and "happens all the time" (31), suggesting that it is the oldest trade in the world.

The casual remark about the man's ownership of the woman and her labor seems disturbing and "patriarchal." Premised on a gender hierarchy, it apparently runs counter to the vaunted equality among humans that is consistent with the ecological resonance between humans and other organisms. But even an egalitarian social ecology cannot dispense with hierarchy. The question is whether the hierarchy is dominant or whether it allows a space of reciprocity and mutuality. In "The Husband," the wife acts like a mother to coax her husband out of his jealousy. Is this a sign of her subordination or an initiative to smooth over the friction? Hierarchy, often embodied in Shen's fiction by

---

59   Kinkley, *Imperfect Paradise*, 29. Further references to this text are indicated by the page number in parentheses in the text.

an authoritative yet caring figure, is a necessary glue of the community.[60] Its purpose is to maintain the social ecology and to keep its members in mutual belonging and solidarity. The same is true of the "ecological family," where humans, though a member of the ecosystem, must take the lead, as the "head of the household," in managing the co-existence and conflict between humans and nonhuman organisms. The hierarchy so created is one of leadership and coordination, and although this "benign hierarchy" degenerates time again into tyranny or barbarism, its essence is far from the "Might is Right" logic of the jungle. Though "human-centered," the human role in ecosystems should be the "central station" for coordinating the balance and reciprocity of all living things.

While this is not the place to explore the possibility of a "benign hierarchy," Shen's approach to the sex trade is remarkably free from moral qualms and favors survival, livelihood, mutual care, and emotion. As the narrator of *Bian Cheng* 邊城 (*Border Town*) observes, "little dames" were brought in from the countryside and the army camps to meet the needs of locals. When night falls, "they'd take their turns serving the merchants and the boatmen, earnestly doing all that it was a prostitute's duty to do."[61] On the other hand, the prostitutes are romantic lovers and passionately committed to their loved ones. They "retained their long-lasting virtues of honesty and simplicity" (17). Serving customers and remaining devoted to the lover go hand in hand and do not clash. They could kill their lovers or take their own lives if they were to discover their unfaithfulness and betrayal. "Short-term commitments, long-term engagements, one-night stands—these transactions with women's bodies, given the simplicity of local mores, did not feel degrading or shameful to those who did business with their bodies, nor did those on the outside use the concepts of the educated to censure them or look down on them" (18).

But the educated, urban outsiders do censure them. The moral, or rather moralistic censure,[62] integral to the May Fourth culture and Confucian

---

60   This view is most remarkable in Shen's nostalgic description of communal and military life. Shunshun, the community leader, an "elder of tested virtue" (20) in *Bian Cheng* (*Border Town*), is a case in point. In "Three Men and a Woman," the military commander is the superior but is level with the foot soldiers.

61   Shen Congwen, *Border Town*, 17. Further references to this source are indicated by the page number in parentheses in the text.

62   I distinguish between "moral" and "moralistic." Ecological relations are "moral" in that humans could be sympathetic with and obliged to nonhumans, whereas the "moralistic" entails the absolutism and rigidity of a specific code of conduct detrimental to humans as well as nonhumans. In "Xiaoxiao," for instance, the girl's sexual vitality and her re-union with the little husband could be read as moral whereas the Confucian penalty is moralistic and inhuman.

morality, misses the bio-evolutionary bonds of human sexual life and nature. Shen Congwen frequently describes sexual acts between men and women not as individualistic, heterosexual intercourse, but as an occurrence propelled by external forces beyond human will or social expectations and decorum. The story "Fufu" 夫婦 (The Lovers) offers a compelling description of how forces of nature inspire and compel sexual acts, which offend the moral sensibility of a rural community. The two lovers are caught having sex in broad daylight and out of doors in a natural setting. A crowd gathers, and people taunt and humiliate the "criminals." The peasants project their own sexual frustration and fantasy on the lovers with sadistic pleasure.

Mr. Huang, an educated gentleman from the city who is visiting the village, intervenes and manages to stop the rush to judgment and punishment by the lynching mob. In his interrogation, the lovers turn out to be newlyweds on their way to the girl's parents residing in a nearby village. The critical moment of their sexual act is paradigmatic of Shen's description of sexuality prompted by natural surroundings:

> When they arrived here, the fine weather persuaded them to rest on a haystack of freshly mown rice straw, to view the wonderful scenery and all the mountain wildflowers. The sweet fragrances in the breeze, the hypnotic chatter of the birds, reminded them of what young people were here for.[63]

Apparently a spur-of the-moment tryst, "the very fact that they are married and had done their thing in broad daylight without covering themselves" (62) is more a welcome voice from inner and outer nature rather than an offense. The passage evidently renders the sexual act to be an innocent fulfillment of libidinal drives in rhythm with the primordial call of the wild.

This vignette of "sex in the haystack" in broad daylight recalls the exuberant scene of *yehe* 野合 (sex in the wild) in Zhang Yimou's film *Red Sorghum*. As the only character perceptive enough to share the narrator's sympathy, Huang discerns the significance of the sex act. He defends the couple and rejects all the suggestions of punishment. But more importantly, he salutes their act and endows it with dignity and sacredness. In parting with the couple, Huang escorts them up the mountain path and asks them if they are hungry. The husband answers that they will soon arrive at the father-in-law's house for

---

63   Shen, *Imperfect Paradise*, ed. and trans. Jeffrey Kinkley et al. (Honolulu: University of Hawai'i Press, 1995), 62. Further references to this source appear in parentheses in the text.

dinner and that they can find their way there by starlight. "At that, all three of them looked up into the heavens. Stars twinkled above the purple mass of mountains in the distance. It was a beautiful night" (64). As Huang sees them off, he catches "the fragrance of wildflowers in the breeze" (64) and feels the urge to ask for a memento of the occasion, which is a wreath of flowers that the young woman still holds. The story ends with a poetic elevation that lifts libidinal and natural vitality onto a sacred plane. Seeing them disappear into a thicket of bamboo, Huang sits down by the bridge, admiring the handful of half-withered flowers whose name he does not even know. "As he smells these blossoms that have been through such a strange experience in the woman's hair, vague pangs of desire unaccountably stirred in his heart" (65). He realizes how narrow his world is and how the narrow-minded country people are unaware and unworthy of the beautiful landscape in which a beautiful love event has just happened.

The story "Sange nanren he yige nüren" 三個男人和一個女人 (Three Men and A Woman) also treats sexuality as rooted in humans' animalistic nature, driven by nonhuman and mythical forces of a supernatural sort. Like "Fufu," the story elevates sexuality to the realm of the mythical and the divine. The plot traces how, in a village, two soldiers and a tofu seller harbor a secret love for a local girl and pursue their impossible dreams of gaining her. Beginning with a drawn-out description of the rain, the narrator hints at the ways the persistent rains forge emotional bonds between the soldiers and local women and facilitate camaraderie between the rank-and-file soldiers and commanders. Staying at a house in a village, the soldiers can joke with a local woman, "laugh a bit, and ask her for a few palm peelings with which we could wrap our feet."[64] The foot solders get a chance to wash their feet "in the same basin as the battalion commander," a liberty against military discipline (253).

The love narrative begins when the two soldiers spot a local girl who is "an angel on earth." Their animalistic desire, associated with the dogs that accompany her, gives rise to their love at first sight. The dogs initially "call forth murderous impulses" (253), hard to suppress, but lead to the delicate voice of the beautiful girl. Later, when the soldiers hang out with the tofu seller, who also desires her, and install themselves for months on end at his shop across the street from the girl's house, they set their eyes on those two white dogs and their mistress, following their "instinctive desires" (256).

More rational and levelheaded than his buddy, the narrator/soldier realizes that the three men's devotion to the girl is a case of "a toad with scabies

---

64 Lau et al., *Modern Chinese Stories*, 253. Further references to this source appear in parentheses in the text.

wishing to eat the meat of the heavenly goose" (256). Yet even this levelheaded soldier, overpowered by desire, finds himself at a loss as to why all three men devote themselves so intensely to this impossible love. One barrier is clearly class hierarchy, as the girl's family is the top ruling house of the village town. But that does not forestall the tofu seller. Coming from a mountain village, the seller has set up his business right in front of the girl's house. Mysterious, solid, and smart, he fits into Shen's archetype of the peasant imbued with honesty, simplicity, and primitive passion—a noble savage. A good man rooted in rural virtues, the seller believes in his masculine qualities as a hardworking and smart bread earner. Each time the girl steps out and glances at him, he would start to "lift the milestone to inspect the axle, thus showing his handsome, muscular forearms" (260). Time and again, "this youthful, honest, and simple man inspected his millstone in exactly the same manner" (26). The hidden truth is that the seller, out of nowhere, has set up and runs the tofu store across the street from the girl's house in order to win her hand. This gambit speaks to the religious intensity of his love-faith.

This love-faith remains hidden from the soldiers until the story's ending. Toward the end, the girl commits suicide by swallowing a piece of gold, a motif from the classical *Dream of the Red Chamber* and probably an act of defiance against an arranged marriage. The story takes a leap from the psychological narrative to rise to a nonhuman, supernatural realm. The tofu seller takes action to realize his dream, and by transcending the boundary between life and death, turns the "obscene to the divine" (265).

Although all three men are traumatized at the news of the girl's death, one of them, the disabled bugler, tries to reconnect with the dead girl by acting on a local myth that the "female victim of suicide by swallowing gold could come back to life if she were hugged and loved by a man within seven days of death" (264). His desire to bring the dead to life is "humanly uncontrollable, but when translated into real action it would still be inadmissible in this world" (264). Well aware of the human taboos involved, the bugler nevertheless toys with the idea of stealing the corpse, but wavers between rational norms and irrational impulses. The second time he goes to the grave, he finds it has been robbed.

News of the robbed grave and stolen corpse spreads and strikes fear. But the supernatural motif intrudes and overturns the human story. "Somebody found the girl's body in a cave about half a *li* away from the grave. She lay completely naked on a stone ledge. Wild blue chrysanthemums were scattered all over her body and on the grounds" (265). From the human and rational perspective, this seems to be superstitious nonsense and a fantastic piece of gossip that embellishes the horrendous event. But unbelievable as it is, the two soldiers know, deep down in their hearts, "what our other friend had done" (265).

Instead of disparaging the tofu seller, the narrator visualizes, in a tone of awe and fascination, the girl's naked body on the stone, enshrined and surrounded by abundant chrysanthemums, "turning the obscene to the divine."

I have attempted here to show that Shen Congwen's work, with its prescient critique of modern culture, urbanization, and alienation, takes on new ecological significance today. Sensitive to how modern culture severs humans' ties to nature and pre-modern life-worlds, Shen affirms an ecological understanding of life in which the writing self must trace its roots to nature and reconnect with other organisms. His animistic language immerses bodily sensations, pleasure, and feelings in nonhuman environs. Pitting nature against the historical teleology of progress, modernization, and consumerism, he reconnects humans to the millenniums-old entwinement of the archaic ways of living with the soil, landscape, and the earth, and targets the modern city's erosion of the simplicity, multiplicity, and vitality of rural life.

Shen Congwen's ecological insight reveals the deep bonds that unite human inner nature and outer nature. Human labor and behavior are described as deeply embedded in the nonhuman world of climate, clouds, plants, animals, rivers, and mountains. This sheds new light on the sympathetic and nonjudgmental depictions of sensuality and sexuality. Shen's love scenes affirm the biological and ecological union between inner nature and outer nature, and testify to the intimacy and conviviality between humans and nonhumans.

Rather than social norms, artificial conventions, fashions, and the mainstream literary language, Shen's work delves into vibrant nature in its restless potential for regeneration and ceaseless renewal. Nature emerges as the primal source of creativity and imagination. Human sexuality, vitality, and sensuality resonate and interact organically with the pulsating life of external environments. In turning the human into the divine, his work does not elevate the human, but gestures toward a religious realm of meaning beyond the pale of anthropocentrism.

Bibliography

Abrams, David. *The Spell of the Sensuous*. New York: Vintage Books, 1997.
Adorno, Theodor. *Aesthetic Theory*. Minneapolis: University of Minnesota Press, 1997.
Anderson, Marston. *The Limits of Realism: Chinese Fiction in the Revolutionary Period*. Berkeley: University of California Press, 1990.
Biro, Andrew, ed. *Critical Ecologies: The Frankfurt School and Contemporary Environmental Crises*. Toronto and London: University of Toronto Press, 2011.
Cai, Yuanpei. *Cai Yuanpei meixue wenlun* 蔡元培美學文論. Beijing: Peking University Press, 1983.

Clark, Timothy. *The Cambridge Introduction to Literature and Environment*. Cambridge, UK: Cambridge University Press, 2011.

Eagleton, Terry. *The Ideology of the Aesthetic*. Oxford, UK: Blackwell, 1990.

Kinkley, Jeffrey. *The Odyssey of Shen Congwen*. Stanford, CA: Stanford University Press, 1987.

Lau, Joseph, C. T. Hsia, and Leo Lee, eds. *Modern Chinese Stories and Novellas: 1919–1949*. New York: Columbia University Press, 1981.

Lu, Sheldon and Jiayan Mi, eds. *Chinese Ecocinema in the Age of Environmental Challenge*. Hong Kong: Hong Kong University Press, 2009.

Shen, Congwen. *Shen Congwen wenji* 沈從文文集. Hong Kong: Sanlian, 1982.

Shen, Congwen. *Imperfect Paradise*, ed. and trans. Jeffrey Kinkley et al. Honolulu: University of Hawai'i Press, 1995.

Shen, Congwen. *Shen Congwen piping wenji* 沈從文批評文集, ed. Liu Hongtao. Zhuhai, Guangdong: Zhuhai chubanshe, 1998.

Thornber, Karen. *Ecoambiguity: Environmental Crises and East Asian Literatures*. Ann Arbor, MI: The University of Michigan Press, 2012.

Wang, David Der-wei. *Fictional Realism in Twentieth-Century China: Mao Dun, Lao She, Shen Congwen*. New York: Columbia University Press, 1992.

Zhu, Guangqian. *Zhu Guangqian meixue wenji* 朱光潛美學文集. Shanghai: Shanghai wenyi, 1982.

CHAPTER 8

A New Vision of Life in Xiao Hong's *The Field of Life and Death*

Todd Foley

If the loosely related vignettes that comprise Xiao Hong's (蕭紅) *The Field of Life and Death* (生死場) are capable of producing a variety of critical responses, one thing is for sure: it is not for the faint of heart. While it does have its lighter moments, including those concerning a lost goat, a stolen melon, and the simple-minded Old Mother Pockface (麻面婆), the work features extensive depictions of suffering that take on a gruesome tone through the disturbingly mundane character of their presentation.

A random sampling of some of the more memorable scenes demonstrates this clearly enough: abandoned by her husband, the paralyzed Yueying (月英) watches maggots thrive on her rotting flesh; Golden Bough (金枝), sleeping on the streets of Harbin and mending clothing for a meager sum, ends up being raped by a lecherous customer; Mother Wang (王婆) drinks poison in a failed attempt to escape her miserable life, only to awaken in her coffin gasping for water. Unsettling as they may be, this sort of description indicates the seriousness of the work's attempt to directly confront an ugly reality, contributing to both its initial success upon publication and the solid presence it has maintained in the canon of modern Chinese literature.

The enduring literary value of the novel is evidenced by the continued production of compelling interpretations, and it is my hope in this chapter to build upon a number of these perspectives to suggest one way that the novel pushes the May Fourth spirit of literary iconoclasm to its furthest extent, inquiring not only into the fundamental problems of society but into the very nature of human existence.

The Field of Life and Death was the first novel Xiao Hong wrote during her short life (1911–1942), and the last to appear in Lu Xun's *Slave Series* (奴隸叢書), published in 1935. It was sandwiched between a preface by Lu Xun and an epilogue by Hu Feng, both of which emphasized the patriotic spirit of the work's depiction of the Japanese invasion of Manchuria—despite the "remarkable" fact that, as translator Howard Goldblatt points out, "less than one third of this short … novel concerns the Japanese at all."[1] In more recent decades, feminist readings of the novel have opened up a penetrating perspective that is able to offer a more complete treatment of the work.[2] These interpretations mainly draw upon the work of Lydia Liu, who argues that Xiao Hong is able to undermine the typical nationalist appropriation of the female body in literature by portraying it in opposition to the Chinese nation.[3] For Liu, the novel demonstrates that Xiao Hong's "dilemma was that she had to face two enemies, rather than one: imperialism and patriarchy. The latter tended to reinvent itself in multifarious forms, and national revolution was no exception."[4]

A third perspective I hope to build upon pays attention to the intriguing relationship between humans and animals depicted in the novel. A number of critics have commented on this prominent aspect of the work as part of their own various approaches. While Liu links representations of females and animals through their shared bodily experiences, Meng Yue and Dai Jinhua are primarily concerned with nature as the mode of production for rural life (鄉土自然生產方式), and they view animality through this lens. They argue that an "animalistic mentality" (動物性心態) comes with a complete erasure of any goals in the natural cycle of life, drawing an essentially spiritual distinction between humans and animals based on this static and cyclical mode of production.[5]

In more recent scholarship, Wang Qin focuses on animality in the novel by setting his argument in contrast to what he characterizes as the feminist perspectives demonstrated by Liu, Meng and Dai, suggesting that the presupposition of a common, fixed identity underlying these readings prevents us from truly and directly confronting the indistinguishable nature of humans

---

1 Howard Goldblatt, *Hsiao Hung* (Boston: Twayne, 1976), 45.
2 For a more complete overview of the novel's critical history, see Amy Dooling, "Xiao Hong's *Field of Life and Death*," *The Columbia Companion to Modern Chinese Literature*, ed. Kirk A. Denton (New York: Columbia University Press, 2016), 189–194.
3 Lydia Liu, *Translingual Practice: Literature, National Discourse, and Translated Modernity—China 1900–1937* (Stanford: Stanford University Press, 1995), 199–213.
4 Ibid., 211. Amy Dooling and Kristina Torgeson reinforce this interpretation, noting that "[Xiao Hong's] sense of the national situation is heavily mediated, if not subordinated, by concerns about gender-based forms of oppression. The suffering of the female characters in this grim narrative is represented not (as it so often would be in the resistance literature of this period) as a pretext for condemning Japanese or foreign incursions on Chinese soil, but as an indictment of the deeply ingrained, homegrown system of patriarchy that still thrived in rural China." *Writing Women in Modern China: An Anthology of Women's Literature from the Early Twentieth Century* (New York: Columbia University Press, 1998), 32.
5 Meng Yue and Dai Jinhua 孟悅、戴錦華, *Fuchu lishi dibiao: xiandai funü wenxue yanjiu* 浮出歷史地標—現代婦女文學研究 (Emerging from the horizon of history: Modern Chinese women's literature), (Beijing: Zhongguo renmin daxue chubanshe, 2004), 178–186.

and animals.[6] "Although this non-dialectical world [of the novel] is unable to progress or develop," he writes:

> This is not to say it is static and closed-off; on the contrary, it is the prerequisite for the possibility of the inversion, transformation, collapse, and generation of life forms—all realizable potential is concentrated within this world.
>
> 但這個既不前進也不發展的非辯證的世界，絕不是一個靜止封閉的世界; 相反, 它是生命形式的一切翻轉, 變形, 生成, 折疊的可能性前提, 將一切 "實現" 的可能性都塌縮其中的世界.[7]

While I share with Wang the idea that examining the relationship between human and animal in the work reveals a literary space for "pure potentiality" (純粹潛能),[8] I instead approach this possibility as an extension of feminist readings.[9] If we are to take seriously the dual oppressive forces of patriarchy and imperialism, then how does a reading of animality in the novel, with its seeming de-emphasis of the human, intersect with these more immediate political concerns? I propose that it offers an answer, however ambiguous, to the more practical question that Amy Dooling suggests is raised by the text: "How can historically oppressed subjects surmount the material and mental circumstances that pin them down in order to break free from an entrenched cycle of poverty, sexual violence, and habitual apathy?"[10] Dooling proposes that war might serve as a paradoxical answer, as it "forces open alternative patterns of human behavior from which new forms of consciousness might

---

6   Wang is careful to note that while Meng and Dai are mainly concerned with modes of production, they do also discuss Xiao Hong's female perspective.
7   Wang Qing 王欽, "'Qianneng,' dongwu yu siwang: chongdu Xiao Hong *Sheng si chang* "潛能"、動物與死亡—重讀蕭紅《生死場》(Potentiality, animality, and death: Rereading Xiao Hong's *The Field of Life and Death*)," *Zhongguo xiandai wenxue yanjiu congkan* 中國現代文學研究叢刊 (*Studies in Modern Chinese Literature*) 10 (2016): 26.
8   Wang's usage of this term, also translated as "pure possibility," refers to the work of Giorgio Agamben, namely *The Open: Man and Animal* (Stanford: Stanford University Press, 2004).
9   In another recent examination, Hangping Xu comments on the role of animality in the novel alongside its representations of females, disability, and the nationalist subject. "Animals," he writes, "become participants in the semiotic system, a phenomenological and experiential web of meaning and signs." "Rescuing Nature from the Nation: Ecocritical (Un)Consciousness in Modern Chinese Culture," in *A Global History of Literature and the Environment*, ed. John Parham and Louise Westling (New York: Cambridge University Press, 2017): 326.
10 Amy Dooling, "Xiao Hong's *Field of Life and Death*," 193.

emerge."[11] I hope to show that a close examination of the relationship between human and animal in *The Field of Life and Death* pushes this line of thinking to a still more radical and theoretical level, suggesting the only way to "break free" is the complete reformulation of human society, beginning from the total reconceptualization of the very notion of the human.

To reach this point, I will first show how Xiao Hong depicts the uselessness of traditional philosophical approaches to addressing the manifold suffering of the villagers, thereby demonstrating the need for a new sort of intellectual paradigm to enable liberation. I will then move on to examine the two most prominent human–animal relationships in the story: that between Old Mother Wang and her mare, and that between Two-and-a-Half Li and his goat. These relationships, I propose, suggest an essential and basic notion of life shared by both humans and animals that can provide a basis for rethinking the nature of human existence.

Finally, I will set my reading of the novel in light of the writings of the feminist anarchist thinker He-Yin Zhen (何殷震), whose thought underscores Xiao Hong's effort to fundamentally rethink the human.

1 The Failure of Traditional Philosophy

The novel opens by presenting a shared reality of physical experience that includes both Daoist and Buddhist elements. A long road (大道) going into the city passes through thick stands of shade trees blocking out the intense midday sun in a cloudless sky, suggesting a visual interplay of *yin* and *yang*. Two-and-a-Half Li's (二里半) goat seeks the shade of the trees while Sorghum, a bowlegged child, and the village peasants in the fields all suffer under the beating rays of the sun. The description of Old Mother Pockface, however, shows that this scene is not some detached, bucolic depiction of rural life, but rather one that depicts the suffering of physical reality. Old Mother Pockface enters the scene with a rather unflattering introduction:

> Perspiration gathered on the face of Old Mother Pockface like pearl drops or peas, seeping into every pockmark and then flowing downwards. Old Mother Pockface was not a butterfly. She could not sprout wings. Only pockmarks. Two butterflies flitted by Old Mother Pockface, and she swatted at them with her wet hands, bringing them down. One fell into the tub and drowned.

11 Ibid.

汗水在麻面婆的臉上，如珠如豆，漸漸侵著每個麻痕而下流. 麻面婆不是一隻蝴蝶, 她生不出磷膀來, 只有印就的麻痕. 兩隻蝴蝶飛飛戲著閃過麻面婆, 她用濕的手把飛著的蝴蝶打下來, 一個落到盆中溺死了！[12]

While the narrator's emphatic statement that "Old Mother Pockface was not a butterfly" gestures toward Zhuangzi's famous "butterfly dream," Old Mother Pockface thoughtlessly bats away any contemplative or philosophical associations the butterflies might carry. Zhuangzi was unsure if he was his human self dreaming that he was a butterfly, or rather a butterfly dreaming to be himself. For Old Mother Pockface, however, as she needlessly swats at the butterflies and continues on with her washing, her existence as a laboring village woman is clearly a harsh reality that has no room for the luxury of philosophical escape.

The same is true for Golden Bough, who is visited by butterflies at the moment she realizes, to her horror, that she is pregnant.

> After she was certain that she was pregnant, her heart shuddered as though it were retching. She was seized with terror. When two butterflies wondrously alighted one on top of the other on her knees, she only stared at the two copulating insects and did not brush them off. Golden Bough seemed to become a scarecrow in a rice field.
>
> 等她確信肚子有了孩子的時候, 她的心立刻發嘔一般顫慄起來, 她被恐怖把握著了. 奇怪的, 兩個蝴蝶疊落著貼落在她膝頭. 金枝看著這邪惡的一對蟲子而不拂去它. 金枝彷彿是米田上的稻草人.[13]

Once again butterflies enter the scene, calling to mind Zhuangzi's dream and its stark contrast with Golden Bough's situation, which is only too real and immutable. Golden Bough sees herself as the butterflies, which are mating just as she herself had so recently done. The biological facts of life are no different for her than they are for the butterflies, driven to procreate, yet the revulsion Golden Bough feels toward the "hideous monstrosity" (可怕的怪物)

---

12 English text from: *The Field of Life and Death and Tales of Hulan River*, trans. Howard Goldblatt and Ellen Yeung (Bloomington: Indiana University Press, 1979), 4–5. Unless otherwise indicated, all English translations are taken from this edition. I have changed Romanized names to their pinyin form. Chinese text from: *Sheng si chang: Xiao Hong jingdian bi du* 生死場：蕭紅經典必讀 (*The Field of Life and Death*: Xiao Hong's must-read classics) (Beijing: Wenhua yishu chubanshe, 2012), 9–10. The text for all quotations from the novel will be taken from these editions, with the page number for the English translation preceding that for the Chinese text.

13 25, 26.

growing in her belly clearly demonstrates the abyss that separates her specific human, female world from that of the insects. While Golden Bough and the butterflies are subject to the laws of nature and procreation, Golden Bough is additionally subject to the human society in which she lives, and which will determine the unfortunate conditions of her pregnancy and life thereafter. The description of her as a scarecrow indicates her complete lack of agency as she is trapped not only in her small village environment, but as a human woman oppressed by the social conditions of a certain time and place from which escape seems impossible. The butterflies here serve as a poignant Zhuangzian metaphor that only highlights the philosophy's inability to offer Golden Bough any measure of practical relief.[14]

Golden Bough does attempt to flee both physically and spiritually, but with no real success. Her husband abuses her and kills their child, and she eventually leaves their village for Harbin. The city, however, offers her no new possibilities of existence: she is still beholden to the vicious cycle of life and death characterized by the patriarchal control of the female body, as she is raped by one of her clients who has hired her to do some mending. Even the avenue of metaphysical escape is closed off to her: in the penultimate chapter, Golden Bough decides to become a nun, but any possibilities for a new, Buddhist existence are immediately dashed when she arrives at the temple. She learns that the resident nun supposedly "ran off with the carpenter who was building the temple," and that the structure now stands vacant. The reason for the nun's departure is essentially the same as the root of all Golden Bough's troubles: a romantic/sexual involvement with a man, which is a crucial touchstone in the novel's cycles of life and death. Further emphasizing this point is the fact that the neighbor from whom Golden Bough learns this information is herself pregnant and alone, her husband having left to join the army (although he unexpectedly returns home at the end of the chapter). Golden Bough's discussion with the woman about the particular danger she faces from the Japanese, who "slit open the women's bellies and take the fetuses with them to battle" (日本子把女人肚子割開, 去帶著上陣), furthermore, writes the specific, local suffering of women into a national context, in which the motherland is being raped by outside invaders.[15] Golden Bough's attempt to enter this monastery shows that her concerns, however, appear to extend beyond those of nation

---

14　The concept of time as cyclical rather than linear enhances the novel's Daoist overtones. Amy Dooling notes that "Time in the rural village is not the progressive, linear chronology of history but is a time suspended in a relentless natural rhythm." ("Xiao Hong's Field," 192.)
15　105, 90. Lydia Liu, commenting on Golden Bough's rape by one of her customers in Harbin, points out Xiao Hong's inversion of "the trope of the raped woman in nationalist discourse" by comparing the work to her husband Xiao Jun's (蕭軍) *A Village in August* (八月的鄉村). "As if in deliberate parody of Xiao Jun's novel," notes Liu, "the rape that

and gender, to an ambiguous metaphysical concern for her own existence: if she knows the Japanese are nearby, as she warns the pregnant woman, then entering this monastery seems like it would offer little practical benefit regarding her physical safety.

The novel makes it clear that withdrawal from the world is impossible, and retreating into Buddhism offers only an empty promise. This is not the first abandoned temple to appear in the story: as Old Mother Wang is leading her old horse to the slaughterhouse in the third chapter, they pass "deserted houses and dilapidated temples."

> In front of one of these small temples lay a dead child, bundled up in straw. The child's head and pitiful little feet extended from the straw. Whose child was this, sleeping in front of this temple in the wilderness?
>
> 經過一些荒涼的家屋, 經過幾座頹敗的小廟. 一個小廟前躺著個死了的小孩, 那是用一捆穀草束扎著的. 孩子小小的頭頂露在外面, 可憐的小腳從草梢直伸出來; 他是誰家的孩子, 睡在這曠野的小廟前?[16]

Buddhist withdrawal from the world is therefore not an option for anyone, as the examples of Golden Bough and the abandoned child demonstrate. The temples are also subject to the harsh realities of life and death, and can offer no real practical or spiritual refuge.

Yet the cyclical suffering in the novel, along with these empty temples, creates a particular existential anxiety if neither Buddhism nor Daoism can offer any sort of relief. For this reason, the role of Buddhism in particular warrants closer examination. Scholars have given varying degrees of significance to the Buddhist implications of the novel's title,[17] as the words life/birth [*sheng* 生] and death [*si* 死] together hint toward the Buddhist idea of samsara, or the

---

occurs in Xiao Hong's work, which is also set on the eve of the Anti-Japanese War, turns out to be committed by a Chinese man rather than by a Japanese soldier." (162)

16 31–32, 31.

17 Xiao Hong herself, however, did not give the novel its title, and two competing claims have been made for this distinction. In his preface to a reprinting of the work, Xiao Hong's husband, fellow leftist writer Xiao Jun, says that he named it, while Hu Feng credited himself for the title while speaking at a fiftieth anniversary celebration to commemorate the work. Jiang Zhijun (蔣志軍), editor of a collection of research on Xiao Hong, weighs the issue in a brief essay and reasons that Hu Feng is more likely to have given the novel its name (52–53). At any rate, both Xiao Jun and Hu Feng describe the selection of the title as having arisen naturally from the contents of the novel itself, so the Buddhist inflection of the title only highlights an aspect of the novel that both men found to be present, rather than attempting to impose a certain lens through which to read the work.

cycles of birth, life, and death which repeat through reincarnation.[18] Lydia Liu generally disregards Buddhist associations,[19] while Gang Yue, in his study of eating and hunger in Chinese literature, dismisses Daoism and Buddhism in the novel by noting that Xiao Hong "is neither a Daoist who cultivates wisdom and seeks immortality by enduring hardship, nor a Buddhist who chooses not to eat in order to deny her flesh and transcend the domain of carnality...." Rather, he says, she "insists on her redemption in the everyday of this world...."[20] While I agree with Yue's materialist view of food and the body that undercuts the liberating possibilities of Daoism and Buddhism, that is not necessarily to say they cannot be employed as interpretive schema. In the introduction to his translation, Howard Goldblatt notes that there is a "strong Buddhist flavor" throughout the novel, stating that "the villagers' fatalistic attitudes, repeated mentions of the four distresses (birth, old age, sickness, and death), and even the title itself ... are unquestionable and, we can assume, conscious references to the Buddhist faith."[21] C. T. Hsia, furthermore, invests the work's Buddhist implications with greater significance, commenting that "in my opinion *The Field of Life and Death* remains Hsiao Hung's most powerful book because of its implicitly Buddhist view of the essential horror of village existence."[22]

While Hsia does not elaborate on this implicitly Buddhist view, there are many indications in the novel that suggest it might be productively read from a Buddhist perspective of suffering and samsara (*lunhui* 輪迴).[23] One of the most prominent references to samsara comes in chapter ten, "Ten Years"

---

18   The novel's connection with Buddhism, however, does not appear to be a major point of discussion in Chinese scholarship.
19   Liu, *Translingual Practice*, 164.
20   *The Mouth That Begs: Hunger, Cannibalism, and the Politics of Eating in Modern China*, (Durham, NC: Duke University Press, 1999), 293.
21   *Field*, xxi. In his biography of Xiao Hong, Goldblatt relegates Buddhism to a footnote (143, n. 36). As far as Xiao Hong's own personal beliefs are concerned, Huang Xiaojuan (黃曉娟) notes that Xiao Hong nowhere in her writings mentions the influence of Buddhism, which leads Huang to what is perhaps an overstatement, saying that "Xiao Hong had no understanding of Buddhism; she merely relied on the innate ability of her spirit to directly grasp this sort of mystery of life" (蕭紅對佛學無所了解, 她幾乎是憑著自己的精神本能, 直接悟出了這樣的生命奧秘) (98).
22   "Hsiao Hung. By Howard Goldblatt," Review, *The Journal of Asian Studies* 37.1 (1977): 103–104.
23   One scholar, in fact, goes as far as creating a chart that matches up the novel's chapters with corresponding sections of the wheel of samsara, suggesting that Xiao Hong deliberately chose it as a formal model for the novel. See Friedrich Bischoff, "Hsiao Hung's Wheel of Life and Death," *Chinese Literature: Essays, Articles, Reviews (CLEAR)* 2.2 (1980): 249–257.

(十年), which consists of only a few sentences. With explicit Buddhist terminology, Xiao Hong writes, "in the village the cycle of life and death went on exactly as it had ten years before" (大片的村莊生死輪迴著和十年前一樣).[24] Perhaps Xiao Hong's most vivid depiction of something like samsara, however, comes in chapter six, "Days of Punishment" (刑罰的日子). Here, the ceaseless cycle of life and death is portrayed through juxtaposed images of humans and animals giving birth. The pain of labor is so great for Old Mother Pockface that she calls for a knife, yet she gives birth to a healthy baby, while another woman produces a stillborn. Sexual desire continues to drive this cycle, mixing pleasure with pain: the villagers listen to a bull in a shed violently battle for its mate, and when Golden Bough is expecting some form of abuse from Cheng Ye, she instead receives a sexual advance. The detached, third-person narrative voice tells us that "in the village, humans and beasts busied themselves at living and at dying" (在鄉村, 人和動物一起忙著生, 忙著死), poignantly summarizing Xiao Hong's attempt to depict samsara through May Fourth realism.[25]

The examination and cessation of suffering lies at the heart of Buddhist philosophy, and if we are to take this Buddhist element of the novel seriously, then the nature of the suffering depicted by Xiao Hong in these ruthless cycles must be examined. The Four Noble Truths—that all life is suffering; suffering is caused by desire; emancipation comes from the elimination of desire; and the way to emancipation is the Noble Eightfold Path—can provide us with an efficient outline for approaching suffering and the possibilities of its cessation.

Suffering is perhaps the most consistently and vividly depicted experience in the novel, making this first "truth" quite apparent. In the May Fourth spirit, the novel clearly identifies the social and political origins of suffering in imperialism and patriarchy, yet the close and persistent juxtaposition of human with animal—specifically regarding birthing, procreation, disease, and death—shows a more basic, natural level of suffering. Hu Feng, in fact, recognizes these distinctions in his afterword, identifying the dual tyrants of nature and humankind, and comparing human beings to ants toiling under the tyranny of both nature and those with two legs.[26] Based in the fundamental level of natural suffering, but also common to all the human-created levels, is the driving "thirst" of sexual desire and the urge to procreate. Finally, we can see Golden Bough's attempted retreat to the monastery at the end of the novel as

---

24   72, 64.
25   56 (Translation slightly altered), 51.
26   "*Sheng si chang* du hou ji《生死場》讀後記 (After reading *The Field of Life and Death*)," *Xiao Hong yanjiu qishi nian: xia juan*《蕭紅研究七十年：下卷》(70 years of Xiao Hong research: Volume 2) (Harbin: Beifang wenyi chubanshe, 2011), 4.

a futile attempt to embark on the Eightfold Path and withdraw from the world of human suffering.

Examining the full extent of human suffering a bit further reveals a kind of reversal of the hierarchy of the wheel of samsara, which normally features humans as part of the three upper realms of existence along with gods and demi-gods, and animals as part of the three lower realms along with hungry ghosts and hell beings. While suffering in the novel is concentrated on the bodies of all females, human females suffer the most.[27] In "Days of Punishment," dogs, pigs, and birds all give birth without incident, while it is the female humans who are all depicted as suffering. Although animals like "cows or horses in their ignorance cultivate their own suffering" (牛或是馬在不知覺中忙著栽培自己的痛苦),[28] they paradoxically seem to enjoy a markedly less tormented existence than humans. This reversal is actually set forth in the second chapter: "For farming people, even a single vegetable or a single straw was worth more than a human being" (農家無論是菜棵, 或是一株茅草也要超過人的價值).[29] Beyond the particular burden that females must bear in the human world, all humans endure additional suffering under certain conditions of their own making. Chinese suffer under the Japanese; Zhao San (趙三) and his fellow peasant participants in the vaguely described "Sickle Society" suffer under the landlord; women and children suffer under men; poor, exploited workers suffer in the capitalist urban environment of Harbin; and even domesticated animals—drawn partly into the realm of human society—suffer under their human masters. These are the social conditions of existence, which are unavoidably adopted and practiced on the individual level, and which are ultimately all-encompassing and inescapable. Demonstrating the uselessness of traditional philosophy in easing the suffering wrought by this society, Xiao Hong at the same time attempts a new intellectual approach that involves a return to the basic relationship between humans and animals.

---

27 Commenting on "Days of Punishment," Liu observes that "In their experience of the body, female animals and women have more in common than women and men do. The agony of having one's flesh torn apart, bones cracked, and life endangered [through childbirth] generates a kind of knowledge impermeable to the male sex." (165–166)
28 56, 51.
29 26, 27.

2   Human, Animal, and an End to Suffering

Many critics who have commented on the relationship between human and animal in the novel have focused on a spiritual distinction between the two categories, and/or interpreted animality through a metaphorical lens. Meng and Dai, for instance, describe the animalization of the novel's characters as part of the natural and cyclical mode of production they identify in the novel, arriving at a standard distinction between human and animal as essentially that between body and soul:

> Their joy is animalistic, and they have no desires other than those of the flesh. Their pain is animalistic, experiencing physical suffering but no spiritual sorrow. [...] The behavior, thinking, and form of all the characters approaches that of animals—like old horses, they are unthinkingly bound by habit.... This animalistic crowd has brains but no thought, desires but no hope or despair, pain but no sadness, memory but no reminiscence, families but no affection, and bodies but no souls.

> 他們的歡樂是動物性的，除肉體的慾望外沒有願望，他們的痛苦是動物性的，只有肉體的苦難而沒有心靈的悲哀 ... 他們的行為，思維，型態也近於動物，他們像老馬般囿於習慣而不思不想 ... 這動物性的人眾有頭腦而沒有思想，有慾望沒有希望或絕望，有疼痛沒有悲傷，有記憶而沒有回憶，有家庭而沒有親情，有形體而無靈魂。[30]

Zhen A'ping and Ye Jianzhong echo this essentially spiritual distinction, attributing the animalization of the novels' characters to a lack of any human meaning beyond biological drive. The example of Golden Bough and Cheng Ye, they argue, demonstrates that the characters "instinctively seek animalistic pleasure, and their behavior does not seem to be a sublimation of another sort of meaningful activity. [...] New lives are simply the byproducts of indulgence in sexual desire" (本能地追求動物般的性快樂，幾乎沒有把他們的行為昇華成任何有意義的活動 ... 新的生命只是性慾享受下的附帶品).[31] Lydia Liu similarly focuses on the physicality of Xiao Hong's descriptions of humans

---

30 Meng, *Fuchu lishi dibiao*, 181.
31 Zheng A'ping and Ye Jianzhong 鄭阿平, 葉建鍾, "*Sheng si chang* yu *Hong gaoliang* de shengming yishi 《生死場》與《紅高粱家族》的生命意識 (Consciousness of life in *The Field of Life and Death* and *Red Sorghum Family*)," *Xiao Hong yanjiu qishi nian: xia juan*. In 《蕭紅研究七十年：下卷》(70 Years of Xiao Hong research: Volume 2), ed. Xiao Chuan (曉川) and Peng Fang (彭放). Harbin: 北方文藝出版社, 2011. pp. 80–85, 81.

and animals, which for her has metaphorical significance, noting that "Xiao Hong's language becomes particularly powerful when metonymy as well as metaphor is used to evoke animals and humans contiguously so that the two species are joined in the homogenous space of the body."[32] Finally, while Wang Qin eschews a priori definitions of identities that would lead to a simple split between body and soul, he does also focus on the materialist implications of this spiritual lack, which is where he locates the generative potential of the possibilities of life. The novel itself, he notes, states this in explicit terms: "In the village, one remained forever unaware. One could never experience the spiritual side of life; only the material aspects gave these people sustenance" (在鄉村永久不曉得, 永久體驗不到靈魂, 只有物質來充實她們).[33]

Two poignant examples of humans' relationships with animals, however, do provide humans with the occasion to experience a spiritual side of life. Not only do they stand as the greatest expressions of love in the novel, but they also place the value of life in affective, spiritual terms that are not unique to the domain of the human. Although the novel's striking depictions of humans and animals gesture toward a Buddhist understanding of life, the explicit failure of this philosophy—at least in its practical instantiation—to provide any tangible relief from suffering forces us not only to reexamine the relationship between humans and animals on its own terms, but also to question how this reexamination can help end the villagers' tortuous cycle of life and death by opening up new intellectual ground.

The third chapter, "The Old Mare's Trip to the Slaughterhouse" (老馬走進屠場), depicts Old Mother Wang's reluctant journey to the city to have her old mare slaughtered for cash.[34] Forced to carry out her task in order to pay the rent, Mother Wang finds herself in emotional turmoil simply because of her feelings for the horse. At the heart of her empathy is her realization of their shared embodied vulnerability. At several points in the chapter, Mother Wang imagines her own body being subjected to the imminent slaughtering the horse will undergo:

> She shivered at the horrible vision of the butcher's knife severing her own spine....

---

32 Liu, *Translingual Practice*, 164.
33 36–37, 35.
34 Amy Dooling understands this scene as an example of Xiao Hong's use of natural symbolism in an attempt to "challenge conventional distinctions between humankind and nature and to underscore the brute existence all living creatures endure." ("Xiao Hong's Field," 192.)

她顫顫寒起來, 幻想著屠刀要像穿過自己的背脊 …

[…]

When Mother Wang saw the cowhide nailed to the wall, she felt as if her heart, too, were suspended in the air, about to crash to the ground.

王婆的心自己感覺得好像懸起來; 好像要掉落一般, 當她看見板墻釘著一張張牛皮的時候.

[…]

The old lady was frightened by the bloodstains and felt as if she herself were entering an execution ground.

被血痕所恐嚇的老太婆好像自己踏在刑場了![35]

Not only does Mother Wang realize that butchering will render the same physical suffering for the horse as it would for her, allowing her to empathize with the old mare in terms of their shared physical embodiment, but she also shares with the animal a sense of helplessness and passivity in the situation. When the chapter opens with the pair heading toward the city, we learn that "Old Mother Wang was not leading the horse. She was following behind, driving it ahead of her with a switch" (老王婆不牽著她的馬兒, 在後面用一條短枝驅著它前進).[36] This reverse ordering, with the mare leading the way, reflects the implication in the chapter's title that both Mother Wang and the mare are stripped of any real agency. "The old horse enters the slaughterhouse," the heading more literally reads, making the horse itself, rather than Mother Wang, the acting subject.

While Mother Wang is obviously driving the horse with her switch, she does so with the same helpless resignation exhibited by the horse: if either of them is to survive, Mother Wang must pay the rent, and this is the only way. Lest we think that Mother Wang stands to gain any profit from the mare, we are told that all the money will "eventually be snatched from Mother Wang's hands by the landlord" (地主又要從王婆的手裡奪去),[37] and we do not have to wait long for this to occur. As soon as she arrives home,

---

35   31–32, 31–32.
36   30, 30.
37   32, 32.

A servant from the landlord was already waiting by the door. Landlords never let even a single penny go to waste on the peasants. The servant left with her money. For Mother Wang, her day of agony was all for naught. Her whole life was all for naught.

家中地主的使人早等在門前，地主們就連一块銅板也從不捨棄在貧貧農們的身上，那個使人取了錢走去。王婆半日的痛苦沒有代價了！王婆一生的痛苦也都是沒有代價。[38]

Clearly, Mother Wang is as helpless in this situation as the mare, and the two are nearly interchangeable. Both have toiled and suffered their whole lives, but for nothing—translated more literally, the final sentence here says that "Mother Wang's life of hardship had no worth." Both human and animal are equally beholden to the cruelty of human society, which not only eliminates all value of life, but forces them to be the agents of this—their own—elimination.

Yet there is an undeniable value to life that is revealed by Mother Wang's tears. Despite having led horses and oxen to the slaughterhouse countless times in her past, this time she "wept all the way home until her two sleeves were completely soaked with tears. It seemed as if she had just returned from a funeral procession" (她哭著回家，兩隻袖子完全濕透. 那好像是送葬禮歸來一般).[39] In the context of the novel, this is a strikingly emotional reaction, the likes of which never appears in relation to human death. Passing by a dead child laid in front of a temple along the path elicits little reaction from Mother Wang, yet the impending death of her horse turns her into an emotional wreck. She does not weep from a detached, philosophical respect for life or from fear of karmic retribution; nor does her reaction seem to be just a metaphorical extension of her own anxieties about death. Why is it that her mare elicits such a reaction?

Interestingly, a third and seemingly unrelated character appears in this chapter: Two-and-a-Half Li. Encountering Mother Wang and the mare on the road to the city, he shakes with emotion as he voices the moral injustice of the situation:

Two-and-a-Half Li felt very sad, and his body trembled. [...] "It's not right to send it to the soup cauldron. It's just not right...." But what could he do? He was at a loss for words. He limped forward and patted the horse's mane. The horse snorted in response. Its eyes looked as if they were

---

[38] 34, 33.
[39] 34, 33.

crying, wet and glassy. Waves of pain stabbed Mother Wang's heart. In a choked-up voice she said: "What is to be must be. If I don't send it to the cauldron, the only alternative is starvation."

二里半感到非常悲痛. 他痙攣著了. 過了一個時刻轉過身來, 他趕上去說: "下湯鍋是下不得的 ... 下湯鍋是下不得 ..." 但是怎麼辦呢? 二里半連半句話言也沒有了! 他扭歪著身子跨到前面, 用手摸一摸馬兒的鬃髮. 老馬立刻響著鼻子了! 它的眼睛哭著一般, 濕潤而模糊. 悲傷立刻掠過王婆的面孔. 哑哑著嗓子, 王婆說: "算了吧! 算了吧! 不下湯鍋, 還不是等著餓死嗎?"[40]

All parties here, human and animal, express a deep sadness despite what could be seen as clearly rational and reasonable circumstances—don't most draught animals get slaughtered at the end of their working lives? Mother Wang's repeated substitutions of herself as the one to be butchered, however, demonstrate that humans share the same lived reality as the horse, as all are subject to the same physical consequences; furthermore, their embodied realities are shown to be completely without value to the world they live in. Stripped down to these bare facts, humans and horses are no different: they are all vulnerable, worthless lives without agency. "The old mare's trip to the slaughterhouse," then, shows the essential commensurability of human and animal in these basic terms.

At the same time, however, the sadness felt by Mother Wang, Two-and-a-Half Li, and the horse indicates that life does have some inherent value. Their emotion demonstrates the basic, shared truth of this value, which is otherwise inexpressible in the world of the novel and can only surge forth as a spiritual excess through their tears. When Mother Wang and the horse finally do make it to the slaughterhouse, they do not want to separate, although they of course have no choice. As Mother Wang turns to leave, the horse follows her out, so she leads it back in and scratches its head. Her subsequent tears mourn the spiritual value of life that is denied expression, yet at the same time they affirm the truth of its existence.

Complementing this chapter is the story of Two-and-a-Half Li and his goat. This relationship actually frames the entire novel, indicating its overall significance. At first, Two-and-a-Half Li's loss of the goat in the opening scene seems like little more than a comedic episode in which he gets beaten by a neighbor for trampling their cabbages and the neighbor's wife, Old Mother Pockface, displays her coarse but well-intentioned stupidity. The goat, meanwhile,

---

40   31, 31.

wanders in blissful ignorance along the road to the city, stopping intermittently to nibble and nap. Two-and-a-Half Li's anger and frustration over losing the goat initially seems as if it is likely born out of practical, economic concerns, but as the story progresses, it becomes clear that his attachment to the goat is emotional rather than practical. This accords with the consistent care and attention he (often gruffly) shows toward all life, even trees:

> In front of his house stood a poplar tree, the leaves of which rustled and shook. Every day, as Two-and-a-Half Li passed beneath the tree, he invariably stopped to listen to the rustling sound of its leaves and watch their movement. So it was with the poplar day after day, and day after day he stopped. On this day, however, he abandoned his routine. His mind was a complete blank. His limp had become more pronounced, and with each stride he seemed to be stepping into a hole.
>
> 他家門前種著一株楊樹，楊樹翻擺著自己的葉子. 每日二里半走在楊樹下, 總是聽一聽楊樹的葉子怎樣響, 看一看楊樹的葉子怎樣怎樣擺動; 楊樹每天這樣 … 他也每天停腳. 今天是他第一次破例, 什麼他都忘記, 只見跌腳跌得更深了! 每一步像在踏下一個坑去.[41]

While Two-and-a-Half Li is so preoccupied by the loss of his goat that he is unable to observe the leaves, the goat still partakes in what is apparently their shared interest, as "it passed under every tree and listened to every whispering leaf" (它經過每棵高樹, 也聽遍了每張葉子的刷鳴).[42] The goat's innocent wanderings are directly paralleled by those of a child making his way through the sorghum field, "a world of verdant sweetness, a world that was obviously cooler than the one outside" (那里綠色的甜味的世界, 顯然涼爽一些).[43] In these first few paragraphs, the napping goat, the wandering child (who turns out to be Two-and-a-Half Li's son), the tree leaves that move and whisper, and the shady road all combine to create a Zhuangzian image of "free and easy wandering" (逍遙遊) that is quickly shattered by the horrific suffering portrayed in the rest of the novel. The initial description of this scene, however, in which the characters are not yet named but merely described as a child (孩子) and farmer (農夫), presents humans, animals, and even trees in a lazy, harmonious image of free-flowing life that has not yet become subject to the cruelty of the human world in which the villagers are trapped.

---

41 4, 9.
42 8, 12.
43 3–4, 9.

The full extent of Two-and-a-Half Li's love for the goat does not become explicit until a later episode, when the villagers gather to take an ambiguous oath in the wake of the Japanese invasion. When a sacrificial rooster cannot be found, some men come to seize Two-and-a-Half Li's goat:

> [The goat] bleated pitifully. Two-and-a-Half Li, looking comical in his sorrow, walked behind the goat with a limping gait as though he were stomping holes in the ground. [...] His wife tried to drag him back but could not.
>
> 二里半可笑的悲哀的形色跟著山羊走來。 他的跛腳彷彿是一步一步把地面踏陷 ... 他的老婆瘋狂地想把他拖回去, 然而不能做到 ...[44]

Not only is Two-and-a-Half Li once again visibly affected by the prospect of losing his goat, but he also demonstrates his complete lack of interest in political affairs: while Zhao San is making a rousing speech about how he is a nationless slave who wants the Chinese flag planted on his grave, Two-and-a-Half Li is out trying to save his goat. After the oaths have all been sworn and the goat is about to be killed, he returns just in time with a rooster. Not only was he "the only person who did not take the oath," but neither did he "seem particularly distressed about the fate of the nation as he led the goat home (只有他沒曾發誓, 對於國亡, 他似乎沒什麼傷心, 他領著山羊, 就回家去)."[45]

For Two-and-a-Half Li, not only are politics and the opinions of others explicitly less important than his goat—at the previous meeting, before his goat is in danger, he "simply could not generate any interest in these matters (二里半對於這些事情)"[46] and dozes off—but his care for life in general also sets him apart from the other men in the village. He is described as being "lenient" (寬容) with his wife, and while he nevertheless doles out a good number of insults, he still stands in contrast to the other, much more violent men. His appearance in the third chapter with Mother Wang and the horse, furthermore, reinforces this portrait of him. He turns up simply to lament the horse's fate and articulate the moral injustice, showing that Two-and-a-Half Li's general concern for all life transcends species boundaries and opposes violence. The life that Two-and-a-Half Li wants with his goat, however, appears to be impossible without taking some sort of action.

---

44   85, 74.
45   87–88, 76.
46   81, 71.

While the penultimate chapter describing Golden Bough's failed attempt to become a nun shows that Buddhist withdrawal does not provide any existential solutions, the final chapter, which centers on Two-and-a-Half Li and his goat, suggests that the origins of any possible answers must first be located in the affirmation of an ontological unity of human and animal. In the final paragraphs of the story, Two-and-a-Half Li decides that "in order to free himself from all worries and ties, it seemed to him that he must kill the goat at once" (他要使自己無牽無掛, 好像非立刻殺死老羊不可).[47] Of course, he is unable to harm the goat, releasing the cleaver in midair.[48] Instead,

> The old animal came up to him and scratched itself against his legs. For a long time, Two-and-a-Half Li stroked its head. He was overcome with shame, and like a Christian, he prayed to the goat. In the morning he seemed to be talking to the goat again. He muttered for a while in the goat pen, then he fastened the gate. The goat grazed in the pen.
>
> 老羊走過來, 在他的腿間搔癢. 二里半許久許久的撫摸羊頭, 他十分羞愧, 好像耶穌教徒一般向羊禱告. 清早他像對羊說話在羊棚喃喃了一陣, 關好羊欄, 羊在欄中吃草.[49]

While destroying the goat—the only meaningful attachment Two-and-a-Half Li has left in the world following the death of his family members—would have freed Two-and-a-Half Li from "all worries and ties," it would have also amounted to his own spiritual destruction. His prayer to the goat, while perhaps not very much like a Christian, indicates the animal's crucial role in his own spiritual constitution. By showing that the goat is clearly an essential part of Two-and-a-Half Li's own conception of his very being, this final scene reveals the ontological underpinnings of the relationship between human and animal that has been variously depicted throughout the novel.

The emotional intensity of the final scene, describing Two-and-a-Half Li's shame followed by his reluctance to part with the goat as "his weeping hands caressed the goat's hair for the last time" (他流淚的手, 最後一刻摸著羊毛),[50] suggests that his decision to leave and join up with the People's Revolutionary Army is not in spite of his love for the goat, but in fact because of it. His explicit

---

47 109, 92.
48 Wang Qin draws an interesting comparison with the story from Genesis in which Abraham is about to sacrifice his son Isaac, but God provides a ram as a substitute. (22)
49 109, 93.
50 110, 93.

political and ideological disengagement earlier in the novel stands in surprising contrast to his final, heartrending decision to leave for the army—as one scholar notes, he is in fact "the opposite of the ideal national subject."[51] Why, then, is Two-and-a-Half Li suddenly so resolute in his commitment? Crippled and unable to see his goat or Mother Wang's horse come to harm, the deadly fate that awaits him in the army seems certain. His decision, therefore, essentially substitutes his own life for that of the goat. As both are part of the same life, an inseparable ontological unity, killing the animal would extinguish the most fundamental element of this life. Putting the human element at risk of death, however, retains the possibility of survival by presenting the chance to break out of the novel's cruel cycle of suffering and death through some sort of revolutionary action. Only the self-destruction of the human can enable the possibility for an entirely new structure and form of life to emerge—a new form of humanity that values life and is free from self-imposed forms of suffering.

3 Conclusion: He-Yin Zhen and Becoming Animal to Reimagine Humanity

It is unclear whether or not Xiao Hong was familiar with the work of He-Yin Zhen 何殷震 (1884–1920),[52] the short-lived but spirited feminist anarchist who published many of her essays between 1907 and 1908 in the journal she founded called *Natural Justice* (*Tianyi bao* 天義報). My aim here is not to trace Xiao Hong's specific intellectual heritage or influences, but rather to demonstrate how reading *The Field of Life and Death* in light of He-Yin Zhen's ideas can suggest a way of approaching the problems of female embodied existence by taking them as problems of the structure of human life in general. Both writers seem to suggest that a return to the most basic, "animal" level of existence can be the starting point for recreating a human structure of life that no longer includes the suffering inflicted by patriarchy, imperialism, modernity, and tradition.[53]

---

51   Xu, "Rescuing Nature," 327.
52   Lydia Liu, Rebecca Karl, and Dorothy Ko point out in their edited volume of a selection of He-Yin's writings that she is better known to many in China as simply He Zhen. Their research has indicated that her preferred name was He-Yin Zhen, which includes her mother's maiden name in her surname. (2–3)
53   Strains of Marxist thought may also link their works, although He-Yin Zhen's active embrace of Marxism—her journal, for instance, was the first to publish a Chinese translation of parts of *The Communist Manifesto*—stands in contrast to the more passive,

In her essays, He-Yin Zhen generally promotes a feminist vision that unequivocally rejects the idea of amending existing social and political systems to "grant" women more freedom and rights: this would both play into and perpetuate the patriarchal power structure already in place, and which was being historically rearticulated through capitalism—the basic functioning of which relies on the power gradient between the rich and the poor and/or disenfranchised.[54] In their introduction to *The Birth of Chinese Feminism*, a collection of translated essays featuring the work of He-Yin Zhen, editors Lydia Liu, Rebecca Karl, and Dorothy Ko offer their own helpful interpretation and summary of He-Yin's thought, describing her notion of "the feminist struggle" as "the beginning and outcome of a total social revolution that would abolish the state and private property to bring about true social equality and the end to all social hierarchies."[55] He-Yin Zhen herself writes simply that "we must first abolish the rule of men and introduce equality among human beings, which means that the world must belong equally to men and to women."[56]

He-Yin Zhen devotes much of her effort to demonstrating the position of women in Chinese society throughout the ages, which she persistently characterizes as one of enslavement. Drawing from a range of texts in the classical canon, she portrays the enslavement of women as a problem of livelihood (生計), arguing that through the perpetual male-dominated accumulation of wealth, women have become property that can now be employed as cheap labor in the modern factories of capitalism. Complementing her presentation of the Chinese tradition—which includes etymological observations linking slavery and women, inequalities in the observance of rites between men and women, and historical examples of the mistreatment of women—are a number of international examples of women's rights movements around the world, and particularly in the West. While she raises these examples primarily to point out the flaws of trying to work for justice within the already established patriarchal social and economic conditions, they also lend her argument a humanistic universalism which reveals the ontological nature of her inquiry.[57]

---

apolitical writing of Xiao Hong, whose identification as a Leftist writer came largely through her personal association with Lu Xun.

54   The approaches to women's rights that did not involve a complete social and economic revolution, such as the feminist writings of men such as Liang Qichao and Jin Tianhe, could only result in "sham freedom and sham equality." (59)
55   Ibid., 10.
56   Ibid., 53.
57   Liu, Karl, and Ko explain that labor in He-Yin Zhen's conception was an inherent aspect of human existence: it was not "an always-already appropriable power for private gain but, rather ... organic to life itself." She was interested, therefore, in the "historic potential to reground labor in a human ontology rather than in human capital." (25)

The first main point of comparison with *The Field of Life and Death* is He-Yin Zhen's focus not just on women in general, but on the physical control and suffering inflicted on their bodies. The Confucian tradition, she says, "has brought insult to women, tortured their bodies, and bound and restricted them," and ultimately allowed men to "control the bodies of all women."[58] "On the Revenge of Women," furthermore, includes an extensive section devoted to classical examples of "women suffering death by corporeal punishment," and in "On the Question of Women's Labor" she laments the fate of slave girls "who can be flogged with a whip; or they can be branded; or their skin can be pierced with sharp instruments; or their bodies can be doused in boiling water."[59] This focus on the body is not only historical; on the contrary, she notes that "in today's system"—what the editors describe in their introduction as her "globally integrated imperialist-capitalist present"—"the bitterness of having both labor power and the body swallowed up is concentrated on the bodies of women of the poor. The bodies of poor women cannot enjoy even an iota of freedom."[60]

He-Yin Zhen's focus on the bodies of women goes further to tie this concern to the question of humanity in general. As slaves, not only had women "lost the right to their bodily freedom," but there was little to separate women from animals, as she notes that historically "there were codes equating slaves with cows and horses."[61] In her description of marriage, she says that the "situation cannot but lead to a point where the idea of woman itself is rendered utterly inhuman," and in her examination of the Confucian commentary on the classics, she ends by rhetorically asking, "Does this not imply that they were banishing women from the realm of the human?"[62] She begins her "Feminist Manifesto," furthermore, with the powerful assertion that "when we look back at China, our men practically treat women as subhuman beings."[63]

For both He-Yin Zhen and Xiao Hong, the physical existence of women shares more in common with draught animals than with humans. The perpetuation and intensification of female suffering, furthermore, is connected to control over the female body through the conditions of patriarchal society, both traditional and contemporary. In the vision presented by both writers, women suffer under the control of social forces that can only be undone by fundamentally reconceiving society. These concerns, therefore, ultimately

---

58 Ibid., 143, 145.
59 Ibid., 76.
60 Ibid., 9, 90.
61 Ibid., 73.
62 Ibid., 118, 131.
63 Ibid., 179.

surpass the specific plight of women to incorporate all human beings in a new social structure in which "men and women are both human."[64]

He-Yin Zhen explicitly sets forth her ideas of how to achieve this new existence, which involves "compelling men to renounce their privileges and power" and abolishing government, as well as an economic revolution that will "overthrow the system of private property and ... replace it with communal property, meanwhile abandoning all monies and currencies."[65]

For Xiao Hong, as the final departure of Two-and-a-Half Li shows, the way forward is not quite so unequivocal or clear. Yet despite He-Yin Zhen's explicit propositions, both writers seem to be lacking in practical answers. He-Yin Zhen's suggestion of "compelling men to renounce their privileges" sounds almost comically impractical in the absence of specific suggestions as to how that might be achieved, and the options open to Xiao Hong's characters are similarly unsatisfactory: Golden Bough cannot withdraw from the world since the nunnery has been abandoned, and it is only a total lack of options that causes Two-and-a-Half Li to begrudgingly part with his beloved goat to go join the revolution. Neither writer seems to advocate violence—He-Yin Zhen doing so explicitly in her essay "On Feminist Antimilitarism"—yet this also seems to present a practical tension with the notion of remaking society.[66]

In summary, He-Yin Zhen's concern for the equality of all human beings requires the complete dissolution of all existing social structures and the revolutionary establishment of something entirely new. I have hoped to show that Xiao Hong's focus on physical suffering, and particularly that of women, when combined with a Buddhist perspective that reflects on the nature of this suffering, also leads to the necessity of creating a new society through its fundamental philosophical reformulation. Both writers reach this point by emphasizing the physical, bodily existence of women to reveal the ways that women's bodies are violently regulated by the societies in which they live; at the same time, their concerns exceed the bounds of gender and extend to all humanity. For both Xiao Hong and He-Yin Zhen, human society must be fundamentally reconstructed from the ground up. While He-Yin Zhen argues for this by demonstrating the insidiousness of female oppression in all previously

---

64 Ibid., 184. He-Yin Zhen ends her "Feminist Manifesto" with this simple statement, followed by the assertion that "By [saying] 'men' (*nanxing*) and 'women' (*nüxing*) we are not speaking of 'nature,' as each is but the outcome of differing social customs and education." For an extensive interpretation of He-Yin's conception of "gender" or "man/woman" (*nannü* 男女), see the editors' introduction.

65 Ibid., 70, 103.

66 This is perhaps also illustrated through the rumor that He-Yin Zhen lived her final years in a Buddhist nunnery (ibid., 51).

realized cultural forms, Xiao Hong's work takes this a step further by positing the reconceptualization of human life that must first undergird any true social reconstruction. For Xiao Hong, this reconceptualization must begin from an ontological unity of human and animal in order to expose and overcome the violent regulation of women's bodies, as well as to propose a new way of existing as humans.

Bibliography

Bischoff, Friedrich A. "Hsiao Hung's Wheel of Life and Death," *Chinese Literature: Essays, Articles, Reviews (CLEAR)* 2, no. 2 (1980): 249–257.

Dooling, Amy. *Women's Literary Feminism in Twentieth Century China*. New York: Palgrave Macmillan, 2005.

Dooling, Amy. "Xiao *Hong's Field of Life and Death*," in *The Columbia Companion to Modern Chinese Literature*, ed. Kirk A. Denton, 189–194. New York: Columbia University Press, 2016.

Dooling, Amy, and Kristina M. Torgeson. *Writing Women in Modern China: An Anthology of Women's Literature from the Early Twentieth Century*. New York: Columbia University Press, 1998.

Goldblatt, Howard. *Hsiao Hung*. Boston: Twayne, 1976.

Hsia, C. T. Review of *Hsiao Hung*, by Howard Goldblatt. *The Journal of Asian Studies* 37, no. 1 (1977): 103–114.

Hu Feng 胡风. "《生死場》讀後記" (After Reading *The Field of Life and Death*), in 《蕭紅研究七十年：下卷》 (*70 Years of Xiao Hong Research: Volume 2*), ed. Xiao Chuan 曉川 and Peng Fang 彭放, 4–5. Harbin: Beifang wenyi chubanshe, 2011.

Huang Xiaojuan 黃曉娟. "心靈的妙悟—論蕭紅與佛學的溝通" (A Spiritual Understanding: On the Connection between Xiao Hong and Buddhism), 《學術論壇》 (*Xueshu luntan*) 5 (2002): 97–101.

Jiang Zhijun 薑志軍. "關於《生死場》的命名問題" (On the Question of Naming *The Field of Life and Death*), in 《蕭紅研究七十年：下卷》 (*70 Years of Xiao Hong Research: Volume 2*), ed. Xiao Chuan 曉川 and Peng Fang 彭放, 52–53. Harbin: Beifang wenyi chubanshe, 2011.

Lee, Leo Ou-fan. "Afterword: Reflections on Change and Continuity in Modern Chinese Fiction," in *From May Fourth to June Fourth: Fiction and Film in Twentieth-Century China*, ed. Ellen Widmer and David Der-wei Wang, 361–384. Cambridge, MA: Harvard University Press, 1993.

Liu, Lydia. "The Female Body and Nationalist Discourse: Manchuria in Xiao Hong's *Field of Life and Death*," in *Body, Subject, and Power in China*, ed. Angela Zito and Tani E. Barlow. Chicago: University of Chicago Press, 1994.

Liu, Lydia, Rebecca Karl, and Dorothy Ko, eds. *The Birth of Chinese Feminism: Essential Texts in Transnational Theory.* New York: Columbia University Press, 2013.

Meng Yue 孟悅 and Dai Jinhua 戴錦華.《浮出歷史地標: 現代婦女文學研究》(Emerging from the Horizon of History: Modern Chinese Women's Literature). Beijing: Zhongguo renmin daxue chubanshe, 2004.

Wang Qin 王欽. "'潛能'、動物與死亡—重讀蕭紅《生死場》" (Potentiality, Animality and Death: Rereading Xiao Hong's *The Field of Life and Death*),《中國現代文學研究叢刊》(*Studies in Modern Chinese Literature*) 10 (2016): 12–26.

Xiao, Hong. *The Field of Life and Death and Tales of Hulan River.* Translated by Howard Goldblatt and Ellen Yeung. Bloomington: Indiana University Press, 1979.

Xiao Hong 蕭紅.《生死場: 蕭紅經典必讀》(*The Field of Life and Death: Xiao Hong's Must-Read Classics*), ed. Wu Yuqin 吳義勤. Beijing: Wenhua yishu chubanshe, 2012.

Xu, Hangping. "Rescuing Nature from the Nation: Ecocritical (Un)Consciousness in Modern Chinese Culture," in *A Global History of Literature and the Environment*, ed. John Parham and Louise Westling, 320–334. New York: Cambridge University Press, 2017.

Yue, Gang. *The Mouth That Begs: Hunger, Cannibalism, and the Politics of Eating in Modern China.* Durham, NC: Duke University Press, 1999.

Zheng A'ping 鄭阿平 and Ye Jianzhong 葉建鍾. "《生死場》與《紅高粱家族》的生命意識" (Consciousness of Life in *The Field of Life and Death* and *Red Sorghum Family*), in《蕭紅研究七十年: 下卷》(*70 Years of Xiao Hong Research: Volume 2*), ed. Xiao Chuan 曉川 and Peng Fang 彭放, 80–85. Harbin: Beifang wenyi chubanshe, 2011.

CHAPTER 9

Aesthetic Cognition and the Subject of Discourse in Lu Xun's Modern-Style Fiction

Nicholas Kaldis

Whatever its successes, failures, and contradictions, the May Fourth stands as a model for a collaborative and thoroughgoing critique of society and cultural traditions. Its literary paragon, Lu Xun, believed that, to effectuate radical social transformation, one must extract the ideological poison from the body politic. Modern science (the study of medicine), though beneficial, could not cure what he saw as a disease in China's social and cultural constitution; instead, he argued that "the best way to effect a spiritual transformation … would be through literature and art."[1] Lu Xun and his literary cohort devoted themselves to deracinating the pervasive and insidious influence of traditional Chinese culture and social relations associated with Confucianism, to which they attributed the ignorance, apathy, social cruelty, and spiritual deadening they perceived in most of their fellow citizens. Accordingly, the "paramount concern of Chinese literary modernity," was "the problem of the Chinese mind (or soul)."[2]

The enormity of this problem was daunting and dispiriting. It is well known that Lu Xun found it difficult to inject optimism into his literary ministrations to the Chinese spirit/psyche.[3] In the famous "iron house" exchange from his "Preface" (自序) to *A Call to Arms* (呐喊 1923), he described being persuaded to write modern-style short stories as a sign of "hope" for the future and of

---

1 Lu, Xun, *Lu Xun: Diary of a Madman and Other Stories*, trans. William A. Lyell (Honolulu: University of Hawaii Press, 1990), 24.
2 Peter Button, *Configurations of the Real in Chinese Literary and Aesthetic Modernity* (Leiden: Brill, 2009), 78. Referring to Button (and other scholars), Carolyn T. Brown observes "The implications of how a writer understands the relationship of the actual world to its textual representation are a major concern of writers and critics of modern Chinese literature," Carolyn T. Brown, *Reading Lu Xun through Carl Jung* (Amherst, NY: Cambria Press, 2018), 176 n38.
3 For more on the history of "spirit" and its importance to Lu Xun and other May Fourth-era intellectuals, see Wendy Larson, *From Ah Q to Lei Feng: Freud and Revolutionary Spirit in 20th Century China* (Stanford: Stanford University Press, 2009), 82–90, and *passim*.

his desire not to infect China's youth with his pessimism.[4] However, as Lin Yü-sheng observes, "nowhere does [Lu Xun] say that he discarded [the] pessimism" of the "Preface."[5] Rather, Lin continues, Lu Xun's fiction is thoroughly pessimistic, exemplifying "an intellectual movement that attacked China's past in toto" (ibid.). Revisiting the iron house allegory, Ling Hon Lam has recently isolated the source of Lu Xun's pessimism in Western enlightenment discourse. In an original recontextualization, Lam paints a scene of Lu Xun and his readers deluded and ensnared by the Western "Enlightenment discourse of awakening," stuck in the "vicious trap … [of] 'external, fixed objectivity,'" gazing down at the "the boxed-in destiny of an entire people," and condemning "a whole civilization to a horrid end … with no hope of jailbreak."[6]

Where Lin and Lam fault Lu Xun for adhering to an unconditional iconoclasm or Enlightenment stance that prevented him from questioning "the validity of a totalistic rejection of Chinese tradition"—and they are not alone here[7]—I argue that Lu Xun's short stories ought to be seen as creative instantiations of a "pessimism of strength," what Leo Ou-fan Lee terms a "counter perspective" and "radical epistemology—a kind of purposeful reversal of

---

4   Andrew F. Jones suggests the iron house image resonates with "purpose-built spaces of modern industrial and disciplinary institutions … [of] Victorian provenance … also the factory workshop, the engine room, the bunker, even the cages in a zoo," in Andrew F. Jones, *Developmental Fairy Tales: Evolutionary Thinking and Modern Chinese Culture* (Cambridge, MA: Harvard University Press, 2011), 37. I would point to possible Chinese literary antecedents with which Lu Xun would have been familiar, such as Liang Qichao's (梁啟超 1873–1929) figuration of China and its people as a decaying mansion on the verge of collapse, in his 1896 "On the Harm of Not Reforming (論不變法之害)," in *China's Response to the West: A Documentary Survey 1839–1923*, ed. Ssu-yü Teng and John K. Fairbank (Cambridge, MA: Harvard University Press, 1982): 154–157, and E Liu's (劉鶚) *The Travels of Lao Ts'an*, trans. Harold Shadick (New York: Columbia University Press, 1990; originally published 1903–1907), 6–8, in which China, in a "ship of state" allegory, is represented as a large decrepit boat on the verge of sinking and drowning all aboard.
5   Yu-sheng Lin, *The Crisis of Chinese Consciousness: Radical Antitraditionalism in the May Fourth Era* (Madison: University of Wisconsin Press, 1979), 118.
6   Ling Hon Lam, *The Spatiality of Emotion in Early Modern China: From Dreamscapes to Theatricality* (New York: Columbia University Press, 2018), 233, 234, 235. Lam does not address Lu Xun's acceding to the possibility of hope, though he does aver that Lu Xun "rejects sympathy as a solution" (232). Many of Lam's thought-provoking insights are themselves trapped in a convoluted labyrinth of jargon and difficult to follow.
7   Lin, *The Crisis of Chinese Consciousness*, 151. There are abundant references in the literature to Lu Xun's pessimism, especially his outlook during his so-called "dark period" and the "ebb tide" of the May Fourth era, as described by Du Ronggen 杜榮根, *Xunqiu yu chaoyue: Zhongguo xinshi xingshi piping* 尋求與超越: 中國新詩形式批評 (Seeking and surpassing: Critique of China's new poetic forms) (Shanghai: Fudan daxue chubanshe, 1993), 88. For phases in Lu Xun's life and intellectual development, see Leo Ou-fan Lee, *Voices from the Iron House: A Study of Lu Xun* (Bloomington: Indiana University Press, 1987), and Leo Ou-fan Lee, ed., *Lu Xun and His Legacy* (Berkeley: University of California Press, 1985).

values."[8] Nietzsche—greatly admired by Lu Xun—wrote: "Is pessimism *necessarily* a sign of decline, decay, degeneration, weary and weak instincts.... Is there a pessimism of *strength*?"[9] Nietzsche posits this in opposition to "a kind of fear of, an escape from, pessimism.... A subtle last resort against—*truth*."[10] Lu Xun struggled to transform entrenched socio-cultural traditions and to persist despite an overwhelming sense of futility. His distinctive praxis was an aesthetic synthesis of personal experience, historical awareness, and imagination. His short stories are not designed to hold a critical mirror up to reality; rather, they are exemplars of aesthetic cognition, efforts to *constitute reality*. For Lu Xun, *"representation is cognition."*[11] "Forms of art," as Walter A. Davis observes, "are original ways of knowing, independent principles of perception and cognition, which give us ... access to experience that exceeds the limits of ... socialized, rhetorical determinations of meaning."[12]

---

8   Lee, *Voices from the Iron House*, 54, and 55–57 *passim*. Lee elsewhere observes that Lu Xun's "entire outlook ... hinged on an unresolved tension between his unequivocal support of all the enlightened 'modern' causes of the May Fourth Movement and the incessant pessimism that haunted his private psyche with regard to the ultimate meaning of life," in "In Search of Modernity: Some Reflections on a New Mode of Consciousness in Twentieth Century Chinese History and Literature," in *Ideas Across Cultures: Essays on Chinese Thought in Honor of Benjamin I. Schwartz*, ed. Paul A. Cohen and Merle Goldman (Cambridge, MA: Harvard University Press, 1990), 134. Theodore Huters likewise reveals the irony of Lu Xun's intellectual project, which drew upon habits inherited from (Neo-)Confucian thought to wage "a battle for the destruction of that thought," all the while aspiring in agony to rescue from the ashes of the battle some modicum of a "nascent optimism" against a reality in which "any prospect for the implementation of change [seemed] exceedingly remote," in Theodore Huters, "Blossoms in the Snow: Lu Xun and the Dilemma of Modern Chinese Literature," *Modern China* 10 (January 1984): 74; and Theodore Huters, "Lu Xun and the Crisis of Figuration," in *Bringing the World Home: Appropriating the West in Late Qing and Early Republican China* (Honolulu: University of Hawaii Press, 2005), 268.
9   Nietzsche, Friedrich. *Basic Writings of Nietzsche*. Trans. and Ed. Walter Kaufmann (New York: The Modern Library, 1992), 17.
10 (Ibid.), 18.
11 Walter A. Davis, *Deracination: Historicity, Hiroshima, and the Tragic Imperative* (Albany: State University of New York Press, 2001), 5, original emphasis. For an expanded discussion of "Aesthetic Cognition" see Nicholas Andrew Kaldis, *The Chinese Prose Poem: A Study of Lu Xun's* Wild Grass *(Yecao)* (Amherst, NY: Cambria Press, 2014), 143–151.
12 Davis, *Deracination*, 152, 216–217. Davis further singles out aesthetic cognition for its uniqueness vis-à-vis other ways of thinking, because it affords "an apprehension of lived experience which preserves 'the whole of things' in an irreducible and concrete totality.... [T]he basic problem is to comprehend the forms of literary creation as original modes of access to experience capable of giving us an understanding of the world which other ways of knowing fail to provide." Walter A. Davis, *The Act of Interpretation: A Critique of Literary Reason* (Chicago: University of Chicago Press, 1978), 97. Similarly, Xiaobing Tang describes "literature as a distinct social discursive praxis with its own logic and historical determinations" ("Lu Xun's 'Diary of a Madman,'" 61, 62).

The concept of aesthetic cognition requires an interpretive method that upholds the primacy and integrity of the literary work, while simultaneously affirming the reader's subjective investment in the process of interpretation, in a dialectical interchange. This method of interpretation has been termed "a hermeneutics of engagement.... Its ruling assumption is that our involvement in our own subjectivity is not a barrier to interpretation but the circumstance that enables us to enter most deeply into a text.... [e]ngaged thinking necessarily does violence to objective commentary because its goal is to reawaken that richer relationship to ourselves that is the basis for a richer relationship to texts."[13]

Xiaobing Tang outlined a similar approach to (Lu Xun's) fiction, describing interpretation as an "intimate relationship with the text" that closely and empathetically follows its "imagery, logic, and reasoning.... as if from within." As the reader decodes and reassembles the text, she is "transformed by the experience," while "the text is produced anew and brought to bear on matters and conditions that are of our own concern."[14]

Carolyn T. Brown has likewise chronicled the profound "impact" and "wrenching reversal of perspective" she underwent when reading Lu Xun's fiction. For Brown, Lu Xun's stories critique Chinese social conditions with "a piercing intellect, a poet's eye, and a complex, nuanced understanding of the human heart...., open[ing] his readers' eyes to seeing and understanding in new ways."[15]

This chapter will keep faith with the underlying premises of Tang's, Brown's, and others' approaches,[16] grounded in my similar encounters with Lu Xun's fiction, which affirm the value and relevance of the concept of aesthetic cognition and a hermeneutics of engagement to the study of modern Chinese literature.

---

13 Walter A. Davis, *Inwardness and Existence: Subjectivity in/and Hegel, Heidegger, Marx, and Freud* (Madison: University of Wisconsin Press, 1989), 4, 7.
14 Xiaobing Tang, "*Excursion I*: Beyond Homesickness: An Intimate Reading of Lu Xun's 'My Native Land,'" in his *Chinese Modernism: The Heroic and the Quotidian* (Durham: Duke University Press, 2000): 77.
15 *Reading Lu Xun*, xiii. See Lyell for a concise description of the stylistic artistry of Lu Xun's fiction: William A. Lyell, "Introduction," in *Lu Xun: Diary of a Madman and Other Stories*, trans. William A. Lyell (Honolulu: University of Hawaii Press, 1990): xxxi–xlii.
16 Jaroslav Průšek ("Basic Problems of the History of Modern Chinese Literature and C. T. Hsia, a History of Modern Chinese Fiction"), Michael S. Duke ("Past, Present, and Future in Mo Yan's Fiction of the 1980s"), Michelle Yeh (*Modern Chinese Poetry: Theory and Practice since 1917*), and others have, each in their own terms, valorized the notion of aesthetic cognition. See also Brown's stated goal of revealing "Lu Xun's way of configuring [his] cultural moment" by means of the projection of private experience and larger historical events onto his fictional "symbolic representations of the Chinese reality" (*Reading Lu Xun*, 19 and passim).

While I cannot do justice to the immense body of secondary literature on Lu Xun's fiction and thought, I will throughout maintain a dialogue with some of the relevant extant interpretations.

Wendy Larson summarizes the majority of Lu Xun's stories as representing "an intricately woven environment in which subjectivity, the physical, the material, and the social interact in a complex way, altering and redefining their relationships moment-by-moment."[17] Peter Button makes a similar observation concerning the "special genius" of Lu Xun's fiction, manifested in "the way he allowed a host of divergent, powerful, and at times contradictory discursive forces to play through his texts."[18] I believe that it is especially edifying and productive to juxtapose some of Lu Xun's repeated portrayals of individuals confronting the discursive forces—namely, the traditional (largely Confucian-inflected) ideologies—that constitute their knowledge, world views, and motivations. Contrasting the interactions of the madman, Ah Q, and Xianglin Sao with these discourses reveals Lu Xun's concern with socioeconomic background, gender, and other constituents of subjectivity that determine a subject's ability to reconcile his or her lived experiences with the available discourses for explaining and understanding those experiences.[19]

---

17   *From Ah Q to Lei Feng*, 81. Xiaobing Tang, in his nuanced reading of "My Native Land" (故鄉), also presents a list of existential issues readers encounter, "questions of subjectivity, language, sexuality, memory, and fantasy.... the condensed psychobiography of a modern Chinese male consciousness" (*"Excursion I,"* 77).

18   *Configurations of the Real*, 86.

19   I am aware of the slippage I have allowed between my somewhat interchangeable uses of "discourse" and "ideology." Ideology employs and is often inseparable from discourse in that it "produces normality by establishing symbolic identities for subjects to embody" (Todd McGowan, *Enjoying What We Don't Have: The Political Project of Psychoanalysis* [Lincoln: University of Nebraska Press, 2013], 122). These identities—associated with "one's personality, beliefs, memories, and attitudes"—are conferred via the dominant discourses through which "ideology causes individuals to believe that they are ... what the social order tells them that they are.... The individual sees itself as it isn't as a result of the operation of ideology—instantiated by the [discourses of the] family, the educational system, the religious institution, the media apparatus, and so on" (Todd McGowan, "Between the Capitalist and the Cop: The Path of Revolution in *Blade Runner 2049*" [forthcoming], 2). Ideology thereby causes "the subject ... [to] feel itself at home within the inherently alienating structure of the social order" (McGowan, *Enjoying What We Don't Have*, 122). The "fundamental task of all ideologies" being to "constitute a social reality free of the traumatic kernel that creates that social reality," a society, in other words, governed by ideological discourses such as Confucianism, patriarchy, etc., where subjects can remain unaware of the injustice, oppression, and violence of the social order, and, especially, of their role in creating and sustaining that order (ibid., 325). Discourses propagate ideology and ideology must make use of discourse: while not identical, there is a great degree of overlap between the two.

From this perspective, "Diary of a Madman" (1918), "The True Story of Ah Q" (1921), and "The New Year's Sacrifice" (1924) can be studied as a trilogy in which Lu Xun explored crises being experienced by modern Chinese subjects as traditional world views clashed with a rapidly changing external reality. These three stories imagine the various efforts of a wealthy educated man, an illiterate poor peasant man, and an illiterate poor peasant woman as each struggles with received traditional discourses and formulates—or fails to formulate—an oppositional consciousness. Oppositional consciousness hinges on the capacity of subordinated subjects to achieve awareness of their oppression within unequal hierarchical systems, and marks the "emergence of freedom out of the ideological illusion of freedom."[20] As such, it is a measure of the degree to which an individual is subject to ideological hegemony under the dominant discourses that determine how one comprehends one's position within an existing social structure. Oppositional consciousness is essential to developing alternative discourses of resistance, rebellion, and revolution.[21]

Lu Xun's debut short story, "Diary of a Madman" (狂人日記 1918), is his first fictional exploration of what it might look like for a Chinese subject to carry out the paramount task being promoted by the May Fourth iconoclasts—rejecting China's traditional (Confucian) ideology in toto, via a thoroughgoing oppositional consciousness.

Using classical Chinese—the authoritative parlance of the elite classes—the narrator introduces diary entries made by an educated young man during a period of madness. He reassures readers that the madman has since recovered and will soon assume a traditional type of official bureaucratic position. The diary—written in a modern colloquial Chinese—reveals that during his madness the young man was convinced the most revered texts of Chinese culture contain the secret exhortation "eat people," and that all of Chinese society is engaged in a cannibalistic conspiracy. The madman's perspective is almost universally interpreted as ironic, his paranoid schizophrenic vision being in fact an accurate allegory of the venerated Confucian ideology upon which Chinese society has been built, an ideology he reveals as barbaric, one that reproduces itself by brainwashing and indoctrinating children at an early age.

Xiaobing Tang has drawn attention to the liberating agency of the madman's breakdown; Tang locates the story's "radicalism" not in its gesturing toward alternative possibilities in the future (saving the children) but in its "unambiguously articulate[d] ... potent" discursive revolt in the present—the

---

20   McGowan, "Between the Capitalist and the Cop," 4.
21   For a variety of essays on oppositional consciousness, see Jane J. Mansbridge and Aldon D. Morris, *Oppositional Consciousness: The Subjective Roots of Social Protest* (Chicago: University of Chicago Press, 2001).

present both of its context (1918 China) and text (each time it is read).[22] "Diary of a Madman," Tang argues, "engender[s] a new form of discourse ... an imaginative energy that always unsettles the dominant discursive order," marking it as "a manifesto of the birth of modern Chinese subjectivity." The madman displays a "playful manipulation of language both to distort and to displace existing texts.... In speaking a language different from that of the encasing context—namely, the preface provided by the writer-narrator—the Madman shows the disruptive force of language itself.[...] The Madman writes in his own language."[23] "Diary of a Madman," in other words, incarnates (a model for) how consciousness might free itself from the dominant ideology, through an ontological-discursive "playful" labor of the negative. Focusing as well on the madman's discursive revolt—his struggle with Confucian ideology— Eileen J. Cheng points out that the madman's enlightenment is incarnated in his subversive manipulation of the dominant discourse, the product of "critical engagement with classical texts."[24] It is the madman's "reading between the lines"—that "inspires his moment of illumination" allowing him to see into the damaging effects of Confucian ideology, i.e., "the violence of traditional literary and cultural practices."[25]

In his inspired readings of traditional Confucian texts, the diarist concludes that, in order to dislodge the insidious "enduring power of traditional ways ... the evil forces of the past,"[26] we (the enlightened/mad) must undertake a drastic intervention into this abhorrent state of affairs—his final entry pleads "save the children...." The madman of course hopes to prevent children from being inculcated into the Confucian social system. But, as Andrew F. Jones has pointed out, Lu Xun is aware that the madman's goal of saving the children is an impossible "utopian scheme" destined to fail, for it can only take place after the processes of "biological and social reproduction" have "already been inscribed upon" the children; salvation will thus necessitate "pedagogy in reverse," subversive "unlearning."[27] I would argue that the madman's plea can also be read as aimed at protecting children from the type of excruciating

---

22 "Lu Xun's *Diary of a Madman*," 67. Tang's reading is not much concerned with the madman's plea to "save the children" in the final lines of the story, which is "generally interpreted as a plea to look toward the future, not the past," Wendy Larson, *Zhang Yimou: Globalization and the Subject of Culture* (Amherst, NY: Cambria Press, 2017), 268 n1.
23 "Lu Xun's *Diary of a Madman*," 66, 57, 68.
24 Eileen J. Cheng, *Literary Remains: Death, Trauma, and Lu Xun's Refusal to Mourn*, (Honolulu: University of Hawai'i Press, 2013), 41.
25 Ibid., 41, 43.
26 Huters, "Blossoms in the Snow," 60.
27 *Developmental Fairy Tales*, 111, 106, 107. Jones highlights the logical contradiction of the situation: "How can the children be saved by adults who have yet to be (and indeed cannot be) redeemed from the taint of cannibalism? ... Who is saved?" Ibid., 110.

psychotic breakdown that he has undergone as an adult in trying to *autodidactically* deracinate the malignant Confucian cultural inheritance.

In either case, cultural salvation via childhood innocence or adult illumination, the narrative is structured so as to mock any glimmer of hope raised by its quasi-heroic madman. The madman has, ironically, been *re-educated*. His state of oppositional consciousness to the discourse of Confucianism, his "madness," has proven only temporary. This conundrum at the heart of the story, concerning the prospects for an individual who has extracted himself from a hegemonic ideological milieu, is among Lu Xun's great insights. Lu Xun here discerned a key epistemological paradox inherent in enlightenment projects, staging *both* how a free subject might "emerge out of an apparently invincible ideological control" to realize its "potential for agency in a world that determines us completely," *and* the monumental difficulty or impossibility of a solitary subject sustaining a state of radical enlightenment while immersed in the ideologically-saturated social structure he has seen through.[28] Via an act of literary perspicacity, Lu Xun imagines the psychological rending that someone would likely endure in attaining a revolutionary, transformational awareness of the destructive nature of Confucian ideology in early twentieth-century China. Such an awareness, he shows, might only be achieved through—and/or perceived as—paranoid schizophrenia. The narrative is structured so that the authoritative language and perspective of China's established male cultural elite introduces a single individual's forging of an oppositional consciousness as a bout of insanity, a temporary aberration. Readers are thereby reassured from the outset that one can "recover" from the crazed purging of one's proper socially-conferred and consensually-validated identity. Thus, even as it presents the diary as a record of radical discursive revolt against the dominant ideology, this framing device simultaneously steers readers toward the conclusion that the psychological agony, not to mention the social ostracism, would make it impossible to sustain such an oppositional consciousness. One would eventually be brought back into the fold.[29]

The madman's paradox uniquely instantiates the dilemma of the May Fourth era intellectual, asking, "If one could indeed break with all received knowledge, identity attributions, with the entirety of one's ideological

---

28   McGowan, "Between the Capitalist and the Cop," 18. 32 n. 14.
29   Huters identifies an embryonic oppositional consciousness in the story's narrative structure, arguing that, despite an undeniably pessimistic representation of the potential emergence of a "new order" in "Diary of a Madman" (and Lu Xun's subsequent three stories published between 1918 and 1919), "the very fact that the narrative voice can establish the past as a distinct entity embodying evil at least holds out the hope of an alternative in the future" ("Blossoms in the Snow," 60).

interpellations, what would remain of a 'self'? What mode or model of cognition can one draw upon in undertaking such radical action? Is there a kernel or residue of unappropriated subjectivity that lies outside of one's socialization and education, outside of all the texts and discourses through which identity is conferred? If so, is there an uncorrupted discourse to employ so that the subject can maintain both ideological individuation (oppositional consciousness) and a connection to reality? What sort of written expression is adequate for representing such a state?"[30] I have left out the qualifier "Chinese" in order to underscore the universal quality of these questions; the genius of this story lies in part in the degree to which readers allow for the possibility of being "transformed by the experience of reading," and recognize issues of shared, ongoing concern, in Xiaobing Tang's formulation.

Having apprehended, through literary imagination, how a well-to-do, educated, highly literate, male member of the cultural elite might undertake the struggle to free his mind from the dominion of traditional Chinese cultural discourses, Lu Xun went on to reconsider the issue from the perspective of a poverty-stricken, ignorant, illiterate male who is oblivious to the operations of those same discourses—Ah Q.

"The True Story of Ah Q" (阿 Q 正傳, 1921) presents us with a diametrically inverse version of the madman in the character of its eponymous (anti-)hero, Ah Q. Button notes Ah Q's complete ignorance of the ideological interpellation that oppresses and eventually destroys him: Ah Q's thoughts and actions "serve as a vivid parody of the (aborted) formation of subjective interiority.... with Ah Q, no such interiority exists. His capacity to 'reflect' upon himself never

---

30 More than seventy years later, similar questions continue to inform aesthetic probings of Chinese society. In Zhang Yimou's 1991 film *Raise the Red Lantern* (大紅燈籠高高掛), the protagonist Songlian (played by Gong Li) can be viewed either as driven mad by the ideology of the Confucian familial structure (the repeatedly invoked patriarchal "household rules/code of conduct [附上的規矩]"), or as opting to sustain a seemingly paranoid-schizophrenic oppositional awareness of that ideology as institutionalized femicide. Her final words before being pronounced "mad/insane" (妳瘋了) by her husband, Master Chen, are "You're all killers!" (你們殺人). We might also see the madman of Yu Hua's 1986 masterpiece, the novella "1986" (一九八六年), as either going insane or opting for what appears as madness: the effort to incarnate and sustain an historical awareness of the destruction wrought on the individual, familial, and collective psyche by the violent political upheaval of the Cultural Revolution. "1986" implies that shocking creative acts such as the psychotic husband/father's public performances of brutal self-mutilation must be undertaken to sustain collective memory of the (recent) past amidst the onslaught of impersonal market-driven culture shown to be replacing political culture.

results in anything other than the complacent assertion of 'victory.'"[31] Ah Q's "victories," I would add, are the fruit of his successful efforts to fit every experience of humiliation, suffering, oppression, and alienation into a world view over-determined by the traditional discourse of Confucianism and its fundamental concepts, such as filial piety (孝).

Theodore Huters sheds light on Lu Xun's careful eschewal of character types or narratives that would conjure up the possibility of an enlightened subject emerging from the darkness of a hidebound "stagnant China." Taking Ah Q as an example, Huters argues that Lu Xun could not "bring himself to embrace" a (deManean interpretation of) Lukácean optimism in the redemptive force and "healing powers of time" that might have conferred meaning on his fictional characters' lives, erased "'the accidental nature of their experiences and the isolated nature of the events recounted,'" and provided them with "'the essential quality of their existence.'" Exemplifying this assertion is "Ah Q's sorry demise and the infinitesimal moment of enlightenment that preceded it," a fleeting "moment of consciousness" that he is neither able to formulate into a nascent understanding nor granted sufficient time to act upon:

> [T]he miserable eponymous main character [Ah Q] can achieve consciousness only at the moment of his own death—a clown unexpectedly given the chance to "peep over the edge" and perceive of meanings he had never so much as imagined before. Even as he is presented with this insight, however, he is given no chance to make use of or even fully to process mentally what he sees at that moment. This marks the terrible inscription of the necessity and pathos of the death of the old. It lies at

---

31   *Configurations of the Real*, 99; 100. Button undertakes a sophisticated tracing of a constellation of theoretical, philosophical, and literary texts and ideas that shed light on the story and its implications for the study of Chinese literary realism. For a thoroughgoing review and analysis of Ah Q and the secondary literature, see Paul B. Foster, *Ah Q Archaeology: Lu Xun, Ah Q, Ah Q Progeny and the National Character Discourse in Twentieth-Century China* (Lanham, MD: Lexington Books, 2006). In her study of Ah Q and Lei Feng, Larson treats Ah Q sympathetically and does not delve into Lu Xun's use of irony (*From Ah Q to Lei Feng*, 77–113, esp. 77–81 and 110–113). Carolyn T. Brown's recent interpretation of Ah Q incorporates the theories of Rene Girard, Erich Neumann, and a number of other thinkers into her larger approach based on Jungian concepts such as the "ego," "shadow," and "Self." See her "Chapter 2: Anatomy of a Scapegoating: 'The True Story of Ah Q'" (*Reading Lu Xun*, 83–134). For a survey of paratextual materials and issues relevant to "The True Story of Ah Q," which includes a fascinating analysis of Ah Q's queue, see Eva Shan Chou, *Memory, Violence, Queues: Lu Xun Interprets China* (Ann Arbor, MI: Association for Asian Studies, 2012).

the point of juxtaposition of the horror that Ah Q suddenly can see, his inability to make out anything from it, and the final narrated inconsequence of his existence. Can there be any redemption in this? If so, what might redemption mean, and could it ever be worth the price?[32]

I fully agree with Huters's assessment of Lu Xun's withering appraisal of the potential for the Chinese everyman to constitute a negative critical awareness. However, I believe that Lu Xun had not yet completed his project of exploring and exposing the complexities of (representing) "the problem of the Chinese mind/soul" in its relationship to then-dominant ideological discourses. He had yet to imagine a female protagonist in this scenario. A consideration of the character Xianglin Sao from "New Year's Sacrifice" (祝福, 1924) as a third installment of this project retroactively colors how we evaluate the madman and Ah Q, for Xianglin Sao embodies a unique stage in Lu Xun's exploration of the [modern] Chinese subaltern subject's potential for developing an oppositional consciousness toward traditional discourses.

Ah Q remains in thrall to those discourses, demonstrating unflagging "allegiance to ritual conventions"[33] as he sings heroic opera songs while being hauled to his death. Still wedded to an identity formulated within the existing power structure, Ah Q is incapable of doubting that structure and freeing his mind. "One is free when one has the ability to doubt, which occurs in the moment that one questions one's ideological manipulation.... Doubt is alienation from identity, ... [which] is always ideological. By alienating the subject from what it thinks it is, doubt locates subjectivity beyond the trap of identity."[34] Far from doubting, the closest thing to alienation that Ah Q experiences is an incomprehensible disconnect—a "blinding" and "buzzing" sensation (兩眼發黑，耳朵裏嗡的一聲)—as he momentarily conflates the predacious gaze of a hungry wolf he encountered years before with the ravenous gaze of the crowd's "monstrous coalition of eyes, gnawing into his soul" (眼睛們似乎連成一氣 ... 咬他的靈魂).[35] He is scarcely conscious of this predatory glint in the eyes of

---

32   Theodore Huters, "Lu Xun and the Crisis of Figuration," in *Bringing the World Home: Appropriating the West in Late Qing and Early Republican China*, (Honolulu: University of Hawaii Press, 2005): 269; 264–265.
33   Brown, *Reading Lu Xun*, 117.
34   McGowan, "Between the Capitalist and the Cop," 7.
35   Lu Xun, *The Real Story of Ah-Q*, 123.

his presumed admiring audience, and unable to turn his faint, ephemeral suspicion into a question aimed at the system that's destroying him.[36]

To Xianglin Sao, on the other hand, Lu Xun grants a more substantive state of enlightenment. Like Ah Q, she experiences a crisis precipitated by the nascent awareness of a disconnect between her lived experience and her traditional world view (a syncretic combination of peasant superstitions, popular Buddhist notions of the afterlife, offerings to the Earth God, etc.). She has been bought, sold, raped (arguably the proper description of her second wedding night, if not her first as well), hunted down and kidnapped, hired and fired at the whims of her employers; she has attempted suicide and buried her only child's eviscerated corpse, been viciously mocked for her traumatized behavior, and callously discarded by the only kin she can claim. Having endured a life of horror, she places all her hopes in a traditional ritual of spiritual purification that has turned out to be a lie. Her ability to understand and justify these experiences within available ideological discourses has consequently collapsed, the latter all having proved deceptive. Utterly alienated from the identity conferred on her by the dominant patriarchal social order, she has begun to doubt.

Whether or not we find Lu Xun's characterization of Xianglin Sao's experiences over-the-top, he has adroitly crafted a situation in which an uneducated and illiterate female commoner could plausibly reject traditional Chinese worldviews and turn wary of those who uphold them. This sets the stage for Xianglin Sao's revolutionary act in the story's key passage, where she puts into words her suspicion of traditional master narratives. In questioning "pious Buddhist" (善女人) Mother Liu's description of the horrors awaiting in the Underworld, Xianglin Sao casts doubt on collective beliefs and prescribed ritual behaviors concerning the soul, salvation, and the afterlife. She even goes a step further, challenging the May Fourth intellectual narrator to posit an alternative empirical knowledge based on his "book learnin'" and worldliness (你是識字的，又是出門人，見識得多), pressing him to confirm or refute popular discourse concerning King Yama and the horrors of hell. Her twin

---

36 Gloria Davies interprets Lu Xun as bestowing upon Ah Q in his final moments a "leap of self-awareness," the "clarity of [a] momentary insight" that allows him for the first time to attain "critical distance from the crowd" and, by association, the social discourses that oppress him (Gloria Davies, *Lu Xun's Revolution: Writing in a Time of Violence* [Cambridge, MA: Harvard University Press, 2013], 306–307). Although the textual evidence is tenuous, Davies's reading is a reminder that we cannot be entirely sure of the state of Ah Q's inner awareness at the end of "Chapter Nine: The Grand Reunion" (第九章: 大團圓). For a history of some of the debates surrounding "The True Story of Ah Q," in addition to Foster, see also Davies's section "Humanness versus Class Traits" in her *Lu Xun's Revolution*, 188–204, esp. 191–198.

challenge to both traditional and modern worldviews, albeit amidst a psychological breakdown, represents a breakthrough in awareness for a woman of her socio-economic position. As evidenced by her pointed questions, Xianglin Sao, though in a state of abject poverty and homelessness, is on the cusp of transformative insight and radical enlightenment, having moved far beyond her subaltern male counterpart Ah Q in developing an awareness that traditional beliefs and social practices are sources of oppression and suffering. Her double subversion of the dominant discursive orders—traditional oppressive and May Fourth enlightened—is arguably even more disruptive than the madman's.

It is further noteworthy that the amount of time Xianlin Sao is allotted to mull over her plight, from when she is cast onto the streets by the narrator's (Uncle's) family until her untimely death, is comparatively much longer than that granted to Ah Q in his final "infinitesimal" flash of quasi-enlightenment. Lu Xun grants Xianlin Sao a more sustained period to "peep over the edge" and perceive meanings she could not have previously imagined, and he has her spending that time immersed in a state of agonizing doubt. This understated temporal distinction indicates a subtle fluctuation in Lu Xun's unwavering rejection of the "healing powers of time" identified by Huters.[37]

The potential radicality in Xianglin Sao's relationship to the discourses of tradition and modernity has been largely overlooked,[38] perhaps owing to the bleak dénouement of the story (she shortly thereafter dies of exposure and starvation) and to Lu Xun's well-known pessimism towards the potential for women's agency or liberation under Chinese patriarchal culture. Recent scholarship continues along the same lines. G. Andrew Stuckey argues that Xianglin Sao is "narrated" via a "powerlessness" he terms "*voicelessness,*" in that her "speech has no power to affect [her] fate[s]."[39] Lu Xun's narrative, in other words, cannot "grant access to the fullness of [Xianglin Sao's] interior psychological state" that would otherwise mark her as possessed of the "personal and modern subjectivity" frequently exemplified by interiority in May Fourth era fiction (ibid.). In positing that her "lack of interiority is reflected in [her] voicelessness and … resulting inability to affect the society

---

[37] "Lu Xun and the Crisis of Figuration", 269.
[38] Brown observes that "Lu Xun … locate[s] the source of moral insight in the lower-class figure" (Carolyn T. Brown, "Woman as Trope: Gender and Power in Lu Xun's 'Soap,'" *Modern Chinese Literature* 4.1/2 [Spring & Fall, 1988] 64). A number of superb and engaging essays that address the plight of women in early twentieth-century China are collected in this special issue of *Modern Chinese Literature*.
[39] Andrew G. Stuckey, "Female Relations: Voiceless Women in 'Liuyi jie' and 'Zhufu,'" *Frontiers of Literary Study in China* 11.3 (2017): 490.

that is changing around [her]," Stuckey overlooks the fact that Xianglin Sao's voice—her pointed and incredulous questioning—does indeed indicate the birth of an oppositional consciousness.[40] As Carolyn T. Brown puts it, Xianglin Sao's discursive disruption presents the challenge of a "peasant, a woman, a voice from the social unconscious" that "breaks into the narrator's awareness with such direct force that the ego-narrator cannot avoid the confrontation."[41] We might even describe Xianglin Sao's attempt to wrest discursive agency away from traditional and modern (patriarchal) ideological discourses as among the earliest—albeit embryonic—*female* fictional embodiments of Yu Dafu's pronouncement that "First among the greatest successes of the May Fourth Movement is the discovery of the individual" (五四運動的最大的成功，第一要算『個人』的發現).[42] The characterization of Xianglin Sao demonstrates Lu Xun's apprehensive apperception of how a (subaltern) female subjectivity might emerge in the space created by traumatic alienation from traditional ideology and the May 4th discourse of enlightenment, both promulgated by male elites, and both seemingly incapable of accounting for gender inequality.

Lu Xun seems to have thoughtfully crafted "New Year's Sacrifice" as a companion piece to "The True Story of Ah Q", as well as a retroactive commentary on "Diary of a Madman." Like the madman, Xianglin Sao is traumatized by the traditional social order, resulting in severe mental anguish and psychological

---

40 Ibid., 491.
41 "Woman as Trope," 139.
42 Yu Dafu (郁達夫), "Introduction" (導言), in *Zhongguo xinwenxue daxi: diqi ji: sanwen erji* 中國新文學大系: 第七集: 散文二集. (*The compendium of modern Chinese literature: Vol. 7: Prose collections II*), ed. Yu Dafu (Hong Kong: Xianggang wenxue yanjiushe, 1935), 2887. Yu continues "Hitherto, a person existed for his lord, existed for the Dao, existed for his parents; but nowadays a person realizes that he/she lives for oneself.... If there is no 'me,' then wherefore society, nation, clan, etc.?" (從前的人，是爲君而存在，爲道而存在，爲父母而存在的，現在的人纔曉得爲自我而存在了.... 若沒有我，則社會，國家，宗族等那裏會有?) (2887). Chen Duxiu similarly referred to "the awakening of [the] full selfhood" (*quan renge de juexing*) (cited in Ping Zhu, "Traversing the Sublime: A Žižekian Reading of Lu Xun's 'Regrets for the Past,'" *International Journal of Žižek Studies* 3.1 [2009]: 19). Mao Dun (茅盾) includes "individualism" (個人主義) as among May Fourth literature's "key objectives" (主要目標), and its "focal point" (中心點), in "Concerning 'Creation'" (關於 "創作"), in *Mao Dun: Collected Miscellaneous Writings on Literature and Art* (茅盾文藝雜論集) (Shanghai: Shanghai wenyi chubanshe [1981], 298. For a nuanced study of the discourse of individualism in early twentieth-century China, see Lydia Liu, *Translingual Practice: Literature, National Culture, and Translated Modernity: China, 1900–1937* (Stanford, CA: Stanford University Press, 1995). Liu argues that modern collective subjectivity and individualism ("nationhood" and "selfhood") were forced to develop from inside the crucible of China's violent encounter with the West (77–99, 150–179, and passim).

breakdown. However, with Xianglin Sao's character, Lu Xun forces readers to revisit and reconsider the material, gendered, and economic conditions of his madman's ideological-discursive crisis and mental collapse.

The madman, we recall, has a large (gated) home and supportive family who protect and care for him during his illness. He is given the best of food, shelter, privacy (his own room), clothing, and medical attention, and he has the autonomy to spend his days resting and convalescing. Most importantly, where his cognitive breakdown and subjectivity are concerned, the madman is a well-educated male with a high level of literacy, and his access to a personal library helps him make sense of his plight and allows him to develop not merely an oppositional consciousness but an entire counter-discourse (albeit a paranoid and schizophrenic one) which appears to have been integral in the alleviation of his suffering and restoration of his mental health. Ironic though his recovery may be, the madman and his diary constitute a permanent *written* record of the possibility of enlightenment, which he may yet re-experience or pass on to the next generation. Xianlin Sao, conversely, conveys her doubts concerning the veracity of traditional Chinese worldviews *orally* to the narrator and shortly thereafter dies. The traces of her oppositional consciousness remain solely within the narrator's memory, and he is only too eager to consign them to oblivion.[43]

Lu Xun creates Xianglin Sao's character and context in what appears to be a point-by-point contrast to that of the madman. Twice forced to marry against her will and twice widowed, her "family" was comprised of a single son who represented her only purchase within the traditional Chinese patrilineal social structure, and he is eaten by wolves. She is economically dependent, a poor servant without social autonomy or agency, she is exploited and scorned by her in-laws and employers, and held in thrall to the terrifying superstitious beliefs conveyed to her by her peers (concerning her dead husbands waiting to tear her in half when she reaches the afterworld). Even her appellation is indicative of her lack of agency and identity—she is referred to "not by her own name but 'Xianglin's wife.'"[44] Overwhelmed by these multiple traumas,

---

43   In ironic contrast to characters such as the madman, Ah Q, and Xianglin Sao, the narrator of "New Year's Sacrifice" represents the acme of modern intellectual cynicism. In clinging to the belief that he knows all he needs to know, as when he congratulates himself on his "can't say for certain" (說不清), he renders himself "unable to engage in the fundamental act of subjectivity—doubting…. for doubt only occurs when we cease relating to ideology with complete cynical distance" (McGowan, "Between the Capitalist and the Cop," 26).

44   Rey Chow, "Lu Xun's 'Zhufu' ('The New Year's Sacrifice') (1926)," in *Woman and Chinese Modernity: The Politics of Reading Between West and East* (Minneapolis: University of Minnesota Press, 1991), 110.

Xianglin Sao goes mad. Of no further use to her employer and with no hometown or dwelling to return to during the New Year (the traditional time of family gatherings, feasting, and celebration), she is made homeless and dies from starvation and exposure. The contrasting plot lines reveal how utterly perilous—indeed, lethal—it is for a (poor) woman in traditional Chinese society to experience mental breakdown and ostracism. Xianglin Sao, lacking the madman's social autonomy, family support, economic means, food, shelter, medical care, literacy and access to texts from which she might make sense of her experiences, cannot develop her embryonic oppositional consciousness or recover from her trauma-induced madness. She dies, while the literate madman works through his dementia at home via textual research and expressive writing, is healed and finds a comfortable job. When these two stories are read in tandem, "New Year's Sacrifice" becomes a dreary commentary on "Diary of a Madman," showing the madman's playful manipulation of language and subversion of the dominant discursive order to be perquisites of the male intelligentsia.

Many of Lu Xun's short stories are exemplars of the concept of aesthetic cognition, and the artistic insights of these texts are most thoroughly engaged and understood when the reader is subjectively invested in the process of interpretation. This is borne out by a close reading of "Diary of a Madman" (1918), "The True Story of Ah Q" (1921), and "The New Year's Sacrifice" (1924), with an eye to how Lu Xun configures his characters' relationships to then-dominant ideological discourses. Such a reading can impart to readers a type of "tragic pleasure" that "lies between the heroic and the pathetic, arising ... out of our response to a character who strives to assume a responsibility [or an awareness] of which he is incapable" (Davis 1978, 133).

Bibliography

Anderson, Marston. *The Limits of Realism: Chinese Fiction in the Revolutionary Period.* Berkeley: University of California Press, 1990.

Brown, Carolyn T. "Woman as Trope: Gender and Power in Lu Xun's 'Soap,'" *Modern Chinese Literature* 4.1/2 (Spring & Fall, 1988): 55–70.

Brown, Carolyn T. *Reading Lu Xun through Carl Jung. Sinophone World Series* 華語語系世界系列. Amherst, NY: Cambria Press, 2018.

Button, Peter. *Configurations of the Real in Chinese Literary and Aesthetic Modernity.* Leiden: Brill, 2009.

Cheng, Eileen J. *Literary Remains: Death, Trauma, and Lu Xun's Refusal to Mourn.* Honolulu: University of Hawai'i Press, 2013.

Chou, Eva Shan. *Memory, Violence, Queues: Lu Xun Interprets China*. Ann Arbor, MI: Association for Asian Studies, 2012.

Chow, Rey. "Lu Xun's 'Zhufu' ('The New Year's Sacrifice') (1926)." In *Woman and Chinese Modernity: The Politics of Reading Between West and East*. Minneapolis: University of Minnesota Press, 1991: 107–112.

Davies, Gloria. *Lu Xun's Revolution: Writing in a Time of Violence*. Cambridge, MA: Harvard University Press, 2013.

Davis, Walter A. *The Act of Interpretation: A Critique of Literary Reason*. Chicago: University of Chicago Press, 1978.

Davis, Walter A. *Inwardness and Existence: Subjectivity in/and Hegel, Heidegger, Marx, and Freud*. Madison: University of Wisconsin Press, 1989.

Davis, Walter A. *Get the Guests: Psychoanalysis, Modern American Drama, and the Audience*. Madison: University of Wisconsin Press, 1994.

Davis, Walter A. *Deracination: Historicity, Hiroshima, and the Tragic Imperative*. Albany: State University of New York Press, 2001.

Denton, Kirk A. "Lu Xun Biography." MCLC [Modern Chinese Literature and Culture] *Resource Center Publication* (Copyright 2002). u.osu.edu/mclc/online-series/lu-xun/.

Du, Ronggen (杜榮根). *Seeking and Surpassing: Critique of China's New Poetic Forms* (尋求與超越: 中國新詩形式批評 *Xunqiu yu chaoyue: Zhongguo xinshi xingshi piping*). Shanghai: Fudan daxue chubanshe (復旦大學出版社), 1993.

Duke, Michael. "Past, Present, and Future in Mo Yan's Fiction of the 1980s." In *From May Fourth to June Fourth: Fiction and Film in Twentieth Century China*, ed. Ellen Widmer and David Der-wei Wang, 43–70. Cambridge, MA: Harvard University Press, 1993.

Foster, Paul B. *Ah Q Archaeology: Lu Xun, Ah Q, Ah Q Progeny and the National Character Discourse in Twentieth-Century China*. Lanham, MD: Lexington Books, 2006.

"Gender, Writing, Feminism, China." 1988. Special Issue. *Modern Chinese Literature* 4.1/2 (Spring & Fall, 1988).

Hanan, Patrick. "The Technique of Lu Hsün's Fiction," *Harvard Journal of Asiatic Studies*, no. 34 (1974): 53–96.

Huters, Theodore. "Blossoms in the Snow: Lu Xun and the Dilemma of Modern Chinese Literature," *Modern China* 10 (January 1984): 49–77.

Huters, Theodore. "Mirages of Representation: May Fourth and the Anxiety of the Real." In *Chinese Literature and the West: The Trauma of Realism, The Challenge of the (Post) Modern*, ed. Theodore Huters and Tang Xiaobing, 1–23. Durham, NC: Working Papers in Asian/Pacific Studies, Duke University Press, 1991.

Huters, Theodore. "Lu Xun and the Crisis of Figuration." In *Bringing the World Home: Appropriating the West in Late Qing and Early Republican China*, 252–274. Honolulu: University of Hawaii Press, 2005.

Jones, Andrew F. *Developmental Fairy Tales: Evolutionary Thinking and Modern Chinese Culture*. Cambridge, MA: Harvard Univ. Press, 2011.

Kaldis, Nicholas Andrew. *The Chinese Prose Poem: A Study of Lu Xun's* Wild Grass *(Yecao)*. Sinophone World Series 華語語系世界系列. Amherst, NY: Cambria Press, 2014.

Kaldis, Nicholas Andrew. "Lu Xun's Fictional Worlds." In *Wiley-Blackwell Companion to World Literature*, Vol. 5: *The Twentieth and Early Twenty-First Centuries*. London: Wiley-Blackwell. Forthcoming.

Lam, Ling Hon. *The Spatiality of Emotion in Early Modern China: From Dreamscapes to Theatricality*. New York: Columbia University Press, 2018.

Larson, Wendy. *From Ah Q to Lei Feng: Freud and Revolutionary Spirit in 20th-Century China*. Stanford, CA: Stanford University Press, 2009.

Larson, Wendy. *Zhang Yimou: Globalization and the Subject of Culture*. Sinophone World Series 華語語系世界系列. Amherst, NY: Cambria Press, 2017.

Lee, Haiyan. "Sympathy, Hypocrisy, and the Trauma of Chineseness," MCLC [Modern Chinese Literature and Culture] 16.2 (Fall 2004): 76–122.

Lee, Leo Ou-fan, ed. *Lu Xun and His Legacy*. Berkeley: University of California Press, 1985.

Lee, Leo Ou-fan. *Voices from the Iron House: A Study of Lu Xun*. Bloomington: Indiana University Press, 1987.

Lee, Leo Ou-fan. "In Search of Modernity: Some Reflections on a New Mode of Consciousness in Twentieth-Century Chinese History and Literature." In *Ideas Across Cultures: Essays on Chinese Thought in Honor of Benjamin I. Schwartz*, ed. Paul A. Cohen and Merle Goldman, 109–135. Cambridge, MA: Harvard University Press, 1990.

Liang Qichao (梁啟超). "On the Harm of Not Reforming (論不變法之害)." In *China's Response to the West: A Documentary Survey 1839–1923*, ed. Ssu-yü Teng and John K. Fairbank, 154–157. Cambridge, MA: Harvard University Press, 1982 (original 1896). (Chinese text: http://www.bwsk.net/mj/l/liangqichao/000/002.htm; accessed 10.11.2018.)

Lin, Yu-sheng. *The Crisis of Chinese Consciousness: Radical Antitraditionalism in the May Fourth Era*. Madison: University of Wisconsin Press, 1979.

Lin, Yu-sheng. "The Morality of Mind and Immorality of Politics: Reflections on Lu Xun, the Intellectual." In *Lu Xun and His Legacy*, ed. Leo Ou-fan Lee. Berkeley: University of California Press, 1985.

Liu, E (劉鶚). *The Travels of Lao Ts'an*. Trans. Harold Shadick. New York: Columbia University Press, 1990.

Liu, Lydia. *Translingual Practice: Literature, National Culture, and Translated Modernity: China, 1900–1937*, 45–76. Stanford, CA: Stanford University Press, 1995.

Lu, Xun. *Lu Xun: Selected Works*. Trans. Yang Xianyi and Gladys Yang. 4 vols. Beijing: Foreign Languages Press, 1980.

Lu, Xun. *Lu Xun: Diary of a Madman and Other Stories*. Trans. William A. Lyell. Honolulu: University of Hawaii Press, 1990.

Lu, Xun. *The Real Story of Ah-Q and Other Tales of China: The Complete Fiction of Lu Xun*. Trans. Julia Lovell. London: Penguin, 2010.

Lyell, William A. "Introduction." In *Lu Xun: Diary of a Madman and Other Stories*. Trans. William A. Lyell, ix–xxxviii. Honolulu: University of Hawaii Press, 1990.

Mansbridge, Jane J., and Aldon D. Morris. *Oppositional Consciousness: The Subjective Roots of Social Protest*. Chicago: University of Chicago Press, 2001.

Mao Dun (茅盾). "Concerning 'Creation'" (關於 "創作"). In *Mao Dun: Collected Miscellaneous Writings on Literature and Art* (茅盾文藝雜論集), 295–312. Shanghai: Shanghai wenyi chubanshe, 1981.

McGowan, Todd. *Enjoying What We Don't Have: The Political Project of Psychoanalysis*. Lincoln: University of Nebraska Press, 2013.

McGowan, Todd. "Between the Capitalist and the Cop: The Path of Revolution in *Blade Runner 2049*." Forthcoming.

Nietzsche, Friedrich. *On the Genealogy of Morals and Ecce Homo*. Trans. Walter Kaufmann and R. J. Hollingdale. New York: Vintage, 1989. Print.

Nietzsche, Friedrich. *Basic Writings of Nietzsche*. Trans. and Ed. Walter Kaufmann. New York: The Modern Library, 1992. Print.

Pollard, David. *The True Story of Lu Xun*. Hong Kong: Chinese University Press, 2002.

Průšek, Jaroslav. "Basic Problems of the History of Modern Chinese Literature and C. T. Hsia, a History of Modern Chinese Fiction," *T'oung Pao*, 49, no. 4/5 (1962): 357–404.

Stuckey, Andrew G. "Female Relations: Voiceless Women in 'Liuyi jie' and 'Zhufu.'" *Frontiers of Literary Study in China* 11.3 (2017): 488–509.

Tang, Xiaobing. "*Excursion I*: Beyond Homesickness: An Intimate Reading of Lu Xun's 'My Native Land.'" In his *Chinese Modernism: The Heroic and the Quotidian*, 74–96. Durham, NC: Duke University Press, 2000.

Tang, Xiaobing. "Lu Xun's 'Diary of a Madman' and a Chinese Modernism." In his *Chinese Modernism: The Heroic and the Quotidian*, 49–73. Durham: Duke University Press, 2000.

Yeh, Michelle. *Modern Chinese Poetry: Theory and Practice since 1917*. New Haven: Yale University Press, 1991.

Yu Dafu (郁達夫). "Introduction" (導言). In *Zhongguo xinwenxue daxi: diqi ji: sanwen erji* 中國新文學大系: 第七集: 散文二集. (The compendium of modern Chinese literature: Vol. 7: Prose collections II), ed. Yu Dafu, 2883–2901. Hong Kong: Xianggang wenxue yanjiushe, 1935.

Yu Hua (余華). "1986" (一九八六年), *Harvest* (收穫) 6 (1987).

Yü Ta-fu [Yu Dafu (郁達夫)]. "Sinking." In *Modern Chinese Stories and Novellas: 1919–1949*. C. T. Hsia, Joseph S. M. Lau, and Leo Ou-Fan Lee, Eds. New York: Columbia University Press, 1981: 125–141.

Zhang, Yimou (張藝謀). *Raise the Red Lantern* (大紅燈籠高高掛), 1991.

Zhu, Ping. "Traversing the Sublime: A Žižekian Reading of Lu Xun's 'Regrets for the Past,'" *International Journal of Žižek Studies* 3.1 (2009): 1–25.

CHAPTER 10

Literary Bombs: a Sketch of the May Fourth Generation and Bomb as Metaphor

Chien-hsin Tsai

> Silence, silence
> Silence is your character
> You've said only one word all your life
> You were never concerned about breaking your flesh and blood to pieces
> In the explosion that startled the heaven and moved the earth
> A new nation of happiness was born
> TAO XINGZHI

∴

> I know of no other bomb but a book....
> I do not think one can use a more effective weapon than literature.
> STÉPHANE MALLARMÉ

∴

A bomb is something that humanity in general wishes to securely store away, keep at a distance, or even eliminate. There have been exceptions. The Russian anarchists and the Irish Fenians in the late nineteenth century detonated bombs to send political messages. Islamic extremists today conduct suicide bombing to instill terror. Against the background of this effort to discourage bombs, how may we begin to understand the proliferation of the bomb metaphor, which seems to take us in the opposite direction? For example, Anne and Paul Ehrlich call their 1968 book that explores the consequences of overpopulation the "population bomb." Debates about environmental capacity and overpopulation did not start with the book, and they have certainly not dissipated because of it. The title, however, sticks. As the three co-authors of *The Housing Bomb*, published in 2013, argue:

> While rising affluence and human well-being defused the population bomb, the same factors only whet our appetite for more houses, larger houses, houses on bigger pieces of land, and houses in beautiful natural landscapes. The factors that defused the population bomb built the housing bomb … a significant force behind wildlife extinction, dependence on fossil fuels (especially oil), unsustainable forest harvest, abusive mining practices, climate change, water scarcity, and the loss of prime agricultural lands.[1]

All the heated debates between supporters of and nonbelievers in environmentalism aside, how are we to understand the bomb metaphor in our everyday language?

According to Erich Kahler, "man himself has developed by means of the perpetual interaction between consciousness and reality, between his interior world and his exterior world."[2] The continuous transformation of environments both natural and manmade prompts a transformation of consciousness, which, Kahler explains, "in its turn exerts a transforming effect upon the outer world."[3] Briefly put, we are what we think we are or what we strive to become, and our actions have consequences.

Metaphor is the exemplar of such internalization of reality. This is the point George Lakoff and Mark Johnson make throughout *Metaphors We Live By*, which strikes a chord with Kahler's observation. Lakoff's and Johnson's study shows that most of our ordinary conceptual system is metaphorical in nature. How we think and what we do everyday is a matter of metaphor. A metaphor "may create realities for us, especially social realities. A metaphor may thus be a guide for future action. Such actions will, of course, fit the metaphor. This will, in turn, reinforce the power of the metaphor to make experience coherent. In this sense metaphors can be self-fulfilling prophecies."[4] In other words, even if there is not a population bomb, a housing bomb, an urban explosion, or an explosive growth of economy, framing the issue so provocatively may make them a reality. And thinking and speaking figuratively about reality has

---

[1] M. Nils Peterson, Tarla Rai Peterson, and Jianguo Liu, *The Housing Bomb: Why Our Addiction to Houses Is Destroying the Environment and Threatening Society* (Baltimore: John Hopkins University Press, 2013), 2–3.

[2] Erick Kahler, *The Inward Turn of Narrative*, trans. by Richard and Clara Winston (Princeton, NJ: Princeton University Press, 1973), 4.

[3] Ibid., 5.

[4] George Lakoff and Mark Johnson, *Metaphors We Live By* (Chicago: University of Chicago Press, 1980), 156.

the potential of changing it. This was one of the reasons that prompted Susan Sontag to write and publish her *Illness as Metaphor*.

In premodern times, people often connected natural disasters and disease to moral depravity and considered them divine punishment. In the twenty-first century, some still do. For Sontag, military rhetoric about disease may further such stigmatization. As medical professionals characterize virus as the "enemy," "invasive" cancer treatment as "the war on cancer" or "defense," a person with HIV, for instance, runs the risk of becoming morally questionable or simply a menace to public health.

Sontag dedicated her book to the liberation from illness as metaphor. In this chapter, I do not advocate for an abandonment of bomb as metaphor. I do, however, wish to offer some elucidation of the bomb metaphor by providing specific contexts in which the May Fourth generation used it. The use of military metaphors—bomb, revolution, explosion, blast, to name only a few—generates crisscrossing entailments: where there is a bomb there is a "target"; "defeating enemies" leads to "victory"; "establishing a new order of things" requires "sacrifices"; and many more.

Metaphor has the power to define the age in which it flourishes. The bomb is an epochal metaphor that has shaped the Chinese reality since the turn of the twentieth century. The ways in which the May Fourth generation used the bomb metaphor should inspire us to reflect on our own usage and what goals we wish to realize thereby.

Aversion to the force of firearms once cost Qing China dearly. At the turn of the twentieth century, Qing China found itself mired in a series of military conflicts. One particular war stands out for its scale. The Boxer Rebellion was an international event that involved tens of thousands of members of a Chinese religious cult facing the assembled forces of eight non-Chinese empires. The Chinese Boxers were convinced that they were impervious to firearms, but their foreign opponents shattered such delusions without hesitation. The violent chaos ended with the Qing court's agreement to many unreasonable demands. Exorbitant war reparations plunged China further into socioeconomic languor.

Against this backdrop, Liang Qichao 梁啟超 (1873–1929) entered the scene. Liang held traditional fiction accountable for China's deterioration. He saw humanity sinking fast in traditional fiction's indulgence in frivolity, and he saw it as his job to rouse people to save themselves. To reinvigorate China, according to Liang, one must first renovate the Chinese people. And to renovate the Chinese people, one must first renovate Chinese fiction. Nothing would be as instrumental, according to his thought, as a new fiction in reforming Chinese people's morality, raising their political awareness, and in due course saving the nation. Many of Liang's contemporaries rose to support his endeavors.

Liang's passionate endorsement of the political nature of fiction failed to save Qing China. His thought nevertheless survived China's transition from an old empire to a young republic, and continued to exert its influence throughout the long twentieth century.

Not all of Liang's successors shared his mild view of revolution. In fact, many Chinese gravitated to the violent aspect of revolution and modeled themselves after the Russian anarchists. Disparate interpretations attracted their own adherents. The Chinese anarchist-revolutionaries, for example, studied bomb making and became suicide bombers in order to deliver a fatal blow to the Qing court, and deliver they did. When the Qing fell in 1911, it fell at the hands of these ardent revolutionaries, who were unafraid of using explosive devices to achieve their goals.

Chen Duxiu 陳獨秀 (1879–1942) was one of these revolutionaries. He was a close friend to Wu Yue 吳樾 (1878–1905), a suicide bomber who tried to take out five imperial commissioners only to accidentally blow himself up in the end. Wu Yue was said to have built the bomb in the house of Chen's stepfather.[5] Besides Chen, there was also Cai Yuanpei 蔡元培 (1868–1940) who plotted with the like-minded to assassinate Empress Dowager Cixi 慈禧 (1835–1908) with homemade explosives. Cai later became disillusioned with using violence for sociopolitical change. He decided to study abroad in Germany in 1907 and eventually became the president of Peking University. During his tenure as the president from 1916 to 1927, Cai initiated a series of fundamental reforms that helped transform the university into a space not just for learning but also for activism, where the sociopolitical significance of "students" began to deepen.[6] And it was these students who initiated the May Fourth movement.

Cai Yuanpei's transformation from a fervent revolutionary to an enthusiastic educator, one emphasizing the high value of aesthetics, was remarkable to say the least. Unlike Cai, Chen Duxiu continued to bask in the revolutionary atmosphere, in practice as well as in theory. In 1917, after Cai appointed him Dean of the College of Letters at Peking University, Chen published an essay, "On Literary Revolution" 文學革命論, which triggered a wave of unprecedented attempts to renovate Chinese literature and society. Chen believed in the power of new literature, and he was more radical than Liang Qichao in his

---

5 Lee Feigon, *Chen Duxiu, Founder of The Chinese Communist Party* (Princeton, NJ: Princeton University Press, 1983), 80.
6 See Fabio Lanza, *Behind the Gate: Inventing Students in Beijing* (New York: Columbia University Press, 2010).

approach. He fanned the flame of revolution, if only metaphorically, to incite change. He vowed to become "the largest cannon in the world" in the Chinese literary revolution.[7] Lurking behind such military metaphors was his former dedication to bomb-making and assassination.

For Chen Duxiu and his supporters, starting a literary revolution meant revolutionizing literature—radically redefining what made Chinese literature "literature." In addition to fictional techniques and matters of topic, what really "destroyed" the old literature for May Fourth intellectuals like Chen was the written vernacular, or *baihua* 白話. They wanted people to write as if they were speaking, and that was something noticeably absent in classical Chinese literature. Classical Chinese was trite.

During the time Chen wrote as well as in the succeeding generation, many writers and critics continued to embrace the notion of vernacular Chinese as though it were a weapon. As the contemporary cultural critic Li Zehou 李澤厚 (b. 1930) points out, written vernacular Chinese was indeed "a tool and a weapon" that accelerated what were seen as the changes needed to save China.[8] Chen Duxiu and Hu Shi 胡適 (1891–1962) were the two pioneering advocates of written vernacular Chinese. Vernacular Chinese and literature written in vernacular Chinese were both regarded as weapons. May Fourth writers and their successors frequently made references to literature as a powerful weapon. Writers were to be brave fighters on the literary front.

Meanwhile, in Taiwan, there were also followers of Chen Duxiu and Hu Shi who worked restlessly to introduce May Fourth literary thought to people in colonial Taiwan. Zhang Wojun 張我軍 (1902–1955) was their representative.[9] In addition to Chen and Hu, Zhang was particularly inspired by Guo Moruo. He wrote many fiery essays that bore Guo's imprint. He followed Guo's example in proudly cultivating the riotous tendencies of a "bandit" 匪徒, unafraid to wreak havoc on establishments. Zhang called classical-style poets outrageous names—dogs, feces lovers, and necrophiles—while he likened himself to a bomb that would wipe out all things archaic. In the end, the high-handed means Zhang took to promote vernacular Chinese did more harm than good.

Hu Shi, incidentally, showed his radical side in a poem he wrote in vernacular Chinese in 1921, commemorating four suicide bombers—Huang Zhimeng 黃之萌 (1888–1912), Yang Yuchang 楊禹昌 (1885–1912), Zhang Xianpei 張先培

---

7 Chen Duxiu., "On Literary Revolution" in *Modern Chinese Literary Thought: Writings on Literature 1893–1945*, ed. Kirk A. Denton (Stanford, CA: Stanford University Press, 1996), 145.
8 Li Zehou, *Li Zehou shinian ji* (Hefei: Anhui wenyi chubanshe, 1994), 3: 95.
9 See Chien-hsin Tsai, *A Passage to China: Literature, Loyalism, and Colonial Taiwan* (Cambridge, MA: Harvard University Press, 2017), 166–170.

(1890–1912), and Peng Jiazhen 彭家珍 (1888–1912)—who died for their beliefs. Hu Shi's familiar image of self-restraint and gentility is nowhere to be found in the poem. There are four stanzas in Hu Shi's "Ode to the Headstones without Inscriptions at the Four Martyrs' Graves" 四烈士塚上的沒字碑歌, and he ended the first three stanzas with these exhortations:

> Their weapons
> Bombs! Bombs!
> Their spirits
> Do it! Do it! Do it![10]

These short lines come from *Experiments* 嘗試集, published in 1920, Hu Shi's first collection and China's first ever collection of modern-style poems written in vernacular Chinese. All the poems from the collection are truly "experiments" in the sense that Hu Shi experimented with abolishing the conventions of classical-style poetry; no parallelism, no rhyme and meter, no allusions, for instance. This poem in particular offers a glimpse into the mindset of an earlier Hu Shi. Before successfully establishing himself as a renowned scholar with suave manners, the younger Hu Shi had harbored revolutionary ideals and was unafraid to call for radical actions.

In this early stage in the making of modern Chinese poetry, or what some refer to as the "new poetry," the bomb and bomb as metaphor held a prominent position, not only because explosion was nearly an everyday occurrence, but also because many writers treated literature as a weapon. The believers wanted to use the new literary weapon to destroy the old conventions that had failed to prepare the Chinese for a fast-changing world.

A young poet by the name of Wang Jingzhi 汪靜之 (1902–1996) published his first poetry collection in 1922. *Orchid Wind* 蕙的風 is a collection of modern-style or new poems that defy social taboos. For that, Wang received a lot of criticism, as well as praise. Zhu Ziqing 朱自清, a noted essayist, called the public's attention to the collection by calling it a bomb. It was a bomb dropped on the old society precisely because it ushered in a brand new way of understanding human emotions.[11] Wang thought Zhu was generous with his praise: "As far as poetry is concerned, *Orchid Wind* was at best a pebble, undeserving of the honor of the 'bomb.'"[12] Yet Wang was also quick to point out that *Orchid Wind*, mediocre as it was, had turned out to be a powerful weapon.

---

10   Hu Shi, *Hu Shi jingxuanji* (Shenyang: Wanjuan chuban gongsi, 2014), 55–56.
11   Chang Tang-chi, *Xiandai wenxue bainian huiwang* (Taipei: Wanjuanlou, 2012), 125.
12   Wang Jingzhi, *Hui de feng* (Beijing: Renmin wenxue chubanshe, 1957), 3.

Lu Xun 魯迅 (1881–1936) was a studious, if fastidious, reader, and he held both writers and critics to very high standards. The above poem by Hu Shi, rudimentary and experimental as it was, would not have met his expectations. Lu Xun did not praise *Orchid Wind*, but he showed his encouragement by criticizing a critic who condemned the collection.[13] New poets who put emphasis more on format than content annoyed him. Frustrated with their pretentions, he held them accountable for the dire situation China faced. In a critical essay, "The Way of Saving the Nation through Literature" 文學救國法, Lu Xun "opens fire" at such new poets and their use of punctuation:

> China is weak, and it is the moaning of the new poets that weakens it.... We must confiscate the lead balls and the copper molds that make the symbols of exclamation in a printing house and completely destroy them. Future manufacture should also be prohibited. This is because they are the very origin of constant moaning. As long as we have solved the root of the problem, the poets cannot "reduce them to the size of germs or enlarge them to the size of cannonballs" as they see fit.... Many poems and essays filled with symbols of exclamation are unpublished. Even so we should still charge them with the attempt to circumvent quarantine or illegal possession of arms. This is to prevent them from spreading infections as minuscule germs and from starting wars as sizeable arms.[14]

Lu Xun was well aware that the new poets were not responsible for the many unequal treaties that had weakened China. Still he chose them as his target to make his case. His overgeneralization aside, the biological and military analogies here are difficult to miss. Many critics have shed light on why and how Lu Xun intended his writings to rid Chinese readers of spiritual maladies. The germ metaphor is an illustration of his belief in the pharmaceutical function of literature.[15] The bomb metaphor, on the other hand, complements the view of literature and writer as weapon that was very much in fashion throughout the entire twentieth century.

Many Chinese writers received inspirations from their Russian contemporaries, and Lu Xun was no exception. His denunciation of the new poets and

---

13 Lu Xun, "Fandui 'hanlei' de pipingjia," *Lu Xun quanji* (Beijing: Renmin wenxue chubanshe, 2005), 1: 425–428.
14 Lu Xun, "Wenxue jiuguofa." *Lu Xun quanji* (Beijing: Renmin wenxue chubanshe, 2005), 8: 163–164.
15 Carlos Rojas, "Cannibalism and the Chinese Body Politics: Hermeneutics and Violence in Cross-Cultural Perception," *Postmodern Culture* 12, no. 3: 2002. https://muse.jhu.edu/ (accessed December 28, 2018).

the press that published their works brings to mind Lenin's characterization of the bourgeois press as a very powerful weapon. Lenin thought the press was "not less dangerous than bombs and machine guns" and that it ought not fall into the hands of the enemy.[16] This again brings to mind Chen Duxiu, who once compared himself to the "largest cannon" in the Chinese revolution. No other comparison was so hyperbolic except Lin Biao's 林彪 (1907–1971) elevation of Mao Zedong 毛澤東 (1893–1976) to the level of the "spiritual atom bomb" in 1968.[17]

Since the late 1920s, endeavors of "literary revolution" that Chen Duxiu and Hu Shi spearheaded gradually gave way to a new focus on "(proletarian) revolutionary literature" (無產階級) 革命文學. Leftist critics such as Li Chuli 李初梨 (1900–1994) and Cheng Fangwu 成仿吾 (1897–1984) began to redefine the role of literature according to Marxist ideology. In their conceptualization, literature was more than a "weapon of art" 藝術的武器; it ought to embody "the art of a weapon" 武器的藝術 for proletarian causes.[18] To the extent that the "weapon of art" turns art into a weapon, the "art of a weapon" accordingly emphasizes the artistic, if not aesthetic, dimension of a weapon that is literature. As dictated by the belief in desperate times call for desperate measure, advocates of revolutionary literature had a proclivity for weapon over art. And as tensions between China and Japan escalated, the legitimacy of bomb as metaphor became all the more irrefutable.

In late 1935, Zhou Yang 周揚 (1907–1989), a rather influential figure in the circle of leftist critics, sent out a call to unite writers who were in disparate ideological campaigns. Zhou rose to fame and power with the founding of the People's Republic of China in 1949. Appealing to a collective cause for the Chinese nation, he proposed the label of "literature for national defense" 國防文學. In his revelation, literature is indispensible in China's struggle with foreign invaders. It is difficult to argue against, let alone dismiss, the label because it taps into the art of pouring out emotional rhetoric in the name of the nation. It is a clever repackaging of an old idea. Strictly from a utilitarian perspective, there was nothing ingenious about Zhou's proposal. Many writers have hoped to use their work to instigate feelings for a wide array of purposes,

---

16 Vladimir Lenin, "Bolshevik Revolutionary Legislation," in *A Documentary History of Communism in Russia: From Lenin to Gorbachev*, Robert Vincent Daniels (Hanover: University of Vermont Press, 1993), 65.
17 Henry He, *Dictionary of the Political Thought of the People's Republic of China* (Armonk, NY: M. E. Sharpe, 2015), 219.
18 Zhang Damin, *Guomindang wenyi sichao: Sanmin zhuyi wenyi yu minzu zhuyi wenyi* (Taipei: Xiuwei zixun, 2009), 9.

and many have. The rivalry among writers for command over the emotions of the crowd has always been present, and it has always been sharp.

Zhou Yang was a talented orator known for his silver tongue, and this reputation, perhaps to his disappointment, elicited little warmth or collegiality—he was not very well liked. In fact, his open seeking of power as well as his cultivation of an exaggerated sense of propriety antagonized many. Instead of uniting writers of all stripes, Zhou's effort led to injurious infighting, notably the "debate of the two slogans" 兩個口號的論戰. This further separated him from such colleagues as Lu Xun and Feng Xuefeng 馮雪峰 (1903–1976). Opposing Zhou's slogan of "literature for national defense" was Lu Xun's insistence on "mass literature of the national revolutionary struggle" 民族革命戰爭的大眾文學.[19] Lu Xun, as Kirk Denton observes, "could not relinquish the May Fourth enlightenment role for literature, especially in the face of the radicals' usurpation of literature as a propaganda weapon, an act Lu Xun found potentially dangerous, both politically and aesthetically."[20]

For those who already disliked him, Zhou Yang only added insult to injury through his call to have others join him. They thought Zhou's call to bring writers together rang hollow, especially because he had just dismantled the League of Left-wing Writers. Zhou's critics were not convinced that he truly wanted people to work together when his hunger for leadership was so glaringly obvious.[21]

---

19   Lu Xun's slogan in 1935 reverberated and expanded an earlier point in a public speech he delivered on the founding day of the League of Left-wing Writers on March 2, 1930. He urged the league to "produce a large group of new warriors" 造出大群的新的戰士 in order to continue the struggle against the old society. Lu Xun, "Guanyu zuoyi zuojia lianmeng de yijian" in *Lu Xun quanji* (Beijing: Renmin wenxue chubanshe, 2005), 4: 241. In the meantime, what Hu Feng 胡風 (1902–1985) in 1937 said about Lu Xun one year after his death is noteworthy: "Lu Xun was not one who introduced or explained new thoughts. He was a warrior who used new thoughts as weapons to 'hit back' at the 'old fort.' Every one of his cuts drew blood. Since the May Fourth movement, Lu Xun was the only person to shake the dark tradition of a thousand years. It was because he had got the fighting spirit of realism from his deep understanding of the old society." Hu Feng, "Guanyu Lu Xun jingshen de ersan jidian: jinian Lu Xun xiansheng shishi yizhounian," in *Hu Feng quanji*, vol. 2 (Wuhan: Hubei renmin chubanshe, 1999), 501. Hu Feng further developed the notion of "the fighting spirit of realism" he mentioned in passing into a more sustained theory of "the subjective spirit of realism" in his 1944 essay, "Realism Today." See Hu Feng, "Realism Today," in *Modern Chinese Literary Thought: Writings on Literature, 1893–1945*, ed. Kirk A. Denton (Stanford, CA: Stanford University Press, 1996), 485–490.

20   Kirk A. Denton, "General Introduction," in *Modern Chinese Literary Thought: Writings on Literature, 1893–1945*, ed. Kirk A. Denton (Stanford, CA: Stanford University Press, 1996), 50.

21   Wang-chi Wong, *Politics and Literature in Shanghai: The Chinese League of Left-Wing Writers, 1930–36* (Manchester, UK: Manchester University Press, 1991), 177–212. Lu Xun has

Zhou Yang, however, still had his supporters. The poet Pu Feng 蒲風 (1911–1942) was one of them. He drew from the works of Byron and Mayakovsky to support Zhou's slogan. On behalf of his fellow poets, Pu Feng asserted: "The land cannot cry out. Our hearts cry out. We must work to express our cry. But we must do more than cry and sing. Rallying and teaching the people are also among our tasks. We are obliged to learn to use our own weapons, to strengthen our forces, to create the defense of the nation and bolster the defense of the nation."[22]

Byron was already a familiar name in China at that time. Vladimir Mayakovsky was not quite as popular, but he was by no means obscure. A Soviet futurist poet, Mayakovsky is remembered by generations of Chinese writers to this day for his comparison of songs and verses to bombs and banners in his 1927 "Gospodin, 'narodnyi artist'" (Mister "National Artist"). In 1953, Chinese critics even organized a symposium on Mayakovsky. The participants praised him as a "beloved comrade and advisor" with a "power and voice like a bomb, like fire, like a flood, like steel" despite the fact that he has gradually moved from a credo of destruction to a rejection of indiscriminating murder in war.[23] Still there was no denying that the younger Mayakovsky was belligerent and influenced by Mallarmé's "bomb as metaphor," as is evident in the epitaph that opens this chapter.

Distrust of Zhou Yang aside, the national crisis, as usual, did motivate writers to use literature as a weapon. Many devoted themselves to literature, especially poetry, for national defense, even if they had no intention of adhering to such a violent metaphor. And whether or not they were emulating Mayakovsky, many Chinese poets did write poems that resounded with "militant clarity and pyrotechnic intensity."[24] How did these dynamic poems help defend China, if they did, especially as the War of Resistance against Japan escalated?

With regard to poetry, we may observe that some enjoy silent reading in privacy and others prefer recitation in public. "Recitation poetry" 朗誦詩 was the most widely practiced and discussed poetic subgenre in wartime China, as John Crespi explains in *Voices in Revolution*. Chinese war poems that mention

---

given Zhou Yang a few monikers, including "the general manager of slaves" 奴隸總管 and "the emperor of the literary field" 文壇皇帝. See Ge Tao and Gu Hongmei, eds., *Jujiao "Lu Xun shijian"* (Fuzhou: Fujian jiaoyu chubanshe, 2001), 143.

22   Bernd Eberstein, Lloyd Haft, Zbigniew Slupski, and Milena Doleželová-Velingerová, eds., *A Selective Guide to Chinese Literature, 1900–1949: The Poem* (Leiden: Brill, 1989), 194.

23   Hong Zicheng, *A History of Contemporary Chinese Literature*, trans. Michael M. Day (Leiden: Brill, 2007), 86.

24   John Crespi, *Voices in Revolution: Poetry and the Auditory Imagination in Modern China* (Honolulu: University of Hawai'i Press, 2009), 107.

bombs and bombardment are too many to count. Recitation poetry as a subgenre of war poetry is most pertinent to the discussion of bomb as metaphor here, because many recitation poets treated their work as an acoustic explosive device.

According to Crespi, "the tradition of patriotic recitation that began during the War of Resistance and was coopted by the Chinese communist literary-cultural apparatus in the 1950s and 1960s seems artistically retrograde."[25] Artistry was not so much a concern as the ability to stir emotions. The sound of colloquial expression, rather than the image of written words, was the essence of Chinese recitation poetry governed by the theme of war and sacrifice. Recitation poets used simple, vernacular expressions to try to reach as many people as they could in the hope of awakening them to the realities of wartime. In colloquial expressions as well as formal writings, "pens" was the popular stand-in for "guns," and "written words" for "bombs." Writers turned to military metaphors not only because they were straightforward and relatable. Many poets, such as Pu Feng, reveled in the violence of war as the primary source of striking imagery because they wanted to arm both the hands and heads of their audience. With "an armed head" 武裝的頭腦, a warrior would understand that the purpose of war is to end the war.[26]

The personification of a bomb is one of the salient features of bomb as metaphor in recitation poetry. Examples of such personification to express anti-Japanese sentiments abound. "Ha! I'm a Bomb!" 啊！我是炸彈 speaks loudly to the slogans of "weapon of art" and "art of the weapon":

> Ha! I'm a bomb,
> Blast! Blast! Blast!
> Blast! Blast to oblivion the cruel dwarf devils!
> Blast! Blast from the water the fierce enemy warships!
> Blast! Blast Tokyo flat!
> Blast! Blast Osaka flat!
> Blast! Blast Kobe flat! …[27]

The line "I'm a bomb" is an example of both objectification and personification. More specifically, in this poem, personification is at the same time objectification. On the one hand, "I'm a bomb" is the bomb's self-introduction. With that, the anthropomorphic bomb then exclaims that it means to exterminate

---

25 Ibid., 10.
26 Eberstein, et al., eds., *A Selective Guide to Chinese Literature*, 195.
27 Crespi, *Voices in Revolution*, 81–82.

the Japanese. On the other hand, "I'm a bomb" is equally an instance of objectification. The poet is identifying with something as mighty as a bomb. War induces fear and anxiety. Such identification begets fearlessness, which may conceivably offer a temporary relief from anxiety. As rage and courage grow, trepidation diminishes. By way of personification and objectification, the poet uses the bomb metaphor to prompt the audience to take up the offense rather than merely seek defense. It is a functional substitute for nationalism, martyrdom, or really any fervent devotion to the well-being of China.

"It's Time, My Comrades" 是時候了, 我的同胞 by Gao Lan 高蘭 (1909–1987), a fierce advocate of recitation poetry, is another resounding example:

> It's time, my comrades!
> The enemy with warplanes and bombs
> Has come again in force to slaughter us!
> We are already dynamite at the point of ignition,
> So how will we bear this burning?
> Explode!
> Explode!
> Let's explode!
> O all who do not want to be the slaves from a fallen nation!
> If you have not yet forgotten the shame,
> If you no longer want to live the inglorious life of a rankling sore,
> Then it's time, my comrades![28]

The line "We are already dynamite" is essentially the same as "I'm a bomb." Both serve to rouse the crowd to fever pitch. The word "explode" the poet uses here is as impactful as the word "blast," which appears frequently in the previous poem. Even if only in writing, the repetition of "explode" or "blast" readily evinces a mental image of bomber planes, constant bombardments, and the deafening noise of explosion. When recited, the repetition has a resounding effect.

In wartime, recitation poets wrote under the stress of nationalism, which compelled them to steep their poetry in righteous anger. Written specifically for public performance, recitation poetry in its entirety is an auditory device, aiming to heighten the other senses of the audience in a chain reaction. A recitation poem as an explosive device triggers memories, which inevitably solicit

---

28 Quoted with minor modification from Mei Chia-Ling, "Voice and Quest for Modernity in Chinese Literature," in *The Oxford Handbook of Modern Chinese Literature*, ed. Carlos Rojas and Andrea Bachner (Oxford: Oxford University Press, 2016), 158.

varied emotional responses. In wartime China, seemingly anything could be a bomb. As Chang-Tai Hung points out in *War and Popular Culture*, a critic at that time by the pen name of Xinbo 新波 likened the force of a cartoon to that of "'a silent bomb,' which, if detonated at the right time, could have an enormous effect."[29] Though trite it may have become, the bomb metaphor retains its ability to tap into the human psyche and stir feelings.

Zhou Yang was close to Mao Zedong in Yan'an, and Mao was someone who consistently resorted to military rhetoric to sustain his ideas and mobilize his followers. Mao gave certain instructions with regard to literary production in the Communist stronghold at Yan'an. He described the key role of writers: "To ensure that literature and art fit well into the whole revolutionary machine as a component part, that they operate as powerful weapons for uniting and educating the people and for attacking and destroying the enemy, and that they help the people fight the enemy with one heart and one mind."[30]

And what best fits literature into the revolutionary machinery and what makes literature as weapon so powerful? Plain diction understandable to workers, peasants, and soldiers with little or no education. The instrumentalization of literature is a commonality shared by Mao's directions for literature and the May Fourth view of literary revolution.[31] Mao's rhetoric shows influence from an existing tradition that has proven itself to be larger than life.

In *The Uses of Literature*, Perry Link writes: "specific formulations came and went in accordance with the 'propaganda objectives' of particular times. For example, in spring 1979, when the post-Mao short story was surging, official critics repeated the cumbersome phrase 'the short story's combat function as a military scout.'"[32] The "cumbersome phrase" from 1979 China was an echo to the Nationalist government's implementation of the policy of "combat literature

---

29   Chang-tai Hung, *War and Popular Culture: Resistance in Modern China, 1937–1945* (Berkeley: University of California Press, 1994), 130.

30   Mao Zedong, "Talk at the Yenan Forum on Literature and Art," in *Selected Works of Mao Tse-Tung* (Beijing: Foreign Languages Press, 1965), 3: 70.

31   Still, as Su Wei points out, "If one were to say that the culture of May Fourth was guided by the Western culture of enlightenment, then between it and 'Yan'an culture' there is a shift toward the revolutionary nationalism of Soviet Russian culture." Su Wei, "The School and the Hospital: On the Logics of Socialist Realism," in *Chinese Literature in the Second Half of the Modern Century: A Critical Survey*, ed. Pang-Yuan Chi and David Der-wei Wang (Bloomington: Indiana University Press, 2000), 67 (also 65–75). Meanwhile, there were intellectuals from the late Qing and May Fourth that had broadcast the Soviet view of revolution and literature. In this regard, Mao's rhetoric is as much a "shift" as a circuitous return to the Soviet culture.

32   Perry Link, *The Uses of Literature: Life in the Socialist Chinese Literary System* (Princeton: Princeton University Press, 2000), 284.

and arts" 戰鬥文藝 in Taiwan in the 1950s despite the ideological misalignment between the Chinese Communist Party and the Nationalist Party. This shows again that literature as weapon has long been a staple in Chinese literary criticism. And clearly it has also been embraced by people with political views that could not be farther from one another.

Where once it was the soldiers who threw bombs, now it seemed that the whole society lofted them. As Link shrewdly observes, "military metaphors eventually seeped even into the language of daily life, where, for example, it became normal in socialist China to propose that friends at a dinner table 'annihilate' (*xiaomie*) the food remaining in a common dish."[33] Military metaphors may have found their ways to the dining table in socialist China, but their permeation has certainly begun well before the Mao era. The May Fourth generation was already cleverly working military metaphors into their everyday writings. To the extent that leftovers are enemies that deserve annihilation, powerful literature has always been a letter bombs that shocks its readers. May Fourth critics have often characterized as bombs publications that stupefied readers.

Among her contemporaries who employed bomb as metaphor in their fictional works or book reviews, Ding Ling 丁玲 (1904–1986), the author of *Miss Sophia's Diary*, stood out for several of her striking contributions. Many critics considered Ding Ling's stories explosive. As one of her contemporaries commented, "It was around 1928 when the woman writer Ding Ling appeared on the literary stage. The publication of her first fiction 'Mengke' stupefied readers. A celebrated newcomer, she continues to publish new pieces. Her style changes all the time. Every one of her changes is like a bomb dropped on this society."[34]

The critic was right: Ding Ling did not stop changing. She continued to reinvent herself as a writer, a critic, a soldier, and a political worker. She continually shocked her audience with each reinvention, or at least alerted them to her latest ideological development. She shifted form writing about female interiority to realistic depiction of war and the Communist contributions to new China in later years. The younger Ding Ling who focused on women's issues may not have thought of her own works as bombs, but the older Ding Ling appeared to have understood the metaphor well. In her acclaimed novel on the Communist land reform, *The Sun Shines over the Sanggang River*, Ding Ling elaborates on the bomb metaphor through a conversation between two comrades:

---

33   Ibid., 284–285.
34   Quoted in Li Jun, "'Shafei xingge' zhengjie: jiantan chuantong wenxue dui Ding Ling zaoqi chuangzuo de yingxiang," *Dongyue luncong*. 34 (no. 12, 2013): 97.

Teacher Liu suddenly put on a happy face and said, "Old Wu, you know everything. Now, bomb, how do you understand this word? Yesterday Comrade Hu told me that the blackboard news should be like a bomb. What did he mean?"

"A Bomb ..." the old man pulled out a small tobacco pipe from his pocket, "why did Comrade Hu say that? Well, you intellectuals don't like to talk straight, as if you don't want people to understand what you say. So he said the blackboard news is like a bomb? Let's see. A bomb.... A bomb blows people up, but how can the blackboard news do that? That's not what he meant. Bombs explode.... He meant the blackboard news ought to be like a burst of flame, setting fire to the reader's heart."[35]

The "blackboard news" refers to news written on a fixed or mobile blackboard. It was a particularly cost-effective way of reaching the people in the countryside where literacy rates remained low. According to Brian DeMare, it was also "[o]ne of the most innovative tools for spreading Communist rhetoric at the local level."[36] Ding Ling as well as her characters understood this well. They treated the blackboard news as an incendiary bomb and used it to educate the audience and rouse them to action. This fictional episode may well be Ding Ling's belated response to the critic who compared her works to bombs decades before.

Ding Ling deserves a little more treatment here because of her involvement, voluntary or not, in a few controversies. Bomb as metaphor connected these controversies and connected her to Zhou Yang, the promoter of literature for national defense. Her relationship with Zhou Yang is complicated.[37] Since the early 1930s, Ding Ling had become rather politically active. The success of "Mengke" and *Miss Sophia's Diary* did not stop herself from self-cultivation. She found in Chinese Communism something worthy of her pursuit and joined the League of Left-wing Writers. From 1933 to 1936, the Nationalist Party arrested and imprisoned her due to her involvement with Communism. She went missing and many thought she had been executed. Zhou Yang soon became the secretary of the Party group in the league, a position Ding Ling held before her disappearance.

---

35   Ding Ling, *Ding Ling quanji* (Shijiazhuang: Hebei renmin chubanshe, 2001), 2: 151.
36   Brian James DeMare, *Mao's Cultural Army: Drama Troupes in China's Rural Revolution* (Cambridge: Cambridge University Press, 2015), 17.
37   See Charles J. Alber, *Embracing the Lie: Ding Ling and the Politics of Literature in the People's Republic of China* (London: Praeger, 2004).

A few years later, in Yan'an, the two met again. Ding Ling arrived in November 1936 followed by Zhou Yang in August 1937. Both devoted themselves to Mao Zedong. Yet they belonged to two factions with opposite approaches to literature. Ding Ling and her group wanted to expose darkness while Zhou Yang and his followers focused on praising brightness.[38] For the Party and to better serve the people, the two worked together harmoniously, at least on the surface.

Something happened years later that fanned Ding Ling's discontent with Zhou Yang. After Ding Ling completed *The Sun Shines over the Sanggan River*, she shared the manuscript with several Communist critics. Zhou Yang was the associate director of the North China Propaganda Brigade at the time, and he also received a copy. While others praised Ding Ling's achievement, Zhou Yang had nothing positive to say. In fact, he said nothing at all, which was unlike his usual vociferous self. Zhou's cold shoulder, given his leadership, stalled the novel's publication, and Ding Ling was understandably upset. Still, with the endorsement of several other critics, the novel went to press, and it eventually won second place in the competition for the 1951 Stalin Prize in Literature. The award spoke volumes about not so much Zhou Yang's lack of discernment as his animus toward Ding Ling, which led him to steer her away from further critical recognition.[39]

Everything that happened between Ding Ling and Zhou Yang in Yan'an was but a "continuation and further development of the old conflicts from the days of the League of Left-wing Writers."[40] In fact, the clash between the two extended beyond Yan'an. During the Anti-Rightest Campaign 反右運動 in the late 1950s, Zhou Yang revisited Ding Ling's disappearance between 1933 and 1936 and used it to question her allegiance to the Communist Party. She was once again interrogated about her motive in joining Mao Zedong in Yan'an. Despite that, it was actually Ding Ling's husband Feng Da who sold her out to the Nationalist Party, and she was suspected to be a Nationalist mole in Yan'an. For Zhou Yang, it was indisputably a "blemish" 污點 that Ding Ling had lived with a traitor.[41]

---

38 Yi-tsi Mei Feuerwerker, *Ding Ling's Fiction: Ideology and Narrative in Modern Chinese Literature* (Cambridge: Harvard University Press, 1982), 166. Tani Barlow, *The Question of Women in Chinese Feminism* (Durham: Duke University Press, 2004), 193.
39 Xing Xiaoqun, *Ding Ling yu wenxue yanjiusuo de xingshuai* (Taipei: Xiuwei, 2009), 92–96.
40 Yuan Liangjun, "Wo suo renshi de Ding Ling," *Chongqing Sanxia xueyuan xuebao*, 17 (no. 1, 2001): 38 (also 38–42).
41 Wei Bangliang, *Dikang yu taodun: Zhongguo wenhuaren de butong xuanze* (Taipei: Xiuwei, 2008), 276.

By way of conclusion, I turn to one last episode that involved Zhou Yang. Writers who wrote about bombardment and employed the bomb metaphor often did so with an untested optimism about the future. In reality as well as fiction, bombing brings about many unpredictable consequences. The leftist writer Ding Kexin 丁克辛 (??–??) learned about this the hard way. Although quite active in the 1940s and the early 1950s, he has largely escaped public memory.

The critic C. T. Hsia is known for his criticism of Communist writers and their fictional work. He often criticized their sacrifice of artistry for the sake of propaganda. In his magnum opus, *A History of Modern Chinese Fiction*, Hsia mentions both Zhou Yang and Ding Kexin to illustrate his aversion to propaganda: "One may be amused by [Zhou] Yang's summary and critique of a story whose main fault, apparently, is to redeem boredom by adding some psychological twist to the propaganda routine."[42] "The Old Worker Guo Fushan" 老工人郭福山 was the story with a psychological twist that boded ill for Zhou Yang.

Instead of giving an example and analyzing what he thinks may have started Ding Kexin off on the wrong foot with Zhou Yang, Hsia gives Zhou a rare opportunity—really a dubious honor—to speak for himself in a lengthy block quotation. Hsia is not so much praising Ding's story or agreeing with Zhou's commentary as showing how challenging it was even for a leftist writer to meet the party's unnerving demands.

Ding Kexin wrote the story to display proudly his support of the Chinese Communist Party's involvement in the Korean War, but it spectacularly backfired. In the story, the son of the old worker, unbeknownst to people around him, suffers from what we today would call PTSD after surviving the War of Resistance against the Japanese. The son, a model party member, hides his suffering by acting tough and giving pep talks to others: "According to Comrade Stalin, Communists are made of special materials. Whatever we do, we must succeed, and we will succeed."[43] Later people find out that the son, who talks an impeccable game, is completely dysfunctional at the mere sound of explosion and machinery.

As the story unfolds and certainly as the title suggests, the old worker is the protagonist and the son is but a supporting role. It is the old worker who requests that the party revoke his son's membership. It is the old worker who sets up an example for everyone around him as he fearlessly dodges the

---

[42] C. T. Hsia, *A History of Modern Chinese Fiction* (Bloomington: Indiana University Press, 1999), 476.

[43] Ding Kexin, "Laogongren Guo Fushan," *Renmin wenxue* 4 (no. 1, 19, 1951), 10.

bombs and bullets in the war against the "American bandits" 美國強盜.[44] It is also the old worker who successfully treats his son's disorder with a stern lecture.

Ding Kexin used bombs, bullets, and episodes of bombardment to illustrate the old worker's devotion to the party, but he overlooked the unpredictability of the bomb metaphor. The fictional treatment of a serious mental condition with a parental lecture was not what displeased Zhou Yang. Zhou picked a bone with the author for letting the father, rather than the party, take credit for the son's reform: "In the whole incident, the decisive factors are physiological and psychological and not political, are in the nature of a family relationship and not of a party relationship. Politically and ideologically, this kind of writing is completely wrongheaded."[45] For Zhou, the party trumps everything, including the bomb.

The May Fourth generation lived with constant bombardment. Their bomb metaphor resonated strongly with air raids and guerilla acts. The era of crisis in which they lived was also one of growing self-awareness. As modern science, Western learning, and imperialism reshaped China, the May Fourth generation felt an urge stronger than ever to make sense of the restless world. They used the bomb metaphor to express this urge meaningfully. They also used it to highlight the opportunity for reconstruction, the effort to initiate or adjust to a new way of thinking and writing, and a new way of life. At the center of the bomb metaphor was a blithe faith in the bomb's positive force.

The bomb resounded with different tones in the hands of different writers and critics, but they were similarly upbeat. There were recitation poets and critics like Guo Moruo and Zhang Wojun, who played up to hyperemotionalism, supercharging the bomb metaphor with ambition and indignation. The May Fourth generation did not make light of the destruction and trauma of the bomb, except in the last instance where Zhou Yang put politics before the people.

The bomb metaphor is so ubiquitous, therefore desensitizing, that it is hard to see the actual bomb as one of humankind's greatest and gravest inventions. Extensive reportage of riots and wars risks turning the excruciations of bombing into banality. The fact of the matter is that not all Chinese writers in the twenty-first century have seen an actual bomb powerfully at work in person, let alone having the knowledge to make one. Despite the similarities and differences between what concerns us today and what concerned the May Fourth

---

44   Ibid., 13.
45   C. T. Hsia, *A History of Modern Chinese Fiction*, 478.

generation a century ago, it is worthwhile to recall their undertakings whenever our own urge to employ the bomb metaphor surfaces.

Bibliography

Alber, Charles J. *Embracing the Lie: Ding Ling and the Politics of Literature in the People's Republic of China.* London: Praeger, 2004.

Chang, Tang-chi. *Xiandai wenxue bainian huiwang.* Taipei: Wanjuanlou, 2012.

Chi, Pang-Yuan, and David Der-wei Wang, eds. *Chinese Literature in the Second Half of the Modern Century: A Critical Survey.* Bloomington: Indiana University Press, 2000.

Crespi, John. *Voices in Revolution: Poetry and the Auditory Imagination in Modern China.* Honolulu: University of Hawai'i Press, 2009.

Daniels, Robert Vincent, ed. *A Documentary History of Communism in Russia: From Lenin to Gorbachev.* Hanover: University of Vermont Press, 1993.

DeMare, Brian James. *Mao's Cultural Army: Drama Troupes in China's Rural Revolution.* Cambridge: Cambridge University Press, 2015.

Denton, Kirk A., ed. *Modern Chinese Literary Thought: Writings on Literature 1893–1945.* Stanford, CA: Stanford University Press, 1996.

Ding Ling. *Ding Ling quanji.* Shijiazhuang: Hebei renmin chubanshe, 2001.

Eberstein, Bernd, Lloyd Haft, Zbigniew Slupski, and Milena Doleželová-Velingerová, eds. *A Selective Guide to Chinese Literature, 1900–1949: The Poem.* Leiden, NL: Brill, 1989.

Feigon, Lee. *Chen Duxiu, Founder of the Chinese Communist Party.* Princeton, NJ: Princeton University Press, 1983.

Feuerwerker, Yi-tsi Mei. *Ding Ling's Fiction: Ideology and Narrative in Modern Chinese Literature.* Cambridge, MA: Harvard University Press, 1982.

He, Henry. *Dictionary of the Political Thought of the People's Republic of China.* Armonk, NY: M. E. Sharpe, 2015.

Hong, Zicheng. *A History of Contemporary Chinese Literature.* Trans. Michael M. Day. Leiden, NL: Brill, 2007.

Hsia, C. T. *A History of Modern Chinese Fiction.* Bloomington: Indiana University Press, 1999.

Hung, Chang-tai. *War and Popular Culture: Resistance in Modern China, 1937–1945.* Berkeley: University of California Press, 1994.

Lanza, Fabio. *Behind the Gate: Inventing Students in Beijing.* New York: Columbia University Press, 2010.

Link, Perry. *The Uses of Literature: Life in the Socialist Chinese Literary System.* Princeton, NJ: Princeton University Press, 2000.

Lu, Xun. *Lu Xun quanji*, vol. 1. Beijing: Renmin wenxue chubanshe, 2005.

Mao, Zedong. *Selected Works of Mao Tse-Tung*, vol. 3. Beijing: Foreign Languages Press, 1965.

Rojas, Carlos. "Cannibalism and the Chinese Body Politics: Hermeneutics and Violence in Cross-Cultural Perception", *Postmodern Culture*, 12, no. 3: 2002.

Rojas, Carlos, and Andrea Bachner, eds. *The Oxford Handbook of Modern Chinese Literature*. Oxford: Oxford University Press, 2016.

Tsai, Chien-hsin. *A Passage to China: Literature, Loyalism, and Colonial Taiwan*. Cambridge, MA: Harvard University Press, 2017.

Wei, Bangliang. *Dikang yu taodun: Zhongguo wenhuaren de butong xuanze*. Taipei: Xiuwei, 2008.

Zhang Damin. *Guomindang wenyi sichao: Sanmin zhuyi wenyi yu minzu zhuyi wenyi*. Taipei: Xiuwei zixun, 2009.

CHAPTER 11

Utopian Language: from Esperanto to the Abolishment of Chinese Characters

Chih-p'ing Chou

Language reform was a critical issue for Chinese intellectuals in the late nineteenth century. In terms of the style of the Chinese language, there was a debate between classical Chinese and vernacular Chinese. In terms of the improvement of the writing system, Romanization and simplification were both proposed. In regard to pronunciation, there was a national language movement that sought to unify various dialects. All these issues were raised during the late nineteenth century as China started to interact with the outside world in an unprecedented way, which prompted the Chinese intellectuals to compare Chinese with other languages. Many believed that the Chinese writing system, when compared to the alphabetical system, was inferior in many ways.

There were numerous proposals for reforming the Chinese language. The overall aim, however, was to phoneticize the Chinese characters. After Lu Zhuangzhang 盧戇章 published the *Yimu liaoran chujie* 一目了然初階 (Basic steps in being able to understand at a glance) in 1892, one of the earliest phonetic systems created by a Chinese intellectual, more than thirty other plans were proposed in the next twenty years. The better-known ones include Wang Zhao's 王照 "Guanhua hesheng zimu" 官話合聲字母 in 1900 and Lao Naixuan's 勞乃宣 "Zengding heshengjian zipu" 增訂合聲簡字譜 in 1905.[1]

Of all the proposals at the time, the most radical one was to replace the Chinese language with Esperanto. As I pointed out elsewhere, "Nothing had confronted the core of Chinese civilization as deeply as the Esperanto movement. Yet nothing had created so few effects on the development of Chinese civilization as the Esperanto movement" (在種種西化或世界化的過程中，沒有比世界語運動更能觸及中國固有文化的核心；然而，也沒有比世界語運

---

1 Ni Haishu, *Qingmo hanyu pinyin yundong biannianshi* 清末漢語拼音運動編年史 (A chronological history of a late Qing movement for a phonographic script) (Shanghai: Shanghai renmin chubanshe, 1959), 3–12.

動更"虛晃一招"而不收任何實效).[2] This seemingly self-contradictory statement reveals that language (and particularly its writing system) is the most conservative element in a civilization. Any attempt to change this system would require the participation of people from all walks of life over a long period of time. A language reform without the participation of the common people is therefore impossible.

The Esperanto movement in modern China appeared to be inspiring and lively, but in reality, it had nothing to do with the common people. Nevertheless, the formation of this radical language reform movement is an important topic in the study of modern Chinese intellectual history and merits our further investigation.

One major reason that the Esperanto movement was able to attract many Chinese intellectuals in the early twentieth century was that Esperanto was understood as a language for the entire world. It was translated as "Shijieyu" (世界語) and "Wanguo xinyu" (萬國新語) in Chinese, which literally means "world language" and "universal new language." The word "Esperanto" was derived originally from the pseudonym used by Dr. Ludwig Lazarus Zamenhof (1859–1917) who created this artificial language in 1887. The original meaning of the term was "one who hopes," which indicated Dr. Zamenhof's hope for a world that is free from language barriers and one that can be united by this language. This was of course Zamenhof's personal wish, one which could not be turned into reality. Yet the Chinese had translated the term as "world language" and this translation transformed Zamenhof's personal wish into a delusion.

This Chinese translation is misleading because it creates the misunderstanding of Esperanto as an "international" or "universal language." In other words, the translation led many Chinese to believe that the Esperanto is a language that is actually used around the whole world.

The word "Shijieyu" ("universal language") was invented by the Japanese and was later adopted by the Chinese. Yet the Japanese had abandoned this translation in favor of a transliteration in Katakana. The Japanese might have done so to avoid misrepresentation. Esperanto was once referred to as "Aisi bunan du" (愛斯不難讀), which literally means "Love it, and it's not hard to read." Qian Xuantong 錢玄同 (1887–1939) suggested in 1918 that the Chinese should simply adopt Esperanto.[3] Nevertheless, except for a few articles published in the *New Youth*, no one really referred to the Esperanto by its transliteration.

---

2 Chih-p'ing Chou, "Chunmeng liao wuhen—jindai zhongguo de shijieyu yudong" 春夢了無痕—近代中國的世界語運動, *Dushu* 讀書 4 (1997): 108–109.
3 Qian Xuantong, "Correspondence" 通信, in *Xin Qingnian* 新青年 4, 4 (1918): 363.

As a result, the term "Shijieyu" became a misleading but common translation of "Esperanto" in the Chinese-speaking context, and it is still used in that way today.

The best example of such a mistranslation/misunderstanding of Esperanto as a real "universal language" is its use by Liu Shipei 劉師培 (1884–1919), who published an article in 1905 entitled "Lun zhongtu wenzi youyi yu shijie" 論中土文字有益於世界 (On the contribution of the Chinese language to the world). In this article, he argued that the etymology used in the Han Dynasty dictionary, *Shuowen Jiezi* 說文解字, has the value of shedding light on the customs of a primitive society. Liu concluded that the Chinese characters contain many references to the structure of the ancient Chinese world, and that this etymological approach was not only applicable to the understanding of the Chinese culture, but also applicable to the study of other languages as well. He thus argued that *Shuowen Jiezi* should be translated into Esperanto, to the benefit of the entire world.[4] Interestingly, Liu Shipei opposed the alphabetization of Chinese script, but he seemed to believe that *Shuowen Jiezi* could be translated into Esperanto, and that once that was done, all people in the world would be able to rely on this Chinese dictionary and appropriate it for their own advantage. While Liu himself had promoted anarchism, it is clear that he believed in the value of this ancient Chinese book, and he was convinced that Esperanto was a truly universal language.

In 1908, Zhang Taiyan 章太炎 (1869–1936) questioned whether Esperanto could be regarded as a real "universal language." In an article entitled "Gui Xinshiji" 規新世紀 (An admonishment on the *New Century*), Zhang wrote, "Esperanto sets its standard according to languages based in Europe, and not those in other continents" (萬國新語者, 本以歐洲為準, 於他洲無所取).[5] He thus suggested that Esperanto should be translated as the "new European language" (歐洲新語) or "new language in diplomacy" (邦交新語). Although these translations are more modest and accurate in reflecting the vision as well as nature of the Esperanto, Zhang still overestimated this "new European language" or "new language in diplomacy," which never achieved the status of a common language, even in Europe, nor can it be used as a language in diplomacy. In other words, while Zhang opposed the Esperanto movement, he still believed in its function and its potential for serving as an international language on a smaller scale.

---

4 Liu Shipei, "Lun zhongtu wenzi youyi yu shijie," *Guocui xuebao* 國粹學報 in xxxx 廣陵書社, (2006/3) 9: 4555–4558.
5 Zhang Taiyan, "Gui xinshiji" 規新世紀 (An admonishment on the *New Century*), *Minbao* 民報 (1908/10/10) 24: 11.

To translate "Esperanto" as "universal language" is like mistaking a mirage for beautiful reality. This had led many twentieth-century Chinese intellectuals to believe that the Esperanto movement was an effective way to introduce China to the modern world. But a mirage, however beautiful, after all, is still a mirage, not reality. After a hundred years, Esperanto did not even come close to gaining the status of a universal language.

In a way, Chinese intellectuals' fascination with Esperanto reflected their belief that the Chinese language and its writing system were inferior to their Western counterparts. "Abandon Chinese characters!" thus became a popular slogan in the 1920s and 1930s, during which the Chinese characters were falsely accused of being the culprit that held China back for more than a hundred years.

1 Language Reforms and Nationalism

The early Chinese language reformers, almost without exception, believed that the implementation of a language reform would modernize China and reduce the rate of illiteracy in the entire country. Therefore, they considered Chinese language reform a matter of national importance that would determine the rise or fall of the nation.

Today, this logic is no longer appealing, and the correlation between the reform of language and national prosperity is difficult to prove. But this kind of claim—that the wealth and power of a nation is determined by its writing system—was common among Chinese intellectuals in the early twentieth century.

At the time, there were only two options that were considered possible: to preserve the Chinese characters and let China perish, or, to abolish the Chinese characters and have China flourish. Under the banner of "saving China from the peril," intellectuals considered any attempt to defend Chinese characters as showing indifference to China's plight. The call to abolish Chinese characters even became tantamount to a declaration of patriotism. Language reform was only a means to a political end; the real goal was to make the country prosper. Proponents of a phonetic and alphabetic writing system thus often exaggerated the flaws of Chinese characters and the benefits of a phonetic-alphabetic language system, arguing that the Chinese characters were nothing more than a tool, and denying that they were entwined with the history and culture.

Carrying as they did the burden of seeking national salvation, the various Chinese language reform movements were characterized both by a strong sense of nationalism and patriotism, and inconsistency among their ideas.

Ironically, many of these Chinese language reformers found themselves espousing the most radical form of internationalism. Abandoning the Chinese script in favor of Esperanto or a Latinized writing system is an obvious example of this inconsistency. On the one hand, these Chinese intellectuals were extremely anti-tradition; yet on the other, they claimed to love China. In order to resolve this conflict, they needed to separate the Chinese script from its history and culture, and to thus consider it a purely linguistic tool.

This kind of utilitarianism was very popular during the May Fourth Movement. Qian Xuantong, for example, wrote in 1918, "My opinion on the writing system is that, like weights and measures, calendars and currency, the more unified the system is, the less effort is required to understand them" (玄同對於文字之觀念, 以為與度量衡, 紀年, 貨幣等等相同, 符號愈統一, 則愈可少勞腦筋也).[6] But equating language and writing with a system of measurement surely oversimplifies humankind's most complex means of communication. Can the development of a language really separate itself from history and culture? The answer is likely to be negative. It is even difficult for systems of measurements to be completely detached from the cultural and historical systems from which they derive.

In 1919, Fu Sinian 傅斯年 stressed that "A writing system is only a tool. It has absolutely no other use" (文字的作用僅僅是器具, 器具以外, 更沒有絲毫作用).[7] Therefore, when speaking of the problem of the Chinese writing, he only spoke of "convenience" (方便) and "benefit" (有益). Fu stated that, apart from these, he "denied that there is any sort of inviolable quality in the Chinese writing system" (絕不承認文字裡面有不可侵犯的質素).[8]

It must be pointed out that any language and writing system is not something that can be easily altered or revamped. Each language has its own features, was developed through thousands of years, and was spoken and used by hundreds of thousands of people. The Chinese language cannot be separated from its writing system (i.e., Chinese characters). Their relationship cannot be severed at will. Qian Xuantong, Fu Sinian, and other May Fourth intellectuals saw only the difficulties brought by the archaic nature of Chinese characters. They did not see how Chinese culture, over the course of thousands of years, relied on the Chinese script to bind together and even intermingle multiple ethnic

---

6   Qian Xuantong, "In reply to Tao Lugong on the issue of Esperanto," *Qian Xuantong wenji* 錢玄同文集 1: 99.

7   Fu Sinian, "Hanyu gaiyong pinyin wenzi de chubu tan" 漢語改用拼音文字的初步談 (A preliminary discussion of replacing Chinese characters with a phonetic system of Roman letters), *New Tide* 新潮 1: 3, 392.

8   Ibid., 402.

groups and dialects, providing Chinese culture with an identifiable contour. As a result, their arguments were mostly sophistry and ungrounded in reality.

In terms of the function of carrying knowledge, Chinese script is only a tool. Yet in terms of reflecting the historical formation of a culture, it represents the fundament of the entire Chinese civilization.

2 The *New Century* Period

In the early twentieth century, the major publication that advocated Esperanto was the *New Century* 新世紀, which was launched by a group of Chinese students based in Paris. In its opening issue, its editor clearly stated that the goal of the magazine was to promulgate anarchism through the Esperanto movement. In other words, Esperanto was then considered a vehicle for promoting anarchism.

On July 27, 1907, the magazine published an article that further indicated that the purpose of promoting the Esperanto was to strive for world peace.[9] Advocating Esperanto at this early stage therefore was more a matter of indoctrinating readers with an ideology than learning a new language. The symbolic significance of the Esperanto movement was thus much greater than its actual impact.[10]

In order to promote Esperanto, Chinese intellectuals exaggerated the backwardness of Chinese characters and highlighted the so-called "scientific nature" of the new artificial language, characterized by its grammatical simplicity. The logic behind this is that an alphabetic language is superior to a graphic one, and that a man-made language is more scientific than a natural one. Wu Zhihui 吳稚暉 (1864–1953) once claimed that "China only has barbaric symbols. It does not have a [more developed] writing system. [We should accept] Esperanto as a Chinese writing system, and those who are concerned about this matter should learn Esperanto themselves and teach others Esperanto" (中國略有野蠻之符號, 中國尚未有文字. 萬國新語, 便是中國文字. 中國熱心人, 願求其同類作識字人者, 自己學萬國新語, 教人學萬國新語).[11]

In the 102nd issue of the *New Century*, Wu Zhihui concluded, "Sooner or later, Chinese script will be abandoned … the best solution is to learn Esperanto,

---

9   Xing 醒, "Wanguo xinyu" 萬國新語, *New Century* (*Xin Shiji*), no. 6 (1907/7/27): 3.
10 Ulrich Lins, "Esperanto as Language and Idea in China and Japan," *Language Problems and Language Planning* 32, no. 1 (2008): 47–48.
11 Wu Zhihui, *Wu Zhihui xiansheng quanji* 吳稚暉先生全集 (Complete works of Wu Zhihui) (Taipei: Zhongyangwenwu gongyingshe, 1969), 2: 2–3.

and the next best thing is to learn the European languages. The worst solution is to add phonetic symbols to Chinese characters" (漢字者為早晚必行廢斥之一物 ... 上策必徑棄中國之語言文字, 改習萬國新語, 其次則改用現在歐洲科學精進國之文字, 其次則在中國文字上附加讀音).[12] Using the Chinese script became the worst solution for China.

At the time, those who promoted Esperanto believed that ideographs and pictographs were primitive and barbaric, while an alphabetic and phonetic system was progressive. These Chinese Esperantists were influenced by Social Darwinism and believed that the Chinese writing system would soon be replaced by a phonetic system. The impact of Social Darwinism was clearly reflected in the argument of language reformers during the early twentieth century: Chinese scholars such as Wu Zhihui and Li Shizeng 李石曾 (1881–1973) had all mistaken this scientific hypothesis as evidence for the evolution of the Chinese language, without considering the fact that biological evolution is not the same as the development of a language.

In 1907, Li Shizeng published an article in the *New Century* titled "Jinhua yu geming" 進化與革命 (Evolution and revolution), in which he argued that in terms of political systems, a "dynasty" will evolve into a "republic" which will eventually become "anarchism." By the same token, he believed that in terms of language development, "pictographs" will evolve into "ideographs" and "ideographs" will eventually become "phonetic." The criterion he used to determine which language was superior was its degree of convenience:

> What matters to a writing system is only its convenience in communication. Therefore, the degree of convenience determines the degree of superiority. There are no guidelines for learning pictographic and ideographic languages. We must learn such languages word by word. Compared to a phonetic system, one can say with conviction that pictographs and ideographs are inferior to the phonetic languages.
>
> 文字所尚者, 惟在便利而已. 故當以其便利與否, 定其程度之高下, 象形與表意之字, 須逐字記之, 無綱領可憑, 故較之合聲之字, 盡括於數十字母之中者為不便, 由此可斷曰: 象形表意之字, 不若合聲之字為良.[13]

12　Wu Zhihui, "Xushu shenzhou ribao dongxue xijian pianhou" 續書神州日報東學西漸篇後 (Afterword to the *Shenzhou Daily* article "On the rise of Eastern learning in the West"), *New Century* (1909), 102: 10.

13　"Zhen" 真 (Li Shizeng), "Jinhua yu geming" 進化與革命, *New Century* (1907) 20: 1.

This kind of conclusion is not only oversimplistic, but also misleading, as it implies that one does not need to learn a phonetic language word by word. The level of difficulty for a Chinese speaker to learn English is no less than that of an English speaker to learn Chinese.

The greatest irony for Chinese language reformers such as Li Shizeng and Wu Zhihui is that, on the one hand they believed in "survival of the fittest," but on the other, they seemed to forget that Chinese characters had "survived" for over three thousand years. By this logic, the simple fact that the system has "lived" for more than three millenniums is strong evidence that it is sound and healthy.

The other blind spot for language reformers of the time was that they could not distinguish between the phonetic and the alphabetic. A phonetic system is written in an alphabet, but an alphabetic system is not necessarily phonetic. English is alphabetic but not phonetic. For example, "to," "too," and "two" all sound identical, but they are spelled differently. Chinese language reformers preferred to replace the Chinese script with a phonetic system, but a phonetic system could never solve the problem of homophones in Chinese.

On October 17, 1908, an overseas Chinese student in Scotland who assumed the pseudonym "Scotland Gentleman" (蘇格蘭君), wrote an article entitled "On the Abandonment of Chinese Characters," in which he argued that in order to save China, the first task was to abandon Chinese characters. The writer believed that if the Chinese script could be abolished in twenty years, China will become a progressive country in the world.[14]

Zhang Taiyan was skeptical of the Esperanto movement. In 1908, he published a long article, "Bo zhongguo yong wanguo xinyu shuo" 駁中國用萬國新語說 (Refuting the adoption of Esperanto in China), in which he argued that Esperanto was by no means a worthy replacement since Chinese pronunciation and the graphic nature of Chinese characters have their values. Zhang's article was well researched and was based on a huge amount of evidence. He criticized those who promoted Esperanto as people who were troubled by their deep-rooted inferiority complex and were willing to be colonized by Western cultures.[15]

Tian Beihu 田北湖 also criticized Esperanto. But his approach was different from Zhang Taiyan's since he deployed a nationalistic perspective. Tian argued

---

14   Sugelan jun, "On abolishing Chinese characters" 廢除漢文議, *New Century* (1908) 69: 11.
15   Zhang Taiyan, "Bo zhonguo yong wanguo xinyu shuo," *Guocui xuebao* 國粹學報, 41: 6–7. For more information on Zhang's views on Chinese language, also see Peng Chunling's 彭春凌 "Yi 'yifan fangyan' dikang 'hanzi tongyi' yu 'wanguo xinyu'" 以 "一返方言" 抵抗 "漢字統一" 與 "萬國新語" (Using dialects as a means of resisting the unification of Chinese script and Esperanto), *Jindaishi yanjiu* 近代史研究 (2008) 2: 65–82.

that a nation's foundation is based on three elements: territory, people, and language. A nation without a language, regardless of its land and people, is by definition not a real nation.[16]

3   The *New Youth* Period

After the discussions on "Wanguo xinyu" (universal new language) in the *New Century* and *Guocui Xuebao* during the early twentieth century, the editors of the *New Youth* also had their discussions on Esperanto. The staunch supporters of the Esperanto movement in the May Fourth period were Chen Duxiu and Qian Xuantong. Although Qian was a student of Zhang Taiyan, who was rather skeptical of this artificial language, Qian was a strong supporter of Esperanto. Like Wu Zhihui, he argued that the Chinese characters should eventually be abolished and replaced by the Esperanto.

The difference between Qian Xuantong and Wu Zhihui is that while the latter only perceived the Chinese characters as a tool, the former claimed that Chinese characters were the mediator of Confucianism. In his correspondence with Chen Duxiu, Qian argued, "If we want to abandon Confucianism, we must first abolish the Chinese characters. If we want to uproot the naive and stubborn thought of the commoners, we must abolish the Chinese script" (欲廢孔學, 不可不先廢漢文, 欲驅除一般人之幼稚的頑固的思想, 尤不可不先廢漢文).[17] As far as Qian was concerned, the Chinese script was the cause of all evils in the Chinese tradition, and therefore it should be replaced. Qian further maintained, "All books written in Chinese characters over the past two thousand years were full of nonsense. This can be detected by reading half of a page in such books" (二千年來, 用漢字寫的書籍, 無論那一部, 打開一看, 不到半頁, 必有發昏做夢的話).[18] It is clear that Qian blamed the "nonsense" upon the Chinese characters without realizing that the Chinese characters also produced profound philosophy and literature.

From Qian's perspective, Chinese characters are worthless and detrimental to China's modernization. "In order to save China," he argued, "we must eliminate Confucianism and Daoism. And in order to do so, it is imperative to eliminate the Chinese characters" (欲使中國不亡, 欲使中國民族為二

---

16   Tian Beihu, "Guoding wenzi siyi" 國定文字私議 (A personal proposal on national language), *Guocui xuebao* 47: 1–2.

17   Qian Xuantong, "Zhongguo jinhou zhi wenzi wenti" 中國今後之文字問題 (China's script problem from now on), *New Youth* (1918) 4, 4: 350.

18   Ibid., 354.

十世紀文明之民族，必以廢孔學，滅道教為根本之解決；而廢記載孔門學說及道教妖言之漢文，尤為根本解決之根本解決).[19] This belief was also shared by Lu Xun when he made his famous statement in 1936: "If we do not abolish the Chinese characters, China will definitely perish" (漢字不滅，中國必亡).[20] While Chen Duxiu agreed with Qian's stance on the abolishment of Chinese characters, he suggested that the reform should start with abolishing the Chinese characters but preserve the Chinese pronunciation by adopting a phonetic system. English words can be used if necessary.[21] Qian, nevertheless, preferred to replace the Chinese language (both script and sound) altogether with Esperanto, since English is only a natural language that is not artificially enhanced. The irregular pronunciation and grammar of English made it unfit to be a true universal language.

Tao Lugong 陶履恭 (1887–1960) was one of the few at the time who opposed the adoption of Esperanto as a replacement for the Chinese language. He argued that it is impossible to create a universal language simply by adopting the words and grammar of the European languages. Furthermore, he indicated that Esperanto and anarchism were two different things.

4   The Revolution of Chinese Character

In 1923, Qian Xuantong published an article titled "Hanzi geming" 漢字革命 (The revolution of Chinese character), in which he blamed Chinese characters for producing all China's backwardness, savagery, and isolation. Chinese characters thus became "a villain through the ages" (千古罪人). Looking back at Qian's accusations almost a century later, we have to admit that the Chinese script was not guilty of all the charges made against it. While China began to play a bigger role in the international society, the Chinese script has not changed much. It did not change from a graphic-based system to a phonetic one.

Li Jinxi 黎錦熙 summarized the problem of Chinese script in 1936: "In regard to the movement of 'mass language,' Chinese script is clearly not a good tool. It is a bad tool. Over the past forty years, studies of various kinds and our

---

19 Ibid., 354.
20 Lu Xun, "Bingzhong dajiuwang qingbao fangyuan" 病中答救亡情報訪員 (Reply to an interview from my sickbed) (1938), in Ni Haishu's *Zhongguo yuwen de xinsheng* 中國語文的新生 (The birth of Chinese language) (Shanghai, Shidai chubanshe, 1949), 119. This article was not included in *Lu Xun quanji*.
21 Qian Xuantong, "Zhongguo jinhou zhi wenzi wenti" 中國今後之文字問題 (On the problem of language in China in the future), *New Youth* (1918) 4, 4: 356.

experience had led us to this conclusion, which is beyond any doubt" (就大眾語文這一點上說, 漢字當然不是好工具, 是壞工具, 四十年來, 經過種種的比較研究, 大家目擊身驗, 鐵案如山, 不必再論).²² The biggest mistake made by the language reformers in that period, Li maintains, is that many people tended to believe that "Chinese script and the masses are absolutely incompatible" (漢字和大眾, 是勢不兩立的).²³ Everyone who sought to eliminate the Chinese characters tended to think that the Chinese script was too difficult to learn for ordinary people. Lu Xun, for example, argued that, "In order to preserve the Chinese script, eighty percent of the Chinese people must suffer the martyrdom of illiteracy" (為了保存漢字, 要十分之八的中國人做文盲來殉難).²⁴

In "Zhongguo yuwen de xinsheng" 中國語文的新生 (the rebirth of Chinese language and writing), Lu Xun repeated his point in a slightly different way, "If we don't want to sacrifice everyone for an old writing system, we must sacrifice the system itself" (如果不想大家來給舊文字做犧牲, 就得犧牲掉舊文字).²⁵ In "Guanyu xin wenzi" 關於新文字 (About a new writing system), Lu Xun used "tumor" (結核), which equates to cancer nowadays, as a metaphor for Chinese characters: "Chinese script is a tumor on the body of the hard-working masses, under which bacteria hide. If we do not get rid of it, we will die eventually" (漢字也是中國勞苦大眾身上的一個結核, 病菌都潛伏在裡面, 倘不首先除去它, 結果只有自己死).²⁶ In 1934, Lu Xun published "Hanzi he ladinghua" 漢字和拉丁化 (Chinese script and Latinization). At the end of the article, he asked: "Should we sacrifice ourselves for the Chinese script, or sacrifice it for our sake? Anyone who has not gone mad can immediately answer this question" (為漢字而犧牲我們, 還是為我們而犧牲漢字呢? 這是只要還沒有喪心病狂的人, 都能夠馬上回答的).²⁷ Although Lu Xun never directly answered the above question, his implication is clear: only madmen would advocate the use of Chinese characters.

But to date, Chinese script has not "sacrificed" any Chinese person, nor have the Chinese people "sacrificed" the Chinese characters. The two coexist peacefully. A hundred years later, we must admit that despite the various plans for a Chinese language reform that had been proposed, Chinese characters remained the only communication tool accepted by "the masses." In fact,

---

22 Lu Jinxi, "Jianshe de dazhongyu wenxue" 建設的大眾語文學 (On a constructive popular language literature) (Shanghai: Commercial Press, 1936), 28–29.
23 Ibid.
24 Lu Xun, "Menwai wentan" 門外文談 (An outsider's chats about written language), *Lu Xun quanji* (hereafter: LXQJ), 6: 98.
25 Lu Xun, "Zhongguo yuwen de xinsheng," LXQJ, 6: 115.
26 Lu Xun, "Guanyu xin wenzi," LXQJ, 6: 160.
27 Lu Xun, "Hanzi he ladinghua," LXQJ, 5: 557.

the Esperanto, Romanization, Latinization, and other language tools are absolutely not compatible with "the masses." This historical fact demonstrates that Chinese characters can be preserved without eighty percent of Chinese people being condemned to illiteracy.

Early twentieth-century Chinese intellectuals wanted to create a new, Latinized writing system because they wanted to make the system "popularized," "scientific," and "international." But the reality is, as soon as the Chinese characters were abolished, any new writing system would be out of reach for the "working masses." Wang Li 王力 (1900–1986) put it well in his 1936 "Hanzi gaige de lilun yu shiji" 漢字改革理論與實際 (Chinese script reform: Theory and reality):

> In the current situation in China, people urgently need to learn Chinese characters. If you teach them a new word, but they do not know how to read Chinese, they will still be illiterate as before.
>
> 在現在中國的環境裡, 民眾所急急要認識的是漢字. 如果你教他們認識一個新文字而不認識漢字, 他們在現在社會裡依舊是些文盲.[28]

Qu Qiubai 瞿秋白 (1899–1935) compared the Chinese characters to a "corpse" (殭屍), and denounced this archaic writing system in sensational language: "Chinese script is truly the most foul, abominable, disgusting, dark-age latrine in the world!" (漢字真正是世界上最齷齪最惡劣最混蛋的中世紀毛坑).[29] After 1949, there was a long period in which the phoneticization of Chinese was seen as the proper path for China to take. As a result, all writings defaming Chinese characters and those promoting the Latinization received official approval. Qu's criticism of the Chinese characters obviously had fallen outside the boundary of academic discussion, but Qu received no criticism for what he had written. On the contrary, Mao Zedong eulogized him as a pioneer for the Communist revolution, and believed that his ideas would greatly benefit the development of Chinese culture in the future.[30] In fact, by that time, language reform movements had become entwined with political trends.

---

28 Wang Li, "Hanzi gaige de lilun yu shiji" 漢字改革的理論與實際 (Chinese script reform: Theory and reality), *Duli pinglun* 獨立評論 (Independent review), (1936/6/14), 205: 7.

29 Qu Qiubai, "Putong zhongguohua de ziyan de yanjiu" 普通中國話的字眼的研究 (A study on the wording in common Chinese), *Qu qiubai wenji* (Collected works of Qu Qiubai) (Beijing: Renming, 1989), 3: 241–247.

30 Mao Zedong's words are printed right after the cover page in the first volume of *Qu Qiubai wenji*.

5   The Esperanto Movement in China after 1949

In August 1979, Hu Yuzhi 胡愈之 gave a talk at the Second National Esperanto Conference. One can observe from his lecture that the Esperanto movement in China after 1949 seemed promising, at least on the surface, but it was actually supported by the government instead of the masses. Hu wrote:

> In the past fifty to sixty years, the Esperanto movement in China did not have much progress. The Chinese Communist Party strongly advocated Esperanto. Without the Party's leadership, Esperanto could not have developed in China. After the establishment of the People's Republic of China, our party, including Chairman Mao, Premier Zhou Enlai, and Vice Premier Chen Yi, all supported Esperanto. There are many Esperanto speakers around the world, but China is the only country in which both the Party and the government had supported Esperanto to such an extent.
>
> 中國的世界語運動搞了五六十年，沒有很大發展，中間走了一些曲折的道路. 中國共產黨對世界語非常重視，沒有黨的領導，世界語在中國不可能發展. 新中國建立後，黨和政府重視世界語，毛主席，周恩來總理和陳毅副總理都支持世界語. 現在世界上許多國家都有世界語者，但黨和政府這樣重視世界語的，恐怕只有中國.[31]

However, Hu Yuzhi may have forgotten that in an article that he published in 1922, he mentioned that "the promulgation of Esperanto, according to its inventor, Zamenhof, shall not rely on power of the government. Thus, the Esperanto movement should be a movement that is entirely initiated by the people around the world" (世界語的傳播，照原始家柴門霍夫的初志，是主張絕不依賴各國政府的勢力的. 所以國際語運動，可以說，完全是國際民眾的運動).[32]

The Alliance of the Proletarian Esperanto-Speakers (普羅世界語者聯) was established in Manchuria on September 18, 1931, as a response to the Japanese colonization of Manchuria. The alliance became a branch of the Cultural Association of the Left-Wing (左翼文化總同盟). This is exactly the aim that Hou Zhiping pointed to in his book, *Shijie yu yuundong zai zhongguo* 世界語運

---

[31]   Hu Yuzhi, "Zai dierci quanguo shijieyu gongzuo zuotanhui shang de jianghua" 在第二次全國世界語工作座談會上的講話 (Talk at the Second Workshop on World Language), *Hu Yuzhi wenji* (Collected works of Hu Yuzhi) (Beijing: Sanlian, 1996), 104.

[32]   Hu Yuzhi, "Guojiyu de lixiang yu xianshi" 國際語的理想與現實 (The ideal and reality of the Esperanto) in *Hu Yuzhi wenji*, 1: 276.

動在中國 (The Esperanto movement in China): "To unite the Esperanto movement with Chinese revolution and its struggles" (把世界語運動同中國革命和全世界人民爭取自由解放的鬥爭緊密地結合起來).[33]

In 1933, the Alliance of Proletariat Esperanto Speakers launched a magazine titled *The World* 世界 in which Esperanto was defined on political terms: "Use Esperanto for the liberation of China" (為中國的解放而用世界語). At this point, the development of Esperanto in China had completely lost its independence and become an instrument of propaganda for the Chinese Communist Party. As a result, there was no criticism of the Esperanto Movement in China after 1949. This kind of politicization around Esperanto had betrayed Zamenhof's original idea of creating a neutral, universal language.

Unfortunately, this concept was ignored by Esperanto supporters in China, where, Chen Yuan argued in a 1988 article, "If people study the language reforms (including the Esperanto movement) in China without understanding their close relationship with national liberation, then they will miss the crucial point" (當人們企圖考察近代中國的語文運動, 包括世界語運動, 而完全漠視它跟民族解放運動緊密結合的特點, 那絕對說不到點子上).[34]

Here, the so-called "crucial point" is nothing more than the idea that the Esperanto movement should serve the cause of "the liberation of China," while in fact, the Communist Party's support of Esperanto had transformed this artificial language into a propaganda instrument.

In 1999 Chen Yuan wrote a preface to a book that commemorates the one hundred years of the Esperanto movement in China, in which he said: "Fifty years after the liberation of China, the Esperanto movement had undertaken a healthy development under the leadership of the Party and the government" (全國解放後的 50 年間, 世界語運動在黨和政府的領導和關注下, 走上健康發展的道路). And the reason that he studied Esperanto was because Esperanto had led him to embark upon the journey of revolution (曾經指引我走上革命的道路).[35] In other words, the development of Esperanto was entirely dependent on the Communist Party's support after 1949.

Esperantists in the 1930s often emphasized Esperanto's proletarian nature. Hu Yuzhi and Ye Laishi 葉籟士 (1911–1994) established the Association of Proletarian Esperanto Speakers and launched a journal under the same

---

33 Hou Zhiping, *Shijie yu yuundong zai zhongguo* (Esperanto movement in China) (Beijing: Shijieyu chubanshe, 1985), 5.
34 Zhangyi 章怡 (Chen yuan; 陳原), "Yuyan de kinrao yu lixiang de zhuiqiu" 語言的困擾與理想的追求 (The puzzlement of language and the pursuit of idealism), *Dushu* (August 1998), 116.
35 Hou, *Shijieyu zai zhongguo yibainian* 世界語在中國一百年 (One hundred years of the Esperanto movement in China) (Beijing: Zhongguo shijieyu chubanshe, 1999), 5.

name. This name, as I pointed out earlier, had led the Chinese to believe that Esperanto was very popular not only in China but also around the world.

But, in fact, Esperanto did not have anything to do with the so-called proletarian class in China. From the overseas Chinese students in France (Wu Zhihui) to the May Fourth intellectuals in Beijing (Chen Duxiu, Qian Xuantong, and Lu Xun), the Chinese supporters of Esperanto were either professors or overseas students. None of them could ever be regarded as proletarian.

The "proletarians" in China in the 1930s and 1940s were mostly illiterate. They could barely read Chinese characters or speak mandarin, let alone use an artificial language. Esperanto, to them, was simply an unrealistic fantasy. To associate "Esperanto" with "proletarian" was the best evidence that the Esperanto movement was politically contaminated after 1949.

6 Ba Jin's Unfulfilled Wishes

In 2005, Ba Jin 巴金 (1904–2005), one of the most influential Chinese writers of the twentieth century, died at the age of 101. Numerous articles were published in his memory regarding his unfulfilled wishes. There was one wish, however, that very few mentioned: his hope and dream that Esperanto could one day become a universal language. In May 1921, Ba Jin published an article entitled "Shijieyu zhi tedian" 世界語之特點 (The characteristics of Esperanto), in which he illustrates his optimistic view of the future development of this language:

> World War I had now ended and world peace had begun. I believe that the great unity is not far away from us. Those of us who believe in world peace should strive to study and promote Esperanto so that everyone can speak this language. If we can implant the idea of anarchism in their heads, the great unity will immediately become a reality.
>
> 今歐戰告終, 和平開始. 離世界大同時期將不遠矣. 我們主張世界大同的人應當努力學 "世界語," 努力傳播 "世界語," 使人人能懂 "世界語": 再把 "安那其主義" 的思想輸入他們的腦筋, 那時大同世界就會立刻現予我們的面前.[36]

---

36 Xu Shanshu, *Bajin yu shijieyu* 巴金與世界語 (Ba Jin and Esperanto) (Beijing: Zhongguo shijieyu chubanshe, 1995), 3.

Ba Jin wrote the above passage at the age of seventeen. His naive optimism is thus understandable. But what surprises us is that throughout his life, which was full of turmoil and chaos, he maintained an unwavering confidence in Esperanto and still believed that it would one day become a universal language. In 1980, at the age of 76, Ba Jin attended the 65th International Esperanto Convention in Stockholm, Sweden. When he returned to China, he published a short article that expressed his belief that Esperanto would become a universal language of mankind.[37]

But his wish that Esperanto would one day become a universal language, I am afraid, will never come true. In the early twentieth century, after the popularization of anarchism, Esperanto had become a utopian language. Throughout his life, Ba Jin had been a firm supporter of anarchism and Esperanto, and his death symbolized the end of an era of utopian thought.

Ba Jin's confidence in the Esperanto movement was similar to a religious belief. Those who endorsed Ba Jin's devotion to Esperanto must have realized that, when it came to using Esperanto as a universal language, his belief was characterized by an often shocking ignorance. Ba Jin's attitude towards Esperanto reflected his lack of knowledge in linguistics and his ignorance of the development of world languages.

The belief in the mission of Esperanto, like all other kinds of utopian discourses, is idealistic. Such discourses are particularly appealing to those who are dissatisfied with the status quo and who hope for a revolutionary change. For example, Kang Youwei's 康有為 utopian writing, *Datongshu* 大同書, aims for an idealism far beyond any possible reality. One can argue that over the last century, Chinese people suffered from such utopian thoughts. When faced with any kind of empty idealism, perhaps we need to be more careful and skeptical.

Some supporters of the Esperanto movement admired Ba Jin's persistence in promoting an artificial language, but they never mentioned that the Esperanto could never function as a universal language. It is only a movement supported by a small group of cultural elites. On November 11, 1982, Ba Jin delivered the opening remarks at the inaugural ceremony of the Esperanto society in Shanghai:

---

37 Ba Jin, "Shijieyu" 世界語 (Universal language), *Tansuoji* 探索集 (Collected works of exploration) (Beijing: Renmin, 1989), 84.

A true Esperantist must not have any false pretense and selfishness. No matter how proficient one becomes in the Esperanto, studying this language for selfish gains will never make one worthy of the glorious title of an Esperantist.

一個真正的世界語者的確是來不得半點口是心非和利己主義的。 為圖私利而學世界語， 無論學得多麼好， 都是同世界語者這光輝稱號不相稱的.[38]

Ba Jin portrayed Esperanto as a moral medium. He even saw it as a symbol of morality itself. It seemed that only an altruistic revolutionary may qualify for the title of Esperantist, while any who study this language for personal gain are selfish. This is precisely why the Esperanto movement in China was unsuccessful and this artificial language is only promoted by a small group of idealistic intellectuals.[39]

Language has nothing to do with "the sublime," "the pure," or "greatness." It is developed through a long period of time and only exists when it is accepted by its common users. In today's world, if there is anything that can be considered a world language, it is English. The monopoly of English can be observed in every corner of the world. This is a reality that cannot be altered by any individual will, desire, or nationalism. Ba Jin promoted Esperanto throughout his life. His intention was pure and great, but it cannot make the Esperanto a true world language.

---

38 Xu, *Bajin yu shijieyu*, 335.
39 See Zhou, *Yuyanxue lunwen ji*, 160. Zhou Youguang 周有光 is one of the few who were honest enough to point out that Esperanto can never be put to real use:
    What language are we going to use in this global village? Can we use Esperanto? No. Esperanto, a so-called universal language, is actually a man-made, artificial language that has simple grammar and is easy to learn; however, it cannot be applied widely in the real world, and it has few linguistic resources at its users' disposal. It only amounts to a small language and cannot function in the fields of modern politics, commerce, and technology. Thus, it cannot be recognized as one of the six languages used by the United Nations.
    用什麼語言作為地球村的共同語呢? "世界語" 行嗎? 不行. 所謂 "世界語" 就是 "愛斯不難讀" (Esperanto). 這種人造語的規則簡單, 學習容易, 但是應用範圍不廣, 圖書資料稀少, 只相當於一個小語種, 不能適應現代政治, 貿易和科技等領域的複雜需要, 所以聯合國 6 種工作語言中沒有它的地位.

Bibliography

Ba, Jin 巴金. *Tansuoji* 探索集. Beijing: Renmin, 1989.

Hou, Zhiping 候志平. *Shijie yu yuundong zai zhongguo* 世界語運動在中國. Beijing: Shijieyu chubanshe, 1985.

Hou, Zhiping 候志平. *Shijieyu zai zhongguo yibainian* 世界語在中國一百年. Beijing: Zhongguo shijieyu chubanshe, 1999.

Hu Yuzhi 胡愈之. *Hu Yuzhi wenji* 胡愈之文集. Beijing: Sanlian shudian, 1996.

Lins, Ulrich. "Esperanto as Language and Idea in China and Japan," *Language Problems and Language Planning* 32:1 (2008).

Lu, Xun 魯迅. *Lu Xun quanji* 魯迅全集. Beijing: Renmin wenxue chubanshe, 1981.

Ni, Haishu 倪海曙. *Qingmo hanyu pinyin yundong biannianshi* 清末漢語拼音運動編年史. Shanghai: Shanghai renmin chubanshe, 1959.

Ni, Haishu 倪海曙. *Zhongguo yuwen de xinsheng* 中國語文的新生. Shanghai: Shidai chubanshe, 1949.

Peng Chunling 彭春凌. "Yi 'yifan fangyan' dikang 'hanzi tongyi' yu 'wanguo xinyu'" 以 "一返方言" 抵抗 "漢字統一" 與 "萬國新語," *Jindaishi yanjiu* 近代史研究 2: 65–82 (2008).

Qu Qiubai 瞿秋白. *Qu qiubai wenji* 瞿秋白文集. Beijing: Renming wenxue chubanshe, 1989.

Wang, Li 王力. "Hanzi gaige de lilun yu shiji" 漢字改革的理論與實際, *Duli pinglun* 獨立評論 205: 7 (1936/6/14).

Wu Zhihui 吳稚暉. *Wu Zhihui xiansheng quanji* 吳稚暉先生全集. Taipei: Zhongyangwenwu gongyingshe, 1969.

Xu Shanshu 許善述. *Bajin yu shijieyu* 巴金與世界語. Beijing: Zhongguo shijieyu chubanshe, 1995.

Zhou Youguan 周有光. *Yuyanxue lunwen ji* 語言學論文. Beijing: The Commercial Press, 2004.

CHAPTER 12

The Immortality of Words: Hu Shi's Language Reform and His Reflection on Religion

Gina Elia & Victor H. Mair

In early twentieth-century China, a young scholar—who had not yet even received his bachelor's degree—quietly started a revolution.[1] Hu Shi was still an undergraduate at Cornell University when he published two essays on language reform in *Xin Qing Nian* (New Youth 新青年), which Hu Shi scholar Jerome B. Grieder describes as "China's leading journal of radical opinion".[2] These articles included "Wenxue gailiang chuyi (Tentative proposals for the improvement of literature 文學改良芻議)" in February 1917, as well as "Li shi de wen xue guan nian lun (On the genetic concept of literature 歷史的文學觀念論)," which was published the following May.[3] These essays paved the way for a plethora of writings on language and broader social reform produced by Chinese intellectuals in the 1920s and 1930s. These writings are considered to constitute the period of Chinese history known variously as the "New Culture Movement," the "May Fourth Era," or more broadly as the "Republican Era," the last of which refers to the brief period of China's history from 1912 to 1949 when it was ruled, at least nominally, as a federal republic. In addition to this earliest accomplishment, for which Hu Shi is probably best known, he was also a scholar of Chinese philosophy and literature, and he served as a diplomat from China to the United States in later periods of his life. Additionally, he served

---

1 "Religion" is placed in quotation marks throughout this article when referring to Hu Shi's worldview. Although "religion" is treated as a constructivist category in contemporary Religious Studies scholarship, with no meaning outside of specific historical, social, and political contexts, we feel that calling Hu Shi's worldview a religion without quotation marks may cause readers to think he identified his ideas with a formal religious tradition—which he did not. "Religion" will be left in quotation marks therefore in order to emphasize the constructivist nature of the term and the idiosyncratic nature of Hu Shi's worldview.
2 Jerome B. Grieder. *Hu Shih and the Chinese Renaissance: Liberalism in the Chinese Revolution, 1917–1937* (Cambridge: Harvard University Press, 1970), 75. Additionally, please note that pinyin in this essay follows the formal rules of pinyin spelling set out by the United States Library of Congress. See "Library of Congress Pinyin Conversion Project: New Chinese Romanization Guidelines," www.loc.gov/catdir/pinyin/romcover.html.
3 Grieder, *Huh Shih and the Chinese Renaissance*, 75–76.

as Chancellor of Peking University (1946–1948) and President of the Academia Sinica (1958–1962).[4]

Hu Shi is most famous for his language reform efforts, but in addition he left behind many writings espousing nuanced perspectives on Chinese and Western society, Chinese modernization and politics, and the responsibilities of the individual to his society. One of his ideas that merits further study in the world of English-language scholarship is Hu Shi's self-styled "religion" (宗教 *zong jiao*). Hu Shi used this term to refer to his belief in the inseparability of the individual and history, and the responsibility of the former to the latter. Hu Shi also called his "religion" a belief in social "immortality" (不朽 *bu xiu*). By this he meant that individuals were immortalized through the deeds they committed and measured by the impact of those deeds on society.

Grieder, the first scholar to write an English-language monograph on Hu Shi, devotes half a chapter of his work to a discussion of Hu Shi's theory of social immortality. While he explains this in great detail, he dismisses Hu Shi's use of the term "religion" as inconsequential, portraying it almost as though he assumes it was picked haphazardly to describe a worldview that is not at all relevant to real "religion." This is clear from what little Grieder writes of this word choice: "The issue here, quite clearly, is not 'religion' as Hu Shih invariably … used the term, to denote an irrelevant and superstition-ridden system of institutions and ideas. The issue, rather, is man's attitude toward himself and his world."[5] Grieder here treats the term "religion" as ahistorical, suggesting that it cannot refer to ideas of "man's attitude toward himself and his world," which is what he claims Hu Shi meant, but rather must always refer to "irrelevant and superstition-ridden systems of institutions and ideas." In other words, Grieder assumes that Hu Shi has misused the term "religion" to denote something it does not actually refer to. It does not occur to him that perhaps the term "religion" *can* be used to refer to attitudes about individuals and the world they live in.

The problem with Grieder's argument is that it assumes there is such a real thing as "religion," that "religion" is a substantive object that exists *sui generis* in the world, the way a plant or a rock does. This is clear from Grieder's assertion

---

4 Victor Mair, "Hu Shih and Chinese Language Reform," Language Log, 4 February 2017, http://languagelog.ldc.upenn.edu/nll/?p=30801.
5 Grieder, *Hu Shih and the Chinese Renaissance*, 116. Note that the spelling "Hu Shih" is an older romanization of Hu Shi's name using the Wade-Giles romanization system. This article gives his name as "Hu Shih" whenever it is quoting from a text that uses the Wade-Giles system.

that Hu Shi's philosophy is not really *about* "religion," but rather is about "something else"—in this case, "man's attitude toward himself and his world."

But since Grieder wrote his book on Hu Shi, the way in which contemporary scholars of Religious Studies talk about "religion" has undergone a sweeping transformation. Today, "religion" is no longer thought of as something that exists in the world, the nature and definition of which it is the job of Religious Studies scholars to pin down. Such a view is considered an "essentialist" mode of understanding religion. Rather, religion now is understood as a constructivist category. Groups categorize certain cultural phenomena as "religious" because there is a specific advantage for them in doing so. In other words, "religion" is a conceptual strategy. People have specific agendas in wanting to designate certain cultural phenomena as "religious," or in other words as not "political," "economic," or "social." One of the main contemporary approaches to the study of religion, "constructivism," seeks to understand why particular groups label certain cultural phenomena as "religious"—in other words, what they gain from doing so. Another possible methodological approach is to consider "religion" from a functionalist perspective, focusing not on who calls what "religion" for what reasons, but rather on what the category of "religion" does to assist specific groups. In other words, functionalist approaches determine what social problems religion helps individuals or groups to solve. In light of this evolution in recent Religious Studies scholarship, this article argues that Hu Shi's use of the term "religion" to describe his worldview should be understood as a rhetorical strategy for enacting the beliefs he espoused on a formal level. By using the term "religion" to describe his worldview, Hu Shi presented it as an idea that was part of the objective reality or truth of the universe—that is, undeniably true. This enabled him to emphasize its importance as well as portray it as an idea that had been true and would continue to be true for all time. In other words, the use of the term "religion" for him is a method of immortalizing his theory of social immortality. This article primarily approaches Hu Shi's use of the term "religion" from a functionalist perspective because of its focus on explaining how Hu Shi used the term to emphasize the importance of his theory. However, the constructivist approach to the study of religion also constitutes a fundamental assumption on which the following arguments are built. Groups call certain cultural phenomena "religious" because they have something to gain from doing so. The following arguments take as their premise that Hu Shi consciously or unconsciously designated his worldview as a "religion" because he had a purpose that was aided by doing so.

At the outset, it should be noted that it is impossible to know Hu Shi's conscious *intentions* in identifying his personal philosophy as a "religion." This article by no means purports to be able to discern his intentions. Rather, it is an effort to examine the possibilities for a deeper understanding of his worldview that are enabled by his decision to designate them as a kind of "religion." The following arguments will demonstrate that the term "religion" served as a rhetorical strategy to highlight his conviction that his worldview was an objective, everlasting reality. In other words, the term "religion" effectively helped Hu Shi to put his worldview into practice, demonstrating on a formal level the immutable status of his idea of social immortality. However, this article cannot make any claims about whether this move was consciously *intended* by Hu Shi, as only he himself would be able to answer that question. It is a study on the rhetorical effects of his choice to use that term to describe his worldview, not an analysis of his intentions in making that choice.

We will first briefly summarize the nature and impact of Hu Shi's essays on language reform, the contribution for which he is best known. Afterwards, we will make use of Grieder's account of Hu Shi's self-styled "religion" as well as essays, letters, and newspaper articles from Cornell University's archives to explain the origins and nature of his belief in social immortality. Following that, we will discuss the theoretical underpinnings of viewing Hu Shi's use of the term "religion" as a rhetorical strategy that underscores the supposed objective truth of Hu Shi's worldview. Finally, the article will conclude with some thoughts about the significance of Hu Shi's choice to label his most central worldview a "religion."

1 Hu Shi's Legacy as a Language Reformer in China

When Hu Shi first left China to study in the United States, it was still customary for Chinese literature to be written in an older form of the language that differed significantly from the spoken language. The name of this literary language is variously translated into English as "Classical Chinese," "Literary Chinese," or "Literary Sinitic." Grieder explains that for centuries in China, Literary Sinitic had been a mark of class and education. Only young men born into some privilege, usually those who were eligible for the Civil Service Exam, possessed the means to study the language, and only they could read it. Educated men were also required to write in this stiff language themselves. These expectations meant that reading and writing were closely guarded as elite acts that only a select few privileged men were capable of performing. While highly-esteemed forms of literature like poetry and official documents were written in Literary Sinitic, however, novels were written in the vernacular language. The Four Classic Novels of China, for example, are written in the vernacular.[6] However, only literature written in Literary Sinitic by elite intellectuals was accepted as the proper medium for written language.[7] Hu Shi says that his own initial exposure to the written Chinese vernacular occurred while he was browsing through some old boxes in the attic of his childhood home, into which someone had carelessly thrown a dog-eared copy of *Water Margin*. Hu Shi was hooked from the moment he started to read it, and from then on he preferred to read literature written in the vernacular to that written in literary Sinitic, which he felt stifled the emotional impact of the literary work.[8]

Despite this early interest in novels written in vernacular Chinese, Hu Shi apparently left for the United States without having yet developed his commitment to Chinese language reform. About five years before Hu Shi was to publish his essay "Tentative Proposals for the Improvement of Literature," he published a biographical sketch of Ezra Cornell in Literary Sinitic, indicating that he was still following China's long-standing written tradition.[9] Hu Shi's decision to write and publish the article that would spur the entire New Culture Movement is generally memorialized as having come about because of an incident that occurred while he was a student at Cornell, although it is highly unlikely that this incident alone caused Hu Shi's worldview to be so radically transformed. An earlier essay of his, written before he left for the United States and entitled "The Problem of the Chinese Language," suggests that he already had long been thinking about the value of switching to a system in which the vernacular language was the mainstream language in which Chinese was written. This incident was likely a catalyst that urged him to finally gather his thoughts on the subject and write up a proposal for language reform.

As for the event itself: Hu Shi was out on Lake Cayuga, near Ithaca and Cornell University in upstate New York, canoeing with some Chinese friends. The canoe capsized at one point, and they all fell into the lake. Nobody was hurt, and they all swam back to shore safely. At this point the young men started a fire so that a young woman in the group could dry her clothing. One of Hu Shi's classmates found this incident charming and wrote a poem about

---

6 *San guo yan yi* (*Romance of the Three Kingdoms* 三國演義) (14th century), *Shui hu zhuan* (*Water Margin* 水滸傳) (late 14th century–1589), *Xi you ji* (*Journey to the West* 西遊記) (c. 1592), *Hong lou meng* (*Dream of the Red Chamber* 紅樓夢) (1791).
7 Grieder, *Hu Shih and the Chinese Renaissance*, 77.
8 Ernest O. Hauser, "Ambassador Hu Shih: China's Greatest Living Scholar Fights a Winning Battle of Wits Against Japan," *Life*, December 1941, 127, *Collected Reproductions of Hu Shih papers at Cornell University*, #41-5-2578, Division of Rare and Manuscript Collections, Cornell University Library.
9 Hu Shi (胡適), "Kang nan er jun zhuan" 康南耳君傳 (A biography of Mr. Cornell), *Chinese Students' Quarterly*, Spring 1915, *Collected reproductions of Hu Shih papers at Cornell University*, #41-5-2578, Division of Rare and Manuscript Collections, Cornell University Library.

it in Literary Sinitic. When he shared it with Hu Shi, to gather his feedback, the latter was struck immediately by how ridiculous it was, in his view, to use such a lofty, academic, weighty language to describe so whimsical an incident. It was immediately following this that he published the essay that was to initiate an entire movement, "A Preliminary Discussion of Literary Reform."[10]

In this essay, Hu Shi distills his philosophy on written Chinese into eight bullet points that together state what constitutes good, clear writing in the language. The eight points, along with some brief explanations by Grieder, are as follows:

1. *Write with substance.* By this, Hu meant that literature should contain real feeling and human thought. This was intended to be a contrast to the recent poetry with its rhymes and phrases that Hu saw as being empty.
2. *Do not imitate the ancients.* Literature should not be written in the styles of long ago, but rather in the modern style of the present era.
3. *Respect grammar.* Hu did not elaborate at length on this point, merely stating that some recent forms of poetry had neglected proper grammar.
4. *Reject melancholy.* Recent young authors often chose grave pen names, and wrote on such topics as death. Hu rejected this way of thinking as being unproductive in solving modern problems.
5. *Eliminate old clichés.* The Chinese language has always had numerous four-character sayings and phrases used to describe events. Hu implored writers to use their own words in descriptions, and deplored those who did not.
6. *Do not use allusions.* By this, Hu was referring to the practice of comparing present events with historical events even when there is no meaningful analogy.
7. *Do not use couplets or parallelism.* Though these forms had been pursued by earlier writers, Hu believed that modern writers first needed to learn the basics of substance and quality, before returning to these matters of subtlety and delicacy.
8. *Do not avoid popular expressions or popular forms of characters.*

---

10   Richard Johnston, "The Influence of the Canoe on the Chinese Literary Revolution," 1941, 3, Collected reproductions of Hu Shih papers at Cornell University, #41-5-2578, Division of Rare and Manuscript Collections, Cornell University Library.

A few years later, Hu Shi published a second article on the subject called "Constructive Literary Revolution—A Literature of National Speech," in which he further simplifies his precepts for good Chinese writing down to just four points, again quoted below with explanations from Grieder:

1. *Speak only when you have something to say.* This is analogous to the first point above.
2. *Speak what you want to say and say it in the way you want to say it.* This combines points two through six above.
3. *Speak what is your own and not that of someone else.* This is a rewording of point seven.
4. *Speak in the language of the time in which you live.* This refers again to the replacement of Classical Chinese with the vernacular language.[11]

One implication of Hu Shi's article is that, if his ideas were implemented, making the vernacular language China's main written as well as spoken language would allow the acts of reading and writing to be accessible to a much wider group of people within China. Thus, many of Hu Shi's peers adopted his article as a call for social as well as linguistic reform. Hu Shi's article paved the way for the following era of the 1920s and 1930s in China, during which time intellectuals produced a rich array of writings on Chinese modernity and modernization. This period is variously referred to as the "May Fourth Movement," the "New Culture Movement," or more broadly as the "May Fourth Era." Kirk Denton summarizes the period as a time in which Chinese intellectuals were forced to grapple with the "technological and military superiority of the West and Japan" in comparison to China.[12] Chloe Starr writes of the period, "… the old ways of society were decried as moribund and collective effort was focused on seeking a new national direction, identity, and system of governance."[13] Denton and Starr succinctly describe the main themes of the New Culture Era, principally the exploration of how to rejuvenate Chinese society. David Wang further highlights the circumstance that Republican Era intellectuals named the traits they considered vital to strengthening Chinese society "modern" to distinguish them from "traditional" Chinese culture. Absorbing a strong sense of anti-traditionalism from the West, they used the term "tradition" to denote

---

11 Grieder, *Hu Shih and the Chinese Renaissance*, 161–162.
12 Kirk Denton, "General Introduction," in *Modern Chinese Literary Thought: Writings on Literature, 1893–1945* (Stanford, CA: Stanford University Press, 1996), 1.
13 Chloe Starr, "Introduction," in *Reading Christian Scriptures in China*, ed. Chloë Starr (London: T&T Clark, 2008), 5.

all aspects of dynastic Chinese society that they viewed as stifling to China's progress.[14] It is no wonder that so many of these intellectuals, inspired by the radical break with tradition on the level of the written language that Hu Shi's article represented, used it as the foundation upon which to build their own diatribes against "traditional" China.

Hu Shi's influence on the development of the Chinese language in the twentieth century cannot be overstated. With these tenets of good writing, Hu Shi's articles elegantly challenged the centuries-old convention among Chinese literati of writing in Literary Sinitic. It turned out that his writing struck a chord with many other young Chinese intellectuals, who quickly adopted Hu Shi's article as part of their own philosophy and began to write in the vernacular language, which was referred to as "*baihua* [白話]" or "plain language." To this day, most Chinese articles and books are written in "*baihua*."

2 The Category of "Religion" in Republican Era Writings

In addition to being a great reformer of the Chinese language, Hu Shi was a well-known intellectual and scholar in both China and the West. This section will contextualize Hu Shi's use of the term "religion" to describe his worldview by first examining how the category was used by other intellectuals who produced most of their best-known works during the Republican Era.

"Religion" generally was one of the ideas relegated by Republican Era intellectuals to the category of "tradition." Zhou Zuoren 周作人 (1885–1967) and Chen Duxiu 陳獨秀 (1879–1942), prolific writers and intellectuals during the Republican Era, both dismissed "religion" as unscientific.[15] In calling the concept of "religion" unscientific, these figures of May Fourth Era literature were effectively calling it "traditional," or in other words, not conducive to the modernization of China or its citizens. Hu Shi was no exception to this trend. Though not especially reviling religion in his writings, he did not consider himself religious and did not express much interest in it throughout his long career.

---

14 David Der-Wei Wang, *Fin-de-siècle Splendor: Repressed Modernities of Late Qing Fiction, 1849–1911* (Stanford, CA: Stanford University Press, 1997), 8–9.

15 Chen Duxiu (陳獨秀), "Jidu jiao yu Zhongguo ren (基督教與中國人 Christianity and the Chinese people)," in *Chen Duxiu zhu zuo xuan pian: di er juan*, 1919–1922 陳獨秀著作選篇: 第二卷, 1919–1922 (Selected writings of Chen Duxiu), ed. Ren Jianshu (任建樹), vol. 2, 1919–1922 (Shanghai: Shanghai ren min chu ban she, 2009), 486; Irene Eber, "Introduction," in *Bible in Modern China: The Literary and Intellectual Impact*, ed. Irene Eber, Sze-kar Wan, and Knut Walf, in collaboration with Roman Malek (Sankt Augustin, Germany: Institut Monumenta Serica, 1999), 13–28.

C. T. Hsia cemented the characterization of Republican Era intellectuals as essentially anti-religious in his monograph *A History of Modern Chinese Fiction* (1961). In fact, he claimed that literature of the period lacked spiritual depth. He writes, "The superficiality of modern Chinese literature is ultimately seen in its intellectual unawareness of Original Sin or some comparable religious interpretation of evil." He comes to this conclusion based on his perception that Chinese people tend to be Confucian rationalists. He argues that, while historically such rationalism has been "kept in check" by such competing, less rationalistic ideologies as Buddhism and Daoism, Republican Era rejection of religion led this so-called Chinese tendency toward extreme rationalism to dominate literary writing and thought of the era.[16]

In the intervening years between the publication of his monograph and the twenty-first century, Marian Galik and Lewis Robinson tried to highlight the idea that, on the contrary, many Republican Era intellectuals did express an interest in Buddhism and Christianity in their work.[17] However, their method was unconvincing—they essentially categorized many instances in which Buddhist or Christian motifs, themes, or imagery were mentioned in Republican Era intellectuals' literature and essays. Because they were not attentive to how these motifs, themes, and imagery were used in each work they mentioned, they included in their studies the work of many authors who were not interested in "Buddhism" or "Christianity" as such, but rather simply utilized the motifs of those religions for specific agendas. For example, Mao Dun's short stories "The Death of Jesus (Yesu zhi si 耶穌之死)" (1945) and "Samson's Revenge (Cansun de fu chou 參孫的復仇)" (1942), written during the Nationalist Regime in China, can be read as critiques of the Nationalist government. Robinson himself points out that Mao Dun may have written them in the form of Christian allegories to hide his criticism from Nationalist censorship.[18] In this case, Mao Dun uses a Christian allegory to evade censorship, not because he has any specific interest in the religion of Christianity. Galik's and Robinson's monographs are comprised of examples like this. They do little more than provide a catalogue of instances of allusion to Christianity and Buddhism in Republican Era literature, without providing analyses of why they chose religious imagery specifically to incorporate into their writings.

---

16 C. T. Hsia, *A History of Modern Chinese Fiction* (New York: Columbia University Press, 1961), 503–504.
17 See Lewis Robinson's *Double-Edged Sword: Christianity and 20th Century Chinese Fiction* (1986) and Marian Galik's *Influence, Translation, and Parallels: Selected Studies on the Bible in China* (2004).
18 Lewis Stuart Robinson, *Double-Edged Sword: Christianity and 20th Century Chinese Fiction* (Hong Kong: Tao Fong Shan Ecumenical Center, 1986), 171–183.

They certainly do not convincingly overturn Hsia's characterization of the Republican Era as essentially anti-religious.

However, at the beginning of the twenty-first century, a number of scholars in various humanistic fields began to challenge Hsia's characterization by approaching the work of Republican Era intellectuals with questions about and an openness to understanding how they used the category of "religion," without trying to pin down the definition of "religion" as either "Christianity" or "Buddhism." This approach reflects a shift in the way "religion" is understood in contemporary Religious Studies scholarship, from a specific object that exists in the world to a conceptual category whose definition is always contingent on specific political, social, and economic circumstances. (See "Hu Shi's Self-Styled 'Religion' of Social Immortality," below, for a more in-depth discussion of the shift in understanding "religion" in contemporary Religious Studies). Understanding "religion" in this way allowed these twenty-first-century scholars to demonstrate that the category of "religion" remained important to Republican Era intellectuals, even if most of them were not writing explicitly pro-Christian or pro-Buddhist essays and stories. For example, historian Rebecca Nedostup argues that many Republican Era intellectuals used the category of "religion" as a way of bolstering their own ideas of what values were necessary to promote in society for China to properly modernize. They designated as "religious" systems of thought that were human-centric and focused on the everyday needs of individuals, which they conceived of as aligned with China's goal of modernization. On the contrary, they disparaged as merely "superstitious" systems of thought that focused on mystical concepts of unfathomable afterlives and other worlds, which they viewed as antithetical to their modernization goal.[19]

In the realm of literature, while much still remains to be accomplished, Zhange Ni and Steven Riep have written several articles critically analyzing the role of the category of religion in the literature of Republican Era intellectuals in general as well as in the literature of Su Xuelin and Xu Dishan specifically. Zhange Ni's essays analyze Su Xuelin's literature and Republican Era literature more broadly.[20] For example, in her essay "Rewriting Jesus in Republican Era China: Religion, Literature, and Cultural Nationalism" (2011), she argues that the choice of several Republican Era authors to incorporate Christian imagery

---

19 Rebecca Nedostup, *Superstitious Regimes: Religion and the Politics of Chinese Modernity* (Cambridge, MA: Harvard University Press, 2010), 28–29.

20 See Zhange Ni's articles "Rewriting Jesus in Republican Era China: Religion, Literature, and Cultural Nationalism." *Journal of Religion* 91.2 (2011), "Making Religion, Making the New Woman: Reading Su Xuelin's Autobiographical Novel *Jixin* (Thorny Heart)" (2014), and "The Thorny Paths of Su Xuelin" (2016).

and motifs into their literature reflect their efforts to indigenize an ideology imported from the West as a way of challenging their oppressors by adapting the religion to suit their own needs.[21] Her work introduces a more nuanced method of understanding allusion to religion in Republican Era literature than the work of Robinson and Galik. Rather than simply pointing out instances of allusion to Christianity in modern Chinese literature, her work represents one of the first substantial attempts in English-language scholarship to read allusions to Christianity in Republican Era literature critically as a way of shedding light on that literature's contribution to the May Fourth enterprise of shaping China into a strong modern nation. Steven Riep employs a similar methodology in his analysis of Xu Dishan's literature, arguing that religious institutions in his works serve as paths through which women can obtain equal social and financial status to men.[22] In both cases, by examining how the category of "religion" operates in Xu Dishan's and Su Xuelin's literature instead of assuming that "religion" in their literature has one specific definition or referent, Ni and Riep are able to make convincing arguments about the importance of the category of "religion" to understanding their works.

Now that the genealogy of recent scholarship of the fields of history and literature on the role of "religion" in the writings of a variety of Republican Era intellectuals has been established, we can return to the topic of Hu Shi and his so-called "religion" of social immortality. Specifically, it can now be understood why Hu Shi's word choice merits further examination. Enough scholars have highlighted the variety of rhetorical strategies for which the term "religion" was employed in Republican Era literature that it should be evident that Republican Era intellectual attitudes toward that concept were varied and complex. The texts named above all use the category rhetorically to various effects, and for various purposes. Given this scholarly context, Grieder's initial dismissal of Hu Shi's use of the term "religion" to refer to his worldview must be revisited. Instead of assuming that Hu Shi's choice of the term "religion" is irrelevant because he was not referring to any pre-existing system of "superstitious thought," as Grieder does, it is necessary to ask what rhetorical strategies and motives are evident in his decision to describe his worldview as a "religion." This inquiry will allow for a better understanding of Hu Shi's worldview and Hu Shi himself.

---

21 Zhange Ni, "Rewriting Jesus in Republican Era China: Religion, Literature, and Cultural Nationalism," *Journal of Religion* 91.2 (November 2011): 230.
22 See Steven Riep's article "Religion Reconsidered: Redemption and Women's Emancipation in Xu Dishan's 'The Merchant's Wife'" (2004).

3 Hu Shi's Self-Styled "Religion" of Social Immortality

When Grieder recounts Hu Shi's self-styled "religion" of social immortality, he is more interested in establishing the exact nature of Hu Shi's worldview than in examining Hu Shi's decision to categorize his theory using the term "religion." The term itself is an import from the West, created by Christian missionaries to talk about cultural phenomena they designated as Christian as though it were a discrete aspect of social life.[23] As for the term "immortality," Grieder points out that it was appropriated from a passage in the *Zuo zhuan* (左轉) (late fourth century BC), a well-known commentary on the *Spring and Autumn Annals* (春秋 *Chunqiu*) (722–481 BC). Grieder writes, "Commenting on the phrase 'to die but not to decay' (死而不朽) the writer of the *Zuo zhuan* suggests that it must refer to the remembrance, even after one's death, of virtuous conduct, meritorious service, and wise words."[24] Although Grieder points this connection out, he does not attribute any particular importance to the term, writing simply that when Hu Shi used it, he meant "little more than" what was written already in the *Zuo zhuan* (103). Even more significantly, Grieder dismisses Hu Shi's decision to call his worldview a "religion" as simply a misuse of the term. While Grieder argues that Hu Shi's designation of his worldview as a "religion" is superfluous, this section will demonstrate that the term serves rhetorically to emphasize his worldview's status, at least in his mind, of being part of objective reality. It is in fact a way for Hu Shi to show his worldview as encompassed within the reality of the immortality of the ideas he envisions, a way of enacting the immortalization of his own ideas. This section will explain the nature, origins, and development of his self-styled "religion," as well as examine how Hu Shi enacts his own belief by denoting his worldview a "religion."

Grieder refers to Hu Shi's "religion" as a conviction of the existence of social immortality.[25] Hu Shi's theory of social immortality crucially relied on distinguishing whether the impact of an individual on his society stemmed from who his family was, or rather came from what his ideas were. His conviction was that it was the latter source, and it was in fact born out of his distaste for the emphasis Chinese society had long placed on filial piety. He felt that this tradition was misguided, cultivating a culture of dependency. He observed, "… [O]ne son makes a name for himself and the whole tribe puts the bite on him,

---

23 See Jost Oliver Zetzsche's *The Bible in China: The History of the* Union *Version or the Culmination of Protestant Missionary Bible Translation in China* (1999).
24 Legge v.507, Paragraph 1, qtd. in Grieder, *Hu Shih and the Chinese Renaissance*, 103.
25 Grieder, *Hu Shih and the Chinese Renaissance*, 103.

like ants swarming over a bone, with no sense of shame but on the contrary thinking this quite natural—what slavishness is this!"[26] The imagery Hu Shi uses here to describe the pattern he observes of interdependency in families suggests his disapproval of the idea of basing one's name and reputation on other members of the family. Rather, he argues that it was the ideas of an individual that determined his contribution to society, not the people to whom he was related. He argues, "Sakyamuni, Confucius, Lao-tzu, and Jesus did not rely on sons to perpetuate their names."[27] Hu Shi is highlighting the idea that many famous men through history have obtained their reputations because of their ideas, not their posterity.

As an extension of these views, Hu Shi felt that the individual has a responsibility not only or principally to himself and his family, but to society, an idea which he found affirmed in the Confucian *Zuo zhuan* several years after he wrote about filial piety.[28] (See the section "Introduction" above for more details on the passage of the *Zuo zhuan* that influenced the development of Hu Shi's worldview on immortality). These ideas form the basis of the worldview that Hu Shi first delineates in an essay entitled "Immortality—My Religion [Bu xiu—wo de zong jiao 不朽—我的宗教]" (1919). Hu Shi confirms his indebtedness to Confucian philosophy for the formation of his self-styled "religion" in a prize-winning paper he wrote while still a student comparing the philosophies of Robert Browning and Confucius.[29]

Hu Shi delineates his worldview in his essay "Immortality—My Religion." He writes that his theory of immortality "does not ask whether the soul can survive after death, but only whether a man's character, his occupation, and his works have permanent value.... Immortality depends entirely upon a man's true worth, not upon the continuation of his family line or the survival of his soul."[30] Hu Shi denounces notions of immortality that depend on the continuation of the soul after death or of the family line. Rather, he stresses the Confucian notion expressed in the *Zuo zhuan* that the individual's contributions to his society constitute his immortality. Hu Shi further writes, "the individual creates history, and history creates the individual."[31] He sees

---

26 Hu Shi (胡適), *Ri ji* (日記 Diary), ed. Shen Weiwei (潘衛威). (Taiyuan: Shanxi jiao yu chu ban she: Xin hua shu dian jing xiao, 1998), 250–251.
27 Ibid., 410–411.
28 Grieder, *Hu Shih and the Chinese Renaissance*, 103.
29 Hu Shi, "The Philosophy of Browning and Confucianism," 1915, Collected reproductions of Hu Shih papers at Cornell University, #41-5-2578, Division of Rare and Manuscript Collections, Cornell University Library.
30 Hu Shi, "Bu xiu—wo de zong jiao" *Xin qing Nian* (New Youth) 6.2 (February 1919): 978–979.
31 Ibid., 981.

the connection between the individual and history as mandating that the individual hold himself to high expectations, since it is by his contributions to history that his "'true worth' would be judged."[32] The individual's impact on history was so profound that Hu Shi saw them as inextricably connected. He referred to the individual as the "lesser self" and history as the "greater self."[33] His word choice suggests that he saw the latter as an extension of the former, a collection of the reverberating impact of the actions of many individuals. An acquaintance of Hu Shi's from the United States named Elmer Eugene Barker further characterized Hu Shi's "religion" as a belief in the "immortality of words." Barker explains that, by this, he means that Hu Shi believed that all words spoken and written, whether good or evil, left a lasting, indelible mark on the "larger self," meaning society.[34] Barker's clarification highlights that Hu Shi was not thinking only or even principally of actions, but also of the lasting legacy of the written and spoken word.

Hu Shi is clear enough that what he refers to as his "religion" is a conviction that all actions and words, spoken and written, good and evil, leave an indelible mark on history, and that accordingly it is the ethical responsibility of the individual to produce "good" actions and deeds that will be beneficial to society. Grieder is under the impression that calling this perspective a "religion" is incorrect, but in fact, no one "essentialist" definition of "religion" is possible because "religion" is not one specific reality, but rather a category of thought used to designate certain cultural phenomena as existing outside of the realm of human social interaction. As such, its definition is always contingent on historically specific political, social, and economic contexts. However, some definition of what kind of cultural phenomena can possibly be designated as "religious" is still necessary to this article. Otherwise, if anything could be considered "religious," then Hu Shi's decision to mark his worldview as a self-styled "religion" would be meaningless. This article employs as its basis philosophy of religion scholar Kevin Schilbrack's definition of "religion." Schilbrack exerts great care to come up with a definition that is narrow enough to exclude some cultural phenomena from the possibility of being considered "religious," while still broad enough to avoid the trap of privileging Protestant-like conceptualizations of "religion."

---

32   Grieder, *Hu Shih and the Chinese Renaissance*, 104.
33   Hu Shi, "Bu xiu—wo de zong jiao," 987–988.
34   Elmer Eugene Barker, "Hu Shih, Incurable Optimist: Personal Recollections of a Great Humanist's Intellectual Development," c. 1962, Collected reproductions of Hu Shih papers at Cornell University, #41-5-2578. Division of Rare and Manuscript Collections, Cornell University Library.

According to Schilbrack, cultural phenomena that can be designated as "religious" by individuals and groups necessarily have two features in common. First, they purport to resolve some social problem, what Schilbrack calls their "promissory function."[35] Second, they acknowledge some ostensible reality that exists beyond the realm of human perception as the justification for carrying out the practices that they claim will resolve social problems. Schilbrack calls this the "superempirical reality" of religious cultural phenomena.[36] Taking Schilbrack's definition as a foundation, we see that when Hu Shi refers to his worldview on "social immortality" as a "religion," he is attributing to it both a "promissory function" and the "superempirical reality" that justifies it. In other words, his use of the term "religion" rhetorically highlights the significance of his conviction by portraying it as a part of so-called "objective" reality. By denoting his worldview as a "religion," Hu Shi also implies that it has a "promissory function," some sort of social problem that it solves. From what Hu Shi has written on his worldview, its "promissory function" is that it provides a blueprint for continued historical and social progress. In his view, if individuals commit to "good" deeds and actions, then their society cannot fail to continually progress and improve.

According to Hu Shi's worldview, all words and actions have a lasting impact on the "greater self" of society, and his own philosophy would of course be no exception. Nevertheless, his treatment of his worldview as a "religion" rhetorically emphasizes the everlasting impact of actions and words by portraying it as existing outside of human society. His "religion" becomes one component of a so-called objective reality that is crucial to resolving the question of how to ensure the continued progression and improvement of society. By using the term "religion," he enacts the immortalization of his own worldview, rhetorically emphasizing its status as an idea that exists objectively in the world and that will continually impact society, in this case through its dictum to individuals to always act for the good of society. This insight is only possible once Hu Shi's designation of his worldview as "religious" is no longer understood as a careless misuse of the term, but rather as a particular rhetorical strategy that helped him to enact his worldview with his words even as he preached it.

---

35   Kevin Schilbrack, "What *Isn't* Religion?" *The Journal of Religion* 93.3 (July 2013): 298–304.
36   Ibid., 312–313.

4 Conclusion

Hu Shi's self-styled "religion" of social immortality is worthy of further inquiry beyond Grieder's initial detailed analysis of it in his critical biography. Understanding Hu Shi's major worldview inevitably leads to a greater understanding of him as an intellectual. For example, it is clear from Hu Shi's worldview that he attached a huge amount of historical importance to all actions and words of individuals, which in turn provides insight into why he was so dedicated to language reform in China. If the potential for society's continued progress and development lay in the good words and deeds of individuals, then it is important for access to those good words and deeds to be as widespread as possible. Further study of Hu Shi's *Diary* and other writings would surely shed more light on the intricacies of his worldview of social immortality. This article takes the first step of challenging the idea that Hu Shi's portrayal of his worldview as a "religion" is insignificant. To the contrary, this rhetorical choice enacts through words the very immortalization of ideas that is preached in the content of his writings on his "religion." Recognizing the important role the term "religion" played in enacting Hu Shi's worldview on a formal level even as he argued for its importance highlights the centrality of this idea of "social immortality" to Hu Shi's intellectual mindset.

Bibliography

Barker, Elmer Eugene. c. 1962. "Hu Shih, Incurable Optimist: Personal Recollections of a Great Humanist's Intellectual Development." Collected reproductions of Hu Shih papers at Cornell University, #41-5-2578. Division of Rare and Manuscript Collections, Cornell University Library.

Chen Duxiu 陳獨秀. 1920, rep. 2009. "Jidu jiao yu Zhongguo ren (基督教與中國人 Christianity and the Chinese people)." In *Chen Duxiu zhu zuo xuan pian: di er juan, 1919–1922* (陳獨秀著作選篇: 第二卷, 1919–1922; Selected writings of Chen Duxiu), ed. Ren Jianshu 任建樹, vol. 2, 1919–1922. Shanghai: Shanghai ren min chu ban she, 2009. Reprint.

Denton, Kirk. 1996. "General Introduction." In *Modern Chinese Literary Thought: Writings on Literature, 1893–1945*. Stanford, CA: Stanford University Press.

Eber, Irene. 1999. "Introduction." In *Bible in Modern China: The Literary and Intellectual Impact*, ed. Irene Eber, Sze-kar Wan, and Knut Walf, in collaboration with Roman Malek, 13–28. Sankt Augustin, Germany: Institut Monumenta Serica.

Galik, Marian. 2004. *Influence, Translation, and Parallels: Selected Studies on the Bible in China*. Sankt Augustin, Germany: Institut Monumenta Serica.

Grieder, Jerome B. 1970. *Hu Shih and the Chinese Renaissance: Liberalism in the Chinese Revolution, 1917–1937*. Cambridge, MA: Harvard University Press.

Hauser, Ernest O. 1941. "Ambassador Hu Shih: China's Greatest Living Scholar Fights a Winning Battle of Wits Against Japan," *Life* magazine, December. Collected reproductions of Hu Shih papers at Cornell University, #41-5-2578. Division of Rare and Manuscript Collections, Cornell University Library.

Hsia, C. T. 1961. *A History of Modern Chinese Fiction*. New York: Columbia University Press.

Hu Shi 胡適. 1915. "Kang nan er jun zhuan (康南耳君傳 A Biography of Mr. Cornell)," *Chinese Students' Quarterly*. Spring. Collected reproductions of Hu Shih papers at Cornell University, #41-5-2578. Division of Rare and Manuscript Collections, Cornell University Library.

Hu Shi 胡適. 1915. "The Philosophy of Browning and Confucianism." Collected reproductions of Hu Shih papers at Cornell University, #41-5-2578. Division of Rare and Manuscript Collections, Cornell University Library.

Hu Shi 胡適. 1916. "The Problem of the Chinese Language," *Chinese Students' Monthly* (June), 567–572.

Hu Shi 胡適. 1917. "Li shi de wen xue guan nian lun (歷史的文學觀念論 On the genetic concept of literature)," *Xin qing nian* (New Youth) 3.3 (May).

Hu Shi 胡適. 1917. "Wen xue gai liang chu yi (文學改良芻議 Tentative Proposals for the Improvement of Literature)," *Xin qing nian* (新青年 New Youth) 2.5 (January).

Hu Shi 胡適. 1919. "Bu xiu—wo de zong jiao (不朽—我的宗教 Immortality—My Religion)." *Xin qing Nian* (New Youth). 6.2 (February).

Hu Shi 胡適. 1998. *Ri ji* (Diary), ed. Shen Weiwei (潘衛威). Taiyuan: Shanxi jiao yu chu ban she: Xin hua shu dian jing xiao.

Johnston, Richard. 1941. "The Influence of the Canoe on the Chinese Literary Revolution." Collected reproductions of Hu Shih papers at Cornell University, #41-5-2578. Division of Rare and Manuscript Collections, Cornell University Library.

"Library of Congress Pinyin Conversion Project: New Chinese Romanization Guidelines." *Library of Congress*. www.loc.gov/catdir/pinyin/romcover.html.

Mair, Victor. 2017. "Hu Shih and Chinese Language Reform," Language Log, 4 February. http://languagelog.ldc.upenn.edu/nll/?p=30801.

Nedostup, Rebecca. 2010. *Superstitious Regimes: Religion and the Politics of Chinese Modernity*. Cambridge, MA: Harvard University Press.

Ni, Zhange. 2011. "Rewriting Jesus in Republican Era China: Religion, Literature, and Cultural Nationalism," *Journal of Religion* 91.2 (November) 223–252.

Ni, Zhange. 2014. "Making Religion, Making the New Woman: Reading Su Xuelin's Autobiographical Novel *Jixin* (Thorny Heart)." In *Gendering Chinese Religions*, ed. Ping Yao, Jinghua Jia, and Xiaofei Kang, 71–99. New York: SUNY Press.

Ni, Zhange. 2016. "The Thorny Paths of Su Xuelin," *Harvard Divinity Bulletin* 39.3–4. Web. 28 July 2016. https://bulletin.hds.harvard.edu/articles/summerautumn2011/thorny-paths-su-xuelin.

Riep, Steven. 2004. "Religion Reconsidered: Redemption and Women's Emancipation in Xu Dishan's 'The Merchant's Wife,'" *Literature and Belief* 24: 1–2. 101–115.

Robinson, Lewis Stuart. 1986. *Double-Edged Sword: Christianity and 20th Century Chinese Fiction*. Hong Kong: Tao Fong Shan Ecumenical Center.

Schilbrack, Kevin. 2013. "What *Isn't* Religion?" *The Journal of Religion* 93.3 (July): 291–318.

Starr, Chloë. 2008. "Introduction." In *Reading Christian Scriptures in China*. Ed. Chloë Starr. London: T&T Clark.

Wang, David Der-Wei. 1997. *Fin-de-siècle Splendor: Repressed Modernities of Late Qing Fiction, 1849–1911*. Stanford, CA: Stanford University Press.

Zetzsche, Jost Oliver. 1999. *The Bible in China: The History of the Union Version, or the Culmination of Protestant Missionary Bible Translation in China*. Sankt Augustin, Germany: Institut Monumenta Serica.

Zuo zhuan. 1960. In *The Chinese Classics*, trans. James Legge. Hong Kong: Hong Kong University Press.

CHAPTER 13

A Historical and Bilingual Perspective on the Concept of Vernacular

Carlos Yu-Kai Lin

The standard narrative of the May Fourth new literature movement, also known as the vernacular literature movement, is that vernacular Chinese (*baihua* 白話) had triumphed over literary Chinese (*wenyan* 文言) in becoming the new literary language for Chinese writers. This narrative is part of the May Fourth intellectuals' efforts to theorize the idea of *baihua*, making it a modern literary concept that can compete with the orthodox status of *wenyan*. While the May Fourth writers had sought to create a new literature that features the use of *baihua* instead of *wenyan*, such efforts nonetheless fostered an impression that *wenyan* and *baihua* are two separate and contrary concepts.

This standard narrative, originally proposed by the May Fourth intellectuals, was by and large inherited by later historians and scholars. To date, researchers, when introducing the achievements of the May Fourth literary revolution, have never failed to mention or reiterate the May Fourth writers' struggle in transitioning from *wenyan* to *baihua* as a medium for literary creation. For instance, Vera Schwarcz, in her often-quoted *The Chinese Enlightenment: Intellectuals and the Legacy of the May Fourth*, wrote, "By choosing to write in the vernacular—by which, using the spoken language called *baihua*—as distinguished from the classical idiom known as *guwen* or *guanhua* (officials' talk)—iconoclastic intellectuals signaled their determination to break with the tradition of their literati predecessors."[1] Merle Goldman also suggested that the "ascendance of the spoken language, *pai hua*, over the classical literary language, *wen yan*, in the May Fourth Movement" is a topic that merits our continual investigation. Geng Yunzhi, a scholar based in China, also stated that "One of the most noted and recognized achievements of the May Fourth literary revolution is that vernacular literature has replaced classical literature, around which some of the most intense debates had been generated" (五四文

---

1 Vera Schwarcz, *The Chinese Enlightenment* (Berkeley and Los Angeles: University of California Press, 1986), 56.

學革命運動，其最顯著最普遍的成果就是白話文學代替了古文文學，而最尖銳的鬥爭也正是圍繞著這一點展開的).[2]

To be sure, this *wenyan-baihua* rhetoric is a literary device designed by the May Fourth intellectuals themselves as a means of either advocating the use of vernacular Chinese or defending the value of literary Chinese. Cai Yuanpei 蔡元培 (1868–1949), a leading May Fourth intellectual, for example, maintained that "on the issue of national language, the most important is the competition between *baihua* and *wenyan*" (國文的問題，最重要的就是白話與文言的競爭).[3] Hu Shi 胡適 (1891–1962), a leading May Fourth intellectual who spearheaded the literary revolution, also sought to juxtapose *wenyan* and *baihua* as two separate concepts in many of his writings. From this perspective, it seems safe to argue that some kind of *wenyan-baihua* binarism has been at work in our standard narrative of the May Fourth literary revolution, shaping the way we narrate and evaluate the achievements of May Fourth writers.

While the new literature movement has been widely interpreted as a struggle between *baihua* and *wenyan*, the fact that a huge volume of discourse had been generated on various issues concerning vernacular literature and language, suggests that the idea of *baihua* was not self-evident or self-explanatory to the Chinese intellectuals at the time. In fact, almost all major Chinese intellectuals in the May Fourth period had written an article or two to participate in this literary debate, indicating that the idea of *baihua* was subject to constant negotiations and interpretations.[4]

---

2 Geng Yunzhi 耿雲志, *Chongxin faxian Hu Shi* 重新發現胡適 (Rediscovering Hu Shi) (Beijing: Renmin chubanshe, 2011), 72.
3 Cai Yuanpei, "Guowen zhij jianglai" 國文之將來 (The future of national language) in *Cai Yuanpei xuanji* 蔡元培選集 (Selected works of Cai Yuanpei) (Beijing: Zhonghua shuju, 1959), 103. Lin Shu 林紓 (1852–1924), the foremost classical essayist at the time, for another example, also argued that certain ancient texts can never be fully interpreted or comprehended through *baihua*: "Can the ancient texts written in seal script be transformed into *baihua*? Mixing the former with the latter is like trying to invite the legendary beauties from the Han and Tang dynasties to have a heart-to-heart conversation with the village women" (篆籀可化為白話耶？果以篆籀之文，雜之白話之中，是試漢唐之環燕，與村婦談心). See Lin Qinnan (Lin Shu), "Lin Qinnan yuanshu" 林琴南原書 ("The original letter of Lin Qinnan"), in Hu Shi's (ed.) *Zhongguo xin wenyi daxi: Wenxue lunzhan yiji* 中國新文藝大系：文學論戰一集 (The compendium of Chinese new literature: Debates on literature, volume 1) (Taipei: Dahan chubanshe, 1977), 243.
4 Even Hu Shi, the foremost scholar in this literary revolution, had elaborated the meanings of the Chinese literary revolution in different ways and languages, indicating that the idea of the vernacular was constantly contested in his discourses.

To demonstrate that the idea of *baihua* was not always presented and understood as a counterpart of *wenyan*, this chapter traces the history of this term from late Ming to late Qing and early Republican (May Fourth) periods, in order to reveal the various definitions of this term and the different ways in which the concept of the vernacular was invoked and circulated. Particularly, this chapter proposes to consider the idea of *baihua* in the May Fourth period as a neologism that implies and combines different meanings. By using Hu Shi as a primary example, this chapter suggests that the idea of *baihua* can and should better be perceived as a kind of quality or potentiality inherent in any living language, and an element essential to the survival of any language. It is for this reason that *baihua* was considered by many May Fourth intellectuals a possible new criterion with which once can judge or predict the health and life span of any language or body of literature.[5]

1   The Concept of *Baihua* in the Ming and Qing Periods

A quick review of the concept of *baihua* in the pre-May Fourth periods reveals that the rise of *baihua* as a counterpart of *wenyan* is a unique product of the May Fourth literary movement. Contrary to the plethora of discussions on *baihua*, there is not much of a record of this term in the pre-May Fourth literature. The term cannot be found in any pre-Qin and Han texts, a corpus of writings that is generally considered the cornerstone of Chinese literary tradition. Even in the Ming (1368–1644) and Qing (1644–1911) dynasties, in which the vernacular fictions prevailed and blossomed,[6] the term was rarely invoked or mentioned.

---

5   While a few contemporary scholars' works were mentioned at the beginning of this chapter, the purpose of this chapter is not to take them at face value but to simply highlight the fact that in our standard narrative of the May Fourth literary revolution, it is sometimes difficult to avoid using a kind of rhetoric that tends to translate the difference and competence between *wenyan* and *baihua* into a theoretical framework that renders the two concepts as diametrically and stably opposed to one another.

6   Scholars had long speculated that vernacular literature might have a long history in China. For example, Zheng Zhenduo 鄭振鐸 (1898–1958) believed that the first golden age of vernacular literature in Chinese history is the Song Dynasty (960–1279). See *Zheng Zhenduo ji* 鄭振鐸集 (Collected works of Zheng Zhenduo) (Beijing: Zhongguo shehui chubanshe, 2004), 12. Hu Shi 胡適 (1891–1962) argues that vernacular literature in China can be dated back to the pre-Qin and Han periods. See Hu Shi's *Baihua wenxue shi* 白話文學史 (History of vernacular literature) (Tainan: Tainan donghai chubanshe, 1976), 1–23.

The term began to be used in a few Ming literary texts such as Feng Menglong's 馮夢龍 (1574–1646) *Xingshi hengyan* 醒世恒言 (Stories to Awaken the World), Xi Zhousheng's 西周生 (dates unknown) *Xingshi yinyuan zhuan* 醒世姻緣傳 (Marriage Destinies to Awaken the World), and Li Zhi's 李贄 (1527–1602) *Chutan Ji* 初潭集 (First Collection by the Pond). For instance, in "Chen Duoshou and His Wife Bound in Life and Death" 陳多壽生死夫妻, a story from Feng's *Stories to Awaken the World*, a sentence containing the term *baihua* was recorded: "Wang Sanlao was chatting with several old men at his door" (王三老正在門首, 同幾個老人家閑坐白話).[7] Here the term *baihua* denotes "chatting" or "talking" and does not refer to a distinctive literary concept or way of expression.

In *Marriage Destinies to Awaken the World*, the term *baihua* was similarly used to denote "talking" or "chatting." For example, in chapter four, a sentence containing the term *baihua* appears: "Now he was talking with Duke Zhou" (如今他正合一個甚麼周公在那裡白話). In chapter five, another sentence reads: "Only Hu Dan and Liang Sheng stood there talking" (只有一個胡旦一個梁生還站住白話).[8] In chapter twenty-nine, the protagonist "dreamed that he was sitting in a house, speaking to a girl who had passed away a long time ago" (夢見到他一個久死的姑娘家裡, 正在那裡與他姑娘坐了白話).[9] In these examples, the term *baihua* invariably means "talking" or "chatting."

In other Ming and Qing dynasty literary texts, the term *baihua* refers to an absurd or nonsensical idea or a narrative that lacks credibility. Take Li Zhi's *First Collection by the Pond*, which is a critical reflection on Confucian ethics, for example. In this work, the author tells a story of an important figure of the Seven Sages of the Bamboo Grove, Liu Ling 劉伶 (221–300 BCE), who was known for his habit of walking around his house without wearing any clothes. Whenever he was criticized by his guests, Liu would reply that he had considered the earth and sky to be his house, and the room his pants, and he would ask his guests in return what they were doing inside his pants. Li Zhi believed that this story was true and argued that what Liu Ling said is "not hyperbole or nonsense" (不是大話, 亦不是白話).[10] Here the term *baihua* refers to a false statement or exaggerated story that appears to be absurd or nonsensical.

---

7   Feng Menglong, *Stories to Awaken the World: A Ming Dynasty Collection, Volume 3*, trans. Shuhui Yang and Yunqin Yang (Seattle: University of Washington Press, 2012), 190.
8   Xi Zhousheng's *Xingshi hengyan*.
9   Ibid.
10 Li Zhi's *Chutan ji*.

In *Honglou meng* 紅樓夢 (Dream of the Red Chamber), the eighteen-century *tour de force* by Cao Xueqin 曹雪芹 (1715–1763), the term *baihua* again refers to a foolish idea or a made-up story. In chapter fifty-seven, the protagonist Jia Baoyu replies to a servant who had falsely implied that Lin Daiyu, Baoyu's beloved cousin, might return to her hometown Soochow soon:

> "You're joking," Baoyu replied with a smile. "Soochow is where her father came from, I know. But the reason we brought her here in the first place was because when my Aunt Lin died there was no one to look after her. There wouldn't be anyone in Soochow for her to go to. You must be lying."

> 寶玉笑道: 你又說白話. 蘇州雖是原籍, 因沒了姑母, 無人照看, 纔接了來的. 明年回去找誰? 可見撒謊了.[11]

Here the term *baihua* can be interpreted as "joking" since it conveys a sense of foolishness and triviality. Yet an implication of absurdity and untrustworthiness is also obvious in this sentence. Not only did Baoyu find the servant's words implausible, he also found them somewhat amusing, as he "replied with a smile." The fact that the term was only mentioned once throughout the entire novel also indicates that the term was not considered important, and its usage was not particularly popular at the time.

It was not until the late Qing period that the term *baihua* began to gain some significance in the discussions on language reform. Starting around the mid-nineteenth century, Chinese intellectuals began to perceive the separation of the spoken and written language as a problem in that it hindered the dissemination of modern knowledge. Inspired by Japan's genbun itchi (the unification of the spoken and written languages) movement, Huang Zunxian 黃遵憲 (1848–1905), a late Qing diplomat to Japan, pointed out that "If [Chinese] fiction writers can use dialects in their writing, speech and script can be unified" (若小說家言, 更有直用方言以筆之於書者, 則語言, 文字幾幾乎複合矣).[12] Here the term *fangyan* 方言 (topolect or dialect) was invoked to refer to the idea of a spoken language.

Lu Gangzhang 盧戇章 (1854–1928), a late Qing linguist, to take another example, invented a spelling system for Chinese writing in 1878, using a set of modified Latin alphabets. In the work in which he introduces his spelling system, he invokes terms such as *tuqiang* 土腔 ("local accent"), *tuyin* 土音 ("local

---

11   Cao Xueqin's *The Story of the Stone, Volume 3*, trans. David Hawkes (New York: Penguin, 1980), 92.
12   Huang Zunxian, *Riben guozhi* 日本國志 (Records of Japan), 1887.

tongue"), and *xiangtan* 鄉談 ("country talk") in order to refer to the idea of the vernacular.[13] It is noteworthy to see that the term *baihua* was not used at all in either Huang's and Lu's writings. Both authors invoked other terms to denote the concept of the vernacular. One possible explanation to this is that the separation of the written and spoken languages was not considered an issue until the late nineteenth century, and the Chinese intellectuals were still looking for a new way to theorize this linguistic issue in Chinese terms.

It was not until the early twentieth century that *baihua* was theorized as a linguistic concept that denotes the spoken languages. In 1900, Wang Zhao 王照 (1859–1933), a Chinese linguist, published *Guanhua hesheng zimu* 官話合聲字母 (Mandarin alphabets), in which he came up with a spelling system. Different from Lu's system, which was based on a local language in Amoy, Wang's was based on Beijing Mandarin. More importantly, he used the term *baihua* to denote the general idea of spoken languages in China. Wang wrote:

> These alphabets were specifically designed to spell *baihua*. To unify the spoken languages, it is better to choose Mandarin, because to the north of the Heilong River, to the west of the Taihang mountains and Wanluo areas, to the south of the Yangtze River, and to the east of the ocean, Mandarin was spoken and can be understood by hundreds of thousands of people living across several thousand *li*.
>
> 此字母專拼白話, 語言必歸劃一, 宜取京話, 因北至黑龍江, 西逾太行宛洛, 南距揚子江, 東傳於海, 縱橫數千里, 百餘兆人, 皆解京話.[14]

The fact that Wang is one of the first to use this term to refer to spoken languages in a scholarly work indicates that the term *baihua* had started to bear a theoretical and linguistic meaning. It is also from this point that the term became a more recognized and commonly used concept. A number of newspapers featuring the use of vernacular Chinese also started to appear in China around the turn of the century, and these newspapers all contain the term

---

13   Lu Gangzhang, *Yimu liaoran chujie* 一目了然初階 (First steps to understand writing at a glance), 1892.
14   Wang Zhao, *Guanhua hesheng zimu*, 1900. In 1908, Zhang Taiyan 章太炎 (1868–1936) created a system of phonetic notation called the "Niuwen yunwen" 紐文韻文, which is based on the Tang dynasty's rime dictionaries and Qin dynasty's seal scripts. Wu Zhihui 吳稚暉 (1865–1953), among others, proposed to eradicate Chinese characters altogether and replace them with a Latinized artificial language called Esperanto. These various trends and proposals of language reforms continued to the 1910s and were fervently discussed by Chinese intellectuals in the May Fourth period.

baihua in their titles. For instance, the first vernacular Chinese newspaper, *Yanyi baihua bao* 演義白話報 (Popular Renditions of Vernacular Newspapers), was founded in 1897. Another, *Wuxi baihua bao* 無錫白話報 (Wuxi Vernacular Newspaper), was launched in 1898. By the end of 1900s, there were already more than a hundred vernacular newspapers published in China. The circulation of these newspapers thus paved the way for the rise of the later May Fourth literary movement.

2   The Concept of *Baihua* in the May Fourth Context: Hu Shi as an Example

Hu Shi's 1917 article, "Wenxue gailiang chuyi" 文學改良芻議 (Some Modest Proposals for the Reform of Literature), is often considered a seminal text that inaugurates the May Fourth movement of vernacular literature. Upon this article's publication in the *New Youth* 新青年, a progressive magazine that introduced Western social thought to China, Chen Duxiu 陳獨秀 (1879–1942), the magazine's editor-in-chief, immediately wrote "Wenxue geming lun" 文學革命論 (On Literary Revolution) to support Hu. Other progressive writers at the time, such as Qian Xuantong 錢玄同 (1887–1939), Liu Bannong 劉半農 (1891–1934), and Fu Sinian 傅斯年 (1896–1950) all wrote in response to the call for a new literary paradigm that features the use of *baihua*. This article thus signifies a new stage of the transformation of the *baihua*.

Hu Shi emphasizes the creative and artistic potential of vernacular writing. Particularly, he warned against any imitation of the classical Chinese literary tradition, and urged writers to write in a way that is aesthetically original without a faithful depiction of reality. For instance, he criticized a poem written by a friend of his who lived in America, Hu Xiansu 胡先驌 (1894–1968). The poem begins and ends with a setting that is typical of classical Chinese poetry:

> Like tiny peas, the twinkling flames of an evening lamp/Cast a flickering shadow on a solitary figure … Enchanted notes lofted above/After lingering momentarily round the columns.
>
> 熒熒夜燈如豆, 映幢幢孤影 … 嫋嫋餘音, 片時猶繞柱.[15]

---

15   See Hu Shi's "Some Modest Proposals for the Reform of Literature" in Kirk Denton, ed., *Modern Chinese Literary Thought: Writings on Literature, 1893–1945* (Stanford, CA: Stanford University Press, 1996), 128–129.

Here "twinkling flames" and "enchanted notes" that lingered "round the columns" are common literary expressions in Chinese poems. But Hu Shi argues that the "evening lamp" could not have "twinkled" "like tiny peas" in America, and there were no "columns" around which the notes could linger in the poet's house. Not only does this imitation of classical Chinese poetry fail to capture the reality, it also disconnects the author and readers from the real world that they see and feel every day. Hu Shi thus argued, "The necessity of eliminating hackneyed and formal language can only be achieved through the creation of new phrases to describe and portray what people see and hear with their own eyes and ears or personally live through" (務去濫調套語者, 別無他法, 惟在人人以其耳目所親見親聞, 所親身閱歷之事物).[16] This emphasis on the relation between individual perception and literary creation henceforth became one of the most important tropes in the May Fourth literary discourses, in which *baihua* was considered the most effective medium to produce a new kind of literature.

While Hu Shi's definition of *baihua* seems to hinge on the notion of classical literature, we should not assume that he must also have considered *wenyan* and *baihua* as two separate and contrary concepts. Recent studies have shown that his learning experiences in the United States (1910–1917) also played an important role in shaping his intellectual discourses. Daniel Fried, for instance, suggests that Hu Shi might have been familiar with American universities' standard literature courses at the time.[17] These courses, which introduced Victorian, Elizabethan, and Romantic poetry, especially the works of Robert Browning and Alfred Tennyson, might be the true source of Hu Shi's theory of vernacular literature. Chih-p'ing Chou, for another example, points out that Hu Shi, as a cultural leader in the May Fourth Movement, reveals a more tolerant attitude toward Chinese cultural tradition in his English writings as compared to his Chinese ones. In fact, in Hu Shi's Chinese works, he tends to emphasize the difference between Western and Chinese civilizations. In his English articles, he tends to highlight the close relationship between modern Western thought and traditional Chinese culture.[18]

---

16 Ibid., 129.
17 Daniel Fried, "Beijing's Crypto-Victorian: Traditionalist Influences on Hu Shi's Poetic Practice," *Comparative Critical Studies* 3, no. 3. (2006): 372.
18 Chou Chih-p'ing, *Guangyan buxi: Hu Shi sixian yu xiandai zhongguo* 光焰不息：胡適思想與現代中國 (Eternal flames: Hu Shi's thought and modern China) (Beijing: Jiuzhou chubanshe, 2012), 304–324.

This recent trend in Hu Shi studies thus points to a cross-cultural and bilingual perspective on May Fourth literary discourses—a view that needs to be further emphasized and explored, as it will enable us to shed light on the various ways in which the concept of *baihua* was articulated in the transnational and cross-cultural May Fourth context. The fact that many May Fourth intellectuals had received their education in foreign countries such as the U.S. (Hu Shi, Yuen Ren Chao, Mei Guangdi), Japan (Chen Duxiu, Lu Xun, Zhou Zuoren), and France (Wu Zhihui), indicates that the May Fourth literary discourses can be valuable resources for transnational studies and cross-cultural analysis. In fact, Hu Shi himself had pointed out that he actually started to develop the idea of a vernacular literary revolution when he was still studying in the United States. According to his memoir, the idea of a literary revolution began to emerge in his mind when he grew interested in language reforms in China. As previously discussed, the issue of Chinese language reform had been debated by Chinese intellectuals since the 1890s, and by the early 1900s, many agendas and plans had been proposed.[19] In 1915, Hu Shi had just finished his undergraduate study at Cornell and was about to transfer to Columbia for his graduate study. At that time, a group of Chinese students in the U.S. founded an organization called the "Research Association of Literature and Science" (文學科學研究會) and were in the process of preparing its annual meeting. Hu Shi, who wanted to organize a panel to discuss Chinese language reforms, invited Yuen Ren Chao 趙元任 (1892–1982), an expert in Chinese linguistics, to join him. Chao was a firm supporter of the Romanization of Chinese character. Yet at that time Hu Shi did not think this plan could be achieved in a short time. As a result, he only chose to present a paper entitled "The Teaching of Chinese as It Is" in this meeting.

---

19   In fact, European missionaries have been using Roman alphabets to write Chinese languages since the early seventeenth century. For example, in 1605, Italian Jesuit Matteo Ricci (1552–1610) published *Xiji qiji* 西字奇蹟 (The miracle of Western letters) in Beijing. In 1626, Nicolas Trigault, another Jesuit visiting China, wrote *Xiru ermu zi* 西儒耳目資 (Aid to the eyes and ears of Western literati) in Hangzhou. Although both works pioneered in Romanizing Chinese languages, they did not have much impact on the Chinese writing system at the time. It was not until two hundred years later that the issue of script reform that involves the alphabetization of Chinese was brought up by Chinese intellectuals. See Victor H. Mair, "Sound and Meaning in the History of Characters: Views of China's Earliest Script Reformers," in *Difficult Characters: Interdisciplinary Studies of Chinese and Japanese Writing*, ed. Mary S. Erbaugh (Columbus: Ohio State University National East Asian Language Resource Center, 2002). Available at http://www.pinyin.info/readings/texts/chinese_writing_reform.html.

This English paper then formed part of a longer essay authored by Yuan Ren Chao—"The Problem of the Chinese Language"—which was later published in the *Chinese Students' Monthly* in 1916, the first English magazine launched by the Chinese students in the U.S.[20] While Hu Shi's 1917 Chinese essay "Some Modest Proposals for the Reform of Literature" had a far-reaching impact on the development of the May Fourth literary movement, the 1916 English essay "The Teaching of Chinese as It Is" perhaps is the first work that Hu Shi wrote in regard to the issue of *baihua*. It is thus important to examine this paper to demonstrate how Hu Shi developed his theory of the vernacular that became crucial to the May Fourth literary revolution in 1917.

Hu Shi wrote at the beginning of this paper:

> I am of the opinion that most of the faults that have been attributed to our language are due to the fact that it has never been properly and scientifically taught. Its critics have been too hasty in their condemnations, and have failed to realize that languages are more conservative than religions and cannot be made and remade by sensational agitations and destructive criticisms ... the teaching of Chinese as it is constitutes a far more urgent problem, because it is the language that records our past and present civilizations, that is the only means of inter-provincial communication, and that is the only available instrument of national education.[21]

It is interesting to see that in this article Hu Shi actually did not see *baihua* and *wenyan* as two separate and contrary concepts, nor does he think that it is necessary for the former to replace the latter. Instead of relying on a binary logic, he held a holistic view that seeks to analyze Chinese language as a whole to reflect on the development of Chinese civilization.

In a Chinese diary written around the day of the annual meeting, Hu Shi mentions this English paper and refers to it as "How to make our country's literary language (*wenyan*) easy to teach" (如何可使吾國文言易於教授).[22]

---

20 "The Problem of the Chinese Language" contains four sections; each has its own subtitle: "The Problem of Chinese Philology," "Chinese Phonetics," "The Teaching of Chinese as It Is," and "Proposed Reforms". Only the third section, "The Teaching of Chinese as It Is," is written by Hu Shi. See Chiang Yung-chen's *Shewo qishui: Hu Shi (diyi bu) Puyu chengbi (1891–1917)* 捨我其誰：胡適【第一部】一璞玉成璧（1891–1917）(The titan: Hu Shi, volume 1: Education) (Taipei: Linking, 2011), 620.

21 Hu Suh (Hu Shi), "The Problem of the Chinese Language (Concluded): III. The Teaching of Chinese as It Is," *The Chinese Students' Monthly*, XI. 8: 567.

22 Hu Shi, *Hushi quanji* 胡適全集 (Hefei: Anhui jiaoyu chubanshe, 2003) 28: 244–245.

If we compare this translation with the original English title ("The Teaching of Chinese as It Is"), we can see that Hu Shi actually used *wenyan* to denote "Chinese language" in general. This means that to him, Chinese language can only be represented by the *wenyan* and *baihua* is only a spoken form of Chinese language that can never replace the written language. This early English paper of Hu Shi thus reminds us that *wenyan* and *baihua* are not always considered opposite to each other in the May Fourth literary discourses.

Hu Shi then proposed two "generalizations" to further the discussions on Chinese language:

> There are a few generalizations that I consider to be of great importance in discussing the problem of teaching Chinese as it is. The first of these is that what we call our literary language is an almost entirely dead language. Dead it is, because it is no longer spoken by the people. It is like Latin in Mediaeval Europe; in fact, it is more dead (if mortality admits of a comparative degree), than Latin, because Latin is still capable of being spoken and understood, while literary Chinese is no longer auditorily intelligible even among the scholarly class except when the phrases are familiar, or when the listener has already some idea as to what the speaker is going to say.

Here, we can see that the definition of "literary language" is founded on a relativistic and cross-cultural perspective, as *wenyan* in China is compared with Latin in Medieval Europe. It is particularly interesting that Hu Shi describes *wenyan* as an "almost entirely dead language" and argues that "mortality admits of comparative degree." This comparative and gradualist perspective on the life span and health of a language is interesting, since it implies that some languages are "more dead" or "more alive," than others, and that the connotation of a "living language" or "dead language" is not absolute but relativistic.

This comparative view was also manifested in Hu Shi's later writings. For example, in his 1920 article "Guoyu de jinhua" 國語的進化 (The Evolution of National Language), Hu Shi uses the term "half-dead" (半死) to refer to any language that does not evolve accordingly with the changing social reality.

> If the growth of [a language] is obstructed by the literary standard of an age, this language will gradually wither and become dead or half-dead. Fortunately, the *baihua* of those country bumpkins and uneducated women had never perished and continued to change with the times: To change means to stay alive; to refuse to change means to die.

進化的生機被一個時代的標準阻礙住了, 那種文字就漸漸乾枯, 變成死文字或半死的文字, 幸虧那些『鄉曲愚夫, 閭巷婦稚』的白話還不曾死, 仍舊隨時變遷: 變遷便是活的表示, 不變遷便是死的表示。[23]

From this example, we can see that concepts such as "dead" or "alive," "*wenyan*" or "*baihua*" in Hu Shi's writings are only relativistic. They are diagnostic terms based on a scale of gradation, and their meanings are symbolic and flexible. A dying language can be turned into a healthy one if it is scientifically taught; a dead language can be rejuvenated by adding some elements of a living language. The concept of a dead or living language therefore is not absolute and fixed but subject to changes according to what and how one compares. Hu Shi continues:

> The second generalization is that we must free ourselves from the traditional view that the spoken words and the spoken syntax are "vulgar." The Chinese word vulgar (see chart 2 [44]) means simply "customary" and implies no intrinsic vulgarity. As a matter of fact, many of the words and phrases of our daily use are extremely expressive and therefore beautiful. The criterion for judging words and expressions should be their vitality and adequacy of expression, not their conformity to orthodox standards. The spoken language of our people is a living language: it represents the daily needs of the people, is intrinsically beautiful, and possesses every possibility of producing a great and *living literature* as is shown in our great novels written in the vulgate.[24]

The chart provided by Hu Shi indicates that the Chinese word for vulgar is *su* (俗), which he defines in English as "customary"—a word that does not contain the pejorative meaning of "vulgarity." It is interesting to see that Hu Shi here sought to change the meaning of a Chinese word by resorting to an English term. The Chinese word, *su*, can, of course, denote vulgarity, and so Hu Shi's definition is selective and strategic. But the fact that he had sought to readjust the meaning of a Chinese word through an English term suggests that his interpretation of *baihua* was actually processed in a bilingual mode that allowed him to challenge the deep-rooted assumption that the vernacular is a vulgar form of language.

---

23 Hu Shi, "Guoyu de jinhua," in *Zhongguo xin wenyi daxi: Wenxue lunzhan yiji*, 314–315.
24 Ibid.

Another interesting aspect of Hu Shi's definition of *baihua* is that he viewed *baihua* as a kind of element. Hu Shi wrote in a diary entry dated August 26, 1915:

> Chinese is a half-dead language. It cannot be taught in the same way one teaches a living language. (The living language refers to words and phrases used in daily lives such as English and French, or *baihua* in our country. The dead language is like Latin in Greece, which is no longer a language of daily use, but a dying one. It is half-dead because it still contains daily-use elements. For example, the character, *quan* [dog], is a dead word, the character, *gou* [dog], a living one; the term, *chengma* [horse-riding], is a dead term, *qima* [horse-riding], a living one. This is why we call Chinese a half-dead language.)
>
> 漢文乃是半死之文字, 不當以教活文字之教法教之. (活文字者, 日用語言之文字, 如英法文是也, 如吾國之白話是也. 死文字者, 如拉丁希臘, 非日用之語言, 已陳死矣. 半死文字者, 以其中尚有日用之分子在也. 如犬字是已死之字, 狗字是活字; 乘馬是死語, 騎馬是活語. 故約半死之文字也).²⁵

In this paragraph, Hu Shi uses an interesting expression, "daily-use elements" (日用之分子), to describe the content of *baihua*. This means that the idea of *baihua* here is perceived as a kind of element that any language should have in order to be qualified as a "living language." If such elements in a language increase, this language can be called *baihua*. If they decrease, the language will slowly die out and became *wenyan*.

This perspective, which views the *baihua* as a kind of element, is particularly useful, since it prevents Hu Shi from falling into the trap of a rigid *wenyan*-*baihua* binarism, allowing him to develop a more nuanced understanding of the Chinese language. Indeed, the way any language develops or decays is a long and gradational process. Any change in the development of a language cannot possibly take place overnight. It is therefore difficult to evaluate the vitality of any language simply by relying on a *wenyan-baihua* binary logic.

Hu Shi's coinage of "daily-use elements" is likely influenced by the terminologies of modern biological science in which "molecule" or "element" is often translated as "fenzi" (分子) in Chinese. Although Hu Shi did not provide additional explanations for this particular expression, it is reasonable to assume that the term "fenzi" here is understood by Hu Shi as an "element" or "molecule"

---

25 Hu Shi, *Hushi quanji* 28: 245.

that can be examined in isolation and extracted from a larger organism. The fact that Hu Shi's writing is influenced by his bilingual thinking can be further proved by his diary entry dated August 26, 1915, in which he wrote:

> Every word has two essentials: one is its sound, the other its meaning. There is no language that can preserve both at the same time. An alphabetical word gives its sound, but not its meaning, while an ideographic word conveys its meaning, but not its sound.
>
> 凡一字有二要: 一為其聲, 一為其義. 無論何種文字, 不能同時並達此二者. 字母的文字, 但能傳聲, 不能達意; 象形會意之文字, 但可達意, 而不能傳聲.[26]

If we compare this passage with the English paper that Hu Shi wrote in 1915 ("The Teaching of Chinese as It Is"), we can notice that it actually derived from that English paper, in which a similar passage can be found:

> Every word, be it Chinese or English, has two elements: its sound and its meaning. A word in an alphabetical language tells immediately its pronunciation, but not its meaning; while an ideographic word in its original form tells immediately its meaning, but not its pronunciation.[27]

While the two passages differ slightly in their wording and sentential structure, the message that the author seeks to convey is the same. The sentence "Every word has two essentials" obviously corresponds to "Every word .... has two elements". The term "essentials" (要) thus can be interpreted as "elements". This example shows that Hu Shi's idea of the "daily-use elements" which is key to his definition of baihua, is influenced by his English thinking and writing.

In another article of Hu Shi, "Du zhang taiyan bo zhongguo wanguo xinyu shuo" 讀章太炎《駁中國用萬國新語說》後 ("After reading Zhang Taiyan's 'Refuting the use of the Esperanto in China'"), he again refers to the English paper that he presented at the meeting in 1915. In this article, Hu Shi discusses in details Zhang Taiyan's essay which compares the differences between the alphabetical and ideographic languages, arguing that Zhang's points resonate a lot with what he believed at the time. To prove his point, he quotes a passage from the original conference paper:

---

26   Hu Shi, *Hushi quanji* 28: 246.
27   Hu Suh, "The Problem of the Chinese Language (Concluded): III. The Teaching of Chinese as It Is," *The Chinese Students' Monthly*, XI. 8, p. 569.

> Every word, be it Chinese or European, has two elements: its sound and its meaning. An alphabetical language, like the English, gives you the sound or pronunciation of the word. But you must get the meaning by sheer memory work …… but when you look at the Chinese characters in their original forms, you immediately perceived their pictorial likenesses. But there is nothing in these pictures which suggests that they are pronounced as they are pronounced.[28]

One can see that this passage, which Hu Shi claimed to have quoted from the original conference paper, is slightly different from the journal paper "The Teaching of Chinese as It Is." The former is more colloquial, the latter more literary. In addition, while the former compares the Chinese with the European languages in general, the latter focuses on the comparison between Chinese and English. This shows that Hu Shi's conceptualization of *baihua* has been evolving and is influenced by his bilingual mode of thinking and writing. The way Hu Shi considers a language to be an organic whole that consists of various elements also reveals his wholistic view on languages.

Last but not least, Hu Shi uses the word "generalization" to describe the basic rules for discussing the issue of Chinese language ("There are a few generalizations that I consider to be of great importance in discussing the problem of teaching Chinese as it is.") This word thus should be interpreted as a "guideline" or "principle" according to which Hu Shi can readjust or intervene in the existing meanings of certain Chinese or English terms, thereby reevaluating the entire cultural tradition of China. From this perspective, Hu's discourse on the vernacular is actually regulated by a wholistic view that is channeled through a bilingual mode of thinking and writing. It should not, there, be simply reduced to a rigid *wenyan-baihua* binarism.

In fact, after Hu Shi published his far-reaching 1917 article, he continued to elaborate the historical meanings of the May Fourth literary movement on various occasions for different audiences. Many of these writings are in English. What is particularly noteworthy is that Hu Shi never had a consistent English translation of the term *baihua*. Instead, he had used many different words or expressions to refer to the idea of *baihua*. For instance, in "A literary Revolution in China," an English article that was published on February 12, 1919, in *The Peking Leader*, he used twelve different English expressions to denote the concept of *baihua*, including "language of everyday conversation," "plain language," "spoken tongue," "vulgate Chinese," "vulgate," "spoken Chinese,"

---

28   Hu Shi, *Hushi quanji* 28: 301.

"popular tongue," "spoken language," "vulgate tongue," "living language," "living spoken language," and *"pei-hua"*.[29]

For another example, in "The Literary Renaissance,"[30] another English essay written by Hu Shi, in 1931, he used "vulgar language of the people" and "living tongue" to refer to the idea of *baihua*. He also used "spoken words," "spoken syntax," "words and phrases of our daily use," and "the spoken language of our people" elsewhere to refer to the concept of *baihua*, indicating that his concept of vernacular in the May Fourth period is subject to the definition of both English and Chinese.

From the various ways in which Hu Shi translates the concept of *baihua* in English, we can see that he was very aware of the different historical situations from which any language develops, and was trying to present the Chinese case in a way that is accessible to the English readers. For instance, in Europe, modern novels rose and matured as early as the eighteenth and nineteenth centuries along with the industrial revolution and the rise of the middle class. Modern English thus became an important medium for literary production, and English writers in the twentieth century therefore did not need to emphasize the aesthetic nature of modern English, whereas in China, the idea of modern Chinese was yet to be fully established and theorized in the early twentieth century. *Wenyan* was still considered an orthodox literary language while *baihua* a trivial and unorthodox one. This is why Hu Shi, as the inaugurator of the May Fourth literary revolution, needed to rely on different cultural and linguistic systems to reverse the common conception of *baihua* in Chinese.

From the examples provided and discussed above, we can see that the widely-held *wenyan–baihua* binarism has its limits in exploring the history of the idea of the vernacular. The idea of *baihua* was not associated with the idea of *wenyan* in the pre-May Fourth context, and it was not always presented as the opposite of literary Chinese in the May Fourth literary discourses, as the case of Hu Shi has demonstrated. The idea of *baihua* is essential to the May Fourth literary movement, but the way it was defined and articulated certainly requires further analysis.

---

29 Chih-P'ing Chou, ed., *English Writings of Hu Shih: Literature and Society, Volume 1* (Heidelberg: Springer and Foreign Language Teaching and Research Press), 3–12.
30 Ibid., 41–50.

Bibliography

Cai Yuanpei. "Guowen zhij jianglai" 國文之將來 (The Future of National language) in *Cai Yuanpei xuanji* 蔡元培選集 (Selected Works of Cai Yuanpei), 103. Beijing: Zhonghua shuju, 1959.

Cao, Xueqin. *The Story of the Stone, Volume 3*, trans. David Hawkes. New York: Penguin, 1980.

Chiang Yung-chen. *Shewo qishei: Hu Shi, Didibu: Puyu chengpi, 1891–1917* (The Titan: Hu Shi, Vol. 1: Education, 1891–1917). Taipei: Linking Publishing Company, 2011.

Chou Chih-P'ing. *Guangyan buxi: Hu Shi sixian yu xiandai zhongguo* 光焰不息：胡適思想與現代中國 (Eternal Flames: Hu Shi's Thought and Modern China). Beijing: Jiuzhou chubanshe, 2012.

Chou, Chih-P'ing, ed. *English Writings of Hu Shih: Literature and Society*, Volume 1. Heidelberg: Springer and Foreign Language Teaching and Research Press, 2013.

Chow, Tse-tsung. *The May Fourth Movement: Intellectual Revolution in Modern China*. Cambridge: Harvard University Press, 1960.

Denton, Kirk, ed. *Modern Chinese Literary Thought: Writings on Literature, 1893–1945*. Stanford: Stanford University Press, 1996.

Feng, Menglong 馮夢龍. *Stories to Awaken the World: A Ming Dynasty Collection, Volume 3*, trans. Shuhui Yang and Yunqin Yang, Seattle: University of Washington Press, 2012.

Fried, Daniel. "Beijing's Crypto-Victorian: Traditionalist Influences on Hu Shi's Poetic Practice," *Comparative Critical Studies* 3, issue 3 (2006): 371–389.

Geng, Yunzhi 耿雲志. *Chongxin faxian Hu Shi* 重新發現胡適 (Rediscovering Hu Shi). Beijing: Renmin chubanshe, 2011.

Goldman, Merle. "Left-Wing Criticism of May Fourth Writers," in *Reflections on the May Fourth Movement: A Symposium*, ed. Benjamin Schwartz, 85–94. Cambridge: Harvard, 1972.

Hu, Shi (Hu Suh). "The Problem of the Chinese Language (Concluded): III. The Teaching of Chinese as It Is," *The Chinese Students' Monthly*, XI. 8 (June 1916): 567–593.

Hu Shi. *Baihua wenxue shi* 白話文學史 (History of Vernacular Literature) Tainan: Tainan donghai chubanshe, 1976.

Hu Shi. *Hu Shi quanji* 胡適全集 (Complete Collections of Hu Shi's Works). Hefei: Anhui jiaoyu chubanshe, 2003.

Hu Shi, ed. *Zhongguo xin wenyi daxi: wenxue lunzhan diyi ji* 中國新聞一大系：文學論戰第一集 (A Compendium of New Chinese Literature: Debates on Literature, vol. 1). Taipei: Dahan chubanshe, 1977.

Huang Zunxian 黃遵憲. *Riben guozhi* 日本國志 (Records of Japan). 1887.

Li Zhi 李贄. *Chutan Ji* 初潭集 (First Collection by the Pond). 1588.

Mair, Victor H. "Sound and Meaning in the History of Characters: Views of China's Earliest Script Reformers," in *Difficult Characters: Interdisciplinary Studies of Chinese and Japanese Writing*, ed. Mary S. Erbaugh. Columbus: Ohio State University National East Asian Language Resource Center, 2002.

Mair, Victor H. "What Is a Chinese 'Dialect/Topolect'? Reflections on Some Key Sino-English Linguistic Terms," *Sino-Platonic Papers*, no. 29 (1991): 1–31.

Schwarcz, Vera. *The Chinese Enlightenment*. Berkeley and Los Angeles: University of California Press, 1986.

Schwartz, Benjamin, ed. *Reflections on the May Fourth Movement: A Symposium*. Cambridge: Harvard University Press, 1972.

Xi Zhousheng 西周生. *Xingshi yinyuan zhuan* 醒世姻緣傳 (Marriage Destinies to Awaken the World). Ca. 1618~1681.

Zheng Zhenduo 鄭振鐸. *Zheng Zhenduo ji* 鄭振鐸集 (Collected Works of Zheng Zhenduo). Beijing: Zhongguo shehui chubanshe, 2004.

Index

Abram, David   167
Adorno, Theodor   165–166
aesthetics/aesthetic cognition   161–162, 166, 170, 210, 222
  discourse   207–226
affect, May fourth as   25–52
alienation   170–171, 181
Alliance of the Proletarian Esperanto-Speakers   259–260
Amane, Nishi   108
analytic reading   33
Anderson, Marston   159–160
animals   193–201
  humanity, reimagining   201–205
  human relationships and   184–186, 185nn8, 9, 201–205
  language   167, 168
  suffering and   193–201
anthropocentrism   20–21, 159, 162
anti-foreign riot (1927)   127
anti-religious movement   147
Anti-Rightest Campaign   242
Arabic, classical   107
Arab Renaissance   106–107
Arinori, Mori   108
Association of Proletarian Esperanto Speakers   260–261
Aurobindo Ghose, Sri   103–104
Austin, John L.   18, 28, 29
Awakening   144

baihua   13–14n14, 14, 32, 35, 46, 49, 84, 97–98, 212, 283–285, 285nn5,6
  definition   290, 295, 297–298
  May Fourth context   289–298
  Ming and Qing periods   285–289
  term   286–289
  see also wenyan
Ba Jin   261–263
Ban Wang   20–21
Bao Yaoming   77
Barker, Elmer Eugene   278
beauty, Shen Congwen and   171–172
Beijing student protest (1919)   8n5
Bengali language   105n16

Benjamin, Walter   38, 48
Bennett, Alan   49
Bian Cheng   163–164, 177, 177n60
biology, sexuality and nature   172–181
The Birth of Chinese Feminism   202
blackboard news   241
Bolshevik revolution   130
bomb
  metaphor   227–246
  personification of   237–238
  silent   239
Borodin, Michael   120
Boxer Rebellion   229
Brandes, Georg   125, 125n35
Brown, Carolyn T.   207n2, 210, 216n31, 219n38, 220
Buchman, Frank   150, 151
Buddhism   149, 189–191, 273, 274–275
  nuns   152
  Xiao Hong and   190–191, 190n21, 200
Button, Peter   207n2, 211, 215

Cai Yuanpei   146–147, 165, 230–231, 284
A Call to Arms   207–208
Cao Juren   78
Cao Xueqin   87, 287
Cao Zhan   87
catching on   35–36, 48
CCP. *See* Chinese Communist Party
Changhe   172–173
Chang-Tai Hung   239
Chan Koonchung   18–19, 54–74*passim*, 59, 69–70
Chan Siu-bak   5
chastity. *See* sexuality
Chen Duxiu   5, 12, 25, 26n2, 42–44, 47, 56, 56n7, 146–147, 220n42, 289
  bomb as metaphor   230–231, 234
  Esperanto   255, 256
  Lu Xun and   83
  vernacular Chinese   85, 98
Cheng, Eileen J.   213
Cheng Fangwu   234
Chen Hongzhe   86
Chen Pingyuan   30–37*passim*, 53, 56

Ch'en Tu-hsiu   130
Chen Yinke   95
Chen Yuan   260
Chiang, Yung-chen   19–20
Chiang Ching-kuo   65–66, 67, 68
Chiang Kai-shek   33, 65, 122, 126, 128–129, 141
children   213–214, 214nn22,27
　parents and   88–90
Chinese characters   250–256
　romanization of   291, 291n19
　revolution of   256–259
Chinese Communist Party (CCP)   40, 26, 55, 58, 75, 132–134, 138, 139
Esperanto and   259, 260
literary-cultural apparatus   237
Chinese cultural tradition, Hu Shi and   290
Chinese Democratic League   58
The Chinese Enlightenment: Intellectuals and the Legacy of the May Fourth   283–284
Chinese language
　meaning   48–49
　reform   291, 291n19
　standardized   14
　see also baihua; wenyan
Chinese Renaissance   95–112, 116–119, 120, 128–129, 129n47, 133, 134
　transcultural reading of   99–103
Chinese Students' Monthly   292
Chinese vernacular. *See baihua*
Chinese writing
　Hu Shi's criteria   270–271, 287
　system   247, 248, 251–255
Chiu-Duke, Josephine   18–19
Chou, Chih-p'ing   19, 22, 290
Chow Tse-tsung   54n3, 103, 138–139
Christianity   138, 146–152, 273, 274–275
　missionaries   150–152
　Yun Daiying and   147, 148, 149, 151
Chutan Ji   286
civil society   8, 55, 55n5
Cixi   7
　assassination plot   230
Clark, Timothy   160
classical Chinese. *See wenyan*
classical poetry   167–168
Cold War   121–122, 134

liberal   121–122
Cold warriors   128
collectivism   12, 27, 113, 131
colloquial Chinese. *See baihua*
Communist regime   144–145
　Hu Shi and   129–130, 132
Configurations of the Real   216n31
Confucianism   33–34, 90, 145, 175–178*passim*, 207, 212, 213, 216, 273
　Chinese characters and   255–256
　morality   138, 177–178
constitutionalism   7, 8n5, 56
　see also democracy, constitutional
"Constructive Literary Revolution— A Literature of National Speech"   271
Cornell, Ezra   269
Crespi, John   236–237
Cultural Association of the Left-Wing   259–260
cultural heritage   128n45
cultural reform   10, 13, 13–14n14, 32, 45
culture, nature vs   172

Dai Jinhua   184, 185n6
Dante   101–102
Daoism   33, 33n21, 165, 189–191, 255
Datongshu   262
Davies, Gloria   18, 218n36
Davis, Walter A.   209, 209n12
"The Death of Jesus"   273
"Debate on Science and the Philosophy of Life"   115, 115n5, 134
DeMare, Brian   241
democracy   28, 46, 49, 55, 56, 67, 81
　constitutional   57nn9,10, 58, 59, 64, 65, 68, 70
　defined   42
　movement   59–60, 69
　dictatorship   42
　religion of   116–117
　socialist   42
Democracy Wall Movement   69
demokelaxi   49
"Deng"   169–170
Deng Zhongxia   152
Denton, Kirk   235, 271
Dewey, John   132
"Diary of a Madman"   212–215, 220

INDEX 303

Di Fuding 28–29, 30
diglossia 97–98, 105–108
  Arab 106, 107
  India 105n15
Ding Kexin 243–244
Ding Ling 21, 240–242
discourse 207–226, 211n19
Doctrine of the Mean 140
doing 140–142
Dooling, Amy 185–186, 188n14
doubt 217, 218
Dream of the Red Chamber 180
"Du zhang taiyan bo zhongguo wanguo xinyu shuo" 296

eco-criticism, Shen Congwen 159–182
ecology and ecosystems 160, 162, 177, 181
Ehrlich, Anne and Paul 227–228
Eightfold Path 191–192
Elia, Gina 22
English
  Indian vernaculars and 107
  modern 298
Enlightenment, European 28, 41, 42, 95, 159–160, 162,165, 239n31
  pessimism and 208–209, 208nn6,7
equality 58, 143, 176, 202, 202n54, 204–205,220
Esperanto 22, 98, 247–258, 261–263, 286n14
  CCP and 259, 260
  post 1949 259–263, 263n39
  proletariet and 260–261
  use 263n39
essentialist mode 267, 278
evolution 6–7, 7n4, 8n5, 172, 178
Experiments 232

fair play 78–79
Fairbank, John K. 133
Fang, Achilles 15
female. *See* women
feminism 185–186, 201–204
Feng Da 242
Feng Menglong 286
Feng Xuefeng 235
Feng Zhizhong 87
Ferguson, Charles 97
The Field of Life and Death 21

filial piety 89–90
final awakening 32, 38
First Collection by the Pond 286
Foley, Todd 21
forgiveness 78–79
Formosa Incident 69
Fourteen Points 1, 2
Fourth literary movement. *See baihua*
Free China Bimonthly 57, 62, 64, 66
Freire, Paulo 40
Fried, Daniel 290
"Fufu" 178, 179
Fu Sinian 12, 13, 25, 26n2, 86, 126, 251, 289

Gabbo Reform 108
Galik, Marian 273
Gandhi 106
Gang Yue 190
Gang Zhou 19
Gannett, Lewis 121
Gao Lan 238
Gao Quanxi 57n10
genbun itchi movement 108, 287
gender 184, 184n4, 204, 204n64, 211, 220, 221
  hierarchy 176–177
  see also women
gilded cage. *See* iron house
GMD. *See* Kuomintang
Goldblatt, Howard 183–184, 190
Goldman, Merle 15–16, 283–284
Gong'an scholars 13–14n14
Grieder, Jerome B. 22, 265, 266–267, 268, 270, 276
"Guanhua hesheng zimu" 247, 288
"Guanyu xin wenzi" 257
"Gui Xinshiji" 249
Guling conference 151
Guocui Xuebao 255
Guomin Dang. *See* Kuomintang
Guomindang. *See* Kuomintang
Guo Moruo 231, 244
"Guoyu de jinhua" 293–294
guwen 35, 283
  see also baihua

Hangping Xu 185n9
"Hanzi gaige de lilun yu shiji" 258
"Hanzi geming" 256

"Hanzi he ladinghua"   257
Hebrew Renaissance   107
Heideggerian, Thomas   39
heterogeneity   39, 46
He-Yin Zhen   186, 201–204
hierarchy   107, 176–177, 177n60, 180
Hillis Miller, J.   29
Hindi   105, 106
Hindustani   106
Hisoka, Maejima   108
historical materialism   40n35
A History of Modern Chinese Fiction   243, 273
Honglou meng   87, 287
hope   38, 207–208, 208n6
The Housing Bomb   227–228
Hou Zhiping   259–260
Hsia, C. T.   61, 190–191, 243, 273–274
Hsiao Hung   190
Huang Xiaojuan   190n21
Huang Zhimeng   231–232
Huang Zunxian   9–10, 287–288
Hu Feng   129, 183, 189n17, 235n19
Hu Shi   6, 10, 11, 12n1, 14, 14n15, 15, 19, 142
　1930s–1940s   121–126
　anti-Hu Shi campaign   129, 133
　bomb as metaphor   231–234 *passim*
　Chiang Kai-shek and   79–82, 80–81nn17,19
　Chinese Renaissance   95, 100–101, 103–104
　education   76–77
　English writing   14–15
　interpretation   114–121
　language reform   266, 268–272
　legacy   56–57, 62, 64, 79, 80, 118, 129–130
　Lu Xun and   82–88
　May Fourth as affect   25, 37–38
　post-1949   126–134
　reassessment   75–94
　religion   265, 265n1, 266–268, 276–279
　Sichel and   99
　social immortality   276–279
　Taiwan   79, 80
　tradition   88–93
　vernacular Chinese   98–102*passim*, 284n4, 285, 285n6, 289–298
　written Chinese   270–271
　Zhou Zuoren and   83

human nature   162, 165, 173–174, 181, 186
humans/humanity   201–205
　animal relationships and   184–186, 185nn8,9
　end to suffering   193–201
　reason   159–160
"Humans and Soil"   172–173
Huntington, Samuel   107
Hu Shih   129, 130, 266n5
Huters, Theodore   209n8, 214n29, 216, 217
Hu Xiansu   289–290
Hu Yuzhi   259, 260–261

Ibsen, Henrik   125, 125n35, 131, 132
ideology   145–146, 211n19
Illness as Metaphor   229
Immortality
　social   22, 279, 280
　words   278
"Immortality—My Religion"   277
India, language   104–106, 105nn15, 16, 107
indigenous practices   152
individualism/the individual   2n1, 56, 57n8, 132, 277–278
　rights   56–57
insight, felt nature of   33, 35
intellectual freedom   32–33
intellectual transformation   122
Ireland, language   104, 107
iron house   62–63, 207–208, 208n4
isms   137
"It's Time, My Comrades"   238
Italy, vernacular   101, 101n10

Jameson, Fredric   28
Japan   1, 108
　CCP and   127–128
　genbun itchi   287
　language reform   108
　Lu Xun and   90–91
　student demonstration   124
　translations   6
Jehovah   148–149
Jianfeng ernian xin Zhongguo wuyoushi, An Uchronia of New China   53–74
Jiang Menglin   25, 26n2, 37–38, 122
"Jinhua yu geming"   253
Johnson, Mark   228–229

INDEX

Jones, Andrew F.   208n4, 213, 214n27
June Fourth   59, 63
June Third   37, 40–41

Kahler, Erich   228
Kaldis, Nick   21
Kang Baiqing   86
Kang Youwei   4–8*passim*, 97, 131, 262
Karl, Rebecca   202, 202n57
Katakana   247
Kinkley, Jeffrey   163, 166–167
Kitching, Gavin   40n35
KMT. *See* Kuomintang
knowing   140–142
Ko, Dorothy   202, 202n57
Korea, language reform   108
Korean War, CCP and   243–244
Kuomintang (KMT)   26, 55, 58,
    67–69*passim*, 75, 117–118,
    123–124, 133, 134, 138
    Hu Shi and   119–122
Kwo-min-Tang. *See* Kuomintang

Lakoff, George   228–229
Lam, Ling Hon   208
Lan Gongwu   114
language   2, 4, 36, 39, 85, 159–160, 263
    literature and novels   20, 268–269, 298
    natural beauty, modern civilization,
        and   163–172
    nature   168–169
    political discourses   9–13
    renaissances   95–112, 128, 130
    revolution   12–13, 33, 98
    time and   39
    utopian   247–264
language reform   247, 253–255
    Hu Shi and   118n11, 266–272
    Japan   108
    nationalism and   250–252
    see also Esperanto
Lao Naixuan   247
Laozi   148
Larson, Wendy   211
Latinization. *See* Esperanto; language reform
League of Left-wing Writers   91–92, 93, 235,
    235n19, 241, 242
Lee, Leo Ou-fan   12, 208–209, 209n8

legacy, Chan Koonchung   53–74
Lei Zhen   64, 81
Lenin, Vladimir   2, 234
Leninism   39, 118, 121, 122, 133, 145
Liang Ch'i-ch'ao   131
Liang Qichao   4–12*passim*, 131, 202n54,
    208nn4,7, 214n54, 229–231
Liang Shaowen   149
Liang Shuming   95
Li Ao   27
liberals/liberalism   16, 34, 57–58
    democracy   42, 55, 56, 56n6, 58, 64, 69
    legacy   53–74
    middle-of-the-road   57–58, 58n11
    reforms   59
On Liberty   5, 6
Li Chuli   234
Li Daoyuan   162
Li Dazhao   46, 47, 114
Li Jinxi   256–257
Lin Biao   234
Lin Changmin   77
Link, Perry   239–240
Lin Shu   4, 11, 12, 284n3
Lin Yü-sheng   208
Lin Yutang   92–93
"Li shi de wen xue guan nian lun"   265
Li Shizeng   253
"A literary Revolution in China"   297–298
"The Literary Renaissance"   298
literary movement. *See* language
Literary Revolution/Renaissance   12–13, 33,
    98, 130
Literary Sinitic, use   268, 269–270
"literature for national defense"   235
Liu, Lydia   184, 188n15, 190, 192n27, 202,
    202n57, 220n42, 256
Liu Bannong   12, 86, 289
Liu Bomin   150
Liu Ling   286
Liu Shaoqi   139, 145
Liu Shipei   249
Liu Zhongyuan   162
Liu Zitong   149
Li Zehou   231
Li Zhi   286
Lu Gangzhang   287–288
Lung-kee Sun   27

"Lun zhongtu wenzi youyi yu shijie" 249
Luo Jialun 25–33*passim*, 26n2, 37–38
Luoming 60
Luo Qing 15
Lushan 148, 149n38
Lu Xun 6, 13, 19, 21, 62–63, 75, 83, 142, 183
    aesthetic cognition 207–226
    bomb as metaphor 233, 235, 235n19, 235–236n21
    Chinese script 257
    education 76–77
    friendships and 82–88
    Hu Shi and 82–83
    legacy 78, 79
    Mao Zedong and 78–79
    May Fourth as affect 38, 38n28, 47
    reassessment 75–94
    tradition, views of 88–93
Lu Zhuangzhang 247

Ma Yuancai 152
Mair, Victor 22
Maissen, Thomas 96
Mallarmé, Stéphane 227, 236
Manchuria
    Esperanto 259
    Japanese invasion 183–184
Manchu rule 55–56, 87
Mao Dun 220n42, 273
Maoism 36
    post-Maoist times 36, 36n25, 44, 45, 48
Mao Zedong 10, 19, 27, 55n5, 66
    bomb metaphors 234, 239, 239n31, 242
    Hu Shi and 76–81, 129–130
    Lu Xun and 75–78
    theory and practice 137–145*passim*
Marriage Destinies to Awaken the World 286
Marshall, George 126
Marxism 7, 39, 40, 133, 144–145, 201–202n53, 234
Mau-sang Ng 16
May Fourth and May Fourth Movement 1–6, 10–12, 49, 265, 271
    as affect 25–52
    contemporary repercussions 18–22
    cross-cultural and bilingual discourses 291

distant reading of 19, 110
historiography 138–140
intellectuals 8, 9, 17
legacy 17–18, 53–74, 113–136, 159
meaning 26
origin 15–16, 15n17
Qing dynasty 4–9
relevance 25
spirit 26, 26n2
theory and practice in 137–156
transnational and cross-cultural flow 14–18
May Thirtieth Massacre 117, 127
Mayakovsky, Vladimir 236
Mayer, Arno J. 2–3
medicine/medical science 13, 207, 229
Mei Chia-Ling 238n28
Mei Guangdi 14n15, 95
Meiji language movement 108
Mencius 132, 140
Meng Yue 184, 185n6
"Mengke" 241
Messrs De and Sai 47, 48
Messrs Democracy and Science 42–45
metaphors
    bomb as 227–246
    military 229
Metaphors We Live By 228
Mill, John Stuart 132
Mills, Wilson 120
Ming dynasty, vernacular literature 13–14n14
Miss Freedom 44–45
Miss Sophia's Diary 240, 241
missionaries. *See* Christianity
Mittler, Barbara 96
modernity 2, 7, 28, 53–54, 55, 110, 131, 146, 161, 163, 181, 271–272
    natural beauty and language 163–172
    Shen Congwen and 159–182
morality 151, 177n62, 177–178
    Esperanto and 263
"Moral Rearmament" 151
Moretti, Franco 19, 110
Morley, John 132
Movement to Liberate Thinking 36
Mr. Democracy 55
muji daocun 33–34, 35, 48

multi-dimensionality and -directionality   54, 55
Mutual Aid Society   149, 151

Nancy, Jean-Luc   38–39
nation   25
nation-state   7, 8, 8n5, 56, 56n7
nationalism   2n1, 13–14n14, 63, 250–252
National Youth Day   27
Nationalist Party. *See* Kuomintang
natural beauty, language, modern civilization, and   163–172
national character   63
nature   163–174, 181
   language of   167, 168–169
   sexuality and biology   172–181
Nehru, Jawaharlal   106
"The New Year's Sacrifice"   212, 217–222, 221n43
New Century period   252–255
New Culture Movement   28, 58, 91, 134, 265, 269, 271
   defined   53–54
New Diplomacy   2
New Literature Movement   12–13, 53, 130, 283
   See also Vernacular Literature Movement
New Tide   15n17, 28–35*passim*, 143
new youth   12
New Youth   42–44, 58, 82, 83, 84, 95, 98, 131, 143, 255–256, 289
Ni, Zhange   274–275
Nietzsche, Friedrich   209, 113

"Ode to the Headstones without Inscriptions at the Four Martyrs' Graves"   232
"The Old Worker Guo Fushan"   243
openness   39, 46
Opium Wars   4
oppositional consciousness   212, 214, 214n29
oppression   185, 212
optimism   216
oranges   172–173
Orchid Wind   232, 233
Oriental History Review, Chen Pinguan interview   34–35
"Oxford Group"   151

Pan-African Renaissance   107
paradise, counterfeit   60, 60n16
parents and children. *See* children
Paris Peace Conference   1, 2, 130
Party-State   26, 60–67*passim*, 60n16
passion   168, 174
patriarchy   184, 184n4, 185, 191, 201, 211n19
patriotism   2n117n21
Peng Jiazhen   232
performative dimension   29, 30, 31, 36–37, 49
personal responsibility   41
pessimism   42, 208–209, 208nn6,7, 219
phenomenal state   161–162
pinyin   187n12, 265n2
poetry/poets   37, 41–49, 232, 233
   recitation   236–239, 244
political discourses to literary revolution   9–13
politics   46, 46–47n45, 118, 122
population bomb   227–228
"On Practice"   144–145
pragmatic time   39, 39n32
praxis   140–142, 209
pregnancy   187–189
"A Preliminary Discussion of Literary Reform"   270
Premchand, Munshi   106
Price, Frank W.   150, 151
privileged pragmatism   113–114
"The Problem of the Chinese Language"   269, 292, 292n20
prodemocracy movement   55–58, 56n6, 70
progress, nature vs   169–170
promissory function   279
prostitution, Shen Congwen and   176–177
public time   39, 39n32
Pu Feng   236, 237

Qian Xuantong   12, 85, 98, 251, 255, 256, 289
Qian Yongxiang   65
Qing dynasty   4–9, 55–56, 132
   conflict   229–230
   intellectuals   4–9
   reforms   141
Qu Qiubai   39–40, 47–48, 258
Qu Yuan   173

radicalism   42, 55, 212–213
Rahav, Shakhar   20
Raise the Red Lantern   215n30
rape   183, 188, 188–189n15
realist fiction   159–160
reality   183, 210n16
    superempirical   279
recitation poetry and poets   236–239, 244
Red Sorghum   178
reformers of 1898   7, 130–131
"Refuting the use of the Esperanto in China"   296–297
religion   22, 147, 279
    Hu Shi   265, 265n1, 266–268, 272–275
    social immortality   22, 276–279, 280
Renaissances   95–112
    Arabia   106–107
    China   99–103, 122, 123
    Europe   99–101, 103
    India   103–105
    Italy   99–100, 101
    other   103–107
Republican Era   141, 265, 271–275
Research Association of Literature and Science   291
"Rewriting Jesus in Republican Era China: Religion, Literature, and Cultural Nationalism"   274–275
Ricci, Matteo   291n19
Riep, Steven   274, 275
Robinson, Lewis   273
Rulinwaishi   87
Russia   128, 129, 227, 230
    conspiracy   126–127
    influence   2, 16, 77, 119, 233–234, 239n31
    literary tradition   16
    resistance   80n17
    see also Leninism; Marxism

samsara   189–192, 190n23
"Samson's Revenge"   273
"Sange nanren he yige nüren"   179–180
"Sange nüxing"   168
Sanskrit   105
Schilbrack, Kevin   278–279
Schwarcz, Vera   54n4, 128, 139, 283
science   12, 28, 207
Searle, John   29

self, concept   20–21
    greater or lesser   278, 279
self-motivation   25, 30
Self-strengthening Movement   4, 4n3, 5
sensuality   162, 167–168, 174, 181
sexuality   176–181, 177n62, 187–188, 191–192
    chastity   43, 78, 88
    Shen Congwen and   174–175
Shen Congwen   21
    ecological perspectives   160–161n6
    modernity   159–182
Shengshi   59, 60, 63
Shen Yinmo   86
Shi bao   26n2
Shijieyu   248, 249
Shijie yu yuundong zai zhongguo   259–260
"Shijieyu zhi tedian"   261–262
Shijing   165
"Shui Yun"   170–171
Shuowen Jiezi   249
Sichel, Edith   99
Slave Series   183
Social Darwinism   7, 7n4
social ecology   176–177
social immortality   22, 276–279, 280
socialism
    Mao Zedong   64, 66
    radical   146–152
Society for Vigorous Practice   141
Some Modest Proposals for the Reform of Literature"   292
Sontag, Susan   229
sovereignty   7, 8n5
Soviet Union   27, 239n31
    Five-Year Plan   120–121
    Hu Shi and   113, 118
speech act theory   18
spirit   38, 131, 207, 207n3, 218
spirituality   104–105, 116–117
    animals and   194–201
    radical practice   146–152
Spring and Autumn Annals   276
Ssu-yü Teng   133
Stalin
    global strategy   127–128
    Prize in Literature   242
Starr, Chloe   271
Stories to Awaken the World   286

Stuckey, G. Andrew   219–220
student movements   32, 118–120, 123–127, 130
subjectivity, constituents of   211
sublime   146–147
suffering   185–192
    end to   193–201
suicide   88, 180, 218
    bombers   227, 230, 231
Su Manshu   12
The Sun Shines over the Sanggang River   240–241, 242
Sun Yat-sen   2n1, 4, 5, 122, 141–142, 144, 151
Su Wei   239n31
Su Xuelin   90, 274, 275
synthesis   104–105, 106, 209

Tagore, Rabindranath   77
Taiwan   27–28, 33, 57, 57n9, 62–70, 231, 240
    Hu Shi and   79
T'an Ssu-t'ung   131
Taoism. *See* Daoism
Tao Lugong   256
Tao Xingzhi   142–143, 227
Taylor, Charles   35–36, 48
"The Teaching of Chinese as It Is"   291, 293, 296, 297
"Tentative Proposals for the Improvement of Literature"   269
The Field of Life and Death   183–206
"The True Story of Ah Q"   212, 215–218, 216n31, 219, 220
theoria   140–142
theory and practice   20, 142–146
Third Force group   58, 58n12, 70
Third International   113, 119, 120
Thomas, Julian   39
Thornber, Karen   162
Tiananmen Square   48
Tian Beihu   254–255
Tibet   60–61
time   188n14
    existential   39
    nature and   172
    now   39, 48
    pragmatic   39, 39n32
    public   39, 39n32
Tong Te-kong   128–129
traditional ways   207, 213–214, 271–272

philosophy of   186–192
    Shen Congwen   159–162, 168–170, 174, 176
transfiguration   43
transformation   56n7
transvaluation   128n45
Trigault, Nicolas   291n19
trilogy about China   61, 61n18, 62, 63
Tsai, Chien-hsin   21
tuqiang   287
Turkish language modernization   109–110
tuyin   287
Twenty-One Demands   1, 2

uchronia   18, 19, 54, 61–62, 66
Ueda, Atsuko   108
urbanization   169–170, 171, 181
Urdu   105, 106
The Uses of Literature   239–240

Vasari, Giorgio   99–100
vernacular Chinese   22, 84–88, 97–98, 105, 107, 114–116, 118n11, 231–232
    use   268–269
    see also baihua
vernacular languages   99
    historical and bilingual perspective   283–300
    Italy   101–102
    Japan   108
    Korea   108–109
Vernacular Literature Movement   12–13, 101, 130
    see also New Literature Movement
Versailles Peace Conference   54
Victorian Age   131–132, 134
violence   185, 199, 204, 211n19, 213, 237
"Voice and Quest for Modernity in Chinese Literature"   238n28
Voices in Revolution   236–237

Wagner, Rudolf   28
Wang, David   62, 163, 172, 271
Wang Guangqi   143–144
Wang Guowei   95
Wang Hui   41–42
Wang Jingzhi   232
Wang Qin   184–185, 185nn6,8, 194
Wang Runhua   15

"Wanguo xinyu" 248, 255
Wang Yangming 132, 140–141, 142–143
Wang Zhao 247, 288, 288n14
War and Popular Culture 239
War of Resistance 236, 237
"The Way of Saving the Nation through Literature" 233
wealth and power 61, 61n19
"weapon of art" 234, 237
Wei Jingsheng 69, 69n29
Wenbo Xuezi 34
Wen Fengqiao 45, 46
"Wenxue gailiang chuyi" 12, 265, 289
"Wenxue geming lun" 12
wenyan 35, 84, 86, 97, 212, 283–285, 285n5, 298
    Hu Shi and 290, 293–297
wenyan-baihua binarism 295, 297, 298
Western Affairs Movement 4
Western civilization 4–5, 95, 113–117, 131
white terror 64, 67
Williams, Edith "Clifford" 115–116
Wilson, Woodrow 1–2
women 88, 201–204
    agency/liberation 219
    body 176, 184, 203–204
    enslavement 202
    feminism 185–186, 201–204
    gender 176–177, 184, 184n4
    rights 202n54
    role 174, 176–177
    traditional Chinese 222
    victimized 174–175
Wordsworth, William 171
Work Study Mutual Aid Corps 143
The World 260
writing system. *See* Chinese writing
Wu Mi 95
Wu Yue 230
Wuxi baihua bao 289
Wu Zhihui 252–255*passim*, 261, 288n14

xiangtan 288
xiansheng 43
Xiaobing Tang 210–215*passim*, 211n17, 213n22
Xiao Hong 21, 183–206, 189n17
Xiao Jun 189n17

"Xiaoxiao" 174–175, 176, 177n62
Xidan Democracy Wall 36
Xi Jinping 17, 17n21, 48–49, 48n47
Xiji qiji 291n19
Xinbo 239
Xingshi hengyan 286
Xingshi yinyuan zhuan 286
Xinhai Revolution 10n6, 40
Xiru ermu zi 291n19
Xi Zhousheng 286
Xu Dishan 274, 275
Xu Youyu 41
Xu Zhimo 77

Yan'an 139n3, 239, 239n31, 242
Yan Fu 4, 5–6, 12
Yang Nianqun 44–45
Yang Yuchang 231–232
Yangzhou group 144
Yanyi baihua bao 289
Ye Laishi 260–261
Yimu liaoran chujie 247
Yin Haiguang 64
YMCA. *See* Christianity
Yoshikazu, Nanbu 108
Yuan Shikai 1
Yu Dafu 220n42
Yuen Ren Chao 15, 291, 292
"Yu Hou" 167–168
Yu-Kai Lin, Carlos 22
Yu Keping 45, 46
Yun Daiying 20, 138–152
Yu Pingbo 86, 129
Yü-sheng Lin 54, 54n4, 55n5
Yuyanxue lunwen 263n39
Yu Ying-shih 95, 103, 110

Zamenhof, Ludwig Lazarus 248
Zeitgeist 172
Zen, H. C. 14n15
"Zengding heshengjian zipu" 247
Zengzi 145
Zhang Dongsun 58n13
"Zhangfu" 176–177
Zhang Fuliang 150–151
Zhang Taiyan 4, 5, 7n4, 249, 254, 254n15, 255, 296–297
Zhang Wojun 231, 244

Zhang Xianpei   231–232
Zhang Yimou   178, 215n30
Zhang Zuolin   47
Zheng Zhenduo   285n6
Zhou Enlai   139
Zhou Yang   234–236, 235–236n21, 239, 241–243, 244
Zhou Youguang   263n39
Zhou Zuoren   13, 13–14n14, 77, 78, 83, 86
Zhuangzi   48, 132, 162
"Zhufu"   174–175
Zhu Guanqian   165
Zhu Jingnong   98
Zhu Ziqing   232
Zuo Shunsheng   149–150
Zuo zhuan   276, 277

Printed in the United States
By Bookmasters